H. L. MENCKEN'S
Smart Set
CRITICISM

H. L. Mencken in 1913. (Courtesy of the Baltimore *Sun*.)

H. L. MENCKEN'S
Smart Set
CRITICISM

Selected and Edited
by
WILLIAM H. NOLTE

GATEWAY EDITIONS
Washington, D.C.

Library of Congress Cataloging-in-Publication Data

Mencken, H. L. (Henry Louis), 1880–1956.
H. L. Mencken's Smart set criticism.

Includes bibliographical references and index.
I. Nolte, William Henry, 1928–   II. Smart set
(New York, N.Y.)   III. Title   IV. Title: Smart set
criticism.
PS3525.E43A6   1987   809   87-23248
ISBN 0-89526-790-X

Published in the United States by
Regnery Gateway
1130 17th Street, NW
Washington, DC 20036

Distributed to the trade by
Kampmann & Company, Inc.
9 E. 40th Street
New York, NY 10016

10 9 8 7 6 5 4 3 2 1

For Alice and Ann

Contents

CONTENTS

Editor's Introduction

I

A favorite cliché among readers and writers is that there will never be another Mencken. When shall we look upon his like again? they ask, without the least trace of hope that an answer might be forthcoming. The literary heavens may be full of stars, but none will ever shine so brightly as that whose light came forth from 1524 Hollins Street in Baltimore. As Mencken might have better put it: Alas, and God damn! About the only argument, indeed, concerns not the man's stature but rather that aspect of his work wherein he *most* excelled.

If no agreement may be found in discussions of his *matter*, at least connoisseurs agree unanimously on his *manner*. As a stylist, Mencken lacks a peer in our time. It would be absurd for me to say that Mencken never wrote a misshapen sentence, that his sense of appropriateness in word choice never failed, or that his humor invariably succeeded. But it would be difficult to name an American writer of this or any other century who wrote with comparable grace and charm or whose good sense is so often in evidence. Putting it more briefly: Mencken's style had vigor, gusto, brilliance, and general persuasiveness. He was a master of American prose.

Style cannot, of course, be totally divorced from content; a man's style, assuming it is more than meretricious novelty, will bear the stamp of the whole man, his personality and knowledge. In all that Mencken wrote, the full personality stands forth, sometimes through understatement, often through exaggeration, now humorous and now biting, but always intelligent and robust.

Mencken's first book article for *The Smart Set* appeared in November, 1908. His final article, entitled "Fifteen Years," appeared in the December, 1923, issue. After having reviewed and criticized some two thousand books in the 182 articles for that periodical, he "resigned" his rôle as America's most influential literary critic for the office of gadflyin-residence. Although he would continue to write reviews for *The American Mercury* and various other magazines, his primary interests lay in other fields. With the founding of the *Mercury* in January, 1924, Mencken entered a second period of his cultural influence, which rose dizzily until he became, as *The New York Times* said in the late twenties, "the most powerful private citizen in America." Walter Lippmann called him "the most powerful personal influence on this whole generation of educated people." With his resignation from the *Mercury* editorship in 1933, he entered the third major phase of his career, this time not as critic or iconoclast but as scholar (*The American Language* books) and as author of the *Days* books.

One should nonetheless view such neat divisions of his work with skepticism, remembering that they are valid only in outline form and useful only as indicators of his *primary* interests. More than any other twentieth-century American, Mencken typified the Renaissance ideal of broadness or catholicity. He was never during his long career any *one* thing—poet, reporter, short-story writer, literary critic, editor, philologist, social philosopher, political analyst, or satirist. During the fifteen years on *The Smart Set*, as book reviewer and, from 1914, as co-editor, he wrote on dozens of topics that concerned literature only incidentally, if at all. There are the lifelong interests in philology, politics, religion, music, philosophy, the biological sciences, journalism—briefly, American civilization. Even more accurately than Emerson, he may be labeled The American as Critic.

Because of this broadness of interest, I suspect, Mencken is not often thought of today as a *literary* critic. Still, he was the most powerful literary critic, in his own lifetime, that this country has produced; and his judgment of individual writers and his analysis of our literary heritage were nigh unerring. So much is evident to us now from our vantage point in time: the writers he praised have lived, and those he panned are forgotten; his assessment of our literary past, so novel at the time it was written, is now almost a cliché. To be sure, his book criticism for the *Mercury* leaves much to be desired, but then he had lost interest in *belles lettres* by the time the *Mercury* attained eminence as the intellectuals' Bible.

II

In his farewell article in *The Smart Set*, Mencken told of his fortuitous entry into the world of professional book criticism.

The assistant editor of *The Smart Set*, in 1908, was the late Norman Boyer, with whom, eight years before, I had worked as a police reporter in Baltimore. One day I received a polite note from him, asking me to wait upon him on my next visit to New York. I did so a few weeks later; Boyer introduced me to his chief, Fred Splint, and Splint forthwith offered me the situation of book reviewer to the magazine, with the rank and pay of a sergeant of artillery. Whose notion it was to hire me—whether Boyer's, or Splint's, or some anonymous outsider's—I was not told, and do not know to this day. I had never printed anything in the magazine; I had not, in fact, been doing any magazine work since 1905, when I abandoned the writing of short-stories, as I had abandoned poetry in 1900. But Splint engaged me with a strange and suspicious absence of parley, Boyer gave me an armful of books, the two of us went to Murray's for lunch (I remember a detail: I there heard the waltz, *"Ach, Frühling, wie bist du so schön!"* for the first time), and in November of the same year my first article appeared in this place.

There is a slight and almost inconsequential error in this remembrance, if we are to believe Mencken's various biographers. Actually, he was first made the offer by mail and asked to call later at the New York office to discuss details. Nor had he given up the writing of fiction and poetry, since he was to write a great deal of both under various pseudonyms during his years on *The Smart Set*.

By the time of this meeting in New York, Mencken had seen two books of prose through the press: a critical interpretation, and the first ever written, of Shaw's plays; and an explication, the first in English, of Friedrich Nietzsche's philosophy. His first published work was a volume of verse, *Ventures into Verse* (1903). He had sold numerous short stories to various magazines—*Short Stories, Munsey's, Ainslee's, Youth's Companion, Everybody's, Hearst's, Red Book*, and *Frank Leslie's Popular Monthly*—and had even impressed Ellery Sedgwick, then editor of *Leslie's* and later editor of the *Atlantic Monthly*, enough that Sedgwick had offered him, in 1901, the post of associate editor of *Leslie's* at a salary of forty dollars a week and a free pass to Baltimore every month. The young reporter must have been sorely tempted, for at that time he was earning less than half that on the Baltimore *Herald*. But he was head of the house in Baltimore, his father having died in 1899, and had to consider his mother and the responsibility of two younger brothers and a younger sister. This is not to say, however, that he was financially responsible for his family, since his

father, August Mencken, had done well as a manufacturer of cigars
and had left his widow well provided for.

Aside from his books (*The Philosophy of Nietzsche*, published in
1908, was a popular and critical success) and his short stories,
Mencken was also acquiring national renown as the country's foremost
journalistic prodigy, having become at the age of twenty-three America's youngest managing editor and at twenty-four the youngest editor
in chief on a big city daily, the Baltimore *Evening Herald*. In 1906 he
moved to the *Sun* and was to be associated with the Sunpapers, except for a three-year absence (1917–1920), down to 1941, when he retired to write his memoirs. In 1948 he reluctantly agreed to cover the
political conventions for the Sunpapers; in the fall of that year he
suffered an almost fatal, and permanently disabling, stroke.

The "anonymous outsider" who recommended Mencken as a possible choice to review books for *The Smart Set* was Theodore Dreiser.
That Dreiser would derive incalculable benefit from Mencken's accepting the job was not then known, of course, but it does indicate a
sort of cosmic justice. When the two men first met, Dreiser was the
editor of the fashionable *Delineator* and of the Butterick Publications.
Among other things, Mencken was acting as a ghost writer for a Baltimore physician and Johns Hopkins graduate named Leonard K.
Hirshberg. Dr. Hirshberg informed Dreiser that he wished to do a
series of articles which would interpret for the lay public, if possible,
some of the more recent advances in medical science. He admitted
that as a medical man he was not a competent writer, but informed
the editor that he had joined with "a young, refreshing and delightful
fellow of a very vigorous and untechnical literary skill," who, as the
Doctor's collaborator, would most certainly furnish Dreiser with articles of exceptional luminosity and vigor. In an explanatory note for
the bound volumes in the Enoch Pratt Free Library, Mencken stated
that Ellery Sedgwick had asked him to find a man at Johns Hopkins
who would be willing to write some medical articles for *Leslie's
Weekly*. He found such a man in Dr. Hirshberg, who provided the
facts for the articles which Mencken wrote. "The combination turned
out to be very successful and pretty soon we were deluged with
orders. Among the magazines we worked for was the *Delineator*, then
edited by Dreiser. Dreiser ordered a whole series of articles on the
feeding and care of children." That series was published afterward as
a book, which was widely popular for years.

As Dreiser tells the story, when he received the first article, it "seemed to me as refreshing and colorful a bit of semiscientific exposition as I had read in years." Some weeks later Mencken called on Dreiser about the articles he had been ghosting. Looking like "a spoiled and petted and possibly over-financed brewer's or wholesale grocer's son who was out for a lark," Mencken promptly ensconced himself in a large and impressive chair placed there to deflate the ego of the overly confident, and from that unintended vantage point beamed on Dreiser "with the confidence of a smirking fox about to devour a chicken." Unable to restrain his laughter at the sight before him, Dreiser asked if his visitor were not "Anheuser's own brightest boy out to see the town." To which Mencken readily replied that he was indeed the son of Baltimore's richest brewer and that his yellow shoes and bright tie were characteristic of his class. Dreiser wrote that they at once dismissed the original purpose of the conference and proceeded to expatiate on "the more general phases and ridiculosities of life, with the result that an understanding based on a mutual liking was established, and from then on I counted him among those whom I most prized—temperamentally as well as intellectually." It is hard to say, as F. O. Matthiessen wrote, which of the two men was farther from his proper work: Mencken as the author of an article on "When Baby Has Diphtheria," or Dreiser as the one who solicited the article.

Not long after he met Mencken, Dreiser was asked by the new editor of *The Smart Set* for advice as to how the magazine could be made better. Dreiser suggested that a book department "with a really brilliant and illuminating reviewer" was just what the magazine needed. And instantly he thought of Mencken as the ideal man for the job. Thus did Mencken begin his fifteen-year association with *The Smart Set*.

In his *The Smart Set: A History and Anthology* (New York: Dial Press, 1966), Carl R. Dolmetsch recounts the fortunes of the magazine from its birth in 1900 to its demise in 1930. Begun as a somewhat risqué journal that pandered to the tastes of the leisure classes, *The Smart Set* entered its golden age in 1913 when Willard H. Wright, a diabolical Nietzschean of indubitable genius, became editor (upon the recommendation of Mencken). During Wright's one stormy year as editor, a year that almost bankrupted the publisher, he introduced a number of foreign writers to the provincial American reader—Wedekind, Schnitzler, D'Annunzio, W. L. George, George Moore, D. H.

Lawrence, May Sinclair, August Strindberg, William Butler Yeats, Robert Bridges, Joseph Conrad, and others. With the dismissal of Wright, whose fondness for the iconoclastic was matched only by an impractical business sense, Mencken and Nathan took the reins. Under them *The Smart Set* became known for its hospitality to young and original writers. For all artistic purposes, the magazine died in 1924 with the resignation of its two most famous editors.

III

Given his strong belief in knowledge for its own sake, his unwavering trust in scientific evidence and rational thought, and his distrust of all forms of supernaturalism and irrationalism, one could hardly expect Mencken to have been either a lover or a competent critic of poetry. Indeed, he sometimes referred to himself as a congenital poetry-hater. Such proclamations were doubtless due in part to his having read so much rimed fustian as editor and critic, and in part to his love for shocking the dilettantes. Moreover, his first book, *Ventures into Verse* (1903), showed a facile if undistinguished hand at composing dithyrambs, and he knew English poetry quite well, much of it by heart. Poetry-haters, needless to say, do not write poetry, nor do they read and memorize it. Nevertheless, critics and literary historians have tended to disparage his poetry criticism.[1] Without attempting to support his critical views, I still think some understanding of the theory on which they are based would help correct an ancient error.

Remembering Mencken's often stated belief that aesthetic beauty has its springs in the emotions, one might expect him to have preferred poetry to prose. Furthermore, poetry comes closer to music than does prose; and music was for him the highest of the arts. Still, Mencken placed poetry beneath prose for the simple reason that all poetry was to some extent ideational; and ideas, he believed, were such sober things that only the rational mind, the skeptical mind, could safely have any truck with them. When a man wants to express, analyze, or expose an idea, he must invariably employ those cerebral centers which communicate in prose. On the other hand, when the

---

[1] In an article, "H. L. Mencken as a Critic of Poetry," that appeared in *Jahrbuch für Amerikastudien* (11:83–95, 1966), Carl R. Dolmetsch defended Mencken against those who dogmatically and irresponsibly dismiss his poetry criticism. Professor Dolmetsch shows the absurdity of the view, rather commonly held by recent critics, that Mencken's criticism had no theoretical foundation.

world of reality is too much with us, we close the door on our rational selves and ask for "a comforting piece of fiction set to more or less lascivious music—a slap on the back in waltz time—a grand release of longings and repressions to the tune of flutes, harps, sackbuts, psalteries and the usual strings." Nothing so comfortably walls out the harsh world as does an emotional binge. Man's *thoughts,* first conceptualized as prose, cannot wear the dress—that is, the phraseology, the meter, the rhythms, etc.—of poetry without being, in part at least, false to themselves. Man's *dreams,* however, flow most convincingly in the sylvan robes of poesy. A reader is most susceptible to the poetic lures when his rational guard is down, exposing his emotional midriff to the blows of the palpably nonsensical. Even though he believed that poetry was thus irrational, and often most convincing by virtue of its beauty, Mencken would never, like Plato, have banned the poet from his republic. Quite the contrary, he would have insisted on his great importance for soothing the tired mind. In effect, poetry played a medicinal part in the intelligent man's life. There are times, Mencken wrote, when all of us go to poetry, just as we go to women, or to "glad" books, or to dogmatic theology.

To avoid laboring a minor point any further, I take a few choice items from "The Poet and His Art," Mencken's most comprehensive statement on the subject. One of the few pieces on literature that he considered worthy of including in his *Chrestomathy,* it appeared originally in the June, 1920, issue of *The Smart Set* and was then included in *Prejudices: Third Series* (1922).

One always associates poetry with youth, for it deals chiefly with the ideas that are peculiar to youth, and its terminology is quite as youthful as its content. When one hears of a poet past thirty-five, he seems somehow unnatural and even a trifle obscene; it is as if one encountered a graying man who still played Chopin waltzes and believed in elective affinities.

In all of [the sonnets of the world] there are ideas that would sound idiotic in prose, and phrases that would sound clumsy and uncouth in prose. But the rhyme scheme conceals this nonsensicality. As a substitute for the missing logical plausibility it provides a sensuous harmony. Reading the thing, one gets a vague effect of agreeable sound, and so the logical feebleness is overlooked. It is, in a sense, like observing a pretty girl, competently dressed and made up, across the footlights. But translating the poem into prose is like meeting and marrying her.

It is the *idea* expressed in a poem, and not the mellifluousness of the words used to express it, that arrests and enchants the average connoisseur. Often, indeed, he disdains this mellifluousness, and argues that the idea ought to be set forth without the customary pretty jingling, or, at most, with only the scant jingling that lies in rhythm—in brief, he wants his ideas in the altogether, and so advocates *vers libre*.

There are whole speeches in the Shakespearean plays whose meaning is unknown even to scholars—and yet they remain favorites, and well deserve to. Who knows, again, what the sonnets are about? Is the bard talking about the inn-keeper's wife at Oxford, or about a love affair of a pathological, Y. M. C. A. character? Some say one thing, and some say the other. But all who have ears must agree that the sonnets are extremely beautiful stuff— that the English language reaches in them the topmost heights of conceivable beauty. Shakespeare thus ought to be ranked among the musicians, along with Beethoven. As a philosopher he was a ninth-rater—but so was old Ludwig.

Poetry is a form of writing in which the author attempts to disarm reason and evoke emotion, partly by presenting images that awaken a powerful response in the subconscious and partly by the mere sough and blubber of words. . . . It is essentially an effort to elude the bitter facts of life, whereas prose is essentially a means of unearthing and exhibiting them. The gap is bridged by sentimental prose, which is half prose and half poetry— Lincoln's Gettysburg speech, the average sermon, the prose of an erotic novelette. Immediately the thing acquires a literal meaning it ceases to be poetry; immediately it becomes capable of convincing an adult and perfectly sober man during the hours between breakfast and luncheon it is indisputably prose.

A sound sonnet is almost as pleasing an object as a well-written fugue. A pretty lyric, deftly done, has all the technical charm of a fine carving. I think it is craftsmanship that I admire most in the world. Brahms enchants me because he knew his trade perfectly. I like Richard Strauss because he is full of technical ingenuities, because he is a master-workman. Well, who ever heard of a finer craftsman than William Shakespeare? His music was magnificent, he played superbly upon all the common emotions—and he did it magnificently, he did it with an air. No, I am no poetry-hater. But even Shakespeare I most enjoy, not on brisk mornings when I feel fit for any deviltry, but on dreary evenings when my old wounds are troubling me, and some fickle one has just sent back the autographed set of my first editions, and bills are piled up on my desk, and I am too sad to work. Then I mix a stiff dram—and read poetry.

IV

Shortly before his twenty-first birthday, Mencken was made drama editor of the *Morning Herald*. Between September, 1901, and October, 1903, he wrote a daily theatre column for that paper, during which time he became a leading dramatic critic. A few years later he acted as dramatic critic on the *Sun*, where his assaults upon theatrical frauds so grossly offended local managers that they complained to the *Sun* publisher, Walter W. Abell, who stood by his young prodigy. In the end, however, Mencken concluded that "the managers were right —that it was a bit unjust after all for me to treat them so hardly. They had to take whatever plays the theatrical syndicate sent them. . . . So I resigned as dramatic critic and have avoided the job ever since. That was in 1909." [2] He later unearthed some of that early criticism to show his *Korpsbruder* Nathan, who found it quite perceptive. In his Personal Note to *Letters of H. L. Mencken* (1961), Hamilton Owens attests to having learned from Mencken's criticism. He concludes, "Some day a scholar will dig out those fugitive reviews and republish them. Most drama critics could learn something from them. Perhaps the late George Jean Nathan did."

It is unthinkable that the young Mencken, just learning his trade, could have read Shaw without being, at first, overwhelmed, just as it was natural that he should have cooled toward the great Irishman as the years disclosed Shaw's extreme didacticism. One can imagine no more fitting subject for Mencken's first book of prose: *George Bernard Shaw: His Plays* (1905). Mencken doubtless learned much from the Shavian style: the iconoclastic wit, the hyperbolic exaggeration, the use of contrast, often outlandish, even fantastic. Moreover, Shaw always gave a good show. His customers invariably went away moved, if not convinced. At a time when Shaw's influence was just beginning to be felt, Mencken wrote of him as he had written of Ibsen:

In the dramas of George Bernard Shaw, which deal almost wholly with the current conflict between orthodoxy and heterodoxy, it is but natural that the characters should fall broadly into two general classes—the ordinary folks who represent the great majority, and the iconoclasts, or idol-smashers. Darwin made this war between the faithful and the scoffers the chief concern of the time, and the sham-smashing that is now going on, in all the

[2] *H. L. M.: The Mencken Bibliography*, compiled by Betty Adler with the assistance of Jane Wilhelm (Baltimore, 1961), p. 46.

fields of human inquiry, might be compared to the crusades that engrossed the world in the middle ages.[3]

Shaw was, Mencken felt, the most gifted of the iconoclasts. Mencken was eager, of course, to take part in the sham-smashing. After all, the two writers who exerted the most influence on his thought—Nietzsche and Thomas Henry Huxley—had spent their lives waging war on popular superstition and prejudice. Like most great satirists, Mencken felt that the iconoclast proved enough when he demonstrated the falsehood of some honored belief; there was no need to hatch a new belief to fill the place of the exploded one. He seemed to imply, if not overtly state, that a discarded belief left as a legacy the freedom to explore and interpret anew. Indeed, Mencken felt that what little progress there was depended not so much on the acceptance of new ideas as on the rooting out of false ones.

In his little book on Shaw, some of the early slap and dash of the Mencken style is evident, particularly in his discussion of *Man and Superman,* which had appeared but recently.

Measured with rule, plumb-line or hay-scales, *Man and Superman* is easily Shaw's *magnum opus.* In bulk it is brobdingnagian; in scope it is stupendous; in purpose it is one with the Odyssey. Like a full-rigged ship before a spanking breeze, it cleaves deep into the waves, sending ripples far to port and starboard, and its giant canvases rise half way to the clouds, with resplendent jibs, skysails, staysails and studdingsails standing out like quills upon the fretful porcupine.

Though in the play Shaw preached treason to all the schools, there was no doubt that he had borrowed from earlier thinkers: "It is a three-ring circus, with Ibsen doing running high jumps; Schopenhauer playing the calliope and Nietzsche selling peanuts in the reserved seats." Calling it "the most entertaining play of its generation," he wondered if Shaw had not written it "in a vain effort to rid himself at one fell swoop of all the disquieting doctrines that infested his innards." Finally, Mencken called it "a tract cast in an encyclopedic and epic mold—a stupendous, magnificent, colossal effort to make a dent in the cosmos with a slapstick." Note that Mencken was aware of the fundamental fact that the play was a "tract."

Mencken later remarked, in 1945, that "there was a good deal of empty ornament in my first prose book, *George Bernard Shaw: His*

[3] HLM, *George Bernard Shaw: His Plays* (Boston, 1905), pp. xvi–xvii.

Plays. There was also plenty of bad writing in my early *Smart Set* book reviews, begun in November, 1908. Soon afterward I began to tone down, and by the time I was thirty I had developed a style that was clear and alive." [4] It is worth noting that as he "toned down" his style, he became less enthusiastic about Shaw. His disenchantment was partially the result, it seems to me, of his realization that Shaw's handling of ideas was too often facile—perhaps of necessity, since he embodied his ideas on the stage. Shaw's facility in handling widely diverse ideas explains his hold on the young, particularly, but that very facility causes the mature student of ideas to be more interested in the Shavian wit than in the gospel being preached. In effect, it is Shaw's manner rather than his matter that continues to please.

The development of Mencken's attitude toward Shaw is most clearly evidenced in his remarks on the plays that appeared between 1910 and 1920. In a review of three plays, in the criticism for August, 1911, entitled "The New Dramatic Literature," Mencken wrote that the prefaces for *Getting Married* and *The Shewing-up of Blanco Posnet* were "far more important than the plays." At the same time, he thought *The Doctor's Dilemma* "an amusing and well constructed piece, in which fun is poked at the medical fellows on the one hand, and that puzzling thing, the artistic temperament, is studied on the other." He concluded by saying that *Dilemma* was the best thing Shaw had done since *Man and Superman*. Still, the antivivisectionist plea in the preface to *Dilemma* drew Mencken's scorn:

Shaw, like every other anti-vivisectionist, is merely a sentimentalist who strains at a guinea pig and swallows a baby. In brief, the wild Irishman sinks to the level of a somewhat ridiculous crusader. The trouble with him is that he has begun to take himself seriously. When he was content to write plays first and discuss them afterward, he was unfailingly diverting. But now that he writes tracts first and then devises plays to rub them in he grows rather tedious.

Reviewing a new edition of *Misalliance* in September, 1914, Mencken summed up the Shaw technique: "The formula of Shaw has become transparent enough—a dozen other men now practice his trick of putting the obvious into terms of the scandalous—but he still works with surpassing humor and address." The play's preface, which ran to something like forty-five thousand words, traversing "the whole

[4] HLM, *Minority Report* (New York, 1956), pp. 292–293.

field of the domestic relations, with side trips into education, journalism, party politics, theology, criminology and sex hygiene," was one of "the best things, indeed, that he has ever done." There was, however, condescension in the praise, since, after all, it was the obvious that Shaw put on display: "This is the special function of Shaw, the steady business of his life: to say the things that every body knows and nobody says, to expose the everyday hypocrisies, to rout platitudes with superplatitudes." The play would not, Mencken felt, lift Shaw any nearer Shakespeare, but it was excellent reading: "You will not do much snoring over this latest book. It will tickle you and caress you and make you tingle with delight. It is bully good stuff."

But by that date it was evident that Mencken no longer looked up to Shaw as the leader of the iconoclasts; he was now just one of the boys, one of the select few, to be sure, but by no means a saint gifted with divine powers. Moreover, Mencken had begun to find the prefaces more amusing than the plays—they were better reading.

Mencken's last critical essay on Shaw was his severest indictment of the platitudinarian aspects of the playwright. "The Ulster Polonius" first appeared in *The Smart Set* in August, 1916, as a review of *Androcles and the Lion* and then in a revised and lengthened form in *Prejudices: First Series*. Here Mencken did little more than polish and elaborate his thesis in the *Misalliance* review. Nowhere in Shaw, Mencken stated, was there an original idea; still, he was constantly abused as a heretic almost of the magnitude of Galileo, Nietzsche, or Simon Magus. Why so?

Because he practices with great zest and skill the fine art of exhibiting the obvious in unexpected and terrifying lights—because he is a master of the logical trick of so matching two apparently safe premises that they yield an incongruous and inconvenient conclusion—above all, because he is a fellow of the utmost charm and address, quick-witted, bold, limber-tongued, persuasive, humorous, iconoclastic, ingratiating—in brief, an Irishman, and so the exact antithesis of the solemn Sassenachs who ordinarily instruct and exhort us.[5]

Shaw offers the playgoer the opportunity to hear truths about himself that he is either too sentimental or too stupid to admit openly. In the play and preface of *Androcles and the Lion*, for example, Mencken felt the complete Shaw formula was exposed: "On the one hand there

[5] HLM, *Prejudices: First Series* (New York, 1919), p. 182.

is a mass of platitudes; on the other hand there is the air of a peep-show. On the one hand he rehearses facts so stale that even Methodist clergymen have probably heard of them; on the other hand he states them so scandalously that the pious get all the thrills out of the busi-ness that would accompany a view of the rector in liquor in the pulpit."

Finally, and most importantly, Mencken objected to the moral note in all Shaw's writings, just as he objected to the moral preachments of all artists. (He was particularly harsh with D. H. Lawrence on this score.) It was dangerous, and usually crippling, he believed, for the artist to allow ethical concerns to dominate a work of art. To be sure, the artist could, if he pleased, present his characters involved in moral problems, but he should do so only to portray character and not some battle to the death between good and evil—the proper subject of melodrama or the Uplift.

At about the same time he encountered the plays of Shaw, Mencken was reading Ibsen, Hauptmann, Sudermann, Pinero, Maeterlinck (whom he later derided unmercifully), and others of the post-Scribe rebellion. In the early years of his pastorate at *The Smart Set*, he wrote dozens of enlightened reviews of Continental, English and American plays. Not long after his tour of duty as drama critic for the Baltimore *Herald* and later the *Sun*, he decided that *reading* plays, just then beginning to appear in print regularly, far surpassed the en-joyment derived from viewing hammy actors cavort about on a stage, the while one's nostrils were assaulted by an odoriferous audience. The numerous reviews of printed plays, a few of which are included in this collection, show Mencken to have been one of our best critics of dramatic literature.

But like poetry, the drama could not satisfy Mencken's hunger for ideas. Moreover, Mencken never tired of insisting that the *causes* of an action were infinitely more important and fascinating than the act itself. A visual art cannot, of course, present the hidden impulse, the atavistic yearning, the fortuitous quirk of fate so clearly or convinc-ingly as can prose fiction—the art form that brought Mencken his greatest triumph as critic.

V

Mencken was always suspicious of iron-clad rules concerning the novel or drama or poetry. He never tired of scornfully dismissing all the dogmatic theorists with their narrow little definitions of what made a book a novel, or what a poem must be before it could be called a lyric, an epic, or whathaveyou. In this he might be called a romantic, though the terms *romantic* and *classicist* are used so vaguely as to be almost meaningless. Though never a pigeonholer, Mencken did have a theory of literature and a theory of criticism, both of which were rather severely revised between the early years on *The Smart Set* and the period of the *Mercury*. When, in his first book article for *The Smart Set*, Mencken chastised Upton Sinclair for mouthing platitudes in his novel *The Moneychangers*, and at the same time predicted that the artist in Sinclair would be destroyed by his messianic delusion, he accompanied his censure with the reminder that "an economic struggle, to make material for fiction, must be pictured, not objectively and as a mere bout between good and evil, but subjectively and as some chosen protagonist sees and experiences it." Stating one of his cardinal beliefs, Mencken insisted that the interest the reader or viewer has in a novel or drama lies, "always and inevitably, in some one man's effort to master his fate." Even in this first book article Mencken was distinguishing between surface realism, which slid easily into melodrama, and what might be called "subjective" realism, which in its interpretation and its concern with the enigmatic in life went far deeper than the photographic could ever go. In criticizing Sinclair, Mencken might well have been thinking of the finest of English novelists, in his judgment—Joseph Conrad. He believed then, as he did later, that *Lord Jim* was the greatest novel in the language.

The great novel, Mencken wrote, must tell, with insight, imagination, and conviction, the story of some one man's struggle with his fate, at the same time displaying, "like a vast fever chart, the ebb and flow of his ideas and ideals, and the multitude of forces shaping them." Such a novel would provide an accurate picture of a protagonist's being driven, tortured, and fashioned by the blood within him and the world without. As an admirer of the fiction of Zola, Dreiser, Hardy, Bennett, and Conrad, Mencken felt that it was the "background" that chiefly marks the good novel; and after the background, the normality of the people under observation. Abnormality was more the subject matter for the psychologist than the novelist; Mencken would never have called many of the highly praised books of today *great*, because they are less concerned, many of them, with the average man and his immemorial struggle with life than they are with the

freaks and "case studies" of the warped minority. Moreover, this typical man must fit in some kind of recognizable environment.

Such a theory was the natural result of Mencken's conviction that
life is a struggle, that each man battles for his place in the sun. What
is more, man's struggle with his environment, although he battles val-
iantly, ends inevitably in his succumbing to it. In other words, fiction
must not endeavor to contradict the most important facts of life. The
influence of Darwin, Spencer, and Huxley on Mencken's thought is
here clearly present. At this stage in Mencken's writing career his aesthetic theory is inextricably bound to biological science. I am referring
to his attitude toward "serious" literature, not comic writing. Although
Mencken later felt that the hero of major fiction was a superior man,
"a salient individual" in conflict with "harsh and meaningless fiats of
destiny" (such phrases appear again and again), he always held to his
belief that recognizable traits of Everyman must be seen in the hero.

If the great novel depicted man heroically struggling with his fate,
it was but a short, logical step to Mencken's belief that the second-
rate novel, or "the average best seller," has for its hero a creature who
is superb, irresistible, and wholly autonomous. "He is the easy master
of every situation that his environment confronts him with; he is
equally successful at killing cannibals, snaring burglars, operating air-
ships, terrorizing the stock market, or making love. He is not the
product and plaything of fate, but its boss. The world is his oyster."
The hundreds of novels which displayed the protagonist as the master
of his fate, the captain of his soul, occasioned high mirth in the skeptical newspaperman and critic. Having viewed society on all its layers,
Mencken concluded that all men are in large part products of a condi-
tioning process. Again, corroboration was readily found in science.

If good fiction then is less concerned with what the characters do
than with what is done to them, we must insist that the novelist have
some view of the world. The writer with no philosophy of life can
hardly be expected to account for what befalls his victim-protagonist.
Did not all the great artists in history have some "comprehensible and
credible philosophy of life, born of a mighty personality"? Also, the
philosophy of an artist will individualize his work. It would be impossible to think of Dickens, for example, "without recalling his sentimental view of the world, with its cardinal doctrine that all human ills
are to be cured by love. And in the same way, we cannot detach
Thackeray from his tolerant cynicism, nor Shakespeare from his proud

resignationism, nor Milton from his lofty idealism, nor Fielding from his buoyant optimism, his belief in mankind, his firm conviction that the mere being alive is sufficient for happiness." [6] Moreover, it is the philosophy of an artist which, underlying everything he writes, enables the reader to gain from reading him and to face life with more understanding and comfort. Mencken felt that the absence of a philosophical viewpoint marred the works of Hermann Sudermann, who shared with Gerhart Hauptmann the distinction of being Germany's leading man of letters in the period just preceding World War I. Although Sudermann was an observer of extraordinary shrewdness, he was unable to interpret his observations satisfactorily. "It is not that he is struck by the notion that life is meaningless—for that notion, as the case of Joseph Conrad proves, is not inconsistent with clear thinking—but that he seeks to read hazy, antagonistic and often puerile meanings into it." One missed in Sudermann's works "the passionate earnestness and certainty, the clear cut logic" to be found in such novels as *Germinal, Barry Lyndon,* and *Anna Karenina.* Rather than present one consistent view, Sudermann sought to be alternately an idealist and a realist, a revolutionary and a reactionary, a pessimist and an optimist; his writings lost vitality because there was no master note in them. In an essay on Sudermann, in *Prejudices: First Series,* Mencken commented again on this absence of any prevailing point of view. He remarked that when Sudermann, like Hauptmann, was finally oppressed by "the emptiness of naturalism," he was unable to change satisfactorily. Rather, he began to dilute his naturalism with a sentimentality that, in *Magda,* his best-known play, recalled Augier's *Le Mariage d'Olympe.*

Like all good critics, Mencken amalgamated theory and practice: while pointing out the weakness or strength in a given work, he would comment on certain broad principles which govern, for example, the creation of character. In criticizing Gertrude Atherton's *Julia France and Her Times* (1912), Mencken revealed his own critical credo when he stated that the fallacy of Mrs. Atherton's method lay in the fact that it left her characters unaccounted for, "that it describes them too much and explains them too little. She shows them doing all sorts of amazing things, and in the showing she is infallibly brisk and entertaining, but she seldom gets into their acts that appearance of inevitability which makes for reality." Mencken did not feel that the novelist

[6] HLM, "A Glance at the Spring Fiction," *The Smart Set,* 30:153 (April, 1910).

had got beneath the surface of her people; to him she had neglected "the first business of a serious novelist, which is to interpret and account for her characters, to criticize life as well as describe it."

The reader of Mencken should be, at this point, aware of what appears to be an essential contradiction in his entire critical credo. Mencken believed that life, in philosophical terms, was flatly meaningless: man's existence was purposeless, merely one of the many results of natural selection; no intelligent, foresighted being created man to fulfill a specific need in the cosmic process. Belief in such an intelligent being is nothing more than anthropomorphism, no matter how you cut it, and Mencken felt that all anthropomorphic gods were creatures of man's imagination. Bearing this apparently nihilistic theory in mind, the reader might assume that Mencken was one of those who then concluded that "everything is permissible," in the manner of a Dostoevskian character.

Mencken concluded no such thing of course; he was much too *ir*religious ever to be a nihilist. (The two men whom Mencken admired most, T.H. Huxley and Nietzsche, were violent opponents, in their different ways, of all that nihilism stood for. It may help to remember that Nietzsche's war on Christianity was in effect a war on the nihilism to which it inevitably led, with its *de*naturizing of both the world and man, its abnegation of *this* life for an imagined afterlife, its elevation of pity as the highest virtue, and its promise of celestial kingship to the weak and the unfit for no other reason than that they were weak and unfit.) The assumption that man resided in a world created for his benefit, for the purpose of his playing at the little game of saints and sinners, was a result of his ability to *imagine* it possible to rescind the laws of physics and biology and move beyond his humanity. Such imaginings were nothing more than evidence of man's almost incredible egotism—and his no less amazing refusal to accept existence as the product of something like chemical necessity. As the contemporary existentialists say, man is free of ultimates; in effect, he is free of anything like divine guidance and its concomitant duty. But unlike the existentialist, Mencken would not extend that freedom to the entire realm of existence, as Sartre, for example, has done.

Sartre seems to say that since man is freed from the shackles of anthropomorphism, he is also free in his existential state, that he is free to choose what course of action he will take, free to *determine* his own fate. Mencken insisted that the anthropomorphic theory, though idiotic, would continue to be popular with the mass mind for ages to come, and probably forever. He would further insist that man's freedom from the gods is really meaningless when we realize that his struggle has always been with nature and its fiats, though at times man translates the terms of natural existence (man as the result of biological and psychological forces) into terms of supernatural dependence (man as the result of divine laws or intelligent design outside the natural order). Sartre says man is pretty much free to do as he wishes, both morally and physically; Mencken said that man was "free" to do whatever he is most strongly motivated to do. Hence his demand that the serious writer provide ample causes to show that his effects are in large degree necessary and thus believable. The comic writer was not so bound, for his success often depended upon his describing actions and events that seemed to contradict the normal cause-effect relationships found in most human activity. Hence, the laughter.

There is really no contradiction between Mencken's numerous remarks about the meaninglessness of life, and his demand that a writer give meaning to his portraiture by having some consistent philosophy of existence. All art was for him an "ordering" of some aspect of the material world—of which man and his irrational impulses were a part. In a word, the artist was a craftsman, a man with a *design* that could be given palpable form.

To see Mencken's critical credo in action, we should examine his criticism of various writers, particularly those whose work he reviewed over a period of years. For the present purpose it would be well to examine his remarks on writers who elicited a mixed blessing. In the objections a critic has to a given work we may readily observe his criteria for the perfect work—which exists as a standard only, never in fact.

Among the writers whom Mencken praised most highly during his first three years as a book critic was H. G. Wells. In April, 1909, he called *Tono-Bungay* one of the best novels to appear in months. In February, 1910, he lauded *Ann Veronica*. In July, 1910, in a review of *Mr. Polly,* he stated that Wells was the successor of Dickens, for he concerned himself with the much neglected English middle class. (The two novelists were, of course, poles apart in their treatment of character: "Dickens regarded his characters as a young mother regards her baby; Wells looks at his as a porkpacker looks at a hog.") "I know very well that the author of *David Copperfield* was a greater artist than the author of *Mr. Polly*, just as I know that the Archbishop of Canterbury is a more virtuous man than my good friend, Fred the Bartender; but all the same, I prefer Wells and Fred to Dickens and the Archbishop. In such matters one must allow a lot to individual taste and prejudice."

Less than a year later, Mencken reviewed *The New Machiavelli* and found in it evidence that Wells had the inside track in the race to claim the laurels of the recently deceased George Meredith. Only Conrad, Hardy, and Moore had as much to say that was worth saying, and they were all entering the twilight of their careers. "If [Wells] keeps on as he has started, the world in ten years may choose to forget that he once wrote thrillers in the manner of Jules Verne, just as it has chosen to forget that Richard Wagner once wrote romanzas for cornet-a-piston." Mencken was more reserved in his praise of *Marriage*, which he reviewed in January, 1913. Wells still promised a great deal, but he was not delivering on schedule. Two more years passed and Mencken began to despair of his white hope. *Marriage* and *The Passionate Friends* were both disappointing after the success of *Tono-Bungay*, and now, in January, 1915, he openly panned *The Wife of Sir Isaac Harman:*

When he abandoned his Jules Verne yarns, back in 1906 or 1907, and set up shop as a serious novelist, he arrested attention at once by the freshness of his point of view, the humorous sharpness of his observation, and the high potentiality (to borrow from electricity) of his writing. There was something magnificently assertive and iconoclastic about him; he seemed likely to put new life and vigor into the novel of manners. . . . We are now familiar with his suffragettes, his tea-swilling London uplifters, his smattering of quasi-science, his Thackerayan asides, his chapter sections, his journalistic raciness. And, being familiar with these things, we begin to grow a bit weary of them. *The History of Mr. Polly* was a comic interlude, a return to cleverness, a reprieve. But *Marriage* and *The Passionate Friends* were sadly lacking in the élan of *Tono-Bungay*, and *The Wife of Sir Isaac Harman*, for whole chapters, is unmistakably dull.

Mencken went on in his review to comment on the numerous English novelists of ability who wrote two or three good books and then moved backwards. As examples he listed Leonard Merrick, W. J. Locke, Galsworthy, Hugh Walpole, and Wells. The only two English novelists who continued turning out good work year after year, mellowing and improving their method, were Joseph Conrad and Henry James—"the one a Pole and the other an American!"

As the months turned into years and as book after book by Wells came off the presses, Mencken became more and more acerb, at last pitiless, in his reviews. Hadn't Wells proved that he could turn out competent work? Then why this continuous flow of fustian, this obsession with every fad of the day? Finally, in December, 1918, Mencken gave up on Wells and composed an essay-review of *Joan and Peter*, which he entitled "The Late Mr. Wells." The same title adorns a rather lengthy obituary in *Prejudices: First Series* in which Mencken endeavored to account for the alarming disintegration of Wells the artist. The essay can stand today as an accurate assessment of the novelist. It was not the War, Mencken asserted, that swallowed Wells; he was patriotic but never went totally insane as so many others had done:

What has slowly crippled him and perhaps disposed of him is his gradual acceptance of the theory, corrupting to the artist and scarcely less so to the man, that he is one of the Great Thinkers of his era, charged with a pregnant Message to the Younger Generation—that his ideas, rammed into enough skulls, will Save the Empire, not only from the satanic Nietzscheism of the Hindenburgs and post-Hindenburgs, but also from all those inner Weaknesses that taint and flabbergast its vitals, as the tapeworm with nineteen heads devoured Atharippus of Macedon. In brief, he suffers from a messianic delusion—and once a man begins to suffer from a messianic delusion his days as a serious artist are ended.

More important than the causes of Wells's artistic decline, at least for the present purpose, are Mencken's remarks concerning the nature of serious art (notice again that his condemnation is accompanied by an aesthetic theory). In this essay, he repeated his belief that a novelist must have not only a point of view, but must have one that is in no way dependent on any craze of the moment. Merely to describe existence was not enough—an answer to those who endeavor to pigeonhole Mencken as nothing more than a "naturalistic" critic, and who define "naturalism" in a most shallow way in the first place. The novelist's point of view, Mencken contended, must regard the internal workings and meanings of existence and not just its superficial appearances. And the writer must be consistent in his over-all view of existence. Even though the artist may be unable to find any meaning in life, still that meaninglessness can be displayed with clarity and consistency—as such skeptics as Conrad, Hardy, Dreiser, and Anatole France have shown. In brief, the sound work of art must do at least two major things: it must represent accurately, and it must interpret convincingly. And "a current of feeling" must coordinate and inform the representation and the interpretation. And here are Horace's *dulce et utile* in modern clothing. The work of art must be both sweet and useful; it must both please in its structure and instruct or interpret in its content. The "current of feeling" is nothing more than the consistent philosophy or manner of viewing life which he insisted must be found in the best art. The two aspects or functions, the *dulce et utile*, are not, of course, mutually exclusive; they are not divorced as structure on the one hand, content on the other. Rather, they are interlocking, dependent on each other.

It would be impossible even to summarize the hundreds of reviews that Mencken wrote in appreciation, and in defense, of realism and naturalism in fiction. Today Mencken is credited, quite rightly, with having been the leader of the forces for realism that triumphed so completely in the nineteen-twenties. But here again it is necessary to examine what he meant by the terms *realism* and *naturalism*. After reading an essay on Joyce's *Ulysses*, which praised it "in high, astounding terms as a complete and exact record of a day in the life of its people," Mencken objected:

It is, of course, nothing of the sort. At least nine-tenths of its materials came, not out of the Bloom family, but out of James Joyce. Even the celebrated unspoken monologue of Marion at the end is his, not hers. There are long sections of it that even the professional psychologists, who are singularly naïve, must detect as false—that is, false for Marion, false for a woman of her position, perhaps even false for any woman. But they are not false for Joyce.[7]

Still, Joyce was a realist, according to Mencken's definition. It was in *The Smart Set* of Mencken and Nathan, incidentally, that Joyce's short stories and poetry first appeared in America. "Realism," Mencken wrote, "is simply intellectual honesty in the artist. The realist yields nothing to what is manifestly not true, however alluring. He makes no compromise with popular sentimentality and illusion. He

[7] HLM, *The Bathtub Hoax and Other Blasts and Bravos,* edited by Robert McHugh (New York, 1958), p. 106.

avoids the false inference as well as the bogus fact. He respects his materials as he respects himself." [8] And Joyce did this. Mencken refused to believe that such a thing as realism grounded on objective fact existed. The artist does not copy the real world (Mencken had almost no respect for what was called "photographic realism"); rather he interprets and criticizes, and his interpretation and criticism are of necessity subjective. It was not the subject matter which determined whether a writer was a realist; it was rather his honesty with his material and, above all, with himself. Thus Mencken believed that Jane Austen was one of the great realists, as were Anatole France and Joseph Conrad, who were often on the border line of the fantastic. It is also clear that in this definition Mencken is taking a swipe at the opponents of realism (mostly academicians, who still constituted a small phalanx in the nineteen-twenties when this was written). Clearly, the implication he makes is that only the nonrealists are dishonest. How Irving Babbitt, Paul Elmer More, and Henry van Dyke must have cried out at such foul casuistry!

Naturalism was something else again. It was a type rather than a method. Mencken saw clearly that the naturalistic novel, so-called, often dabbled in filth for the simple hoggish joy of being repulsive (he spoke of the "meticulous nastiness that is so often the undoing of the naturalistic novelist" and of "flea-hunting naturalism"), but he also saw the enormous value of such writers as Zola. In a long essay-review (in *The Smart Set* for August, 1912) of three new translations of Zola's minor works, Mencken paid tribute to the great novels of the "Rougon-Macquart" series and especially to his influence on other writers.

Allow all you please for Zola's ardent pursuit of scientific half-truths, for his air of an anatomist dismembering a corpse, for what Nietzsche, in a bitter moment, called his "delight to stink" and you still have an extraordinarily acute and penetrating observer of the human comedy, a creator of vivid and memorable characters, an accomplished workman in large forms, the high priest of a new cult in art. Zola, I am aware, did not invent naturalism—and naturalism, as he defined it, is not now the fashion. But it must be obvious that his propaganda, as novelist and critic, did more than any other one thing to give naturalism direction and coherence and to break down its antithesis, the sentimental romanticism of the middle Nineteenth Century—*Uncle Tom's Cabin, David Copperfield, La Dame aux Camélias*—

[8] *Ibid.*

and that his influence today, even if he has few avowed disciples, is still wide and undeniable.

That influence, Mencken felt, could be seen in the works of Moore, Hardy, Wells, and Bennett in England, Sudermann and Wedekind in Germany, Norris and Dreiser in America, Gorki and Andreyev in Russia, and in a whole school of writers in Scandinavia. His impression on individual writers was not so great, however, as the effect he had had on the novel as an art form. He was one of the first great writers to view man as a mammal, "swayed and fashioned, not by the fiats and conspiracies of a mysterious camorra of arbitrary gods, but by natural laws, by food and drink, by blood and environment. He taught his fellow-craftsmen to sit down in patience before a fact, to trace out its cause, to see it largely, not as something *in vacuo,* but as something fitting into an inevitable and unemotional process."

Though perhaps an exaggeration of Zola's influence, this statement perfectly illustrates Mencken's concern with character motivation. It was not a character's acts that were of first concern; rather, it was the novelist's depiction of the causes of action that mattered. In his extraordinary essay on Conrad in *A Book of Prefaces* (1917), Mencken concentrated on the novelist's interest in the subjective, rather than objective, "fact." As Mencken stated, Conrad certainly could paint a scene; he could make the reader see and feel an event, an object, a personage as probably no other artist in the realm of fiction could do; but the mere outward show of the phenomenal world was secondary to his art. He was concerned with "the inextricable movement of phenomena and noumena between event and event"; with "the obscure genesis, in some chance emotion or experience, of an extraordinary series of transactions"; with the "effect of some gigantic and fortuitous event upon the mind and soul of a given man"; with showing "how cause and effect are intricately commingled, so that it is difficult to separate motive from consequence, and consequence from motive." It was the process of the mind rather than the actual fact that interested him. He was concerned foremost with subjective impulses, and only secondarily with the objective acts resulting from the impulse. All this, it should be remembered, was written fifty years ago, when Conrad was still thought of as a "romancer."

There was, Mencken believed, a danger in following too closely any kind of "objective" naturalism. In his reviews of various writers

Mencken remarked the inability of the naturalist to do the one thing necessary to the highest form of art: involve his reader emotionally with the central figures of his creation. No matter what the art form, the "viewer" must be "taken in" by the artist and become one with the subject. In an exceptionally acute essay on Bennett that appeared in *Prejudices: First Series*, Mencken further clarified his position on the necessity of emotional involvement in the plight or fate of the fictional hero. Likening Bennett's "extraordinarily fluent and tuneful" journalese to that of Wells, Mencken then contrasted the "manner" of the two men.

Wells has a believing mind, and cannot resist the lascivious beckonings and eye-winkings of meretricious novelty; Bennett carries skepticism so far that it often takes on the appearance of a mere peasant-like suspicion of ideas, bellicose and unintelligent. Wells is astonishingly intimate and confidential; and more than one of his novels reeks with a shameless sort of autobiography; Bennett, even when he makes use of personal experience, contrives to get impersonality into it. Wells, finally, is a sentimentalist, and cannot conceal his feelings; Bennett, of all the English novelists of the day, is the most steadily aloof and ironical.

In this aloofness Mencken saw both the great strength and the no-less-great weakness of Bennett the artist. On the one hand the irony set him free from the messianic delusions that had "engulfed such romantic men as Wells, Winston Churchill and the late Jack London, and even, at times, such sentimental agnostics as Dreiser." But on the other hand it had left him "empty of the passion that is, when all is said and done, the chief mark of the true novelist." Unable to involve himself in his characters' struggles against destiny, Bennett was unable "to arouse in the reader that penetrating sense of kinship, that profound and instinctive sympathy, which in its net effect is almost indistinguishable from the understanding born of experiences actually endured and emotions actually shared." Not possessing this sympathy for his characters, Bennett was unable to create a figure that haunted the memory as did Lord Jim or Carrie Meeber or Huck Finn or Tom Jones. In explaining why Bennett was unable to create memorable characters, Mencken expressed a theory that is near being irrefragable. The reason for this inability:

It lies in the plain fact that [Bennett's characters] appear to their creator, not as men and women whose hopes and agonies are of poignant concern, not as tragic comedians in isolated and concentrated dramas, but as mean figures in an infinitely dispersed and unintelligible farce, as helpless no-bodies in an epic struggle that transcends both their volition and their comprehension. Thus viewing them, he fails to humanize them completely, and so he fails to make their emotions contagious. They are, in their way, often vividly real; they are thoroughly accounted for; what there is of them is unfailingly life-like; they move and breathe in an environment that pulses and glows. But the attitude of the author toward them remains, in the end, the attitude of a biologist toward his laboratory animals. He does not *feel* with them—and neither does his reader.

Actually, Bennett's chief concern was not so much with individuals as it was with large groups. In the long series of Five Towns books he had done his best work. "Better than any other man of his time he has got upon paper the social anatomy and physiology of the masses of average, everyday, unimaginative Englishmen." But in depicting this middle-class milieu Bennett employed an irony that was finally dis-quieting to the reader. Striving for what Mencken called a French ob-jectivity, Bennett eventually arrived at a cynicism that was crippling to his art. Finding life without meaning, he seemed to conclude that it was futile to read a meaning into it. In effect, he concluded that art and life are one and the same. On the contrary, Mencken asserted that art was a purposeful organization of some aspect of the universal meaninglessness.

Art can never be simply representation. It cannot deal solely with precisely what is. It must, at the least, present the real in the light of some recogniz-able ideal; it must give to the eternal farce, if not some moral, then at all events some direction. For without that formulation there can be no clear-cut separation of the individual will from the general stew and turmoil of things, and without that separation there can be no coherent drama, and without that drama there can be no evocation of emotion, and without that emotion art is unimaginable.

VI

Mencken scorned the criticism that sought to improve the mind or "uplift" the reader. Both in theory and practice he adhered to the Di-onysian rather than the Apollonian view: the critic's first duty was aesthetic, not moral or pedagogic. He felt that the true critic helped his reader to appreciate, in a judicious manner, the work of art. But he stood foursquare against the pedant and the pedagogue, those who

sought to schoolmaster art and artists. Nonetheless, for over two dec-
ades Mencken acted as Harvard and Yale, minus stuffiness and dead
matter, to American readers, and helped create a sophisticated reading public. In his autobiography Ben Hecht referred to Mencken as
"The Republic's One-Man Renaissance." Hecht called him, quite simply, "my alma mater." Literate members of Hecht's generation would
doubtless subscribe to the following encomium and then append their
own personal footnotes: "No single American mind has influenced existence in the Republic as much as did his. That he influenced us
without declaring wars, starting panics or drumming up a job-hungry
constituency to help him is fine proof that brave words can still lift
the soul of man." [9]

The following selection from the *Smart Set* files provides a rollick-
ing survey of just what went on in the world of letters—and various
other "worlds" as well—between 1908 and 1923. In gathering these
criticisms, reviews, comments, barbs, horselaughs, prophecies, and as-
sorted miscellanea, which constitute about one sixth of Mencken's
Smart Set literary criticism, I was guided by a desire to collect material that deals with books or men still of interest, or that vividly displays what was of special interest in the period, or that helps us to
understand better the multifarious personality of Mencken. I have
avoided articles that are solely or largely concerned with aesthetic
theory or with literature in its broadest sense. Hence, I pass over the
June, 1920, article, "Reflections on Poetry," which was later included in
a *Prejudices* volume and from which I quoted in part II of this Preface. I also exclude those articles on our literary past which eventually
composed the long essay "The National Letters" (in *Prejudices: Second Series*), certainly one of the better analyses of our cultural heritage; Huntington Cairns included it in his excellent reader, *H. L.
Mencken: The American Scene* (1965). A few of these pieces later
appeared, usually in revised form, in the *Prejudices* books, and still
later in the various collections of Mencken: *A Mencken Chrestomathy*
(1949), Alistair Cooke's *The Vintage Mencken* (1955), and James T.
Farrell's *Prejudices: A Selection* (1958). The vast majority of the contents, well over 90 per cent, appears here for the first time in book
form.

Certain passages in the preface and head notes herein appeared
originally in articles in *The Southwest Review* (Spring, 1964) and *The*

9 Ben Hecht, *A Child of the Century* (New York, 1954), p. 175.

Texas Quarterly (Autumn, 1964) and then later in *H. L. Mencken, Literary Critic* (Wesleyan University Press, 1966), Copyright © 1964, 1966 by William H. Nolte. I thank the editors for permission to pour some old wine in this new bottle.

W. H. N.

Columbia, South Carolina
October 1967

Note to the Second Edition

That there has been a great resurgence of interest in the multifarious works of Mencken is apparent in the fact that today most of his many books are back in print, and both selections from and biographical and critical studies of both the man and his oeuvre continue to roll off the presses. In just the past few months four new volumes of his letters have been published, bringing the total to seven so far. Whether this heightened interest in Mencken should be attributed to the spirit of the times or, as is more likely the case, to his artistry, I leave others to decide. But the fact is plain: Mencken is still very much with us.

This collection of Mencken's *Smart Set* criticism first appeared nearly twenty years ago. Since it has been out of print, I have received numerous requests from readers both at home and abroad for aid in locating copies that not even the professional bookfinders were able to provide. Needless to say, I am delighted that this selection from our most delightful critic is once more being made available to readers everywhere.

W.H.N.

Columbia, South Carolina
April 1987

H. L. MENCKEN'S
Smart Set
CRITICISM

I

American Culture

The two pieces that follow are used as an introduction to all that Mencken wrote on literature. In the first article, which appeared in February, 1919, Mencken laments the absence of "a native aristocracy, either political or intellectual, of any permanent position or influence." This lament sounds throughout his work. Though the idea that America suffered, and suffers, from the lack of a self-reliant and intelligent group of standard-makers was certainly not original with Mencken, he probably did more to publicize the need than any other single American.

Mencken assesses briefly our literary past and then comments on salient figures and symbolic events of the present. During the *Smart Set* years Mencken constantly exhorted his fellow critics and literary historians to provide realistic appraisals and re-evaluations of our cultural past, which would then, he felt, influence the present. An "historical sense" imbues all of Mencken's pronouncements on the subject of literature. It is also noteworthy that when given the opportunity as editor of *The American Mercury*, Mencken published a large number of articles on Whitman, Twain, Crane, Melville, and other major figures of the nineteenth century.

One more note: within three years after writing this rather despairing article on the national letters, Mencken found reasons for a more optimistic view. During the great upheaval of the nineteen-twenties, he felt, our literature showed a truly native character for the first time.

In "Our Literary Centers," Mencken develops what might be called a "geographical argument" to explain the vitality of writing in some areas of the country and the timorousness elsewhere. The article further illustrates Mencken's interest in young writers of the nation.

Diagnosis of Our Cultural Malaise

I

The hope business formerly carried on *appassionato* by Randolph S. Bourne seems to have been taken over, of late, by Van Wyck Brooks. It is apparently many months since Dr. Bourne last enjoyed his old dream, once so gaudily set forth in the *New Republic,* of a proud and heaven-kissing super-America, standing solidly on its own bottom and pledged eternally to beauty, that sweet one, and to all the high exercises of the unadulterated intellect. When he prophecies at all, in these bilious current days, it is only to lament like Johann in Herod's rain-barrel, for what he sees around him and ahead of him is naught save a general boiling-down and debauchment of the spirit, so that all ideas yield to an insidious standardization, and the national soul ceases to soar, and even such professional bawlers as I am take the veil and become secret Methodists. But Dr. Brooks, despite certain discreet hems and haws, still cherishes a good deal more confidence and is truer to the glad metaphysic of his (and Bourne's) native New Jersey—as you will discover by a glance through his new book, *Letters and Leadership.* At the moment, he admits, there are unmistakable shadows athwart the American scene, and it may be argued plausibly that we "present to the world at large the spectacle of a vast, undifferentiated herd of good-humored animals"—Knights of Pythias, Presbyterians, Ph.D.'s, Prohibitionists, readers of the *Saturday Evening Post,* admirers of Massenet, sitters on committees, weepers at Chautauquas, wearers of badges, honest householders, children of God. But in the course of time, he believes, this unanimous lethargy of the psyche will be thrown off, and men of powerful and original soul will leap from the mass, and a great art and a great philosophy will begin to bubble, and America will stand out as sharply and as brilliantly as Renaissance Italy or Periclean Greece,

and the world will view the phenomenon with sentiments of approbation, and "we shall become a luminous people, dwelling in the light
and sharing our light."

II

Well, I shall be very glad, for one, to see this luminosity turned on,
but for the present, I must confess, I observe no hand upon the
switch. On the contrary, it seems to me that the shadows were never
darker than they are today, and that we must linger in their blackness
a long while before ever they are penetrated by authentic shafts of
light. My reasons for this depressing belief—for this sad but ineradicable doubt that a grand intellectual awakening is upon us—are two
in number, and I may as well state them at once. The first will require
a long and perhaps somewhat tedious sentence, for which my apologies. It is that the United States, alone among the great nations of
the earth, past or present, has come to its full growth without developing a native aristocracy, either political or intellectual, of any permanent position or influence, and that, in consequence, the banal
ideas and cautious, stupid habits of mind of the great masses of inferior men prevail among us as nowhere else on earth and attain to a
dignity and a power that far surpass their intrinsic worth, and that, in
secondary consequence, almost insuperable obstacles are put in the
way of that disdainful reaction against them which lies at the heart of
all sound art, of all sound philosophy and of all sound progress, here
as elsewhere, world without end, Amen. The second reason, I am glad
to say, may be stated less formidably. It is simply this: that the
United States, despite all the current highfalutin about melting pots
and national destinies, remains almost as much a colony of England,
intellectually and spiritually speaking, as it was on July 3, 1776, and
that all talk of developing an independent culture in such a colony,
superior to the old or even equal to the old, is merely so much windy
gabble, and as absurd as teaching one's grandmother to suck eggs.

In brief, the makings of such a culture are simply not here. We
haven't got the machinery for it and we haven't got the heart for it.
The things we lack are precisely the things that all other groups of
colonists, however rich and potent, lack, to wit, self-confidence, the
indomitable will to self-expression, intellectual courage, pride amount-
ing to disdain, and, above all, a thorough organization of society in all
its ranks. The upper rank is always missing; it remains anchored to the

motherland; there is no incentive to its migration. And with it are all
the other things, for they are inevitably in its keeping—confidence,
courage, true pride. The aspiring colonist thus faces dismay the moment he essays that look inward which must precede the projection of
individuality outward. The sense of difference that he notes, and that
must be the kernel of any genuine self-expression, immediately translates itself into a sense of inferiority. In the motherland—in any
motherland, in any wholly autonomous nation—there is a class of men
like himself, devoted to translating the higher manifestations of the
national spirit into ideas—men differing enormously among themselves, but still united in common cause against the stupidity of the
mass. But in a colony that class, if it exists at all, lacks coherence and
certainty; its authority is not only disputed by the inertia and suspiciousness of the inferior orders, but also by the superior authority
overseas; it is timorous and fearful of challenge. Thus it can offer no
protection to an individual of assertive originality, and he is forced to
go as a suppliant to a quarter in which nothing is his by right, but
everything must go by favor—in brief, to a quarter where his very
application must needs be regarded as proof of his inferiority, and the
burden of proof upon him is hence made double. This attitude must
almost inevitably affect his view of himself; he must be a man of the
very first class to hold to his ideas in spite of it. Such men occasionally
appear in a colony, but they always stand alone; their worst isolation,
indeed, is at home. For the colonial of less vigorous soul the battle is
too severe. Either he submits to subordination and so wears docilely
the inferior badge of a praiseworthy and tolerated colonist, or he deserts the minority for the far more hospitable and confident majority,
and thus becomes a mere mob-leader.

III

So much for the theory; now for a few applications of it. As examples of colonials strong enough to shake off the handicap of colo-
nialism I give you Whitman and Poe—and after I have given you
Whitman and Poe I can think of no other—perhaps Whistler may also
sneak in. The salient thing about each of these men was this: that his
impulse to self-expression was so powerful that it carried him beyond
all ordinary ambitions and prudences—in brief, that the ego func-
tioned so enormously that it even disregarded the welfare of the individual. Neither Poe nor Whitman made the slightest concession to

what was the dominant English taste, the prevailing English authority, of their time. And neither yielded in the slightest to the maudlin emotions that passed for ideas in America; in neither will you find the least reflection of the things that Americans were saying and doing in their day—even Whitman, preaching democracy, preached a democracy that not one actual democrat in a hundred thousand could so much as imagine. Well, what happened? *Imprimis,* English authority dismissed them loftily; they were, at best, rare freaks from the colonies. *Zum zweiten,* American stupidity denounced them as mere naughty fellows; both were unpopular and Whitman came near landing in jail. The accident that maintained them was an accident of personality and environment. They happened to be men accustomed to social isolation and of the most meagre wants, and it was thus difficult to deter them by neglect and punishment. So they stuck to their guns —and presently they were "discovered," as the phrase is, by men of a culture wholly foreign to them and perhaps incomprehensible to them, and thereafter, by slow stages, they began to win a slow and reluctant recognition in England (at first only from rebels and iconoclasts), and finally even in America. That either, without this French prompting, would have come to his present estate I doubt very much. And in support of that doubt I cite the fact that Poe's high talents as a critic, not having interested the French, have never got their deserts either in England or at home.

It is lesser men that we chiefly have to deal with in this world, and it is among lesser men that the lack of a confident intellectual viewpoint in America—a culture genuinely autonomous, and arising out of a natural and unfettered aristocratic reaction against the stupidity of the native masses—makes itself most evident. Examples are numerous and obvious. On the one hand, we have Fenimore Cooper—first making a cringing bow for English favor, and then, on being kicked out, joining the mob against sense: he wrote books so bad that even the Americans of 1830 admired them. On the other hand, we have Henry James—a deserter made by despair; one so depressed by the tacky company at the American first table that he preferred to sit at the second table of the English—the impulse was, and is common; it was only the forthright act that distinguished him. And in the middle ground, showing both seductions plainly, there is Mark Twain—at one moment striving his hardest for the English *imprimatur,* and childishly delighted by every favorable gesture; at the next, returning to the na-

tive mob as its premier clown—monkey-shining at banquets, cavorting
in the newspapers, shrinking poltroonishly from his own ideas, obscenely eager to give no offense. A much greater artist than either Poe
or Whitman, so I devoutly believe, but a good deal lower as a man.
The ultimate passion was not there; the decent householder always
pulled the ear of the dreamer. His fate has irony in it. In England
they patronize him: he is, for an American, not so bad. In America,
appalled by his occasional ascents to honesty, his stray impulses to be
wholly himself, the dunderheads return him to arm's length, his old
place, and one of the most eminent of them, writing in *The New York
Times,* argues piously that it is impossible to imagine him actually believing the commonplace heresies he put into *What Is Man?*

IV

These antagonistic and yet correlative pulls—for they both make
war upon the artist's primary yearning to express himself freely and
fully; they both cramp him by threatening him—explain the general
flatness and flatulence of American literature, even at its best. The literary artist, if he would come to any sort of repute at all—and it is
only the colossus who can put repute wholly out of his mind—has a
hard choice before him: either he must submit himself to the current
standards of a culture that is at odds with his actual environment, or
he must submerge himself in a pseudo-culture that is ineradicably hostile to all decent artistic striving. One sees the effects of the heart-
breaking conflict in scores of talented men—Howells, with his paralyzing surrender to Boston notions of what is nice, *i.e.,* to Boston notions of English notions of what is nice; Percy Mackaye, with his surrender to the mob notion that the aim of art is to lift up fat women
and green-grocers; Owen Johnson and company, with their even
worse surrender to the mob notion that what is most popular is most
worth doing. But even more clearly the effects are visible in American
criticism, which condenses into plain and damning propositions the
seductions that betray the actual artist. On the one hand there are
Brownell, Paul Elmer More and the rest of the honorary pallbearers
of letters—bogus Oxford dons, jitney Matthew Arnolds, deceiving
only themselves. And on the other hand there are the Mabies, Lyon
Phelpses and so on—amiable but pathetic spokesmen of the artistic
faith that lies in surburban pastors, fresh-water college professors and
directors of the Y.M.C.A. The stars of the first posse seem to be on

evil days. Though their culture is second-hand, it is at least a culture, and so they appear as foes to that grand movement against "privilege"—*i.e.*, the class-consciousness of the civilized minority—which now goes on. The second batch have the bleachers with them; the doctrines they preach in the *beaux arts* match perfectly the doctrines whooped in the Chautauquas. No observant man, indeed, had excuse for surprise when the Creel Press Bureau, as a war measure, employed an Iowa Aristotle to prepare a ukase declaring Puritanism to be the official faith of the country, and denouncing any writer who flouted it as a hireling of the Hohenzollern. This was the logical conclusion of the "we churchgoers" aesthetic of Dr. Phelps.

V

Well, what is to be done about it? As for me, I can't see that anything is to be done about it. Nor does it seem to me that there is any excuse for tragical attitudinizing in the fact. After all, there is no inherent reason why the culture of America should be distinct from the culture of England, save the reason that we, as Americans, find in our mere vanity. It would be just as sensible to argue that the culture of New Jersey or Arkansas should be distinct from that of the rest of the country, such as it is. In such things, when the chance offers, wise nature ordains a division of labor. A nation shut in by racial and linguistic isolation—a Sweden, a Holland or a France—is forced into autonomy by sheer necessity; if it is to have any intellectual life at all it must develop its own. But that is not our case. There is England to hold up the torch for us, as France holds it up for Belgium, and Spain for Latin America, and Germany for Switzerland. It is our function, as the younger and less confident partner, to do the simpler, rougher parts of the joint labor—to develop the virtues of the more elemental orders of men: industry, piety, docility, endurance, assiduity and ingenuity in practical affairs—the wood-hewing and water-drawing of the race. It seems to me that we do all this very well; in these things we are better than the English. But when it comes to those larger and more difficult activities which concern only the superior minority, and are, in essence, no more than products of its efforts to *demonstrate* its superiority—when it comes to the higher varieties of speculation and self-expression, to the fine arts and the game of ideas—then we fall into a bad second place. Where we stand, intellectually, is about where the English non-conformists stand; like them, we are marked

by a fear of ideas as disturbing and corrupting. Our art, say in the
novel, is imitative and timorous; when a challenge appears, as in
Dreiser, it is immediately denounced, not as unsound but as immoral.
Our political theory is hopelessly sophomoric and superficial; even English Toryism and Russian Bolshevism are infinitely more profound
and penetrating. And of the two philosophical systems that we have
produced, one is so banal that it is now imbedded in the New
Thought, and the other is so shallow that there is nothing in it either
to puzzle or to outrage a school-marm.

Unpleasant facts, but I see no reason for setting up vain denials of
them. However much we may protest against them, it must be very
plain that the English are aware of them. When, of late, they had
occasion to woo the American *intelligentsia*, what agents did they
choose? Did they nominate Thomas Hardy, Joseph Conrad, George
Moore and company? Nay, they nominated Conan Doyle, Coningsby
Dawson, Alfred Noyes, Ian Hay, Chesterton, Kipling and company.
In the choice there was high sagacity and no little oblique humor. The
valuation they set upon the *illuminati* of These States was exactly the
valuation they were in the habit of setting, at home, upon MM. of the
Free Church Federation; they saw the Wesleyan beneath the master's
gown and mortar-board. Let us look closely, and we shall see him,
too. In church and state, in letters and philosophy, he is eternally on
guard. Objectively, he gives us Prohibition, Comstockery and all the
other grotesque flowers of mob morality. Subjectively, he gives us that
distrust of ideas which cripples all honest inquiry among us, and sub-
ordinates all speculation to the safety and happiness of the stupid,
and makes it almost as dangerous to advance a new thought as to
practice a new vice.

This, of course, can't last forever. The levelling process has probably
gone almost as far as it will ever go; the backwash will leave a
nascent aristocracy on the shore, rubbing its eyes and spouting water.
But it will take a long time for that aristocracy to be organized, and
still longer for it to get itself oriented and effective. Until those periods elapse I am full of doubt that there will be any emanation of the
luminosity described so hopefully by Dr. Brooks, heir and assign to Dr.
Bourne.

(February, 1919)

Our Literary Centers

I

The Literary Aspirant

Some time ago, being full of devilment, I issued a challenge to the neglected literary geniuses of the Republic, inviting them to send me their scorned masterpieces, and promising to read them all with attentive eye and to procure the instant publication, by some reputable publisher and on fair terms, of each and every one that showed the slightest solid merit. This challenge I printed in an eminent public journal, and it was reprinted, as I expected, by a great many other journals, including all of the little "literary" magazines that devote themselves to bad authors. The result was a tidal wave of manuscripts. They gushed upon me from all parts of the country, and I was weeks working my way through them. Finally I finished reading them—that is, all those that it was humanly possible to read at all—and cast up accounts. I found that, in the whole lot, there had been exactly one manuscript showing genuine sense and skill. It was, in fact, a very excellent piece of work, and the first publisher that I sent it to accepted it forthwith, as any other intelligent publisher would have done. But this lonesome exception, alas, did not quite meet my specifications, for it was surely not the work of a neglected genius. On the contrary, it was the work of a man who had already had one novel printed by a reputable house—a novel duly reviewed and praised at the time in this place, though I had forgotten the fact by the time I read the author's second. Thus the net yield of my quest: that not a single sound manuscript by an author hitherto unpublished came to me—that I could not find a single author in the whole country who could offer reasonable proof that his or her genius had gone neglected by publishers.

This result, I need not say, did not surprise me. I am by profession a hunter-out-of and helping-hand-giver to nascent literati, and my agents are as busy in the Greenwich Villages and on the Telegraph Hills of the nation as ever the spies of Metternich were in Hesse-Darmstadt. I read manuscripts constantly, and not only manuscripts but also many long and bombastic letters from aspirants. The net product of all this diligence and suffering is the firm conviction that there is no other country in the world in which the literary neophyte has so easy a time of it, that the publishers of no other land are one half so hospitable to half-baked and phosphorescent talent. I simply can't imagine a new work of any genuine merit at all going unpublished in the United States for so long as six months. If there is any such work in existence, then the author thereof has followed an incredible imbecility in trying to market it: he has sent a pornographic novel to Fleming H. Revell, or a biography of Treitschke to Putnam, or an attack upon spook-chasing to Henry Holt. Even so, it has escaped very narrowly. So thoroughly convinced am I of all this that I am tempted to reissue my challenge. What restrains me is the knowledge that the bad authors and bogus geniuses of America are not only stupid, but also petty grafters. More than half of the manuscripts that reached me as a result of my former defiance were sent in violation of its primary condition. This condition was that each should be accompanied by a stamped and addressed envelope for its return. In order to save a few cents author after author put me to trouble and expense. And only one of all these jitney Bennetts and Conrads thanked me. A good many sent me abusive letters after I had returned their manuscripts, but only one thanked me for my exertions.

II
Letters and the Map

My examination of this mountain of garbage bore out an observation that I have often made in reading manuscripts for *The Smart Set*, to wit, that literary skill in the United States is segregated geographically—that there are regions in which it tends to appear, and regions in which it is almost unheard of. One of the latter is the Los Angeles neighborhood. Many more manuscripts come out of Los Angeles every month than out of any other American city of its size—perhaps six or eight times as many. The town seems to swarm with literary aspirants. Every writer of movie scenarios out there is at work upon a novel, and nine-tenths of the fair, frail and fat victims of the local swamis appear to have an itch for the short-story. Perhaps it is because the place is full of half-educated idlers—the wives, widows and daughters of Iowa hog-stuffers, Oklahoma oil-thieves, Wyoming sheep-raisers, and so on. One quickly discerns the note of moony mysticism, by the Wilsonian idealism out of the Chautauqua, in the poetry there manufactured. It is about avatars and poltergeists quite as often as it is about spooning behind the door. But the subject matter of this Los Angeles literature is not what gives it distinction; the thing that genuinely marks it is its infernal badness. Long experience has made me so suspicious of it that I always open a new bale with misgivings, and am seldom disappointed. The town really enjoys a unique eminence: it houses more bad authors than New York. During the past five years I have read the manuscripts of probably four or five hundred different Los Angeles geniuses, and in the whole number there have not been six of even the most meagre talents. I daresay that the place is full of literary societies, and that these harsh words will cause them to pass resolutions denouncing me as the worst critic that ever lived. If so, I shall induce Dr. Nathan to print a Los Angeles number of this great literary and moral periodical, made up of the first thirty manuscripts that reached me from there after noon of a certain day.

Another literary Alsatia is in the South. The South, of course, is by no means illiterate. On the contrary, it swarms with authors, and many of them are very fecund; there was one, a few years back, who sent me a manuscript a day for two or three months. But the quality of the stuff thus produced is simply frightful. Nothing in understandable English could be more windy, more banal, more childish. The bad authors of the North at least choose respectable models: their eyes are on Henry James, or Huysmans, or Whitman, or Dreiser, or even George Moore. But their brethren of the sub-Potomac wilderness are still in the age of Mrs. E. D. N. Southworth; if they have a model, it must be the Julia Magruder of the *Ladies' Home Journal* serials of thirty years ago. Love down there is still a duet for flute and harp; there is no sign that the fictioneers of the region have yet become aware of its new pathological, medico-legal and scandalous aspects, so fiercely studied in Greenwich Village. Perhaps the influence of Sir Walter Scott, which, as Mark Twain was fond of declaring, caused the Civil War, is still raging. For a Southerner to deal with his neighbors realistically, as Masters and Anderson have dealt with theirs in the Middle West and many a scrivening old maid has dealt with hers in New England, would be almost unbelievable. If it is ever done, it will be done by the new school of Aframerican novelists, now struggling heavily to emerge. A few sound authors, of course, live in the South, just as Dreiser lives in Los Angeles, and Poe once lived in Richmond and even Baltimore. But they are not genuinely Southern; the main stream of Confederate *Kultur* flows around them and takes no color from them. The typical Southern author remains an archaic sentimentalist of the farm-paper variety.

Well, then, where is the good writing that goes on in the Republic done? In New York? Not much of it. New York is the home of literary artisans, not of literary artists. Many of the manufacturers of best-sellers live here, and most of the manufacturers of machine-made stuff for the cheap fiction magazines. But, considering its population, the big town produces very little literature of genuine significance. Compare it to London or Paris, and at once it shrinks to the size of a staphylococcus. Greenwich Village, for all its noisy pretensions, is quite sterile. It has never produced a first-rate poet, or a first-rate novelist, or a critic worth a hoot. Even its drama, in the main, is hollow and imitative; all its little theatres, taken together, have not averaged one good play a year. What the Village lacks, of course, is a civilized culture, with the skepticism that goes therewith. It follows every new craze like the proletariat following a circus parade. I believe, and have often argued, that its influence is for the good. Some of the novelties it embraces are worth examining, and it gives them a chance. Best of all, it keeps a certain bawdiness in letters, which always threaten, in the United States, to become too respectable. But this influence bears its fruits elsewhere. The Village itself has enthusiasm and curiosity, but it lacks ideas, it lacks brains.

Draw a circle of two hundred miles radius around Chicago, and you will enclose four-fifths of the real literature of America—particularly four-fifths of the literature of tomorrow. Draw a circle of a hundred miles around Boston, and you will enclose nearly all the rest. I seldom read a manuscript from the Boston region that fails to show some touch of civilized feeling, some proof of sound reading, some sense of style. I seldom read a manuscript from the Chicago region that is wholly without ideas. The bean-eaters are urbane, cultivated, sophisticated, somewhat aloof and cold. The hog-skinners are eager, curious, penetrating, iconoclastic, impatient of finesse, close to the ground. Ah, that one could have both groups of qualities! The American Thomas Hardy would be born that day, perhaps even the American Ibsen. My notion is that it would pay to ship forty or fifty head of young New England authors to Chicago, and let them breathe the ozone of the stockyards; it might electrify them as it electrifies the young peasants of Indiana, Iowa and Illinois, and there would be something in them that was better worth electrifying. The contrary movement produces only decay. William Dean Howells, migrating from the Ohio saleratus belt to Boston and then to New York, was ruined in his literary infancy; he became a model of correctness and ineffectiveness, the perfect colonial. Hamlin Garland was ground to death in the same nickel-plated sausage-machine, and I believe that it also snipped a few schnitzels from Dreiser and from George Ade, both of whom fled westward before it was too late. The young *muzhik* is simply scared to death by the pomp and circumstance of the seaboard Brahmins; their overwhelming manner makes him feel as puny and ineffective as a coroner's physician at a Christian Science revival. But I doubt that the West would have the same paralyzing effect upon immigrants from the East. The latter would at least have the confidence that goes with respectability; it may be true that one learns nothing worth knowing at Harvard or Yale, but one at all events gets a certain assurance. The reaction between this assurance and the startling panorama of life in the heart of America should produce precisely the tingling sense of awareness that is at the bottom of the artistic impulse. The immigrant would be thrilled and stimulated, but not abashed.

I proceed from the theory to a case: that of Robert Herrick. Herrick is a typical New Englander of the thoroughly Harvardized subspecies—a professor absolutely true to form. I have never had the honor of sitting under him in class, but his occasional discussions of public problems in the Chicago *Tribune* prove that the *Weltanschauung* of the Boston *Transcript* has entered into the very marrow of his bones. Nevertheless, this Cambridge pedagogue, moving to the stockyards, was so shaken up that he began to write novels, and his Eastern culture made some of them very good novels. Henry James would have been vastly improved by a few whiffs from the same stupendous abattoirs. James, finding New England all culture and no soul, decided to escape, but he made the mistake of going in the wrong direction. In London he was in exactly the same situation as a young Westerner in Boston—that is, he was confronted by a culture more solid and assured than his own. It kept him shaky all his life long; it almost kept him fawning, as his letters inconveniently reveal. He died a sort of super-Howells, with a long row of laborious but essentially hollow books behind him. The notion that James was a master mind is confined to the sort of persons who used to regard Brown-

ing as the greatest of poets. He was a superb technician, as Joseph
Conrad has testified, but his ideas were always timorous; he never
overcame his bashfulness in the presence of such superior fauna as the
Lord Chancellor, the Master of Pembroke and Mrs. Humphrey Ward.
Thus his painful psychologizings, translated into plain English, turn
out to be chiefly mere kittenishness—an arch tickling of the ribs of
elderly virgins—the daring of a grandma smoking cigarettes. But I believe that the makings of a genuinely first-rate artist were in James,
and that Chicago would have developed him. What he needed was intimate contact with the life of his own country. He was unhappy in
New England because he was an American, and New England, then
as now, was simply a sort of outhouse of old England—a Devil's
Island of intellectual poor relations, eternally wearing out the English
chemises and pantaloons of season before last. A very defective
psychologist—like most professional psychologists—he made the blunder of jumping from the frying pan into the fire. The West would have
amused, intrigued and finally conquered him. He would have been a
greater artist in his own country. . . .

As I say, the Boston vicinage and the Chicago vicinage produce
practically all of the decent writing done in America. There are isolated outposts of the enlightenment in a few cities, but not in many.
Who could imagine a good book written in Kansas City? Or in Atlanta, Ga? Or in Cleveland, O.? San Francisco once disputed the
primacy of Chicago, but no more. The glamorous color of the town
produces a great deal of aesthetic activity, but the climate is so sensuous that it seldom gets very far. The San Franciscans either slide
down the well-vaselined chute into the *Saturday Evening Post* or sink
into a sort of dilettantism. They lack staying power. Life out there is
so gloriously pleasant that the hard rooting and straining and puffing
that the fine arts demand is simply impossible. One could not write a
fugue in San Francisco. As well try to read Einstein with the band
playing, and a gal on one's knee, and a slave squirting one with attar
of roses, and another wheeling in a barrel of Pilsner.

(November, 1920)

II

Critics and Criticism

Throughout his years as a literary critic, Mencken commented on the function of criticism and its relevance to literature as a whole. His most significant statements on the subject are to be found in "Criticism of Criticism of Criticism," which first appeared in *The Smart Set* in 1917 and was then extended for the first volume of *Prejudices* in 1919 and in "Footnote on Criticism" in *Prejudices: Third Series.*

The following pieces should enable the reader to better understand Mencken's critical credo, for they amplify most of the ideas expounded in the two major essays. I have included nothing here on James Huneker, a dazzling critic of the seven arts whom Mencken liked to contrast with the academic critics of the period, since Huneker warrants a section to himself. Rather, I have chosen pieces on lesser critics—both wild and tame, as Mencken would say—who seem representative of the fifteen-year period covered in this collection.

William Lyon Phelps and Others

When, in the year ten of this damndest of centuries, there appeared a book by a college professor in which it was openly admitted that Mark Twain was a greater writer than Oliver Wendell Holmes, I hymned the prodigy as one full of exhilarating portents and anointed the good professor himself with lavish cataracts of cocoa butter, vase-

line, neats'-foot oil and curve grease. His name was William Lyon
Phelps, A.B., A.M., Ph.D.; he was Lampson professor of English
language and literature in Yale College. I hailed him as the first herald
of the academic enlightenment, the bold forerunner of a new renaissance, the pioneer of intelligence in the professorial chair. Let me
now, with a wry face, withdraw and swallow the great bulk of those
unguents. Let me take back and purge myself with those caressing
pomades. Down, down they go! I was honest, brethren, but I was
somehow wrong. The Phelps of 1917 has gone back to orthodoxy and
the stale fruits of the scholastic grove. A mugwump and iconoclast no
longer, he now chants the standard liturgy of Harvard and of Yale,
of Princeton and of Columbia, of literary embalmers and of his witless
order, of heavy platitude and of pious bosh. His book of 1910, *Essays
on Modern Novelists*, had novelty and the breath of life in it; there
was more than one show of independence in its judgments; it rang
clear. His book of 1917, *The Advance of the English Novel*, is a flat
reboiling of old respectabilities, a hack job for literary ladies and college boys, a mass of mush. It might have been written by Hamilton
Wright Mabie or Edwin Markham, even by Brander Matthews, even
by that fair Ella (I forget her last name) who interprets literature to
the women's clubs out in Chicago. It might have run serially through
the paleozoic columns of the Boston *Transcript;* one can even imagine
it following Dr. Mabie's "White List of Books" in the *Ladies Home
Journal.* In it the estimable professor goes back to the tasteless herbs of
his New England youth; once more he is the pedagogue who edited
The Poetry and Prose of Thomas Gray and *The Best Plays of Chapman* for sweating and god-forsaken school-boys. In it, after that memorable aberration at forty year, he returns to his drowsy bath in the
academic Lethe, there to wait the last, sad bugle-call.

    Et tu quoque, my dear Mon Chair! . . . Do I bawl and snuffle? Do
I call the professor names? Then consider what a blow has found my
ribs. For seven years I nursed this serpent. For seven years I cried
him up as one who had drunk at college pumps and yet lived. For
seven years, in season and out of season, I kept a spotlight on him,
displaying him to the nobility and gentry as a college professor shaken
free of the class-room, a pundit emancipated from superstition, the
White Hope of the seminaries. And now he turns upon me and sets
fire to the deck beneath my feet. Now he adopts the criteria of the
Literary Supplement of *The New York Times*. Now he is sicklied o'er

with the pale cast of Harvard and the *Nation*. . . . I assume the
black cap and proceed to issue judgment upon him in due form of
law. May his work be tagged and chewed up for posterity, when his
time comes to die, by his successor as Lampson professor of English
at Yale. May his books be adopted as texts in all the fresh-water colleges west of the Wabash, and many generations of plow-boys learn
to venerate him between Dr. Robertson Nichol, the Methodist Taine,
and Dr. Mabie, the Hannah More of Summit, N.J. May he find no
books to read in the purgatory of professors—a deep and roaring hole,
I surely hope—save the novels of James Fenimore Cooper and the
critical works of Paul Elmer More. May he live to see his verdicts solemnly accepted by readers of books, and O. Henry put above Frank
Norris, and Owen Wister above Theodore Dreiser, and Charles D.
Stewart invested with the late toga of Mark Twain, and W. J. Locke
revered as a great Christian moralist. To the calaboose, Mr. Catchpoll!
Out, out! . . .

In detail, it is hard to deal with this curiously hollow and uninspired book. It proceeds upon no intelligible plan; it is incoherent and
uninforming; it is prejudiced and ignorant; its valuations are often
preposterous, and sometimes almost fabulous. What is one to think of
a critic who devotes a whole page to a discussion of H. G. Wells's *The
Wife of Sir Isaac Harmon,* and then fails to mention *The New Machiavelli* at all? Of one who hails Mrs. W. K. Clifford's *Love Letters of
a Worldly Woman* as a "masterpiece," and then forgets to name a single work by Hugh Walpole, J. S. Beresford or W. L. George? Of one
who describes O. Henry as a "genius" who will have "abiding fame,"
and then rigorously avoids any mention of Dreiser, or Robert Grant,
or Thomas Nelson Page? Of one who speaks seriously of the "highest
reaches" of the "art" of Henry Bordeaux, the French Harold Bell
Wright? Of one who gravely accepts General Lew Wallace as a first-
rate novelist? Of one who signs his name to the doctrine that "the
American novelist most worthy to fill the particular vacancy caused by
the death of Mark Twain is Charles D. Stewart"—the author of a
volume of vaudeville anecdotes called *Finerty of the Sandhouse?* Of
one who—but there is no need to multiply examples. A few such
judgments are sufficient. Worse, they are accompanied by a lot of
puerile moralizing, an endless dallying with the notion that the aim of
art is to perfume and sweeten the beholder. The *Encyclopaedia Britannica*'s astounding discovery that *A Mummer's Wife* is a tract

against gambling is gone one better by the discovery that *Esther Waters* has "a nobly ethical tone" and makes the reader "feel a moral stimulation." (God help poor old Moore! Imagine the *Stammvater* of the literature of Texas as an evangelist!) Samuel Butler's *The Way of All Flesh*, we are told, will be "of real service to Christianity." (O, shades, liver and lights of Shaw!) Joseph Conrad's "The Point of Honor" is "an allegory of the struggle between good and evil, with the triumph of good." W. J. Locke, since *The Morals of Marcus Ordeyne*, has been converted to Christianity, and is "an ethical philosopher," and his *Simon the Jester* is "illuminated with deep religious feeling." . . . Pish, tartuffery, cant! It reaches its climax in a passage on Zola. "He was found, in the morning, lying half out of bed, his face on the floor buried in his own vomit. . . . An excellent illustration of the limits of his art." . . . Ah, the sweet, the savory, the "moral" Puritan!

Enough, and too much! What must the English think when they read contemporary American criticism—such piffle as Mabie's pious prattle for high-school girls, More's staggeringly ignorant "criticism" of Nietzsche, the late *History of American Literature Since 1870*, by Professor Fred Lewis Pattee, the reviews in such journals as the *Times* and the *Outlook*, such lame and pointless stuff as is in Dr. Phelps's present volume? One of the amusing characteristics of the books by professors is their unanimous failure to so much as mention Dreiser. The thing, indeed, takes on the aspect of an organized movement; the fellow becomes a sort of bugaboo to the rev. pundits, to be put into Coventry with Beelzebub. It will be curious to see how long this moral exile lasts. Already the British violate its terms. The London *Academy*, taking the professors from the rear, calls *Sister Carrie* the greatest of American novels. The *Fortnightly*, the *Spectator*, the *Saturday Review* and the *Athenaeum* heap praises upon its successors. Arnold Bennett, H. G. Wells, W. J. Locke, Frank Harris and others of their kidney venture upon the atrocity of putting Dreiser above Howells—a blasphemy, but by experts, ladies, by experts! Over all roars the voice of Theodore Watts-Dunton, surely a respectable man! . . . Let us reserve our snickers until the day the first drover of rah-rah boys swallows the bilious Indianan, as Dr. Phelps swallowed old Mark in 1910. Let us see what university sends its "professor of English language and literature" to do that noxious job. Let us stay our guffaws a bit longer. . . .

A sad, sad lot, these Yankee tasters of beautiful letters—but stay! A

few months ago, taking the air in Fifth Avenue, I dropped into one of
the stores given over to marked-down books. On the 50-cent counter
reposed a volume entitled *The Spirit of American Literature,* by John
Macy. The name of this Macy was known to me; I had received reli-
able reports from my Boston agents that he was a man of sense.
Nevertheless, his publishers had not thought it worth while to send
me his book when it was published in 1913, and it now reposed upon
the bargain counter, among a lot of other forlorn "remainders." I
bought it, steered for Lüchow's, sent Gustav for a *Seidel* of Hoboken
malt, and inquired within. . . . What I found was a first-class book of
criticism, a book sparkling with the ideas of a well-read and intelligent man, a book by a genuine lover of books, a true joy and delight.
Not a trace of academic fustian! Not a line of flapdoodle! Not a hint of
the college professor! Here was sharp and shrewd judgment. Here
was clear and independent thinking. Here was enthusiasm unashamed
and contempt undisguised. Here, above all, was sound writing—a
graceful flow of sentences, a stock of new phrases, a piquant and intriguing style. No book of criticism that I have read in ten years has
given me more pleasure. No book has set my own notions to bubbling
more furiously. None has left me with a more vivid sense of vigorous
and worthwhile intellectual experience. . . . I recommend it to you
without qualification. Macy is the antidote to the pedagogues. He will
be discovered, I daresay, in fifteen or twenty years. But once discovered, he will not be quickly forgotten.

(June, 1917)

The Professor Doctors

The curse of criticism in America, and of literature with it, is the infernal babbling of the third-rate college professor, which is to say, of
the overgrown sophomore. I am not one, of course, to deny the usefulness of the learned Ph.D. in the palace of beautiful letters, or, at all
events, in the ante-chambers thereof. He, too, is one of God's creatures, and he has his high utilities. It is his business, *imprimis,* to
ground unwilling school-boys in the rudiments of knowledge and

taste, that they may comprehend the superiority of Ralph Waldo
Emerson to Old Cap Collier, and know wherein the poems of Crabbe
transcend "Only a Boy." It is his business, *secondamente*, to do the
shovel and broom work of literary exploration—to count up the weak
and strong endings in *Paradise Lost*, to guess at the meaning of the
typographical errors in Shakespeare, to bowdlerize Hannah More for
sucklings, to establish the date of *Tamburlaine*, to prove that Edgar
Allan Poe was a teetotaler and a Presbyterian, to list all the differences between F_1 and F_2, to edit high-school editions of *Tales of a
Traveler*, *Die Jungfrau von Orleans* and *La Mort de Pompée*. But it is
not his business to sit in judgment upon the literature that is in being,
for that job requires, above all things, an eager intellectual curiosity, a
quick hospitality to ideas, a delight in novelty and heresy—and these
are the very qualities which, if he had them, would get a professor
cashiered in ten days. He is hired by the God-fearing and excessively
solvent old gentlemen who sit on college boards, not to go scouting for
what is new in the world, but to concentrate his mind upon the defense of what is old and safe. It is not his job to inflame his pupils to
the pursuit and testing of ideas, but to make them accept docilely the
ideas that have been approved as harmless, and his security and eminence in the academic grove run in direct proportion to his fidelity to
that programme. If you want to know what happens to a professor
who departs from it in the field of social theory, examine the life,
crimes, trial, condemnation and execution of the late Scott Nearing,
B.S., B.O., Ph.D. And if you want to measure the extent of the pres-
sure in the field of the arts, think of what would have happened to a
Princeton instructor who pronounced Walt Whitman a great artist in
1867.

It is the curse of American criticism, as I have hinted, that our rev.
professors do not stick to their last—that they are forever poaching
upon the preserve of criticism proper, and that a large body of public
opinion follows them in their gyrations there. Fool that I am, I once
welcomed that extension of function, and even mistook it idiotically
for a proof that the professors were growing intelligent. I now know
better, and recant without reservation. This roving of the birchmen
has been, almost invariably, a damage and a nuisance. It has set up
and fortified the formulae of the college pump in the precise field
where all formulae are most dubious and most dangerous. It has
created a caste of class-room big-wigs whose ponderous stupidity and

mania for senseless labelling have corrupted the taste of two-thirds of our people. And it has worked steadily, maliciously and lamentably against the recognition of every new writer who has had anything sound and original to contribute to the national letters, from Poe to Whitman, from Whitman to Mark Twain, and from Mark Twain to Dreiser, George Ade and Montague Glass, and in favor of every platitudinizing old woman who has offered tripe in the market-place, from John Greenleaf Whittier to George E. Woodberry, the New England spinsters and Henry van Dyke.

(December, 1917)

Paul Elmer More

Paul Elmer More's *A New England Group* offers simply one more solemn statement—the eleventh in the order of the Shelburne Essays of his familiar ideas. More is the Bourbon of criticism in These States: he never learns anything and he never forgets anything. Let hell bubble and Rome howl: he sticks to his guns. What occupies him primarily is a war that was fought to a finish, with both sides fearfully beaten, fully a century ago, to wit, the historic war between the classicists and the romantics. His side is that of the classicists (which he constantly identifies with that of the New England blue-noses), and to the business of supporting it he brings a learning fit for a German professor and a diligence beyond compare. The new roaring that goes on in the world of letters does not reach his ears; he knows nothing about all the wild movements of the moment, and cares less. So far as his books offer any evidence, he has never heard of Dreiser and the Dreiser following, or of Amy Lowell and her janissaries, or of George Bernard Shaw, or of any of the new novelists in England, or even of Joseph Conrad, Thomas Hardy or George Moore, or even, God help us all, of Ibsen. The only living authors mentioned in his index are Arthur Symons, W. B. Yeats, Henry Holt, Viscount Morley and Ernest Poole. The Goths and the Huns are at the gate, but More is deaf to them. High above the gory battlements whereon the artists of forty schools fight, slay and devour one another, he sits in an ivory tower reinforced with steel and concrete, and there shut off from the world he piles up his monumental proofs that there is "peril in following the electric thrill of freer feeling" and that what man needs most is order, restraint, discipline, the goose-step. There is no boyish curiosity in him, no sneaking desire to go out and take a hand in the current row, no lust for mere combat. His method is wholly judicial, scientific, *ex parte*. Year after year he goes on reiterating the faith that is in him, seldom so much as changing a word.

So much for his principles. In detail, of course, he occasionally ventures upon a novelty. This time it takes the form of a strange politeness to the late Friedrich Wilhelm Nietzsche, the scoundrel who plotted the Great War twenty-five years ago, and then launched it suddenly fourteen years after his own death, to the colossal surprise of the French War Office and the British Admiralty, neither of which suspected that anything of the sort was afoot. Ten years ago More had many harsh things to say about Nietzsche, in whom he discerned a lingering romantic, by Wagner out of the Chopin waltzes; now he salutes and almost embraces the brute. Well, perhaps it is not so astonishing, after all. Wasn't it Nietzsche who said "Be hard!"? And isn't this, at bottom, the substance of the Morean aesthetic? More, I suspect, misunderstood Nietzsche in those first days (as, indeed, I presumed to tell him at the time); now he knows better. At all events, he gives the Prussian Antichrist a very courtly bow, and even forgets to blame him for causing the war, to the surprise, as I have said, of the French War Office and the British Admiralty, not to mention the Russian Foreign Office. . . . Even stranger than this new flirtation with Nietzsche is a long (and, I regret to report, rather flabby) chapter on the adventures of the venerable Henry Holt among ghosts. Here, of course, More is a bit cautious. "No doubt," he says, "there has been a vast amount of deliberate deception in the table-turning and other so-called mediumistic phenomena." Nevertheless, the combined effect of so much evidence, even though it be dubious in severalty, is powerful, and there remains "a residue of facts which cannot be accounted for by the ordinary faculties." But even so, the strangeness is not wholly strange. Didn't Jonathan Edwards believe in witches, and wasn't he "the greatest theologian and philosopher yet produced in this country"? Assuming that man has an immortal soul—a gaseous part that resists both the metabolism of the worm and the hot coals of the crematory—isn't it reasonable to assume further that this soul may occasionally long to tread its old paths on the earth, and that, so longing, it may make the attempt? The first assumption is certainly one that no defender of the New England enlightenment can reject. Jonathan Edwards not only believed in witches; he also believed in souls, and in spooks to boot. Thus it is not surprising to find More disinclined to flout the last-named. He warns Mr. Holt to be careful and upbraids him for certain romantic generalizations, but is quite willing to allow a high dignity to his quest.

This More is a man who always entertains me. I couldn't imagine a man whose ideas stood at greater variance with the prejudices and superstitions that I personally cherish, but I always forget his specific notions in admiring the pertinacity with which he holds and maintains them. The vacillating type of man, believing one thing this year and the contrary next year, and always ready to be converted back and forth—this fellow I dislike intensely. I dislike him most when he flops suddenly to my side, and so embarrasses me with a fiery enthusiasm for ideas that I always mix with doubts. More will never flop. With his last gasp he will cry out against "the electric thrill of freer feeling" and declare anew his immovable belief in a moral order of the world.

(June, 1921)

Private Reflections

The longer I live the more thoroughly I become convinced that criticism is anything but an exact science. The things I remember chiefly, looking back over my own somewhat longish service in the critical trenches, are not my occasional sound judgments, but my far more frequent imbecilities—some of them, seen in retrospect, quite astounding. I have often misunderstood men grossly, and I have misrepresented them when I understood them, sacrificing sense to make a phrase. Here, of course, is where even the most conscientious critic often goes aground; he is apt to be an artist before he is a scientist, and the impulse to create something passionately is stronger in him than the impulse to state something accurately. As for me, I am not noticeably conscientious. But I do not apologize for the lack. Is any

other critic now in practice in America? I can recall none. Certainly
those who, in the exercise of their office, perform upon my own books
are not much better in this respect than I am. A good many of them
denounce me violently, simply because they disagree with my politics.
Others, less prejudiced, fall into profound errors as to my aims, and
credit me constantly with ideas that are as abhorrent to me as they
would be to a Methodist bishop. What is the remedy for this distressing piling up of nonsense? Perhaps the best way out would be for
every writer to attempt a clear statement of his own ideas, confining
himself to fundamentals. The thing is often done by painters and sculp-
tors. I have before me half a dozen catalogues of art exhibitions by
new men—one-man shows of novel stuff. Each of the exhibitors prints
a preface over his sign manual explaining just what he is about—
often, alas, somewhat muddily, for artists seldom know how to write,
but always earnestly and sometimes even indignantly. I find such
expositions very interesting and instructive. Even when one of them is
downright idiotic it at least sets forth the useful fact that the author is
an idiot.

As for me, my literary theory, like my politics, is based chiefly upon
one main idea, to wit, the idea of freedom. I am, in brief, a libertarian
of the most extreme variety, and know of no human right that is one-
tenth as valuable as the simple right to utter what seems (at the
moment) to be the truth. Take away this right, and none other is
worth a hoot; nor, indeed, can any other long exist. Debauched by
that notion, it follows necessarily that I can be only an indifferent citizen of a democratic state, for democracy is grounded upon the instinct
of inferior men to herd themselves in large masses, and its principal
manifestation is their bitter opposition to all free thought. In the
United States, in fact, I am commonly regarded as a violent anti-
patriot. But this is simply because most of the ideas upon which
American patriotism bases itself seem to me to be obviously sentimental and nonsensical—that is, they have, for me at least, no intelligible relation to the visible facts. I do not object to patriotism when it
is logically defensible. On the contrary, I respect it as a necessary
corollary to the undeniable inequality of races and peoples. Its con-
verse, internationalism, appears to me to be almost insane. What an
internationalist says, stripping it of rhetoric, is simply that a lion is no
more than a large rat.

My literary criticism has been almost exclusively devoted to attacking and trying to break down the formal ideas, most of them wholly devoid of logical content, which formerly oppressed the art of letters in the United States very severely, and still hang about its flanks— ideas of form and method, of aim and purpose, of mere fashion and propriety. This attack, carried on for many years, has got me the name of a mere professional ruffian: I am constantly accused, and sometimes quite honestly, of tearing down without building up, of murdering a theory without offering in its place a new and better theory. But it must be plain enough that the objection, however earnestly made, is quite without merit. My business, considering the state of the society in which I find myself, has been principally to clear the ground of mouldering rubbish, to chase away old ghosts, to help set the artist free. The work of erecting a new structure belongs primarily to the artist as creator, not to me as critic. It may be (and, alas, it is often the case!) that after he has been set free it turns out that he actually has nothing worth hearing to say. (I could name names, but refrain in decency). But it is certainly better to utter even nonsense as a free man than to keep on repeating formulae like a boy in school.

Here the astute reader may file a caveat: if I am so hot for freedom, then why do I belabor fellows whose sole crime, at bottom, is that they express their honest ideas in a banal and oleaginous manner? The answer is simple: it is not their sole crime. I do not belabor them for expressing their own ideas; I belabor them for trying to prevent other men expressing *theirs*—that is, for trying to set up standards and taboos that hinder the free play of the creative impulse. This effort seems to me to be intrinsically immoral, however exalted the purpose behind it. The essence of sound art is freedom. The artist must be allowed his impish impulse, his revolt, his perversity. He stands in fundamental opposition to Philistine correctness; if he is bound by it he is nothing. But I by no means engage to agree with him: all I ask is that no one oppose him with weapons foreign to the world he inhabits, *e.g.*, the ballot, the policeman's club, the schoolmaster's rattan, the bishop's mitre. I am even against proscriptions on purely aesthetic grounds. Thus when Miss Lowell and her friends essayed to set up the doctrine that the only decent way to write poetry was the way they personally wrote it, and that all exponents of other ways were ignoramuses—when this theory appeared in the learned groves and barbershops I joined the professors in opposing it. But the great majority of such attacks upon freedom are not made by revolutionists, but by advocates of an established order: for one Futurist who launches bulls like a pope there are a hundred pedagogues who issue proscriptions like an American Attorney-General—for one Miss Lowell there are whole herds of Comstocks. Thus my critical labors, in the main, have been on the side of the younger generation. I have protested *sforzando* against the schoolmastering of letters—against setting the artist in bondage to his inferiors. For this service, I am convinced, I shall be rewarded by a just and intelligent God when I have been translated from these sordid scenes. If it turns out that I am in error about it, then I confess frankly that I shall be very greatly disappointed.

(December, 1922)

Professor Pattee and Professor Sherman

Two professors next. One is Prof. Dr. Fred Lewis Pattee, of the Pennsylvania State College, with *Sidelights on American Literature;* the other is the venerable brother, Prof. Dr. Stuart P. Sherman, of the University of Illinois, with *Americans.* Each puts a burden upon me, as reviewer, by making me the villain of his discourse. Dr. Pattee, it must be added, is very polite about it. In fact, he is often *too* polite— for example, when he reprints long extracts from my juvenile verse, perhaps the worst piffle ever written in America before the New Poetry Movement began, and argues solemnly that it has some merit. If it has, then there is also merit in the state papers of the Hon. W. G. Harding. But it is my later prose that concerns Dr. Pattee most seriously. What he finds in it chiefly is a waste of God-sent talents—a fine gift for ingratiating utterance degraded to the uses of anarchy and atheism. His hope is that increasing years may bring me back to the good, the true and the beautiful. Who, indeed, can tell? Some die of diabetes; some die of growing good. The professor is an earnest man, and he shakes me not a little. But he would have shaken me a great deal more had he not grounded his case against me (see his page 77) upon a note on criticism that was written, not by me, but by Colleague Nathan. You will find it in *The World in Falseface,* page 39, § 93. Need I add that I dissent from its doctrine absolutely, and regard

it with even more abhorrence than Dr. Pattee does? . . . The rest of
his book is less open to question. He has a capital chapter on O.
Henry and a still better one on Jack London. His essay on Philip
Freneau is more conventional—the sort of paper that is read before
annual conventions of teachers of English. What remains is even
worse.

Just what ails Prof. Dr. Sherman it is rather difficult to determine.
During the war it was easy to recognize him as a patriot driven to a
desperate and heroic resistance by the Kaiser's plot to destroy Christianity, conquer Europe and enslave the United States. Like many
another brave pedagogue of the time he was moved by this threat to
throw down his rattan and mount the stump. The historian will find
an eloquent record of his sweatings for democracy in one of the publications of the Creel Press Bureau, by title, *American and Allied
Ideals.* This brochure, which was distributed to the conscripts of the
Republic before the battle of Château-Thierry, to heat up their blood,
is now somewhat rare, but fortunately it is not copyrighted, and so I
may reprint it later on, with a gloss. But all that, as I say, was in war-
time, and Sherman followed a large and clearly visible star. Now,
however, with the ideals of the Allies in a somewhat indifferent state
of repair, it is hard to make out precisely what he is in favor of, and
what he is against. On the one hand he lays down the Ku Klux doctrine that no American who is not 100 per cent Anglo-Saxon can ever
hope to write anything worth reading and on the other hand he
praises the late Andrew Carnegie, who was no more an Anglo-Saxon
than Abraham Cahan is, and reads a severe lesson to Paul Elmer
More, who is the very archetype of the species. The truth about Dr.
Sherman, I fear, is not to be sought in logical and evidential directions. It lies deeper, to wit, among the emotions, or, as Prof. Dr.
Freud would say, in the unconscious. What afflicts him, no doubt, is
what afflicts many another Americano of his peculiar traditions and
limitations: the uneasy feeling that something is slipping from under
him. The new literature of the Republic, both in prose and in verse,
tends more and more to be written by fellows bearing such ghastly
names as Ginsberg, Gohlinghorst, Casey, Mitnick and Massaccio. To
put down these barbarians by purely critical means becomes increasingly difficult, for the scoundrels begin to practice criticism themselves, and some of them show a lamentable pugnacity. Well, then, let
us put them down by force. Call out the American Legion! Telephone

the nearest Imperial Wizard! Set the band to playing "The Star-Spangled Banner"!

Such impulses, I venture to say, are at the bottom of the learned pedagogue's frequent public exhibitions of anguish. He longs secretly, I suspect, for the gone but happy days of the Creel Press Bureau, when the easy way to get rid of a poet who wrote against the Anglican Holy Ghost was to allege that his grandfather was a Bavarian. That scheme is no longer effective, and so it has to be changed. But Dr. Sherman, as yet, has not devised any effective substitute, and in consequence his writings show the uncertainty and inconsistency that I have mentioned.

Two courses lie before him, if he would avoid exhausting himself by chasing his own tail. On the one hand, he may join the Ku Klux openly, and perhaps become its Literary Grand Cyclops or Imperial Kritik. On the other hand, he may undertake a conquest by peaceful penetration, as he has already attempted, indeed, in the cases of Sinclair Lewis (a Hun at heart) and Dr. Ludwig Lewisohn. But neither device, I fear, will really achieve much for the sacred cause of the Anglo-Saxon. If he adopts the second, that cause will be swallowed up. And if he adopts the first, he will simply get himself laughed at for his pains. For what distinguishes the American Goths, Wops and Kikes above all other barbarians, as Dr. Sherman himself accurately argues, is their defective respect for the purely spiritual inheritance of their Anglo-Saxon compatriots. On the material side they are less contumacious. They respect and even venerate the American bathroom; they esteem the ease with which money may be cadged in America; they admire the professional efficiency of bootleggers. But they regard James Russell Lowell, alas, with much lack of reverence; they snore over Irving and Cooper; they find Emerson too often windy and the rest too often bores. Ignorance? I doubt it. Certainly the gems of the Yanko-Saxon heritage have been on display enough during the past eight years for all literate men to be aware of them. But awareness is not always translated into admiration; sometimes it may be translated into snickers.

But I forget Dr. Sherman's book, which starts off by charging that I am the Grand Cyclops of a vast horde of extremely toothsome but unhappily antinomian young gals from the foreign missions and mail order belt, descending upon New York in perfumed swarms to hear me defame Jonathan Edwards, the *Stammvater* of Billy Sunday and Paul

Elmer More. Ah, that it were true—but the facts are the facts! No
such sweet ones ever appear; I have yet to see a single ankle of the
kind the professor so lasciviously describes; all the actual arrivals are
overweight and of a certain age. But to proceed. From this Freudian
nonsense the learned critic goes on to sober, correct papers on Franklin, Emerson, Hawthorne and Joaquin Miller, to somewhat waspish
notes on Carl Sandburg and Roosevelt, to delirious dithyrambs on
Andrew Carnegie, and to a final essay on Dr. More, before alluded to.
A respectable book, and mainly quite safe and sound in doctrine. But
I doubt that it accomplishes its patriotic purpose. The members of
what the professor calls "the Loyal Independent Order of United
Hiberno-German-Anti-English-Americans," having faced the Department of Justice in its palmy days, are not likely to be shaken by peda-
gogical denunciations now. Moreover, if a thirst for the golden elixirs
of Sassenach snivelization ever seizes them, they are very apt to seek
satisfaction for it, not at an Iowa silo but at the *Urquell* in the
Motherland.

(March, 1923)

III

The Art of Fiction

As I attempted to show in part IV of the Preface, Mencken did not separate theory and practice in his criticism. Rather, he combined the two in his examination of novels and collections of short stories. The review of Upton Sinclair's *The Moneychangers,* the initial review of Mencken's first book article for *The Smart Set,* illustrates at least two characteristics. First, in the opening paragraphs Mencken endeavors to lure or charm his reader into reading and following his arguments. The first desideratum for all writing, especially critical writing, was that it be charming. Secondly, the review illustrates Mencken's aversion for the didactic and his insistence on some particular point of view.

"A Definition" comments further on the nature of fiction, provides certain standards against which novels may be judged, and then passes judgment on Mary Johnston's *Lewis Rand.* As is often the case with good criticism, the value of this essay does not depend upon the work being criticized; it depends rather upon what the critic says about the work.

The brief review of the O. Henry book assesses that writer's weaknesses and strengths and at the same time shows Mencken's early interest in the craft of writing. In "The Raw Material of Fiction," Mencken compares the "melody" of music with the "story" of fiction and remarks their respective importance to various composers and novelists before examining Conrad's *Chance.* Here is an example of book criticism at its best. Much of what Mencken says in the final piece, on Maugham's *The Moon and Sixpence,* has been repeated many times since.

The Novelist as Messiah

Platitudes have their uses, I have no doubt, but in the fair field of imaginative literature they have a disconcerting habit of denouncing and betraying one another. Separate a single platitude from the herd, and you will find it impeccable, inviolable and inevitable; comforting, amiable and well-mannered. But then lead out another, and try to drive them tandem; or three more, and try to drive them four-in-hand; and you will quickly land in the hospital—your collar-bone broken, your head in a whirl and your raiment muddy and torn.

Consider, for example, the ancient and pious platitude that it is wrong for the rich to rob the poor, for the strong to exploit the weak. Examining it from all sides, you are bound to admit that it is true. It is the fruit of countless ages of hard thinking and bitter experience; it appears in Holy Writ; it is embalmed in the platforms of all the great parties; it bears the O.K. of your pastor and of Mr. Roosevelt, and your own experience with gas companies, beef trusts and janitors convinces you of its eternal verity. But just attempt to harness it with some other platitude—say, for instance, with the one which announces that only the poor are happy and see where the two will carry you. You will have, then, (a) the doctrine that it is wrong to make the poor poorer, and (b) the doctrine that the poorer a man grows the happier he becomes. Now, let x equal the word "poorer" and y equal the word "happier," and try a little equation, thus:

(It's wrong to make the poor x) = (The x a man grows the y he becomes.)

An inspection of the second part of this equation, in its original form, shows that x and y are exchangeable terms. Therefore, let us substitute y for x in the first part. This gives us: "It is wrong to make the poor y," which, being restored, becomes: "It is wrong to make the poor happier."

I have a suspicion that there is some truth in this last hybrid, as there is in all untruths, but of that it is best to say nothing. The real point is that our two platitudes have led us to a conclusion which, whatever its logical soundness, is undoubtedly impossible, not to say immoral.

But what have platitudes to do with the divine art of literature? And, in particular, what have they to do with Upton Sinclair's new romance, *The Moneychangers*? Simply this: that hordes of the *bacillus platitudae* have entered Sinclair's system and are preying upon his vitals. They have already consumed his sense of humor and are now fast devouring his elemental horse sense. The first result is that he is taking himself and the world seriously, and the second result is that he is writing tracts. Saving only explanatory programs for symphony concerts, tracts constitute the lowest of all forms of literature. To write a play, a novel, a poem or even a newspaper editorial, one must first ensnare an idea. To write a tract one needs but leisure, a grouch and a platitude.

If Sinclair were a natural tractarian, born to the vice, it would be scarcely worth while to waste space upon him. But he is not, for his past performances upon the literary turf—and his present book, too, in more than one place—prove that he has a genuine gift for writing better things. His feeling for form and climax is sure; he sees the essential thing in the heap of unessential things; and—though he doesn't always do it—he knows how to write simple, straightforward, natural dialogue. When he started out he loomed big. There seemed to be something of the vigor of Frank Norris, even of Zola, in him. He appeared to sense the sheer meaninglessness of life—the strange, inexplicable, incredible tragedy of the struggle for existence. But then came the vociferous success of *The Jungle*. The afflatus of a divine mission began to stir him, and he sallied forth to preach his incomprehensible *jehad*. Today he is going the road of Walt Whitman, of Edwin Markham, of the later Zola, all of whom began as artists and ended as mad mullahs.

The Moneychangers is the second volume of a trilogy which began with *The Metropolis*. Its hero, Allen Montague, is a young Southern lawyer who goes to New York to try his fortune. He soon finds, however, that in the money marts of Manhattan, the chivalry of the Confederate States has no place—that it is impossible, in brief, to make a million there and yet remain a Southern gentleman. So he abandons his original enterprise and sets up shop as a sort of virtuoso of virtue in the midst of the jackals. They pass before him in review, scheming, swindling and betraying, dog eating dog. He sees them at close range, in their homes and in their offices, at their play and at their trade. Over all the muck of promoters, liars, thieves, robbers and seducers towers the epic figure of Dan Waterman, master of Wall Street. Waterman preys upon the lesser jackals, and these, in turn, feast upon the people. It is a grim and moving picture, and despite its melodrama, it somehow bears an air of truth.

Mr. Sinclair's story, indeed, is passionately and riotously veracious. It purports to show how certain money kings caused the panic of last autumn—and it shows all this more clearly and plausibly than any Presidential message or leading article yet inflicted upon the public. It purports to show the evil influence of money madness upon the human soul—and it shows. It purports to show that, when the dollar barons fight, the common people die in the trenches—and the proof is there. But why show and prove such things? Why demonstrate the obvious? Why go over ground that is trodden smooth by every campaign spellbinder and magazine muckraker? Why mouth platitudes and draw the willing tear with banalities?

Carried away by his notion that his own sophomoric theory of human existence is a Mosaic revelation, and his secondary, but equally virulent, notion that all other theories are criminal and of the devil, Mr. Sinclair has hopelessly confused the functions of the novelist with those of the crusader. His story, despite its interest and its craftsmanship, is not a moving picture of human passions, not an analysis of the human soul under suffering, but a somewhat florid thesis in sociology, with conclusions that were stale in the days of St. Augustine. His characters are at once too familiar and too elusive. Very evidently they impinge upon his own consciousness, not as real persons, but as incarnations of the more elemental virtues and vices. To the reader they appear as mere names in a brief for the prosecution, and in reality and vitality they are one with John Doe and Mary Roe.

Let Mr. Sinclair, after his trilogy is done, choose between crusading and writing. If he yearns to go down into history with Marx and Debs, Mohammed and Dowie, Billy Sunday and Sam Jones—well and good. But if he wants fame to know him as an anatomist of the human soul—as a novelist comparable with Norris of *The Octopus*, for example—let him remember that an economic struggle, to make material for fiction, must be pictured, not objectively and as a mere bout between good and evil, but subjectively and as some chosen protagonist sees and experiences it. A novel as well written as *The Moneychangers*, but with Dan Waterman filling the picture—a novel laying bare his mind and showing us why, how and by what manner of ratiocination he arrives at his deviltries—would be a novel of the first rank. And by the same token a novel showing, specifically and with insight, the exact manner and means whereby Waterman's deviltries blast some given poor man—John Smith or William Brown— would be of the first rank, too. For in the novel, as in the drama, the interest lies, always and inevitably, in some one man's effort to master his fate. From the acts which make up this effort, the reader may hope to deduce some syllable of philosophy for his own use. But out of a tract he can get nothing but a platitude—a platitude which he knows to be true, and which he also knows to be untrue.

Mr. Sinclair may maintain that Allen Montague is the protagonist in *The Moneychangers*—that the drama is played in his soul—that the philosophy is distilled from his lips. If such is his notion, it may be well to recall to his mind certain things he was taught at college about the Greek drama, and particularly certain things concerning the difference between a protagonist and a chorus.

(November, 1908)

A Definition

We will begin with what the architects of rituals call a responsive service, to wit:

Q.—What is a novel?

A.—A novel is an imaginative, artistic and undialectic composition in prose, not less than 20,000 nor more than 500,000 words in length, and divided into chapters, sections, books or other symmetrical parts, in which certain interesting, significant and probable (though fictitious) human transactions are described both in cause and effect, with particular reference to the influence exerted upon the ideals, opinions, morals, temperament and overt acts of some specified person or persons by the laws, institutions, superstitions, traditions and customs of such portions of the human race and the natural phenomena of such portions of the earth as may come under his, her or their observation or cognizance, and by the ideals, opinions, morals, temperament and overt acts of such person or persons as may come into contact, either momentarily or for longer periods, with him, her or them, either by actual, social or business intercourse, or through the medium of books, newspapers, the church, the theater or some other person or persons.

The definition represents the toil of several days and makes severe demands upon both eye and attention, but it is well worth the time spent upon it and the effort necessary to assimilate it, for it is entirely without loophole, blowhole or other blemish. It describes, with scientific accuracy, every real novel ever written, and by the same token, it bars out every last near-novel, pseudo-novel and quasi-novel, however colorable, and every romance, rhapsody, epic, saga, stuffed short story, tract and best-seller known to bibliographers.

This definition, in truth, has a quarrel with the great bulk of current fiction. One and all, the books that pour from the presses, in their bright gauds of gilt and red, are labeled novels, but often their labels mislead sadly.

Now and then, however, there appears upon the bookstalls a new book which meets upon fair ground those great books of other years which set the bounds of fiction's symphonic form—a new book which tells, with insight, imagination and conviction, the story of some one man's struggle with his fate—which shows us, like a vast fever chart, the ebb and flow of his ideas and ideals, and the multitude of forces shaping them—which gives us, in brief, a veritable, moving chronicle of a human being driven, tortured and fashioned by the blood within him and the world without—a chronicle with a beginning, a middle and an end, and some reasonable theory of existence over all. Such a book is *The Pit*—a true novel. And such a book is Miss Mary Johnston's new novel, *Lewis Rand*.

Lewis Rand, it must be admitted at the start, is far from flawless. In form, for example, it is immeasurably below *Henry Esmond;* in its painting in of color and character it is inferior to *Huckleberry Finn*— the greatest work of fiction yet produced by an American; and in its analysis of incident and motive it is not to be compared to *Lord Jim*. But while it thus falls short of the first rank, it is unquestionably at the top of the second rank. There is sincerity in every line, and there is an epic sweep and breadth to it. Planned lavishly and written with infinite pains, it is not only a good story of a strong man's losing battle with Fate, but an illuminating study of an epoch and a conflict of civilizations.

The man we see is a poor white of the Virginia of Jefferson's day. Born to toil, he is rowelled, from early youth, by high ambitions, for

mingling with his father's plodding burgher blood there is a more fiery
strain from his mother. A chance meeting with the Sage of Monticello
gives shape to his yearnings and he enters upon the study of the law.
In Virginia a lawyer is, *ipso facto*, a politician, and Lewis Rand is apt
at both trades. From the very start, he is a young man of obvious
promise, and as the years drift past this promise is realized. That rising of the yeoman against the baron which has Jefferson for its philosopher, finds in Rand, in so far as Virginia is concerned, its prophet
and hero. With his horde behind him, he triumphs over the old ruling
caste with ease and the State is at his feet.

But in all this delirium of success Rand finds disquiet. He is the
master, true enough, at the polls, and if he gives the word he may be
Governor of Virginia and the peer of princes, but in the face of all
that worldly glory is he the equal, after all, of his foes? He has carried
the war into the enemy's country by making a daughter of the Churchills his wife, but isn't it a fact that the Churchills and the Rands are
still of different castes, as unlike as the Roman and the Hun? The
thought drives Rand into bitter rage and fills his mind with plans for
vast, fantastic revenges and conquests.

It is at this time that Aaron Burr—sleek, confident and plausible—
crosses his path. Burr dreams of an empire beyond the Mississippi,
and Rand sees in it his opportunity. He will cast in his lot with the
dreamer and then trample the dreamer down. Jacqueline Rand, of the
Churchill clan, will become an empress! He, Rand, disdaining accep-
tances as a mere equal, will lift the Churchills up! Governor of Virginia? Jefferson's heir? Pooh!

But then Fate steps in, with her grim smile. Burr is arrested, the
empire vanishes, and Rand faces the cold, accusing eye of Jefferson. It
is only by his betrayed patron's generosity, indeed, that he escapes a
trial for treason. Even as it is, the story of his gigantic plot reaches the
ears of one of his foes—and that man is Ludwell Cary, most serene of
the baronial caste and most noble of vanquished rivals in love. It is
not because Cary has loved Jacqueline that Rand hates him, for Jacqueline's love and loyalty are perfect, but because in him is visualized
the supremely desirable and the eternally unattainable. One day, rid-
ing along a lonely road, Rand and Cary meet. Next morning Cary is
found dead—and as the story closes we see Rand preparing to enter
felon's dock to answer the charge of murder.

A very clever woman of my acquaintance, reading this sound and

moving novel, objected to Rand's sudden slaying of Cary without immediate provocation as a mere trick of the theater. But to me it seems
anything but that. It is, indeed, one of the surest touches in the book.
From the start the murder is as inevitable as Hamlet's slaying of the
king, and one glimpses its gathering shadow in scene after scene.
Rand's fight, it is ever plain, is not for kingship over the rabble, but
for acceptance by his vanquished foes. All his vast energies and talents are shaped to that end, and when, after his narrow escape from
disgrace, it slowly dawns upon him that the barrier before him is not
an artificial thing, to be torn down at will, but a wall impenetrable
and everlasting, his rage becomes ungovernable. In its very breaking
of all restraint, indeed, appears proof that the barrier is real—that, after all, the difference between caste and caste is fixed, not by man
himself, but by Providence. A Cary, in all ages, has his passions in
hand, even when they are most fiery; but a Rand, unschooled by generations of formula and inhibition, is their slave. And so Lewis Rand
kills Ludwell Cary—because he can't help it.

In detail, *Lewis Rand* is of uneven texture. Here and there the story
lumbers, and now and again it runs thin, but for the greater part Miss
Johnston's technique suffices for her plan. She is obviously writing, not
to meet the current fashion, but to please herself—and it is just such
writing that makes the best of reading. With a stage sparsely peopled,
she has opportunity to give her characters rotundity, and out of it
grows reality. One may quarrel, at first blush, with Jacqueline's good-
ness, but if one recalls the ideals of feminine duty which obtained in
the sub-Potomac palatinates of her day, she grows in plausibility. So,
too, the Carys and the Churchills. The century-long battle has been
won by the Rands and the old aristocracy is no more, but the conflict
was very real while it lasted, and in Miss Johnston's understanding of
its savagery and significance lies the chief value of her novel. The
siege of caste by caste is not merely a part of the story's machinery.
On the contrary, the story itself is but a fable visualizing the siege,
just as in *Nostromo* one's mind is made to dwell, not upon the adventures of Nostromo himself, but upon that maddening world-riddle—
that unanswerable question as to the meaning of life—which lies beneath them.

                                                      (January, 1909)

O. Henry

O. Henry (Sidney Porter), author of *Roads of Destiny*, is an insoluble riddle. I give him up. Either he is the best story teller in the world today, or the worst. Sometimes I think he is the one and sometimes I am convinced that he is the other. Maybe he is both.

And why the best? Because no other man now living equals him in the invention of preposterous intrigues and the imagining of fantastic characters. He can borrow an idea from Stevenson—as in the title story of the present book—and give it so many novel and outlandish twists that it becomes absolutely new. He can construct a farce plot that would have sent Offenbach flying to his music paper, as in "Next to Reading Matter"; and he can bring back again, with all its sentimental melodrama, the Golden West of Bret Harte, as in "Friends in San Rosario." Always his stories have action in them—action and "an air." They are full of queer ambuscades and surprises. The end is never visible at the beginning.

And why, being so marvelously ingenious and resourceful, is Mr. Porter also so bad an artist? Chiefly, because his fancy is a bucking broncho without a rider. He has no conception of the value of restraint. He lays on his effects with a shovel. As he writes, innumerable comic ideas occur to him—bizarre phrases, impossible slang, ridiculous collocations—and he slaps them in at once. If they fit, well and good; if not, he uses them all the same. The result is that his characters all speak the same tongue. At the beginning of a story, now and then, he manages to keep them differentiated, but before long they are all spouting Porterese.

Again, this same exuberance leads to a painful piling up of snickers. In "The Discounters of Money," for example, a capital story is spoiled by too much smartness. There are twenty wheezes to a page. Instead of helping on the tale, they make it bewildering and unreal. You grow interested in a character study—and the author asks you to halt at every third line and marvel at some banal wit from Broadway.

But it is an ungrateful task to point out defects in a writer so amusing as Mr. Porter. At his worst, true enough, he is very, very bad, but at his best he is irresistible. Some day, let us hope, he will acquire resolution enough to stick to the letter of his text, no matter how great the temptation to fly off into literary roulades. Meanwhile, it might benefit him to give a month or two of hard study to a book called *In*

Babel, by George Ade—a book containing some of the best comedies in the English language.

(July, 1909)

The Raw Material of Fiction

Without running any very grave risk of being posted publicly as a liar, one may venture to say, I take it, that, just as melody is the raw material of music, so the thing we call the story is the raw material of prose fiction.

In the most elemental forms of fiction, as in the most elemental forms of music, we get that raw material and nothing more. Sometimes, indeed, it is inherently so nearly perfect, both in substance and in pattern, that nothing more is needed. Thus it was a sure artistic instinct which led Mark Twain to tell the famous story of the jumping frog exactly as he had heard it from Old Ben Coon, the half-wit of Angel's Camp. The slightest attempt to augment and bedizen it, or, as the musicians say, to develop it, would have been ruinous to it. And thus it is that we are wholly satisfied, however richly nourished upon unresolved sevenths, by such homely songs as "Dixie," *"Stille Nacht"* and "Annie Laurie." They are as primitive as Aesop's *Fables* or the first book of Genesis, but nevertheless it is unimaginable that any reinforcement of their naked simplicity could improve them, or even fail to spoil them. At least one of the three— "Annie Laurie," to wit—is almost if not quite flawless as it stands, and hence it must be ranked with the greatest works of art that music can show.

But such perfection, of course, is quite as rare in art as it is in nature. The world has been producing songs innumerable for hundreds of years, and yet its "Annie Lauries" are still very few, and sometimes a quarter of a century goes by without any new one being added to the stock. So with its great stories. Of such infrequency, in fact, are accessions here that it is common to say that all of the really great ones have been told. But meanwhile the demand for both music and tales—or, as we now say, novels—keeps up as strongly as ever, and very tempting rewards, both in money and in fame, are offered to whoever can meet it. Two avenues of approach to these rewards lie open to the ambitious fictioneer. On the one hand, he may throw all intelligible standards of merit to the winds, and devote himself to manufacturing new stories that are frankly bad, trusting to the fact that nine persons out of ten are utterly devoid of esthetic sense and hence unable to tell the bad from the good. And on the other hand, he may take stories, or parts of stories that have been told before, or that, in themselves, are scarcely worth the telling, and so encrust them with the ornaments of wit, of shrewd observation, of human sympathy and of style—in brief, so develop them—that readers of good taste will forget the unsoundness of the material in admiration of the ingenious and workmanlike way in which it is handled. The authors of the first of these classes achieve the mawkish romances and incredible detective stories which leer at us from all the book counters. The authors of the second class achieve such things as *Tom Jones, Huckleberry Finn, Barry Lyndon, Germinal* and *The Brothers Karamazov.*

It is in music, however, rather than in fiction, that this triumph of skill over materials is best to be observed, and in music, again, that the occasional failures of the process are most striking. The opening movement of the greatest orchestral work ever written, Beethoven's Fifth Symphony, has nothing at the bottom of it save a little melody of two tones, one of them three times repeated—a melody so childishly simple that one has to stretch the meaning of the term to call it a melody at all. And yet, out of that austere material, Beethoven constructed a piece of music so noble and so beautiful, so rich in imagination and so lofty in style, that it remains today, after more than a century, a masterpiece that no other man has ever equalled, and that few have even so much as approached. But this same Beethoven, in the symphony immediately following, made a failure almost as note-worthy as his success in the incomparable Fifth. Here, in the so-called Pastorale, he started out with a melodic idea of decided grace and charm—in other words, with what seemed to be excellent material —but when he essayed to embellish and develop it, his usual resourcefulness failed him, and all he managed to do was to repeat it over and over again, with inconsiderable changes in tonality and instrumentation. The result was a composition which remains famous to this day, despite many beauties in its other movements, chiefly for its forbidding monotony. It is hard hearing, just as certain books by undoubtedly competent authors are hard reading.

All of which may well serve as overture to a few discreet remarks upon the subject of Joseph Conrad, an artist who falls far short, perhaps, of the Beethoven stature, but is still a fair match for—well, let us say Brahms. Like most other great novelists, Conrad belongs to the second of the two classes of story tellers that I mentioned a moment ago. That is to say, his actual story, thrilling though it may be, is always a great deal less important than the way he tells it. It is what he thinks about it and says about it, and in particular, the great laws of conduct and destiny that he sees within and behind it, that make it on the one hand a work of art and on the other hand a profound study of human motive, instinct and emotion. The uncanny fascination of *Typhoon,* for example, does not lie in the storm which batters the steamship *Nan-Shan,* nor even in the melodramatic battle which goes on among the terrified Chinamen in her hold, but in the action and reaction of these external phenomena upon the muddled mind of Captain MacWhirr. The whole of that colossal tragi-comedy, indeed, is played out there. MacWhirr himself is not only the stage of the play, but also the entire stock company. And it is because Conrad is able to imagine clearly every move in so fantastic and rarefied a drama, and to make it comprehensible and poignant to the reader, that he earns the respect which belongs to a first-rate artist.

As I have said, the mere story, to such a novelist, is of secondary importance. The thing he demands of it is not that it be novel and enthralling in itself, but that it lend itself readily to artistic development, and be fruitful in situations which offer opportunity for elaborate psychological exploration. Just as Beethoven, in the Fifth Symphony, began with a fragment of tune so primitive that it scarcely had any separate existence at all, so Conrad is in the habit of using the most commonplace materials of melodrama. At the bottom of "Falk" you will find nothing more than the old, old story of the shipwrecked sailors who fight for the last crust and then proceed to devour one another. And in *Heart of Darkness,* again in "An Outpost of Progress," again in *Almayer's Folly,* again in *An Outcast of the Islands,* and yet again in *Lord Jim* the fable is the simple one of the white man who sheds his civilization when thrown among savages. Here, in truth, Conrad has used the same story, or what is substantially the same story, no less than five times—and it appears as a sub-motive, as it were, in still other of his tales. So again, in *The Secret Agent, Under Western Eyes, Nostromo,* "Youth," and *The Nigger of the "Narcissus":*

the primary material is conventional blood and thunder, and in other hands it would probably make us smile. But in Conrad's hands it becomes the warp and woof of a fabric so complex and yet so delicate that the stuff out of which it is made is forgotten and we stand enchanted before the marvelously beautiful pattern. Such a story as "Youth," told by an O. Henry, or even by a Kipling, would be nothing more than an exciting story. But told by Conrad it is at once a subtle philosophy of life and a stately poem, with something in it of the eternal wisdom of Ecclesiastes and something of the surge and thunder of the *Odyssey*.

Obviously, there are dangers attending the use of this method, for the moment the author begins to lose his grip on his story it becomes an empty and a tedious thing. How Beethoven slipped into platitude in the Pastorale we have seen; a hundred other musical examples might be drawn from the works of Schubert, Mendelssohn, Tschaikovsky and even Wagner, to say nothing of the Italians. And among the novelists there are many who suffer intermittently, and a few almost chronically, from attacks of the same depressing banality—for instance, Edith Wharton and Arnold Bennett among the former, and Eden Phillpotts and Gerhart Hauptmann among the latter. Even Conrad, like Meredith and Zola before him, has his off days, his times of clumsy floundering, his haltings upon intellectual dead centers. At such times a novelist is thrown, so to speak, upon his manner. That is to say, he has to go through the motions of saying something without actually having anything to say. The result is inevitably painful to the faithful reader. He gets a specious effect of profundity, a sonorous and deceptive soothing. He is ready, and even eager, to believe that he is being led down tortuous and enchanting paths. But the truth is, of course, that he is standing stock still, or rather, revolving like a teetotum, and after a while his head begins to swim and his knees to give way, and he presently falls into a fitful and unrefreshing slumber.

Something of this aching emptiness is to be met with in the latest of the Conrad novels, *Chance* by title, or, at any rate, in its first hundred pages or so. Here we have the Conrad manner at its worst, and with no compensating richness of matter. The author hides a story within a story, and then turns aside from that second story to tell an irrelevant third story. Chapter after chapter is given to platting the psychological charts of Mr. and Mrs. Fyne, brother-in-law and sister to the redoubtable Captain Roderick Anthony, despite the plain indication, from the very start, that the main business of the chronicle is to be with the Captain, and not with the Fynes. And in the same way we are introduced with the utmost elaborateness to one Captain Powell, whose only visible function, at least for a long while, is to impede and obscure the progress of events. In the end, true enough, it is seen that each of these persons has had a considerable influence upon the life of Anthony, but the point I wish to make is that the part they are to play is but dimly foreshadowed in the earlier portions of the story, and that in consequence their doings take on an air of irrelevance. In brief, Conrad proceeds to his development section before he has clearly given out his themes, and that habit makes for chaos in the novel quite as surely as in music.

The actual story, like that of *Lord Jim,* is plain melodrama. Captain Anthony, who is master and part-owner of a sailing ship, falls in love with Flora de Barral, the only daughter of a ruined financier. De Barral has been sent to prison and Flora is at the mercy of atrocious relatives. She is by no means in love with Anthony, but in order to escape these relatives she marries him and goes to sea with him. When her father is released from prison, he, too, is taken aboard the ship. Old De Barral, his mind a bit unbalanced by his downfall, takes a violent dislike to Anthony, and insists upon regarding him as the jailer of Flora. Finally he goes to the length of trying to poison Anthony. His intentions are discovered, and, panic-stricken, he swallows the poison himself. The cause of his death is concealed from Flora, and Anthony chivalrously offers to release her. But meanwhile she has fallen in love with him and is eager to become his wife in fact as well as in name. Thereafter they live happily, traveling up and down the world, until Anthony loses his life in a shipwreck.

Out of these simple materials, so familiar to all students of the *Seaside Library* of thirty years ago, Conrad has fashioned a characteristically complex and searching piece of fiction. Exasperatingly mystifying at the start, it gathers clarity as it goes on, and in the latter half is some of the best writing that he has done since *The Mirror of the Sea.* Is it only by coincidence that this increase of momentum comes with the departure of Anthony and Flora on their first voyage? I am inclined to see a greater significance in the fact. The story, true enough, is scarcely to be called a sea story. All that goes on aboard the ship *Ferndale,* or, at least, all that is essential to the tale, might have been made to occur with equal probability in a house ashore.

But the first breath of ocean air seems to give Conrad, in some occult manner, a new grip upon his characters. After all, the fact is perhaps not strange. The sea is his element; the whole of his youth was spent upon it; its mark is upon all the ideas and impressions that make up his literary stock in trade. He has written superb land stories—setting aside *The Secret Agent* and *Under Western Eyes,* there is always "The Point of Honor"!—but the things that lift him wholly above his contemporaries, and give him what would seem to be a secure place in the front rank of English novelists, are his incomparable tales of the sea—"Falk," *Typhoon, The Nigger of the "Narcissus", Lord Jim.* Here, indeed, are masterpieces for you. Here a true genius is spinning yarns.

But not, of course, simple yarns—not yarns as yarns are ordinarily understood. The fascination of a Conrad story lies, not in its merely narrative elements, but in its interpretative elements. "My task," said Conrad once, "is, by the power of the written word, to make you hear, to make you feel—it is, before all, to make you *see.*" And what he makes us see is precisely what is least upon the surface—the subtle play of forces in the dim region of human motive and emotion, the inordinately tangled reactions between will and environment, the blind and irresistible play of the cosmic currents. He is a psychological polyphonist, an explorer of strange disharmonies, of startling progressions, of inexplicable overtones. All this, of course, explains the difficulty he presents to the idle novel reader, and even to the reader of more serious purpose. He is so intent upon the remoter effects and implications of his story that he sometimes allows the story itself to lose direction and clarity.

The same phenomenon is a familiar one in music: how often, indeed, do we see a composer involve himself in unintelligible snarls of sound in his free fantasia! The device employed to help out the baffled hearer might help out the baffled reader, too. Why not print a sort of thematic analysis before each of the Conrad novels, clearly marking off its main outlines? What an aid that would be to the comphrehension and enjoyment of *Lord Jim!* As it is, the Conradian neophyte must read it twice to get at its true greatness—once to gather in the bare substance of the story, and once to search out the extraordinarily twisted and elusive paths of its inner content. The second reading is a joy, but the first must needs be somewhat arduous. Why not avoid the necessity for it by setting forth the author's principal materials in advance, as Sir George Grove has set forth those of

Beethoven and a host of commentators those of Wagner? I throw out
the suggestion and no more. Perhaps it may help Conrad's publishers to
that popularization of him which they plan.

(March, 1914)

Point of View

The best of them, and by long odds, is *The Moon and Sixpence,* by
W. Somerset Maugham, an absurdly vague and vapid title for an extremely sound piece of work. This Maugham, half a dozen years ago,
was well-known as a writer of bad comedies of the lighter, smarter
variety, by Oscar Wilde out of the Tom Robertson tradition—the sort
of thing that John Drew used to do—labored epigrams strung upon a
thread of drawing-room adultery. In the intervals between them he
wrote third-rate novels: *The Explorers, The Magician,* and others, all
now forgotten. One day, entirely without warning, he gave London a
surprise by publishing a story of a quite different kind, to wit, *Human
Bondage,* [*sic*] an interminably long, solemn and inchoate but nevertheless curiously sagacious and fascinating composition—very un-
English in its general structure, almost Russian in some of its details.
This book came to me for review, but when I observed its count of
pages I quietly dropped it behind the piano. Two or three years later
a woman of sound taste in fiction advised me to unearth it and read it,
and I made a futile search for it. Another year passed and a second
woman began talking it up. Having been long convinced that women
are much better judges of novels than men—who ever heard of a
woman who read detective stories?—I now got hold of the book and
read it, an enterprise absorbing the leisure of a whole week. I left it
very much impressed. The story was too garrulous; it often threatened
to get beyond the author; it was, in more than one place, distressingly
young; but all the same there was a fine earnestness in it, and a great
deal of careful observation, and some passages of capital writing. The
Maugham of the shallow comedies for West End theaters was nowhere visible. This Maugham of *Human Bondage* was a man who
was trying very hard to present his characters honestly, and to get be-

neath their skins, and to put behind them a living and recognizable background, and what is more, he was, in chapter after chapter, coming pleasantly close to success. In brief, a very unusual book—something worthy of being mentioned in the same breath with such things as Walpole's *The Gods and Mr. Perrin,* George's *The Making of an Englishman,* Bennett's *Whom God Hath Joined,* and Wells' *Ann Veronica.*

Now, in *The Moon and Sixpence,* Maugham takes another leap forward. That leap is from the uncertainty of the neophyte to the sureness of the accomplished craftsman, from unsteady experimentation to fluent and easy technic. It is, indeed, an astonishing progress; I know of no other case that quite parallels it. The book, if it were hollow as a jug otherwise, would still be remarkable as a sheer piece of writing. It has good design; it moves and breathes; it has a fine manner; it is packed with artful and effective phrases. But better than all this, it is a book which tackles head-on one of the hardest problems that the practical novelist ever has to deal with, and which solves it in a way that is both sure-handed and brilliant. This is the problem of putting a man of genius into a story in such fashion that he will seem real—in such fashion that the miracle of him will not blow up the plausibility of him. Scores of novelists have tried to solve it, and failed. Every publishing season sees half a dozen new tales with Nietzsche, or Chopin, or Bonaparte, or Wagner for hero—and half a dozen creaking marionettes, no more real than your aunt's false teeth. But Maugham, with his painting genius, his Kensington Gauguin, somehow achieves the impossible. One gets the unmistakable feeling that the fellow is extraordinary—not merely odd, but of genuinely superior quality—and yet there is nothing operatic and fabulous about him; he remains an authentic man in the midst of all his gaudiest doings. It is a novelistic feat of a high order, and, as Woodrow says, I should be lacking in perfect frankness if I did not admit that I have been a good deal surprised by Maugham's performance of it. It is as if John Philip Sousa should suddenly spit on his hands and write a first-rate symphony. It is almost as if a Congressman should suddenly become honest, self-respecting, courageous and intelligent.

Naturally, the thing is done very simply. Maugham's success, in fact, lies a good deal less in what he positively does than in what he discreetly leaves undone. He gets the colors of life into his Charles Strickland, not by playing a powerful beam of light upon him, but by leaving him a bit out of focus—by constantly insisting, in the midst of every discussion of him, upon his pervasive mystery—in brief, by craftily making him appear, not as a commonplace, simple and completely understandable man, but as the half comprehended enigma that every genuine man of genius seems to all of us when we meet him in real life. The average novelist, grappling with such a hero, always makes the fatal error of trying to account for him wholly—of reducing him to a composite of fictional rubber-stamps. Thus he inevitably takes on commonness, and in proportion as he is clearly drawn he loses plausibility as a man of genius. Maugham falls into no such blunder. Of Strickland, the unit of human society—the Strickland who eats, sleeps, travels about, reads the newspapers, changes his shirt, has his shoes polished, dodges automobiles and goes to business every morning like the rest of us—we get a portrait that is careful, logical and meticulous—in brief, that is brilliantly life-like. But of the vaster, darker Strickland who is a man of genius—the Strickland who deserts his family to go to Paris to paint, and there plods his way to extraordinary achievement, and then throws away his life in the South Seas —of this Strickland we see only an image made up of sudden and brief points of light, like flashes of Summer lightning below the horizon. He is, in one aspect, made convincingly vivid; he is, in the other, left in the shadow of mystery. That is precisely how we all see a man of genius in real life; he is half plain John Smith and half inscrutable monster. It remained for Maugham to get the thing into a novel. If there were no other merit in his book, it would stand out from the general for that unusually deft and effective character sketch.

As for the machinery of the effect, part of it is borrowed from Joseph Conrad, to wit, the device of presenting the story through the medium of an onlooker, himself fascinated and daunted by the enigma of it. This device, of course, was not invented by Conrad, but it seems to me that he has employed it to better purpose than any other novelist writing in English. Consider, for example, how magnificently it is used in *Typhoon*, in *Lord Jim* and in *Heart of Darkness*. These stories, straightforwardly told, would still be stories of very high quality, but I believe that a good deal of their present strange flavor would be gone; they would cease to suggest the sinister and inexplicable. There appears to be a theory among novelists that the precisely contrary method is the more convincing—that the way to write a tale that will carry the air of reality is to do it in the autobiographical form. But that is surely not true. When he adopts the autobiographical form the novelist is compelled to account for his protagonist completely; he must attain to realism by pretending to omniscience. That pretension has brought many an otherwise sound novel to disaster. I am almost convinced that it would have brought even *Lord Jim* into difficulties. What holds our interest in Jim to the last, and leaves us with a memory of him that glows for long days, is the dark wonder of him. We learn enough about him to see him clearly, but we never quite penetrate his soul—we are never quite certain about the interplay of motives that brings him to his romantic catastrophe. Take away the droning Marlow, and he would come too close to the camera. Thus there lies, beyond the crude realism of white light, the finer, softer realism of delicately managed shadows. More than half the charm of Conrad, I daresay, is due to his superb capacity for managing them. At the end of every one of his incomparable tales there is a question-mark. He leaves us to answer as we will, each according to the light within. . . . I think that Maugham, borrowing that device, has employed it with noteworthy success. He is, God knows, no Conrad, but he has written a very excellent novel, and in it there is plenty of evidence that its quality is no mere accident, but the product of very deliberate and intelligent effort.

(November, 1919)

IV

The Drama and Some Dramatists

Having discussed Mencken's early interest in the theater and the great changes that were taking place at the turn of the century, I need only add here that the following excerpts and reviews were chosen to illustrate Mencken's interest in foreign products. Following in the wake of Huneker and Percival Pollard, who died in Baltimore in 1911 at the early age of forty-two (Mencken was with him at the end and, along with the satanic Ambrose Bierce, attended his cremation), Mencken helped to spread the foreign news to his provincial countrymen.

On Playgoers—And on
Hauptmann, Synge, and Shaw

Upon the depressing stupidity and vulgarity of New York first nighters my colleague, Mr. Nathan, has lately discoursed with great eloquence. As for me, I am no New Yorker, save intermittently and unwillingly, and so I do not have to sit beside such animals very often; but they have thousands of relatives, of the first, second, third, fourth, fifth and sixth nights, in the provinces, and the fair city I inhabit has its full share of them. They may be distinguished from truly civilized theatergoers by various signs. In the first place, their women always smell of unearthly coal tar perfumery; in the second place, they themselves always wear dinner coats; in the third place, they break into explosive laughter whenever the word "damn" is uttered on the stage; in the fourth place, they make a peculiar, indescribable, throaty sound whenever the proceedings become what they call "suggestive"; in the fifth place, they always speak of a play as a "show," and in the sixth and last place, they distinguish but two classes of "shows," to wit, good "shows" and rotten "shows." In the former class —I speak especially of the provincial species—they put all plays with rubber stamp plots, all plays of bullring buffoonery and all plays of frank obscenity; and into the latter class they put all plays of ideas.

Because of the presence of these simple folk, playgoing in our fair land is often a trying adventure. Not only do they make it necessary for our managers to give us far more bad "shows" than good ones, but they also have a habit of spoiling the "show" whenever it happens, by any chance, to be good. In the presence of such a drama as Ibsen's *Hedda Gabler,* Shaw's *Man and Superman* or Walter's *The Easiest Way* their one thought seems to be to smell out indecencies. Compared to their covert snickering, their incessant shuffling, their asinine whispering, the frank booing of the English gallery god is soothing as a sound and intelligent as a criticism. The less boorish theatergoer, trying to get himself into the mood for receiving and enjoying a work of art, is constantly annoyed and exasperated by the proximity of these killjoys. The actors on the stage, following the custom of their trade, always do their best to make the play absurd; the overdressed hinds in the auditorium complete the crime. To see Hervieu's *Connais Toi* as I have seen it in Baltimore, with bad actors obfuscating it and a fat *entrepreneur* beside me sighing, "Oh, hell!" at intervals of three minutes, is not unlike hearing the funeral march of the Eroica Symphony done by honest union men at the "lodge of sorrow" of some barroom fraternal order.

Fortunately there is no need for the partisan of the drama to submit himself to such assaults from stage and stalls. When the theater itself becomes unbearable he may flee to his own home, and there, in peace and quiet, read the plays which the vileness of man makes it painful, if not downright impossible, for him to see. Time was when Shakespeare was the only dramatist read by Americans—if, indeed, even *he* was read—but that time is happily no more. We have been taught, by enforced familiarity with the printed pages of Ibsen and Shaw, to visualize costumes and scenery, false whiskers and talcumed noses, in the

library. We have learned a new trick and we joy to perform it. Not so
many years ago the printing of a contemporary play of any value was
a rare occurrence. Today they pour from the presses in a steady
stream—English plays, translated Continental plays, even a few American plays—and the fact that they do so is proof that there is a public
waiting for them. I have, in a collection by no means exhaustive, more
than four hundred modern plays, and fully two hundred of them, I
believe, are good plays. Of good plays the theaters of my town, taken
together, offer about ten a year. It would thus take me twenty years to
see two hundred there. But stretched at ease in the old homestead, a
pillow under my head, I may read two hundred on two hundred
nights, and then begin all over again and enjoy a hundred and sixty-
five a second time before the year runs out.

Here, for example, is Gerhart Hauptmann's very impressive drama,
The Weavers, done into English by Mary Morison. So far as I know,
The Weavers has never been played in English in our theaters. Hauptmann's *Hannele* has been seen (the first time it was produced in New
York the moral ferrets of that town demanded that it be prohibited by
the police), and his *The Sunken Bell* was once presented by Sothern
and Marlowe; but *The Weavers,* undoubtedly the greatest of all his
works and one of the most striking and influential of modern German
plays, remains a stranger to our stage. For a dollar, however, one may
now have it in a pretty little book, to read and study at one's leisure,
and without having to hear bad actors mouth its lines or to sit among
donkeys who find it incomprehensible. Mr. Huebsch's edition is a reprint of the London edition of William Heinemann. Let us hope that
he will also reprint the other plays in the series—*Hannele, The
Sunken Bell* and *Lonely Lives.*

Better still, here comes an American edition of the plays of John
Millington Synge, beautifully printed and bound and extremely modest in price. Synge, like Hauptmann, is practically unknown to our
theatergoers, and yet he wrote, during his short life, at least two
dramas of the first rank; and they were written, not in German or
French or Norwegian, but in honest English. Reading his *Riders to
the Sea* and *The Tinker's Wedding* you will make acquaintance with
the one undoubted genius of the Neo-Celtic movement—not a fantastic, pale green mystic like W. B. Yeats, or a maker of crude folk plays
like Douglas Hyde, but a noble poet plus a great dramatic craftsman,
a man who got the universal note into scenes from the lives of simple

Irish peasants, an Irishman who wrote an Irish tragedy so poignant that it lifted his people to a Grecian dignity, and a comedy so searching and merciless that it made his people scream. That tragedy is *Riders to the Sea*, a mere fragment, a thing of twenty-eight pages, and yet, if I do not err, a work of art of the very highest quality. I have never seen it on the stage, and if ever it is given in my vicinity I shall apply to be jailed during the performance, for it is impossible to imagine such marvelous prose coming from the mouths of actors, those sworn foes of all beauty. It is prose that enchants the ear with queer rhythms and exquisite cadences—prose that, for variety and movement, freedom and color, has been unapproached in our time. Synge once said that he had learned to write it by listening to West Coast Irishmen through a crack in the floor of his inn chamber. I don't believe it. As well imagine Marlowe getting Faustus's great speech before Helen from the horseboys of the Bankside.

Synge wrote, in all, but six plays—the two mentioned, *The Playboy of the Western World* (a masterpiece of comedy), *The Shadow of the Glen, The Well of the Saints* and *Deirdre of the Sorrows*, which last I have yet to read. In addition he wrote two books of travel, *The Aran Islands* and *In Kerry and Wicklow*—notebooks, as it were, for his plays. Strangely enough, the incomparable Synge prose, which appears in such magnificent flower in the speeches of his stage characters, is almost missing from his accounts of his own wanderings. Here and there one encounters a glowing page of it, but for the most part his descriptions are commonplace and sometimes even clumsy. Synge died in Dublin on April 1, 1909, at the early age of thirty-eight. He had been writing less than five years. What he would have come to had he lived fifteen years longer no man can tell. But once you have read his plays you will agree, I think, that his was one of the most original and arresting talents of our day and generation.

Another Irishman of parts—George Bernard Shaw, no other—comes before us with a new book of some four hundred pages, containing three plays and three long prefaces. In the case of *Getting Married* and *The Shewing-up of Blanco Posnet* the prefaces are far more important than the plays. *Getting Married* shows, in spots, a plentiful cleverness, but elsewhere it shows mere smartness—and smartness, once its quality is reinforced by quantity, begins to grow tedious, like the kisses following the first dozen. As for *Blanco Posnet*, it is a somewhat cheap effort to shock the pious, in the course of which Mr. Shaw

reveals the abysmality of his ignorance of spoken American. Where he
got the dialect of his unearthly Westerners I don't know, but I venture
to suspect some German version of the Italian libretto of *The Girl of
the Golden West*. There remains *The Doctor's Dilemma,* an amusing
and well constructed piece, in which fun is poked at the medical fellows on the one hand, and that puzzling thing, the artistic temperament, is studied on the other. Shaw's hero is a great artist who is also
a shameless scoundrel. To serve his art he preys upon all available
game—his wife, his friends, mere strangers. At the very gates of success he falls ill, and eminent physicians are called in to wrestle with
the bacilli which infest him. One of these physicians, the only one
who can cure him, falls in love with his wife. What to do? Kill the
scoundrel and get the wife, or save the artist and lose the wife? You
may rest assured that Shaw neglects none of the opportunities that
this amazing problem offers. The play, indeed, is the best he has done
since *Man and Superman.*

But in the preface, in which he undertakes to dispose of medical
experimentation, the brilliance of his rhetoric does not conceal the
weakness of his cause. Not that he employs the old, old arguments,
depends upon the old, old false testimony, wrings the old, old tears.
Far from it, indeed. With characteristic originality he seeks ammuni-
tion in the very latest discoveries of the pathologists—particularly in
Sir Almroth Wright's discovery of opsonins and of the so-called negative phase in the process of immunization. But after reading fifty
pages of his engaging paralogy, one suddenly finds at the end that it
is mere nonsense, after all—that Shaw, like every other anti-vivisectionist, is merely a sentimentalist who strains at a guinea pig and swallows a baby. In brief, the wild Irishman sinks to the level of a somewhat ridiculous crusader. The trouble with him is that he has begun
to take himself seriously. When he was content to write plays first and
discuss them afterward, he was unfailingly diverting. But now that he
writes tracts first and then devises plays to rub them in he grows
rather tedious.

(August, 1911)

Getting Rid of the Actor

Why waste a whole evening, once or twice a week, in a stuffy and over-red theater, breathing zymotic air, sniffing discordant perfumery, looking at idiotic scenery, listening to the bleeding English of ignorant and preposterous actors? Have you ever, in all your life, seen five leading men who actually looked like civilized gentlemen, or even like the authentic valets, head clerks or unburied corpses of civilized gentlemen? Have you ever sat through a whole performance without wishing it were possible to take at least *one* of the actors out into the alley, there to do execution of the *lex non scripta* upon him? *Eheu, Postume,* what all of us have suffered at the hands of such strutting mummers and mountebanks! How we have writhed and squirmed beneath their astounding outrages upon the vulgate! What is worse than an actor? Two actors? Three actors? A whole stage full of actors! An endless succession of actors! . . . How we have leaped and squealed under their broad *a*'s, their fearful renderings of proper names, their obscene attempts at boarding school French! How our paws have itched to grab them by the collars of their advanced coats, and to strangle them with their futurist shirts, and to anatomize them with the razor edges of their superbly ironed pantaloons! . . .

There are, of course, such things as good actors. Let us be just and admit it. I have seen and known a few myself, and have heard of a few more. There are half a dozen in England and as many in France. In Germany, I dare say, the police have the names of twenty. (One memorable night, in that strange land, I saw two on the stage at once!) But is the good actor, either at home or abroad, the normal actor, the average actor? Of course he is not. He is the rare actor, the miraculous actor, almost the fabulous actor. Examine a hundred bartenders and you will find that fully sixty of them actually know how to tend bar: they can mix a cocktail that, whatever its faults, is at least fit to drink, and they have the craft needed to draw a *Seidel* of Pilsner and to beat the cash register. But in the allied art of acting there is no such general dispersion of talent. A handful of outstanding super-actors have it all. The rest of them not only don't know how to act, but they don't know that they don't know.

Argue with them for years, and you will never convince them that the mushy jargon they speak is not English. Chain them to mirrors until they die, dry up and blow away, and they will never notice that the clothes they wear are not worn by cultured white men, and that the way they walk, gesticulate, make love, blow their noses, commit murders, crawl, lope, die, eat, trot, pace, jump out of a window, climb up a rainspout, sing, sneeze, roar, whoop, swear, pray, sit down and get up is not the way affected by the free citizens of any Christian commonwealth. No; the average actor never notices these things. He never notices anything—saving only the doings of other actors. These rivals, whom he despises (and usually with reason), he devotes himself to imitating. The result is the so-called art of acting—an art as thoroughly dehumanized as that of cutting tombstones.

But how to escape these assassins of English, these libelers of dramatists, these pestiferous gnats and gadflies of our hours of ease? The thing is as simple as marrying a widow! Don't *see* plays; *read* them. Don't go to a theater for your dramatic entertainment, but to a bookstore. Don't pay two dollars for a seat between two fat women; seventy-five cents will buy you the play, and you may read it in comfort and at your leisure, spread out in your own quiet library, miles away from plush and perfumery, a jug and a siphon at your side, your nose untortured, your mind untroubled, your soul ripe for adventures among masterpieces.

Time was when it was difficult. Time was when it was almost impossible. But no more. The Ibsen plays led the way and the Shaw plays followed after. Today a new play is published almost as soon as it is performed—and sometimes even before. And if, now and then, it is not published—if a dramatist or a manager, growing wise, fears to let your eyes compete with his actors—then don't let it worry you. You will not be missing much. All of the good plays, with very few exceptions, are being printed today. Most of the bad ones—the cheap and tawdry melodramas, the machine-made sentimental comedies, the "strong" variations upon borrowed themes, the tedious adaptations of French and German farces, the *Aztec Romances* and *Master Minds*, the exquisite confections of David Belasco and Charles Klein—are *not* being printed.

You can now get, in any bookstore, all of the dramas of Henrik Ibsen, John Millington Synge, John Galsworthy, Lady Augusta Gregory, William Butler Yeats, Granville Barker, Leo Tolstoi, Maxim Gorki, Alfred Sutro, St. John Hankin, Stephen Phillips, Percy Mackaye, Maurice Maeterlinck, Oscar Wilde, Israel Zangwill and Henry Arthur Jones, and all save one or two of George Bernard Shaw, Arthur Wing

Pinero and Arnold Bennett. A complete edition of Gerhart Hauptmann, admirably translated, has now reached its second volume and
seventh play, and several other Hauptmann plays are to be had separately. Of the dramas of August Strindberg, at least fifteen have been
translated—twice as many as have ever been acted in English—and
two or three further volumes are announced. The principal plays of
Eugène Brieux have been in English for two years or more, and his
complete canon is soon to follow. So with the plays of Hermann
Sudermann: I read his *Heimat* in the vulgate so long ago as the year
1900. So with Frank Wedekind. So with Arthur Schnitzler. So with
Björnstjerne Björnson. So with José Echegaray. So, to finish the foreigners, with Anton Tchekoff, Leonid Andreieff, Paul Hervieu, Ed-
mond Rostand and Hugo von Hofmannsthal.

All the best plays of the late Clyde Fitch, including *The Climbers*,
The Truth and *Nathan Hale*, are now to be had in pretty little cloth-
bound books at seventy-five cents apiece. For the same price you can
get most of the pieces presented by the New Irish Theater Company,
and such excellent things as Stanley Houghton's *Hindle Wakes*, and
Melchior Lengyel's *Typhoon*, and Jerome K. Jerome's *The Passing of
the Third Floor Back*, and Franz Adam Beyerlein's *Lights Out*
(Taps), and Nikolai V. Gogol's *The Inspector-General*, and Herman
Heijermans's *The Ghetto*, and Laurence Housman's *Pains and Penal-
ties*, and the amusing light comedies of Hubert Henry Davies, W.
Somerset Maugham and R. C. Carton. For a dollar or $1.25 you can
get Edward Sheldon's *The Nigger*, Paul Heyse's *Mary of Magdala*,
John Masefield's *The Tragedy of Nan*, Charles Frederic Nirdlinger's
version of José Echegaray's *El Gran Galeoto* (*The World and His
Wife*), Edward Knoblauch's *Kismet*, Rudolph Besier's *Don* and *Lady
Patricia*, Arthur Schnitzler's *Anatol*, William Vaughn Moody's *The
Great Divide*, Githa Sowerby's *Rutherford and Son*, and Josephine
Preston Peabody's *The Piper*. And if your taste is for more elemental
things, there are *Arizona* and *Alabama*, the best plays of Augustus
Thomas, not to mention *As a Man Thinks*, his worst; and Anthony
Hope Hawkins's *The Adventures of Lady Ursula*, and Richard Har-
ding Davis's *The Dictator*, and B. McDonald Hastings's *The New Sin*,
and Charles Rann Kennedy's *The Servant in the House*, and Louis N.
Parker's *Disraeli*, and most of the pieces of Haddon Chambers, Syd-
ney Grundy and Madeline Lucette Ryley. In England, as on the Continent, practically all of the living dramatists now print their plays. So

far as I know, indeed, there is but one of distinction who refuses to do so, and that one is Sir James M. Barrie.

(September, 1913)

Chesterton's Picture of Shaw

If you approach Gilbert K. Chesterton's *George Bernard Shaw* as serious biography, you will find it amazing in the things it contains and irritating beyond measure in the things it doesn't contain; but if you throttle your yearning for facts and look only for entertainment you will fairly wallow in it. The cleverest man in all the world, with the second cleverest as his subject, is here doing his cleverest writing. The result is a volume as diverting as Nietzsche's *Also Sprach Zarathustra,* and as obviously unauthentic. It belongs, not to history, but to philosophic fable. I have shelved it among my more furious epics, cheek by jowl with *The Estimable Life of the Great Gargantua,* the Book of Revelation, *Fécondité* and *The Story of Mary MacLane.*

The Shaw that Mr. Chesterton draws for us is a valiant and heaven kissing hero, a metaphysical Hugh de Vermandois, a moral Knight Hospitaller, an economic Carrie Nation, an Irish Luther, earnest, lion-hearted and chemically pure. He staggers toward the light of a remote future, the weight of a universe upon his shoulders. It is his business to clear the path, to tear up the brambles, to knock the old gods down, to prick and pulverize the old delusions. He is, in a word, none other than Zarathustra Himself, actually come to life. In every word he utters there is some ghastly stab at pretense, convention, smug content, in his every act, grimace and attribute; in the very raisins of his bill of fare and texture of his woolen shirt there is some note of impatient revolt. The man is bitter. He thinks deeply and, as Max Beerbohm once said, indignantly. He is the armed and mobile foe, not alone of sloth and *laissez-faire* but also of peevish dissent and stupid remedy. He hates the reformer almost as much as the unreformable. It is only, indeed, his sublime faith in his own infallibility that saves him from bilious pessimism.

Mr. Chesterton's word picture of this entirely imaginary colossus spreads itself over some two hundred or more delectable pages, and in the course of drawing it he takes occasion to prove that he, too, is a philosophic Sandow. There are, in fact, lengthy passages in which Shaw recedes into the background, losing his character as a hero and taking on the shadowy outlines of a mere text. In these passages Mr. Chesterton maintains anew his familiar theses—that the only real truths in the world are to be found in the Nicene Creed, that science is a snare and human reason a delusion, that Hans Christian Andersen was a greater man than Copernicus, that sentiment is more genuine than hydrochloric acid, that all race progress is an empty appearance. Of his dialectic manner, it is not necessary to give examples, for every habitual reader of books knows it well, and enjoys it hugely without letting it convince him. He is the world's foremost virtuoso of sophistry and paralogy. Not since St. Augustine have the gods sent us a man who could make the incredible so fascinatingly probable.

Getting back to his vegetarian muttons, Mr. Chesterton undertakes to estimate the damage that Shaw has done to the human race and the benefit that he has conferred upon it. In three ways, he says, the author of *Man and Superman* has worked harm. First of all, he has made his followers too fastidious. That is to say, he has inoculated them with a tendency to peck at things and to turn up their noses. The Shawian, when it comes to morality, is too all-fired dainty: he is disgusted by the good old hoggish virtues. In the second place, Shaw has encouraged that anarchy which now torments the world. Seeing his vast success, thousands of lesser sages have sought to win fame by denouncing the true, the good and the beautiful, and the result has been a needless slaughter of ideals. In the third and last place, he has been too much the joker. Mankind, as a species, has no sense of humor whatever, and so Shaw's elaborate hoaxes and wheezes have been taken seriously, and headaches have been the fruit of them.

On the credit side, Mr. Chesterton finds three high and honorable services. Number one is the service of making philosophy intelligible and popular; number two is that of stirring up the philosophical animals, and number three is that of obliterating the mere cynic, with his ineffective sneers. Without entering into a long consideration of Mr. Chesterton's exposition and demonstration of these ideas, I may be permitted to record, perhaps, my modest conviction that only the second of his trio of services has any real existence. Shaw has not stamped out cynicism, and he has not made philosophy popular. The palpable survival of eminent cynics proves the first proposition, and the second finds its proof in two obvious facts, the first being that Shaw is not a philosopher, and the second being that philosophy remains today, as it was in Carthage and Mesopotamia, entirely beyond the ken of the plain people.

So far as I have been able to discover, the central problem of philosophy—What is truth?—has never even occurred to Shaw. Search his writings from first to last and you will find no answer to it and no attempt at an answer. At one moment he seems to subscribe to a sort of rationalism, and at the next moment he is a thoroughgoing empiricist. He flirts with mysticism, agnosticism, sensationalism; he is, in turn, Kantian, Nietzschean, Haeckelian. When he talks of one thing he is a violent dogmatist; when he talks of something else he is a pallid skeptic. Taking him by and large, he is probably a sort of pragmatist—which means, not a philosopher at all, but a man from whom all the philosophical juices have been squeezed.

But when he credits Shaw with a beneficent stirring up of the animals I agree with Mr. Chesterton affably and completely. Shaw's method is that of the Suffragettes. He heaves bricks, horsewhips demigods, howls from carttails and has himself arrested. He has a great contempt for the respectable, an abysmal loathing of the usual. And he has the wit and humor, the command of epithet and skill at fence, to make his onslaughts dangerous. Such a man, I believe, does a lot of good in the world. His light thrusts go home; he sheds blood where blood letting is needed; he is a resourceful and horrific foeman to platitude, conscious virtue, orthodoxy, tradition, superstition and all the other vile impediments to human progress. He is honest enough to laugh now and then at himself; he can find the heart to turn his squirt gun upon his own creed. He is riotously human and sentimental, and yet he can lift himself above emotion and look at men and things with a clear eye. Such men are rare. Ibsen was one, as *The Wild Duck* proves. Shaw is another. You will not find many more.

(January, 1910)

Shaw as Platitudinarian

The general formula of George Bernard Shaw, to wit, the announcement of the obvious in terms of the scandalous, is made so palpable in his new book, *Androcles and the Lion,* that even such besotted Shawolators as George Jean Nathan will at last perceive and acknowledge it. Here, indeed, the Irish Herbert Kaufman indulges himself in a veritable debauch of platitudes, and the sickly music of them fills the air. In the long and indignant preface to *Androcles* (it runs to 114 pages) all he manages to say about Christianity is what every man of the slightest intelligence has been thinking for years; and yet he gets into his statement of all this trite stuff so violent an appearance of radicalism that it will undoubtedly heat up the women's clubs and the newspaper reviewers, and inspire them to hail him once more as a Great Thinker. It is amusing to rehearse in cold blood some of his principal contentions: (a) that the social and economical doctrines preached by Christ were indistinguishable from what is now called Socialism, (b) that the Pauline transcendentalism visible in the Acts and the Epistles differs enormously from the simple ideas set forth in the Four Gospels, (c) that the Christianity on tap to-day would be almost as abhorrent to Christ, supposing Him returned to earth, as the theories of Nietzsche, George Moore or Emma Goldman, (d) that the rejection of the Biblical miracles, and even of the historical credibility of the Gospels, by no means disposes of Christ Himself, and (e) that the early Christians were persecuted, not because their theology was unsound, but because their public conduct constituted a nuisance. Could one imagine a more abject surrender to the undeniable? And yet, as I say, these empty platitudes will probably be debated furiously as revolutionary iconoclasms, and perhaps even as blasphemies, and the reputation of Shaw as an original and powerful metaphysician will get a great boost.

In this new book his method of making a scandal with embalmed ideas is exactly the same that he used in all his previous prefaces, pontifications and pronunciamentos. That is to say, he takes a proposition which all reflective men know and admit to be true, and points out effects and implications of it which very few men, reflective or not, have the courage to face honestly. Turn to *Man and Superman* and you will see the whole process. There he starts out with the self-evident fact, disputed by no one, that a woman has vastly more to gain by marriage, under Christian monogamy, than a man, and then proceeds to manufacture a sensation by exhibiting the corollary fact that all women know it, and that they are thus more eager to marry than men are, and always prove it by taking the lead in the business. The second fact, to any man who has passed through the terrible decade between twenty-five and thirty-five, is as plain as the first, but its statement runs counter to many much-esteemed conventions and delusions of civilization, and so it cannot be stated without kicking up a row. That row stems from horror, and that horror has its roots in one of the commonest of all human weaknesses, viz.: intellectual cowardice, the craven yearning for mental ease and safety, the fear of thinking things out. Shaw is simply one who, for purposes of sensation, resolutely and mercilessly thinks things out—sometimes with much ingenuity and humor, but often, it must be said, in the same muddled way that the average "right-thinker" would do it if he ever got up the courage. Remember this formula, and all of the fellow's alleged originality becomes no more than a sort of bad-boy audacity. He drags skeletons from their closets, and makes them dance obscenely—but everyone, of course, knew that they were there all the time. He would produce an excitement of exactly the same kind (though perhaps superior in intensity) if he should walk down the Strand bared to the waist, and so remind the horrified Londoners of the unquestioned fact (though conventionally concealed and forgotten) that he is a mammal, and hence outfitted with an umbilicus.

This is all I can get out of the long and highly diverting preface to *Androcles*: a statement of the indubitable in terms of the not-to-be-thought-of-for-an-instant. His discussion of the inconsistencies between the Four Gospels is no more than a *réchauffé* of what everyone knows who knows anything about the Four Gospels at all. You will find all of its points set forth at great length in any elemental treatise upon New Testament criticism—even in so childish a tract as Ramsden Balmforth's. He actually dishes up, with a grave air of sapience, the news that there is a glaring inconsistency between the genealogy of Jesus in Matthew, I, 1–17, and the direct claim of Divine Paternity in Matthew, I, 18. More, he breaks out with the astounding discovery that Jesus was a good Jew, and that Paul's repudiation of circumcision (now a cardinal article of Christian faith) would have surprised Him, and perhaps even shocked Him. Yet more, he takes thirty or forty pages to prove that the essential ideas of Jesus, stripped of the interpolations of Paul and all the later volunteers, were the ideas of a militant communist, and hence of a Socialist—a notion so obvious that it occurred to me (a man but little concerned with either Socialism or Christianity) fully a dozen years ago, and so much a part of my common stock of platitudes that I embalmed it in print last April in a tedious, rubber-stamp review of John Spargo's *Marxian Socialism and Religion*. Of such startlingly "original" propositions the preface to *Androcles* is all compact. Searching it from end to end with eagle eye, I have failed to find a single fact or argument that has given me any sense of novelty—despite the circumstance, as I say, that I pay little attention to exegesis, and so might be expected to be surprised by its veriest commonplaces.

Nevertheless, this preface makes bouncing reading—and for the plain reason that Shaw is a clever workman in letters, and knows how to wrap up old goods in charming wrappers. When, in disposing of the common delusion that Jesus was a long-faced tear-squeezer like John the Baptist or the average Methodist evangelist, he arrives at the conclusion that He was "what we should call an artist and a Bohemian in His manner of life," the result, no doubt, is a shock and a clandestine thrill to those who have been confusing the sour donkey they hear every Sunday with the genial, good-humored and likable Man they affect to worship. And when, dealing with the Atonement, he argues against it that it puts a premium upon weakness, and that the man who doesn't accept it is apt to be a more careful and unflinching fellow than the man who does, he gets the easy dramatic effect of a raid upon the very sanctuary, and so achieves a pleasant devilishness. But, as I have said, these ideas are not, in themselves, new ideas, nor are they really very naughty. I have heard the first of the two maintained by a bishop, and as for the second, I myself urged it against a chance Christian encountered in a Pullman smoking-room three or four months ago, and snickered comfortably while he proceeded from an indignant repudiation of it to a reluctant confession of its practical truth. I remember well how staggered the poor old boy was when I complained that my inability to accept the orthodox doctrine put a heavy burden of moral responsibility upon me, and forced me to be more watchful of my conduct than the elect, and so robbed me of many good chances to make money. I was very considerate in dealing with this pious gentleman. So far as I remember, I avoided tackling him with any idea that was not wholly obvious. And yet, in half an hour, he was full of the same protesting (and subtly yielding) horror that afflicts the simple folk who support the fame of Shaw.

A double joke reposes in the Shaw legend. The first half of it I have expounded; the second half is to be found in the fact that Shaw is not at all the heretic his fascinated victims see him, but an orthodox Scotch Presbyterian of the most cock-sure and bilious sort. In the theory that he is Irish I take little stock. His very name is as Scotch as haggis, and the part of Ireland from which he comes is peopled almost entirely by Scots. The true Irishman is a romantic; he senses religion as a mystery, a thing of wonder, an experience of ineffable beauty; his interest centers, not in the commandments, but in the sacraments. The Scot, on the contrary, is almost devoid of that sort of religious feeling; he hasn't imagination enough for it; all he can see in the Word of God is a sort of police regulation; his concern is not with beauty, but with morals. Here Shaw runs true to type. Read his critical writings from end to end, and you will not find the slightest hint that objects of art were passing before him as he wrote. He founded, in England, the superstition that Ibsen was no more than a tin-pot evangelist—a sort of brother to General Booth, Mrs. Pankhurst, Mother Eddy and Billy Sunday. He turned Shakespeare into a prophet of evil, croaking dismally in a rain-barrel. He even injected a moral content (by dint of abominable straining) into the music dramas of Richard Wagner, surely the most colossal slaughters of all moral ideas on the altar of beauty ever seen by man. Always this ethical obsession, the hall-mark of the Scotch Puritan, is visible in him. He is forever discovering an atrocity in what has hitherto passed as no more than a human weakness; he is forever inventing new sins, and demanding their punishment; he always sees his opponent, not only as wrong, but also as a scoundrel. I have called him a good Presbyterian. Need I add that, in *Androcles*, he flirts with predestination under the scientific euphemism of determinism—that he seems to be convinced that, while men may not be responsible for their virtues, they are undoubtedly responsible for their sins, and deserve to be clubbed therefor? . . . And this is Shaw the revolutionist, the heretic, the iconoclast! Next, perhaps, we shall be hearing of Woodrow the immoralist, of Pius the atheist, of Nicholas the Hindenburgista!

(August, 1916)

Strindberg—A Final Estimate

When August Strindberg died in his native Stockholm, little more than a year ago, but a scant half-dozen of his plays had been done into English, and his novels and other writings were practically unknown to us, but since then our translators have been working in eight-hour shifts, like coal miners, and the result is already a formidable shelf of books. What is more, there is a feverish and senseless duplication of effort, so that most of the more important Strindberg plays are now to be had in two or three different versions—for example, *The Father, The Stronger, The Outlaw, Pariah* and *Easter*. In the case of the sardonic *Fröken Julie,* so beloved of ambitious leading ladies, there are no less than four translations on the market, and the rival translators have shown their originality by translating the title in four different ways, not one of which is exactly accurate. Edwin Björkman makes it *Miss Julia,* Arthur Swan makes it *Julie,* Charles Recht makes it *Countess Julia* and Edith and Wärner Oland make it *Countess Julie.* My own talent for Swedish, like my talent for the pianoforte, is very slight, but I have employed learned philological counsel at enormous expense, and they all tell me that *Fröken* does not mean Countess, and that, as Strindberg uses it, neither does it mean Miss. True enough, it is now assumed by all unmarried Swedish ladies, even including cook ladies, but its orthodox meaning is "the daughter of a noble," and it was precisely in that sense, no doubt, that Strindberg intended it to be taken, for Julie is a count's daughter, and the fact is insisted upon throughout the play. There are no counts in the English nobility, but the earls correspond to them exactly, and an earl's wife is still called a countess. Well, what is his daughter called? Is she called Miss Mary, or the Hon. Miss Mary, or Countess Mary? Not at all. She is called *Lady* Mary. . . . I offer the suggestion to future translators of *Fröken Julie:* make it *Lady Julie* and have done. And don't change the "Julie" into "Julia"! "Julia" has a virtuous, domestic flavor, in Swedish as well as in English—and this Julie What's-her-name has no more virtue than a congressman. Strindberg called her Julie, indeed, for the very purpose of indicating that she was Frenchy and devilish. Don't try to whitewash her, messieurs!

No less than four non-dramatic works of the terrible Swede are in the current crop—*The Confession of a Fool, The Inferno, Married,* and *Zones of the Spirit*. All save *Married* are autobiographical, and even there the flavor of personal reminiscence is often very marked. The most coherent and interesting of the four is *The Confession of a Fool*, an extremely frank account of Strindberg's first marriage, to the Baroness Siri von Essen. The author was an innocent young librarian of twenty-five or twenty-six when he met this charmer, and she was the wife, at the time, of a Swedish army officer, and the mother of two children. She and her husband, who got on badly, seem to have worked a sort of refined badger game upon poor Strindberg. At all events, she gave him a pretty plain invitation, and was not at all shocked when his youthful ardor carried him over Hurdle No. 7. Nor was the Baron's indignation very violent. After a few melodramatic sobs, in fact, he began calm negotiations for a divorce, and when it was granted Strindberg married the lady. Their life together was one darn thing after another. They raged and roared through France, Switzerland and Germany, to the scandal of a score of fourth-rate watering places. The birth of children marked their occasional truces: they acquired, by and by, a family of half a dozen or so. But in the long run, of course, such guerrilla warfare was bound to end in disaster, and after seventeen years they were divorced. Strindberg was twice married later on, and twice divorced. No wonder he came to view marriage as a combat of wolves!

His account of this first marriage is one long record of quarrels and suspicions. No doubt there was often a substantial basis for them: on one occasion, indeed, the ex-baroness confessed that she had been unfaithful to him during a visit to Finland, her old home. But toward the end he piles up accusations with such prodigality, and they grow so wild and preposterous, that his wife's counter-accusation of insanity begins to take on a considerable plausibility. It is further borne out by *The Inferno* and *Zones of the Spirit*, which followed *The Confession of a Fool* at intervals of ten and twenty years. The first is obviously the daybook of one who has got more than halfway to lunacy. It tells of the author's chemical experiments in Paris, of his efforts to turn the baser metals into gold, of mysterious plots against him by unnamed and incredible enemies. He lives in a squalid garret in the Latin Quarter, supported by the charity of fellow Swedes and suspicious of their very kindness. When he goes upon the streets he reads dark portents in the shop signs, in the handbills on the lampposts, in the way passers-by wear their hats, in the remarks of waiters in obscure cafes. Finally he turns to religion as a solace, plowing through the incomprehensible balderdash of his countryman, Emmanuel Swedenborg. In *Zones of the Spirit*, ten years later, we find him steeped in pious credulity to the gills. He is ready to believe anything, even Sir William Crookes's reports of his seances with "Katie King"! He denounces the critics of faith as persons who have slipped their trolleys (I report his own figure). He dismisses science and art as so much feeble bosh. One carries away a picture of a man passing slowly into senile dementia, of the final break-up of a mind always a bit unsound, of the pathetic last act of a mental tragedy.

The twenty short stories in *Married* go back to the years 1884–88, before the accumulating bile of the author had quite dethroned his reason, and so they show him at his best. The first of them, "Asra" by name, is the story of two brothers, the one given to the sins of the flesh and the other chemically pure. Mark Twain treated the theme humorously in his twin stories of the good and the bad little boy; here it is treated with all of Strindberg's bitter and magnificent irony. You will go a long way, indeed, before you will find a more cruel fable: it is a devastating counterblast to all the Sunday school books. The same hot acids are to be found in some of the other stories—"Unnatural Selection," "A Natural Obstacle," "Corinna" and "Compulsory Marriage" among them. Not a touch of human kindness relieves the brutal pessimism of these tales. The author hasn't the slightest affection for his characters; he hasn't even any pity for them. His one aim seems to be to strip them to the bone; to make them dance naked to point his sardonic morals. But in certain other of the stories, for all their ruthlessness, a note of sentiment still creeps in. For example, in "Autumn," a study of the transformation which the years work in love, purging it of passion and making it a thing of mutual help and mellow contentment. And again in "A Doll's House," a sort of *reductio ad absurdum* of the bumptious feminism which Strindberg saw, perhaps falsely, in Ibsen's play of the same name. But these are exceptions. The general tone of the collection is that of furious misogyny. The author fancied that he had suffered much from women, and here he sought to get his revenge. Good reading for ribald and defiant old bachelors—and even better reading, I suppose, for young lovers.

But not, when all is said and done, a work of genius, nor even, perhaps, the work of a genius. I begin to fear, indeed, that some of the early estimates of Strindberg will have to be revised before long, and radically at that. I myself had the honor of being one of his first whoopers-up in this fair land; I wrote about him at great length so long ago as the year 1901, quoting Ibsen's saying that "here is one who will go further than I." But was this discreet and pondered praise, or merely a sort of emotional taking fire? I incline more and more to the fire theory. Very little of Strindberg was then to be had in English—and perceived through the muddy German veil, he took on colors that really didn't belong to him. The defects of his style were concealed; his gross and frequent blunders in construction were overlooked; ignorance conveniently took no account of his vapid essay in spiritism and theology, the general looseness and absurdity of his more serious thinking. A re-examination of him strips off most of his gauds. He left us one dramatic masterpiece—*The Father*—and half a dozen extremely clever plays—*Lady Julie, The Stronger, The Link, The Dream Play,* and the two parts of *The Dance of Death.* But he also left a lot of very shallow and silly stuff—for example, *Lucky Pehr* and *Easter*—and in his non-dramatic writings he left us far more of it. *The Inferno* and *Zones of the Spirit* (properly, *The Blue Book*) are one-fifth sense and four-fifths nonsense, and such books as *The Confession of a Fool* are interesting only when they are insane. There remain his short stories, of which some of the best are in *Married.* Are they short stories of the first rank? Are they comparable to "Youth" and "Heart of Darkness," to "The Attack on the Mill" and "The Blue Hotel"? To be sure they are not. The best thing in them is the courage of their cynicism; the author must be remembered for the hearty way in which he roared his objurgations. But there is no profundity of thinking in them; they do not impress us with any sense of their eternal verity; they are not great human documents.

The trouble with Strindberg, in brief, was that he was a second-rate artist. Over and over again he spoiled a good idea by treating it clumsily and superfically. Half of the stories in *Married* do not belong to literature at all, but merely to journalism. They suggest a busy man writing against space, with no time for that careful weighing and polishing of materials which is two-thirds of art. And many of the plays leave the same impression. They are written buoyantly, but they are not writtten very skillfully. There, indeed, is Strindberg in a nutshell. He was a man of striking originality and unbounded courage, and always magnificently in earnest, most of all in his lunacies. But he was

without the critical faculty. He lacked a feeling for form. He was not
an artist of the first caliber.

(August, 1913)

The Greatest Stylist of Modern Times

The curse of popularity lingers like a pall over Joseph Conrad
Korzeniowski and John Millington Synge, ready to swoop down at
any minute, like the Pharaonic chicken (*Neophron percnopterus*) of
Holy Writ, and bear them off to the department stores and the quar-
tered oak bookcases. A metaphor perhaps of lamentable heteroge-
neity, but none the less you gather the idea behind it, and, let me
hope, perceive the danger.

It would never do for Conrad, for one, to reach and inflame the
vulgar, for the reason that the vulgar would at once translate his True
Romance into shoddy romance, just as they translated Ibsen's *A Doll's
House* into a suffragist tract and *Huckleberry Finn* into bad Oliver
Optic. Imagine *Lord Jim* illustrated by the Cruikshanks of the best
sellers, with Jim stretching seven feet three inches into the blue, and
wearing patent leather slippers in the midst of the Bornese jungle!
Imagine *Heart of Darkness* done into a drama of fustian by some literary *demi-mondain*—and Kurtz carried upon the stage by four supers
in burnt cork and black undershirts! Imagine the elocutionists of the
Chautauquas—may the Fire be hot for them Beyond!—giving read-
ings from *The Nigger of the "Narcissus"* and *Typhoon!* And yet such
scandals impend, for the publishers, awaking from their lewd dreams
of new Oppenheims and undiscovered McCutcheons, announce extensive second editions of various Conrad tales—and by the same token,
Synge appears in an elegant library edition, suitable for the built-in
bookcase beside the open fireplace of any *Ladies' Home Journal* bungalow in the land.

Four or five years ago, while Synge still lived, the people of his own
country tore up their theater seats and threw them at him, and the
people of America dismissed him suspiciously, as but one more of the

recondite devils praised by James Huneker, that agent of the incomprehensible and immoral. Only in such savage places as Vienna, Munich and Copenhagen was he hailed as artist. But now, as I have said, he appears suddenly in all the panoply of *The Works of* . . . —four stately and highly respectable volumes, bound in buckram and with uncut leaves—and before long, perhaps, we shall hear that the Ancient Order of Hibernians has forgiven him, and that he has been elevated to the national valhalla, along with Charles Lever and Mr. Dooley. Wherefore, and as in duty bound, I pronounce a curse upon the publishers who thus make him so seductive to the newly intellectual, and at the same time offer them my congratulations for doing it so well. They have put into these four volumes not only *The Playboy of the Western World, Riders to the Sea* and the other plays of Synge, but also his sketch books of Kerry, Wicklow and the Aran Islands, his scattered poems and some of his translations from the French and Italian, not to mention four fine portraits of him, all in photogravure. In the volume on the Aran Islands the drawings by Jack B. Yeats are reproduced, but Mr. Yeats's equally excellent illustrations for the Kerry and Wicklow sketches are omitted. Other defects are the absence of an adequate introduction, reciting the circumstances of Synge's strange life and showing his precise relation to the other Neo-Celts, and the lack of a bibliography. But allowing for all this, it is a very satisfactory edition, done soberly and in good taste, and so it should get a welcome, despite its invitation to the Goths and Huns.

Synge made his flash so unexpectedly and so recently, and it was so blinding when it came, that it is difficult, this near to it, to achieve a sound estimate of it and him. Down to 1903 or thereabout he was an obscure intellectual waster, living idly in Paris on four dollars a week or doing hack work for second rate periodicals. No one save a few Irish editors and poets had ever heard of him, and only W. B. Yeats believed that there was anything in him. Even the production of *In the Shadow of the Glen* and *Riders to the Sea* in Dublin (at the end of 1903 and the beginning of 1904, respectively) brought him the notice of only a few specialists in the drama. But when these one-acters were published in a modest shilling pamphlet, in 1905, whispers about him began to go abroad, and when *The Playboy* followed two years later, to the tune of Celtic yelps and cat calls, Synge began to come into his own. That was rather less than six years ago. Today this fantastic and eerie fellow, whose whole published work fills less space than *Vanity Fair* and little more than *Peer Gynt,* is accepted as a genuine genius by all the critics of Christendom, and more than one of them, forgetting Sheridan and Goldsmith and disdaining all lesser men, has called him the greatest dramatist working in English since the age of Elizabeth. Staggering praise, and, to me at least, praise considerably overladen, but nevertheless its very exuberance shows that it has some basis in fact. Synge, in truth, was an artist of extraordinary talents, a dramatist who apparently accomplished with ease what others failed to accomplish by the severest painstaking, a sharp and relentless observer of human character, a contributor of new music to the English tongue—and if he had lived ten years longer, there is no doubt whatever that he would have justified the enthusiasm of some of his least compromising admirers, and taken his secure place beside Marlowe, Scott, Congreve, Coleridge and the other sublime second-raters, who are no less venerable because they are not of the true blood royal.

I have spoken of Synge's apparent ease of manner, but I do not mean thereby that he struck the perfect note by intuition and without effort. As a matter of fact, he was an extremely conscious and conscientious craftsman, and if we had his notebooks we should probably find, as we have from Ibsen's, that much careful toil intervened between his first grappling with an idea and its ultimate incomparable expression. In *Deirdre of the Sorrows,* indeed, there is proof of this, for Synge died before the play got its final touches, and so its dialogue, instead of showing an advance upon that of *Riders to the Sea,* shows an actual retrogression. It lacks the perfect music; one trips, now and then, upon a harsh progression, an awkward cadence. But where Synge exceeded all other dramatists of his time was in his capacity for attaining to that perfect music when he bent his whole endeavor to the task. He was not the inventor of his medium, by any means. You will find the same haunting Irish-English, with its queer enallages and hyperbata, its daring use of ancillary clauses, its homely vocabulary, its richness in idiom, in the plays and fairy tales of Lady Augusta Gregory—and particularly in her Kilkartan Molière—and in the plays, too, of a number of other Neo-Celts, including Lennox Robinson and Seumas O'Kelly. But it was Synge, and Synge alone, who lifted it to consummate beauty, who penetrated to its farthest possibilities, who made it sing like the angels. No man, in truth, ever brought to the writing of English a more sensitive ear, a more certain feeling for color and rhythm. Read *Riders to the Sea* or *The Well of the Saints* or one of the translations from Villon, and you will go drunk with the sheer music of the words, as you go drunk over the Queen Mab speech in *Romeo and Juliet,* or Faustus's apostrophe to Helen, or the One Hundred and Third Psalm. Here any merely intellectual analysis must needs fail. The appeal is not to the intelligence at all, but to the midriff and the pulses. One *feels* such stuff more than one ever understands it.

But Synge, it should be said, is not all manner; there is matter in him, too. Translate it into ordinary English and *The Playboy* would still be a well built and effective comedy, with real Irishmen in it and irresistible humor. *Riders to the Sea,* structurally, is an almost perfect piece of craftsmanship. Even *Deirdre,* the least of the plays, is immeasurably better made than Lady Gregory's *Grania,* or, to come still nearer home, the *Deirdre* of Mr. Yeats. As P. P. Howe points out, in *J. M. Synge: A Critical Study,* the dramatist's acute sense of form, his instinct for balance, proportion, rhythm, is visible in the way his plots are managed as well as in the way his dialogue burbles and flows. But here it is easy to overestimate him, and Mr. Howe succumbs to the temptation. As dramatic contrivances and even as studies of character his plays have been more than matched by the inventions of other dramatists. Nothing that Synge ever wrote, not *The Playboy* nor *Riders to the Sea,* shows the superb design of Galsworthy's *Strife,* Strindberg's *The Father* and Ibsen's *Ghosts,* and in the delineation of Irish peasant types, for all his wanderings over the countryside, he has nothing to teach to Lady Gregory. It is only as stylist that he leaves all rivals behind him, but here his lead is so great that he really has no rivals at all. He got into words the surge and splendor, the ground bass and overtones, of mighty music. He made prose that had more of Aurora's light in it than nine-tenths of English poetry.

(October, 1912)

V

Poetry

Mencken's analysis of Miss Reese's "Tears" perfectly illustrates his belief that the poet attempted "to disarm reason and evoke emotion, partly by presenting images that awaken a powerful response in the subconscious and partly by the mere sough and blubber of words." Any attempt to translate the content of poetry into prose would be disastrous, just as a *literal* reading of poetry would deprive it of its appeal. Given his poetical theory, Mencken should have sympathized with the imagistic movement in poetry—as, in fact, he did. He was an early admirer of Ezra Pound, even though he felt Pound's violence was at times comic, and he generally approved of Amy Lowell's efforts for the imagistic cause.

As an example of Mencken's poetry criticism, I include "The Troubadours A-Twitter." Every eight or ten months he gave over his book article to numerous books of verse which had come to him since the last poetry round-up. Hence, a book seldom got more than five hundred words of attention, and most received only a line or two. In "Holy Writ" Mencken argues convincingly that all attempts to translate the Bible into standard English prose will invariably work against the proposed aim of spreading the faith.

Lizette Woodworth Reese

A certain English critic achieved the other day the awe inspiring feat of writing a long and learned essay on contemporary English poetry without once mentioning the contribution of Rudyard Kipling. The thing enchanted by its daring, but not, I regret to say, by its novelty, for something of the same sort had been done before by Americans, and more than once.

If you don't believe it, examine the files of the literary monthlies for the past ten years. There you will find numerous and copious dissertations, chiefly by woman college professors and earnest young bachelors of arts, upon the gentlemenly strophes of Richard Watson Gilder, the colossal blank verse masterpieces of Cale Young Rice, the somnambulistic rhapsodies of Dr. S. Weir Mitchell, the passionate stanzas of Professor Woodberry, and the pompous piffle of a horde of other pundits—and seldom a word about Lizette Woodworth Reese! And yet I am firmly convinced, despite all these constituted and self-constituted authorities, that Miss Reese is of vastly more dignity and worth as a poet than any of the meistersingers mentioned, and that there is more merit in a single one of her sonnets than a diligent search will discover in the collected rhythmic writings of the whole congregation. In support of which conviction I hereby suspend my rule against quoting books long enough to print the sonnet in question. It bears the title of "Tears" and forms part of Miss Reese's latest collection, *A Wayside Lute*. Here it is:

> When I consider Life and its few years—
> A wisp of fog betwixt us and the sun;
> A call to battle, and the battle done
> Ere the last echo dies within our ears;
> A rose choked in the grass; an hour of fears;
> The gusts that past a darkening shore do beat;
> The burst of music down an unlistening street—
> I wonder at the idleness of tears.
> Ye old, old dead, and ye of yesternight,
> Chieftains and bards and keepers of the sheep,
> By every cup of sorrow that you had,
> Loose me from tears, and make me see aright
> How each hath back what once he stayed to weep:
> Homer his sight, David his little lad!

It is a vain thing, of course, to attempt to point out the beauties of a work of art when they must be patent to any sane observer, but in the present case I can't resist calling attention to the fine simplicity of this exquisite sonnet, to the quite remarkable beauty of its phrases, to its haunting rhythms, to the noble dignity which lifts it up and certifies to its author's possession of something rarer and more worthy than mere craftsmanship. Like most other poems from Miss Reese's pen, it is written in the severely plain and almost austere tongue of early England. A deliberate attempt to avoid the sounding Latin is evident; setting aside the two proper names, there is scarcely a word not of Anglo-Saxon origin. But the effect of barrenness, which is so apt to follow such a choice of vocabulary, is nowhere to be noted. The words, in brief, are short and common, but there is music in them and more music in their felicitous collocation.

No doubt the sciolist will find much fault with "Tears." There is room, I suppose, for furious debates over its rhyme scheme, and excuse for objecting to its seventh line on the ground that it does not scan. May the curse of Cadmus fall upon all such pedantries! That seventh line is one of the glories of the sonnet. It is a perfect example of the broken rhythm which Sidney Lanier, with his sensitive musician's ear, found to be the sweetest of all the sweets of English poetry. What a beautiful line it is, indeed! Change it; get rid of a syllable; make it scan—and see how much it loses! And what could be more nobly sonorous than the tenth line, or more nakedly simple than the first, eighth and ninth lines, or more eloquent than the whole of the concluding sestet? Believe me, we have here a sonnet that no other American has ever approached. To find its mates we must go to Keats's sonnet on Chapman's Homer, to Milton's on his blindness, to Wilde's "Easter Day."

"Tears" is not new. I remember reading it fully ten years ago, and it is to be found in Stedman's *Anthology*, despite the fact that the magazine Hannah Mores have yet to discover its superlative merit. I used to spend a good deal of time wondering why it appealed to me so strangely, for its beauties of phrase could not alone explain that appeal, and the idea at the bottom of it was one which my private creed rejected utterly. That is to say, I was profoundly convinced that we poor mortals would *not* find a place of recompense beyond the grave, where Homer was no longer blind and David no longer a father bereft; and yet, as I have said, this sonnet moved me as few other poems had ever moved me. Why? The answer tarried until I happened upon the theory that the overpowering impressiveness of certain lofty poetry depends largely, if not entirely, upon the very fact that it is incredible.

Look for this gorgeous unveracity and you will find it often. Suppose the *Odyssey*, for example, were reduced to straightforward prose; what would be the result? Simply a long string of tedious impossibilities. So, too, with the *Iliad*, the *Divine Comedy, Paradise Lost* and the Psalms. And so, too, with that greatest of poems in prose— the one delivered on the heights to "great multitudes of people from Galilee and from Decapolis and from Jerusalem and from Judea and from beyond Jordan." In the whole of the Sermon on the Mount, indeed, there are scarcely half a dozen promises or statements of fact which admit of literal acceptance. The meek, as we all know by bitter experience, do *not* inherit the earth, and everyone that asketh does *not* receive, and it is *not* safe to take no thought for raiment. Thus with all the noblest work of the bards and bishops. It is overpoweringly beautiful, but it is also untrue, and its very potency and beauty lie in its bold untruth.

Here I come to the toxic theory of art preached of late by Willard Huntington Wright, a critic of whom more will be heard anon. Wright says that all art is a sort of autointoxication—a voluntary enchantment brought on by the artist to enable him to escape from the sour facts of life. An artist, in other words, is one who, with bravado and eloquence, denies Nature and all her works, and creates for himself a new cosmos, dripping with the fictions that he wishes were true. If his medium happens to be alcohol, he turns night into day, cold into warmth, hunger into satiety, drabs into goddesses; if it is music, he converts unclean German violinists, with union cards in their pockets, into choirs of angels, and the low notes of the trombone into the voice of the Lord God Himself; and finally, if it is the written or spoken word, he adds his magic to a palpable falsehood and makes of it a thing more beautiful than truth. "The Lord abideth back of me, to guide my fighting arm"—so sings Mulholland. Balderdash! But what a thrill is in it!

The prosodists and grammarians, sensing all this in their dull way, speak vaguely of hyperbole and call it a figure of speech. But hyperbole means nothing more than an extravagant accentuation in degree, while the thing I am discussing is essentially a complete transvaluation of value. Thus Robert Loveman, when he sang of Valerie that "past the telling of the tongue is the glory of her hair," was merely enthusiastic, but Robert Browning, when he ventured the assertion that all was right with the world, was in a state of artistic self-enchantment, for the world in his time was plainly imperfect, and its very imperfection was its most insistent characteristic. Facing that disagreeable fact, he sought to make it bearable in the fashion of a true artist. That is to say, he boldly denied it, insisting that he saw only perfection and making a beautiful song upon it. The chief charm of his song, I believe, lies in its palpable untruth. Reading it, one arrives at some measure of his own agreeable toxemia, and as the poppy goes coursing through one's veins, one sees only blue skies and leafy forest aisles and nesting birds. It is pleasant. It soothes. It makes life more bearable.

But away with all such theorizing! Miss Reese's fine stanzas rise above it. There are sonnets in her book that are worthy to stand with "Tears," even though they fail to equal it. And there are other verses of abounding merit, too. She has a hand for telling epithet; she knows how to draw a vivid picture with a few phrases. The poem called "Wild Geese" offers an example. It is a Whitmanish series of irregular and often disconnected lines, and yet how plainly one sees that drab sky, that ancient village, that lonely wagon track, that honking flock of gray birds! The book stands head and shoulders above the common run of verse. It is worth reading and rereading—and Mr. Mosher has printed it in a fashion that does him credit.

(May, 1910)

Ezra Pound

Ezra Pound, author of *Provença,* tells us frankly that his chief aim is to sound a revolt against that puerile kittenishness which marks so much of latter day English poetry. Nine-tenths of our living makers and singers it would seem are women, and fully two-thirds of these women are ladies. The result is a boudoir tinkle in the tumult of the lyre. Our poets are afraid of passion; the realities of life alarm them;

the good red sun sends them scurrying. Instead of celebrating with their wind music "great deeds, strong men, hearts hot, thoughts mighty," they

> dream pale flowers,
> Slow moving pageantry of hours that languidly
> Drop as o'erripened fruit from sallow trees.

Such is Mr. Pound's complaint against the bards of our decadence. In his little book he attacks them, not only with precept, but also with example. That is to say, he himself writes in the clangorous, passionate manner that he advocates—and it must be said for him in all honesty that his stanzas often attain to an arresting and amazing vigor. The pale thing we commonly call beauty is seldom in them. They are rough, uncouth, hairy, barbarous, wild. But once the galloping swing of them is mastered, a sort of stark, heathenish music emerges from the noise. One hears the thumping of a tom-tom. Dionysos and his rogues are at their profane prancing. It is once more the springtime of the world.

Naturally enough, Mr. Pound finds poets—and heroes—to his liking in the Middle Ages—those spacious days of feasting, fighting and hard loving. A ballad of the gibbet, in the manner of Villon and with good François himself the gibbet bird, is one of the best things in the book. Again we have a fine song of the open road, credited to some Wanderer of the Campagna in 1309. Yet again there is the last song of Arnaut of Marvoil, troubadour to the Countess of Beziers in the twelfth century. From the Provençal of Bertrans de Born comes a lament upon the death of Prince Henry Plantagenet, elder brother to the Lion Heart; from Lope de Vega comes a song to the Virgin Mother; from Jaufre Rudel and Arnault Daniel certain fantastic canzon forms. Bertrans bawls vociferously in a battle song:

> Hell grant soon we hear again the swords clash!
> And the shrill neighs of destriers in battle rejoicing,
> Spiked breast to spiked breast opposing!
> Better one hour's stour than a year's peace
> With fat boards, bawds, wine and frail music!
> Bah! There's no wine like the blood's crimson!

"The Ballad of the Goodly Fere" (*i.e.*, mate, companion) is Mr. Pound's only venture into the old English ballad form, but here he achieves a remarkable imitation, not only of the form, but also of the

naif spirit of the early tales in rhyme. It is Simon the Apostle that
speaks, "some while after the crucifixion." A few stanzas follow:

> A son of God was the Goodly Fere
> That bade us his brothers be.
> I ha' seen him cow a thousand men,
> I ha' seen him upon the tree.
>
> He cried no cry when they drave the nails
> And the blood gushed hot and free;
> The hounds of the crimson sky gave tongue
> But never a cry cried he.
>
> . . . . .
>
> A master of men was the Goodly Fere,
> A mate of the wind and sea;
> If they think they ha' slain our Goodly Fere
> They are fools eternally.
>
> *I ha' seen him eat o' the honeycomb*
> *Sin' they nailed him to the tree.*

Mr. Pound is an American, but he had to go to England to gain
recognition. The present volume, I believe, is the first book from his
hand to be printed in this country. It has defects a-plenty. More than
once the very earnestness of the poet destroys the effect he essays to
produce. His violence at times grows almost comic. One recalls the
early profanities of Kipling. But, considered as a whole, this little collection of verses is one of the most striking that has come from the
press in late years. Here we have a poet with something to say and
with the skill to say it in a new way, eloquently, sonorously and sometimes almost magnificently.

(April, 1911)

The Troubadours A-Twitter

Harps, lutes, psalteries, ophicleides, dulcimers, fifes, viols d'amore, shawms, sackbuts, hautboys, banjoes, tabors, balalaikas, citoles, rebecs, cornets, castanets, tambourines, saxophones, bagpipes, bassoons, bugles, lyres, guitars, trumpets, spinets, glockenspiels, harmoniums, trombones, clavichords, citterns, cymbals, crwths, cervelats, chalumeaus, clarinets, oboes, chimes, harmonicas, virginals, piccoloes, barrel organs, mandolins, zamrs, whithorns, flageolets, hurdy-gurdies, rybybes, huslas, tom-toms, snare drums, tubas, waldhorns, serpents, buzines, zithers, flutes, Jew's harps, archlutes, tenoroons, rattles, tympani, cow bells, xylophones, triangles and "the usual strings": I can hear them all in the ante-chamber. The oboe sounds its baaing A; the rest reach for it, snuffle at it, tunnel under it, slide over it. It is the eve of May Day; the bock beer mounts in the maples; the zephyrs chirp in the trees; the birds blow softly from the South; the poets are back again. . . .

Let them in one by one, Zarathustra, old top—and don't spare your club if they crowd! Poets are a naif and eager lot, with their veins full of incandescent star dust. Unpoliced, they would run amuck, knock down the hall of audience, trample one another to death. So be careful as you admit them. There: that's the way: one at a time. . . . And who, prithee, is No. 1? No. 1, it appears, is the talented Prof. Edwin P. Haworth, of Kansas City, Mo., the Edgar Allan Poe of those parts. In his hand is a copy of his latest work, *Sunshine and Roses;* under his arm is a viola da gamba, gnarled and mellow. He opens fire at once and his choice is a lay of amour. To wit:

> Azmarine! Enchantress, she
> Leads me through the glens,
> Coaxing and beguiling me
> With some power not human's . . .

Hold up, good professor! Let us hear that again. "Through the glens . . . power not human's"? What sort of prosody is this? Hast the effrontery in this high-toned company to rhyme "glens" with "humans," even with "hu*mans*"? The ideer! . . . Out with him, Zarathustra! Down the chute with him! Over the fence with him! To the lions with him! . . . But halt! The rules, it seems, save him, or, at any rate, reprieve him: two chances for every candidate at the bar. Even

Shakespeare sometimes slipped, as witness—but no need to offer examples. Let us hear this Prof. Haworth de Kansas City again:

> It is only an artificial rose,
>   Witherless, fadeless, unreal,
> Wanting the fragrance and freshness, forsooth,
>   Genuine roses reveal.
> It is only the artistic handwork of man,
>   Imitation of nature and life,
> And yet in this art is concealed for a heart
>   The mem'ry of love and of strife.

"Only an artificial rose"? "Only the artistic handwork of man"? Off with him, Zarathustra! He has had his second chance! To the lions, tigers, wolves, leopards, lynxes, jaguars, cougars, hippopotami! . . . So, he has departed. Now a chair and a polite bow for No. 2—an estimable lady poet, Miss Jessamine Kimball Draper. Hear her begin:

> Gray clouds scudding,
> Milk cows cudding . . .

What! Milk cows *cudding*? Can you point to such a word in Webster, Miss Jessamine? There is *cud,* a noun (from the AS. *cwidu,* a stomach, a gizzard), but where is *to cud,* a verb? No doubt you mean *ruminating* (from the L. *rumen,* a throat, a gullet, an aesophagus). But *ruminating,* of course, doesn't rhyme with *scudding*—nor, for that matter, with any other word in English. . . . However, let it pass. Every poet has two chances. Thus Miss Jessamine's response to her second:

> To be alone—what is it, then,
>   In this vast universe?
> Is't when we walk a lonely road,
>   Or sit in solitude,
> Or find there's none to lift our load,
>   Or give us, hungry, food,
> We suffer with this curse?

Suffer *with*? How can one suffer *with* a curse? *Under* it, *from* it, even *despite* it, but surely not *with* it. Is the curse itself, then, also suffering? Let Miss Jessamine look into the matter a bit more carefully, and report upon it at length at our next annual meeting. . . . Meanwhile, No. 3 is waiting, the same being Prof. Horace Traubel, of Philadelphia, Pa., with his *Chants Communal* under his arm. This

Prof. Traubel, it appears, disdains all the ordinary and orthodox forms of poetry. He refuses to saw up his threnodies and exultations into stove-lengths, nor will he dally with the corrupting voluptuousness of rhyme. It also appears that he disdains all rewards or emoluments for his labors. Witness:

You think I am fighting a fight for wages. For pay. For a glass more of beer. For better cigars. For costlier clothes. To get rid of rags. Well. So I am. But only incidentally. I am really fighting for life. As long as wages are only wages high wages and low wages are all one. But when wages are life I embody my plaint in a different song. I am fighting for life. I have fought fights for wages. But I have fought my last fight for wages. I have seen that no fight for wages can be the fight of freedom. There is only one fight left. *The fight against wages.*

With the highest respect for a venerable and bald-headed bard, Pish! All this tall talk against wages is merely so much buncombe, academic and empty. In point of fact, no one has offered Prof. Traubel any wages. No man with a heart would dare to offer *any* poet wages. The revenues and usufructs of the true maker and singer do not come in the form of pounds, shillings and pence. They reach him as the music of heavenly harps and sackbuts, inaudible to earthly ears; as the sweet ticklings and caressings of ineffable winds; as the pungent, swooning scents of indescribable flowers; as the cosmic leaps and gurgles of the blood in his own arteries; as the rolling surges of remote and illimitable oceans; as the deafening applause and clapper-clawing of the angels and archangels, the cherubim and seraphim; as the blinding sweeps and flashes of a light that never was on land or sea. The poet is paid in ecstasy, in afflatus, in divine madness, in transcendental unguents, in hydrogen; not in cash. As well talk of paying off the Twelve Apostles on Saturday night! . . . But let us hear Prof. Traubel again:

I want to be counted. I do not want to stand out from the rest. I am willing and glad to remain in the crowd. I am willing to serve and for no one to know me. The humblest job in the cause is not too proud a job for me. The proudest job in the cause is not too humble a job for me. Here I stand. I am ready. I want to be counted.

Here the poet is easier to comprehend—and to accommodate. Let us count him at once: he is No. 3. And before ordering him to that lowest hell where Socialists are doomed to shine the shoes of the late

Karl Marx forever and ever, let us remove his little brass identification
tag and mail it to his weeping heirs and assigns, that they may know
he died the *Heldentod* for poesy. . . . After him comes another rebel,
to wit, No. 4, Miss Nanna Matthews Bryant, whose *Phantasies* fill 94
pages. Miss Bryant's rebellion, it appears, is against the pain and
bother of seeking an idea before inditing a poem. All she needs is a
pen and piece of paper. In a few moments she has set down a few
pointless and empty lines, and her poem is done. For example:

> The dusk falls over all,
> A hush is o'er the dying day,
> The cricket's drowsy chirp
> Makes evensong along the dusky way.

Again:

> Silent waters,
>   Deep shadows,
> Strong light,
>   Great might.

Toward the end of her book Miss Bryant dispenses with intellectual
content altogether, and her poetry is conveniently written with a rubber stamp. To wit:

> A gray sea,
> A gray sky,
> And I am sailing, sailing, sailing.

> A gray sea,
> A gray sky,
> The winds are wailing, wailing, wailing.

What could be easier to write than this sort of verse? Given the
rubber stamp, a child of six should be able to manufacture it by the
yard. It represents the supreme triumph of words over sense. To find
its match one must go to the New Thought dithyrambs of Prof. N.
Vachel Lindsay. For example:

> Whangaranga, whangaranga,
> Whang, whang, whang,
> Clang, clang, clangaranga,
> Clang, clang, clang.
> Clang—a—ranga—

Chang—a—ranga—
Clang,
Clang,
Clang.

This specimen of the poetry of the future is from Prof. Lindsay's *The Congo and Other Poems,* the which seems to be arousing a lot of excitement in the women's clubs and other such centers of advanced thinking. But as for me, low, beery brute that I am, I can find little in it save a lot of strutting and empty doggerel, some of it almost on all fours with the primitive strophes that schoolboys chalk upon schoolhouse fences. Nor is it helped out by the ludicrous stage directions that the author offers to possible elocutionists. *Zum Beispiel:*

To be bawled in the beginning with a snapping explosiveness, ending in a
   languorous chant.
Lay the emphasis on the delicate ideas. Keep as light-footed as possible.
All the *o* sounds are very golden.
Like the wind in the chimney.
Like a train-caller in a Union Depot.

Miss Harriet Monroe, in a preface to the book, says that it represents an attempt to restore "poetry as a song art, an art appealing to the ear rather than the eye." Nonsense! Poetry has never ceased to be a song art; it is inconceivable save as a song art. The moment it becomes so stiff and formal that it fails to woo and tickle the ear, it is no longer poetry in any genuine sense, but merely prose chopped into lengths. The strident, hop-legged puerile bosh that Prof. Lindsay here sets before us falls into this category, for it lacks entirely that inner and pervasive music which is at the heart of all authentic poetry. Mere rhythm, however assertive, is not music. If it were, then a college yell would be comparable to Beethoven's Fifth Symphony. Music is "a concord of sweet sounds"; it must have melody and harmony as well as rhythm. And beneath its melody and harmony and rhythm there must be a certain emotional dignity, an elevation of mood, an exaltation of the soul. You will find that exaltation in things as widely apart otherwise as Whitman's *"Salut au Monde,"* and Miss Reese's "Tears," Kipling's "Diego Valdez," and the Queen Mab speech in *Romeo and Juliet,* "Annie Laurie" and *"Die Wacht am Rhein."* But you will not find much of it in *The Congo and Other Poems.*

In his *rôle* of prophet of a new school of comic versifiers, Prof. Lind-

say is even more inept and unsuccessful. Miss Monroe mentions
with approbation the theory of Signor Marinetti, the Italian futurist,
that the germs of a new art are to be found in the extravagances and
eccentricities of American vaudeville, and she seems to be of the belief that Prof. Lindsay is pointing the way to it. But consider the following specimen of his humor:

> The Lion is a kingly beast,
> He likes a Hindu for a feast.
> And if no Hindu he can get,
> The lion-family is upset.
>
> He cuffs his wife and bites her ears
> Till she is nearly moved to tears.
> Then some explorer finds the den
> And all is family peace again.

What could be more hollow, more silly, more banal? Ranged beside
it, such a vaudeville song as "My Wife's Gone to the Country" seems a
veritable masterpiece of humor. Besides, Prof. Lindsay is years too
late with his "popcorn, glass balls and cranberries," as he calls them.
Let him study the songs of Otto Julius Bierbaum, Erich Hartleben and
the other clever fellows of the Berlin *Uberbrettl'*, before he spills any
more ink; he has a lot to learn from them. . . . And meanwhile, let
him have his hat, his poet's cloak and his rain-check. . . .

Of the next comers we get but a flashing glance. Zip! and they are
gone! An inspection of the entry-list reveals the names of Walter Ma-
lone, author of *Hernando De Soto,* and Richard Osborne, author of
The Conquest. Two epics, suave, elegant, scholarly, but oh, so long!
The Conquest runs to 3,500 lines; *Hernando* to no less than 18,500.
Why should any sane man struggle through such endless jungles of
words? The thing, indeed, is against all reason. A poem of 18,500 lines
is as essentially absurd as a novel in ten volumes or a symphony of
twenty movements. The sense of beauty is not made of rubber: it
cannot be stretched *ad infinitum.* Even the classical epics, when all is
said and done, are hoary old bores. They belong to the childhood of
poetry, and their chief appeal is still to the childish—*e.g.*, to pedagogues. To say that they represent a height of achievement which the
poetry of our own time has not surpassed is just as ridiculous as to say
that Aeschylus' band of lyres, trigonons and sambukas made better

music than the Boston Symphony Orchestra. . . . Let the epicians depart!

And after them, hurriedly a whole troop of poets who have little to say, and say that little tediously—John Curtis Underwood, with his *Americans;* H. E. Walker, with his *Intimations of Heaven;* Robert De Camp Leland, with his *Ballads of Blyndham Town;* Patrick R. Chalmers, with his *Green Days and Blue;* Louise W. Kneeland, with her *Sunlight and Shadow;* Ed. Blair, with his *Sunflower Siftings;* Joseph Noel, with his *Love's Breadline;* Blanche Goodman Eisendrath, with her *Poems;* George Herbert Clarke with his *At the Shrine;* Walter Conrad Arensberg, with his *Poems;* Charles Henry Mackintosh, with his *Song of Service.* I can find nothing in all this vast emission of strophes that is worth noting. They say the old things, conventionally, flaccidly, without invention. Prof. Noel solemnly compares the city to a harlot. Prof. Leland solemnly hymns the Maytime and sentimentally woulds that he were a boy again. Prof. Chalmers offers us 173 pages of indifferent newspaper verse. Prof. Walker announces his hope of Heaven in 150 uninspired sonnets. Miss Kneeland greets us with this:

> Joy of the earth! Exquisite flower!
> In the wildwood I found thee,
> Nestling alone, and thy strange power
> Weaves still its spell around me.

And so on and so on, sometimes better than this and sometimes worse. The one effort at originality is made by Prof. Underwood, whose "one hundred representative Americans of today . . . address themselves directly to the reader in speaking parts of thirty lines or less." Thus the School Teacher:

Near three-quarters of a million, fifty thousand on part time,
Average classes fully fifty; that's the black collective crime.
Crowds your schools, and crowds your prisons; crowds your cities, lifetimes too.
We can teach the life you lend us, but the rest remains for you.

And the Chorus Girl:

Chorus girls are human beings, just the same as you.
Some are straight and some are crooked, some between the two.

Is this poetry? If so, then I take the count! . . . Curiously enough, another poet, Edgar Lee Masters, has attempted much the same thing—but with how vastly greater success! Mr. Masters' *Spoon River Anthology* has yet to be published in book form, but it has appeared serially in the St. Louis *Mirror,* and so we may let him in today. The anthology is made up of stanzas of irregular metre and length, each bearing the name of some citizen of Spoon River (a real village in Illinois), and setting forth, as it were, his outlook upon the world. Thus the contribution of Rutherford M'Dowell, the village photographer:

> They brought me ambrotypes
> Of the old pioneers to enlarge.
> And sometimes one sat for me—
> Some one who was in being
> When giant hands from the womb of the world
> Tore the republic.
> What was it in their eyes?—
> For I could never fathom
> That mystical pathos of drooped eyelids,
> And the serene sorrow of their eyes.
> It was like a pool of water,
> Amid oak trees at the edge of a forest,
> Where the leaves fall,
> As you hear the crow of a cock
> From a far-off farm house, seen near the hills
> Where the third generation lives, and the strong men
> And the strong women are gone and forgotten.
> And these grand-children and great grand-children
> Of the pioneers!
> Truly did my camera record their faces, too,
> With so much of the old strength gone,
> And the old faith gone,
> And the old mastery of life gone,
> And the old courage gone,
> Which labors and loves and suffers and sings
> Under the sun!

Here is true poetry, albeit as gnarled and unadorned as the pioneers it celebrates. It has sincerity; it has a delicate fancy; it shows a genuine feeling for beauty. Superficially, it deals with the lives and loves of petty and unconsidered men, but what one gets out of it, in the end, is a sense of spaciousness, of epic sweep and dignity, of universal tragedy. The general, indeed, elbows out the particular: Mr. Masters, upon his little stage, sets a drama that must move all of us. . . . Let him have a bay leaf, Zarathustra, and a card of invitation to next year's *Sängerfest.* . . .

Which clears the audience chamber for the Imagistes—a round dozen of them. Rebellious ladies and gentlemen, making faces at orthodoxy in all its forms! It is Miss Amy Lowell who speaks for them. "Away," says she, "with didacticism, rhyme schemes, hobbling metres, ancient forms." The aim of poetry is "to head-up an emotion until it burns white-hot"—and that sort of heading-up is not to be done in corsets, hoop-skirts, straight-jackets. Give the poet room! Make him free to "find new and striking images, delightful and unexpected forms."

Take the word "daybreak," for instance. What a remarkable picture it must once have conjured up! The great, round sun, like the yoke of some mighty egg, *breaking* through cracked and splintered clouds. But we have said "daybreak" so often that we do not see the picture any more, it has become only another word for dawn. The poet must be constantly seeking new pictures to make his readers feel the vitality of his thought.

A sound enough idea, and, what is more, it actually seems to be producing excellent poetry. In sooth, you will go a long, long way, beloved, before ever you find anything better than the opening poem of *Les Imagistes*—a thing called "Choricos," by Richard Aldington—a sonorous and beautiful apostrophe to Death, noble in its conception and exquisite in its details. I have room for only the closing lines:

> And silently,
> And with slow feet approaching,
> And with bowed head and unlit eyes,
> We kneel before thee:
> And thou, leaning toward us,
> Caressingly layest upon us
> Flowers from thy thin, cold hands,
> And, smiling as a chaste woman
> Knowing love in her heart,
> Thou sealest our eyes
> And the illimitable quietude
> Comes gently upon us.

Nor is Mr. Aldington the only Imagist to strike this clear note. There is true beauty, too, in F. S. Flint's rhapsody upon London, in Ezra Pound's strange fancies from the Chinese, in John Courno's rhythmic prose, above all in Miss Lowell's "In a Garden." This also appears in Miss Lowell's book of *Sword Blades and Poppy Seeds,* and with it there are half a dozen other things of notable quality. What could be more brilliant than the procession of colors in "The Pike"—a truly magnificent evocation of visual images by the magic of words? And what could be better done than "Music," with its subtle suggestion of the cold, pale beauty of flute tones? When she attempts conventional rhymes and metres Miss Lowell is a good deal less successful. Her long ballads, indeed, are frankly third-rate. But in the new forms she offers work of unmistakable distinction. . . .

(May, 1915)

Holy Writ

I

Enough good intentions are concealed in the *Riverside New Testament,* a translation "from the original Greek into the English of today" by the Rev. William G. Ballantine, D.D., LL.D., to pave all the avenues and side-streets of Hell from the Jonathan Edwards monument to the Boulevard of the Popes. It is the pious and laborious work of a divine now in his seventy-fifth year, and its laudable purpose is to clear Holy Writ of its howlers and archaisms, and so bring it within the understanding of the average American reader of today. Exactly the same purpose, I hope I may say without insolence, prompted me to make my own translations of the Declaration of Independence and Lincoln's Gettysburg Address into the American vulgate; my aim was to rescue both of these great papers from the Johnsonian English in which they were couched, and thus make them comprehensible to the great masses of the plain people, who had apparently forgotten the doctrines set forth in them, and were, in fact, tarring and lynching men who presumed to preach them. But my scheme failed, and for a simple reason. The plain people, hearing the Declaration in Bald American, were outraged and alarmed by the ideas in it, and proceeded only to fresh assaults upon the fanatics who voiced them. So long as the Declaration had been mainly incomprehensible to them, so long as they had apprehended it, not as a statement of concrete ideas but as a mere series of highfalutin dithyrambs, they were able, when drunk enough, to stand it, but the moment they read it in the language of their everyday life they leaped as if stuck with pins. And not only the common people. I was also denounced by *Gelehrten* in all parts of the country, and one of them, Prof. Dr. Scott, of the University of Michigan, hastened to assure a group of visiting English professors that I was a low and contumelious fellow, and that my dissemination of notions in contempt of the Motherland was thus not to be taken gravely. It seems to me that Dr. Ballantine's new version of the New Testament will come to grief in the same manner. What he hopes to accomplish by it, as he says, is to bring what he calls "divine truth" down to the grasp of persons who get "no meaning at all or a meaning that is mistaken" out of the Authorized Version—that is, down to the generality of Americans, lay and clerical. But I greatly fear that what he will achieve, if this translation is widely circulated, is rather the propagation of agnosticism. For when they are put into plain English some of the most venerated passages in the New Testament begin to seem banal and dubious, and others begin to seem silly, and yet others begin to seem downright idiotic. In the Authorized Version their imbecility is concealed by the extremely elevated and beautiful dialect in which they are set forth, but in the speech of everyday it is only too plain.

Worse, it appears to me that Dr. Ballantine often makes a mess of his work, even when he is most faithful to his purpose—that he often fails at his primary business of converting the archaisms of the Authorized Version into phrases that even a Methodist clergyman should understand. I turn at random, for example to Matthew VIII, and encounter one of the most familiar and moving speeches of Jesus: "The foxes have holes, and the birds of the air have nests, but the Son of man hath not where to lay his head." Dr. Ballantine seeks to improve this by changing *nests* into *coverts* and *hath* into *has*. What a botch, indeed! *Nests* is the natural, the inevitable word; it instantly conjures up a living image; it is absolutely simple and clear. But how many Christians in America, without resort to the dictionary, could give a sound definition of *coverts?* Certainly not 5 per cent. I doubt, in fact, that Dr. Ballantine himself could do it, for he uses the word in a very far-fetched sense. *Covert* means, primarily, cover for ground game—a shelter in a thicket or copse. The birds of the air do not resort to *coverts;* they resort to *nests,* as the estimable Matthew plainly says. I find many other such inept renderings without leaving the First Gospel. In Matthew V. 17, for example, there is the historic pronouncement: "Think not that I am come to destroy the law, or the prophets; I am not come to destroy, but to fulfill." Dr. Ballantine converts the last clause into the incredibly clumsy and confusing: "I have not come to do away with them, but to fill them full." To *fill them full?* What on earth does that mean? With what is he going to fill them? It would be hard to imagine any worse nonsense than that. But there *is* actually worse. In the fortieth verse of the same chapter— "And if any man will sue thee at the law, and take away thy coat . . ."—the venerable translator changes *coat* into *tunic!* Will this help the morons—or simply stump them? In the next verse—"And whosoever shall compel thee to go a mile . . ."—*shall compel* is changed to *commandeer,* which has been current English only since the Boer War and is still quite incomprehensible to millions. Finally, still remaining in Matthew, I come to the Lord's Prayer in Chapter VI, the version read daily in the public schools of all the American states that are Christian, and familiar even to Congressmen, bishops and the inmates of houses of correction. Here, if you don't know it, is the Authorized Version:

Our Father which art in heaven, Hallowed be thy name. Thy kingdom come. Thy will be done in earth, as it is in heaven. Give us this day our daily bread. And forgive us our debts, as we forgive our debtors. And lead us not into temptation, but deliver us from evil: For thine is the kingdom, and the power, and the glory, forever. Amen.

And here (omitting the doxology, which is not found in the oldest Greek MSS) is Dr. Ballantine's horror:

> Our Father in heaven,
> Thy name be kept holy:
> Thy kingdom come;
> Thy will prevail;
> As in heaven, so on earth.

> Our bread for the coming day
> Give us today;
> And forgive us our failures
> As we forgive those who fail toward us;

And bring us not into trial,
And save us from evil.

II

But this almost inconceivably fatuous effort to gild the lily is not the worst of Dr. Ballantine's offendings; he is far more dangerous to the faith, I believe, when he achieves his avowed purpose—that is, when his version of the Greek original is actually clearer and better than the rendering of the King James Version. What misleads him here is a misapprehension of the nature of religious feeling. He seems to think that it is the product of an intellectual process, that it arises out of ideas; it really has its origin in a sense of mystery, a complete escape from ideas. It seizes upon the mind most powerfully, indeed, when the evidences of its objective truth are most vague and unconvincing—in brief, when it is apprehended, not as fact, but as poetry—the negation, or at all events, the antithesis of fact. The success of Christianity in the world, as I have often argued, is due chiefly, if not wholly, to the incomparable beauty, as poetry, of its sacred books. It is hard to think of any other oriental religion that is not logically more plausible and persuasive, but not one of them has a sacred literature that is even remotely to be compared, for sheer gaudy loveliness, to that of the decadent Judaism which, alone among them, has enchanted the West. There are single Psalms that have ten times more beauty in them than the whole literature of Brahminism, ancient and modern; in the story of the Christ Child there is greater poetry than ever was heard of in Greece or Rome. It is this profound and disarming poetry, this irresistible evocation of the unattainable and ever to be desired, that gives Christianity its undiminished strength, despite the gradual destruction of all its so-called evidences. Poetry, I repeat, does not fetch a sentient man by convincing him; it fetches him by robbing him of the wish to be convinced—by lulling his critical faculties and setting him off upon an emotional debauch. Certainly there are few educated men left in the world who believe literally that Mary was got with child by God, or that the shepherds on the hills were guided to the manger by a dancing star, or that wise men came from the East to hail the new-born King in the manger at Bethlehem; nevertheless, that man must be a dull clod, indeed, who is not moved by the simple and charming story, and made to wish a bit wistfully that such things could really be. It is, of all stories ever devised by man, enormously the most beautiful. The Jews, when they invented it, conquered the whole Western world.

Now, poetry, as everyone knows, is a fragile flower, and will not bear transplanting—certainly not anatomizing. It cannot be reduced to plain propositions without losing everything that makes it what it is—without becoming, in fact, the very reverse of itself. Try the experiment with any poem you admire, even with "Mary Had a Little Lamb." In prose all its bloom is gone; it becomes simply nonsense. This is true, of course, of great poetry as well as of poetry that is not great, as every attempt at a prose translation of the *Odyssey* bears witness. It is preeminently true of the vast body of poetry which makes up the sacred books of Christianity. Try it with any of the Psalms, with the Sermon on the Mount, with the story of the Nativity, with the roaring strophes of Revelations. The thing becomes, in the speech of everyday, a mere absurdity. It is not only not moving; it is even somewhat laughable. To get the savor of it one must have the archaic language that it stands in, with its curiously inverted syntax, its strange and often barbaric phrases, its mysterious and scarcely comprehended terms. In other words, to get the savor one must have the savor. Dr. Ballantine, in his translation, has squeezed it all out. His New Testament, ceasing to be a great poem, becomes nothing more than a series of improbable anecdotes. I cannot imagine it making any new believers, save perhaps among idiots; on the contrary, it will very likely unmake not a few old believers. This is saying that it fails of its central aim, certainly and disastrously—that all the piety of the learned and reverend translator has gone into an enterprise that will delight and prosper the devil. Seeking to make customers for theology, he has only succeeded in scaring off customers for poetry. I am convinced, indeed, that even a congregation of Presbyterians, if his banal prose were read to them aloud, would begin to cough, shuffle their feet and look at their watches.

Well, let us not heap opprobrium upon him. When he stands up to answer for his crime on the Judgment Morn, he will at least be able to say that he followed lofty precedent and thought himself in good company. The dock, indeed, will be full of holy men who sought to promote the faith by bringing the Bible to the multitude. A great folly. Poetry is always better heard than read—and it is best heard where the lights are dim and a certain spookiness prevails. Let the priests read it, with vows to protect them, and then tell simple folk

what is suitable for simple folk to hear—above all, what is within the
limits of their imagination, their sense of beauty. Whoever it was that
translated the Bible into excellent French prose is chiefly responsible
for the collapse of Christianity in France. Contrariwise, the men who
put the Bible into archaic, sonorous and often unintelligible English
gave Christianity a new lease of life wherever English is spoken. They
did their work at a time of great theological blather and turmoil,
when men of all sorts, even the least intelligent, were beginning to
take a vast and unhealthy interest in exegetics and apologetics. They
were far too shrewd to feed this disconcerting thirst for ideas with a
Bible in plain English; it was deliberately artificial even when it was
new. They thus dispersed the mob by appealing to its emotions, as a
mother quiets a baby by crooning to it. The Bible that they produced
was so unutterably beautiful that the great majority of men, in the
face of it, could not fix their minds upon ideas. To this day it has enchanted the English-speaking peoples so effectively, that, in the main,
they remain Christians, at least sentimentally. Paine has assaulted
them, Darwin and Huxley have assaulted them and a multitude of
other merchants of facts have assaulted them, but they still remember
the Twenty-third Psalm when the doctor begins to shake his head,
and they are still moved beyond compare (though not, alas, to acts!)
by the Sermon on the Mount, and they still turn once a year from
their sordid and degrading labors to immerse themselves unashamed
in the story of the manger. It is not much, but it is something. I do
not admire the general run of American Christians—Methodists,
United Brethren, Baptists, and such vermin. But try to imagine what
the average low-browed Methodist would be if he were not a Methodist but an atheist!

The Latin Church, which I constantly find myself admiring, despite
its occasional astounding imbecilities, has always kept clearly before it
the fact that religion is not a syllogism, but a poem. It is accused by
Protestant dervishes of withholding the Bible from the people. To
some extent this is true; to some extent the church is wise; again
to the same extent it is prosperous. Its toyings with ideas, in the main,
have been confined to its clergy, and they have commonly reduced the
business to a harmless play of technicalities—the awful concepts of
heaven and hell brought down to the level of a dispute of doctors in
long gowns, eager only to dazzle other doctors. Its greatest theologians remain unknown to 99 per cent of its adherents; the great theo-

logians of Protestantdom—Wesley, Billy Sunday and the like—are as vulgarly familiar as Babe Ruth. Rome, indeed, has not only preserved the original poetry in Christianity; it has also made capital additions to that poetry—for example, the poetry of the saints, of Mary, and of the liturgy itself. A solemn high mass is a thousand times as impressive, to a man with any genuine religious sense in him, as the most powerful sermon ever roared under the big-top by a Presbyterian auctioneer of God. In the face of such overwhelming beauty it is not necessary to belabor the faithful with logic; they are better convinced by letting them alone. Preaching is not an essential part of the Latin ceremonial. It was very little employed in the early church, and I am convinced that good effects would flow from abandoning it today, or, at all events, reducing it to a few sentences, more or less formal. In the United States the Latin brethren have been seduced by the example of the Protestants, who commonly transform an act of worship into a puerile intellectual exercise; instead of approaching God in fear and wonder these Protestants settle back in their pews, cross their legs, and listen to an ignoramus try to prove that he is a better theologian than the Pope. This folly the Romans now slide into. Their clergy begin to grow argumentative, doctrinaire, ridiculous. It is a pity. A bishop in his robes, playing his part in the solemn ceremonial of the mass, is a dignified spectacle; the same bishop, bawling against Darwin half an hour later, is seen to be simply an elderly Irishman with a bald head, the son of a respectable police sergeant in South Bend, Ind. Let the reverend fathers go back to Bach. If they keep on spoiling poetry and spouting ideas, the day will come when some extra-bombastic deacon will astound humanity and insult God by proposing to translate the liturgy into American, that all the faithful may be convinced by it.

(October , 1923)

VI

Music

In a letter to Fanny Butcher, dated February 20, 1921, Mencken stated his often-repeated preference for music over other art forms: "I'd rather have written any symphony of Brahms' than any play of Ibsen's. I'd rather have written the first movement of Beethoven's Eroica than the Song of Solomon; it is not only far more beautiful, it is also far more profound. A better man wrote it. I believe that Anatole France and Joseph Conrad are the best writers now living, but neither has written anything so good as the first act of *Der Rosenkavalier* or the last ten minutes of *Electra*. In music a man can let himself go. In words he always remains a bit stiff and unconvincing." He often remarked that on the day of his hanging his one regret would be that he had not been better trained in musical theory as a child. As a member of the rather famous Saturday Night Club in Baltimore, he rarely missed a weekly meeting over a period of nearly fifty years. Without doubt he was more deeply moved by the tonal art than by any other human invention or activity.

And yet I still doubt that a career in music would ever have been so satisfying as his affair with words. Like Voltaire and Nietzsche, Mencken was a natural iconoclast. Moreover, he was forever fascinated by the play of ideas, particularly those ideas that men paid homage to. Despite all his playful disclaimers and his warnings against taking any idea too seriously, Mencken remained, even when most humorous, an extremely *cerebral* human being. True enough, any appearance of intellectual *straining* is difficult to detect in his writings, but that absence of strain is nothing more than art—an art that appears artless, which is, of course, the highest form. As Jacques Barzun once remarked, Mencken's style "reveals its subject and conceals its art." Music, it seems to me, can never be ideational in the sense that language is. The appeal of music, as Mencken admitted, must be largely emotional rather than intellectual. Poetry, which Mencken compared to music, has the same emotional appeal. I find it impossible to imagine Mencken fully "expressing" himself except in prose. If that prose, at its best, happens to be vibrant, muscular, with a horn note sounding now and again through it, so much the better. But it is nonetheless prose.

Louis Cheslock has put together an excellent selection of Mencken's writings on music, entitled *H. L. Mencken on Music* (New York: Alfred A. Knopf, 1961), in which he includes an account of Mencken's musical studies and a history of the Saturday Night Club, which Mencken and three other amateur musicians founded around 1902. The Club grew until it numbered close to two dozen members, several of whom were professionals. Cheslock's book covers a most important aspect of Mencken's life.

Additional material on Huneker forms a later section of this collection. The two reviews of Van Vechten's books are interesting, if for no other reason than the comments on Igor Stravinsky, whose compositions cost Mencken many uneasy hours at the piano.

Huneker in Motley

A few books on music drift in, but, alas and alack, no more than a few, for we of English speech are but little given to that sort of reading matter, and not many of our publishers trade in it. German is the language of musical theory and criticism, and it is rapidly becoming the language of music itself, despite the old kingship of Italian. When A. W. Thayer finished the first volume of his monumental life of Beethoven, he at once had it translated into German, and in German it was published. To have printed it in English, at that time, would have been almost as fatuous as printing *The Complete Bartender* in Arabic. And even today, the American who can't read German misses the best there is in current musical literature—for example, Richard Strauss's revision of Berlioz's classical treatise on the orchestra. We take music lightly, futilely, sensuously, without intellectual interest. It is not habitually discussed among us, as books, sports, politics, morals and even painting are discussed. In any American society of pretensions to culture, a man who couldn't give a reasonably accurate definition of "sonnet" or "epic" or "etching" would be set down an ignoramus, but nothing would be thought of it if he failed to define "sonata." I doubt, indeed, if there are five thousand persons in the whole United States who could do it, even including all the professional musicians and music teachers—two distinct classes, by the way, though they have in common their hatred of music. And yet the sonata form lies at the heart of all the greatest music in the world, and no intelligent comprehension of that music is possible unless its plan and its possibilities are clearly understood. To listen to the "Moonlight Sonata" and not know exactly what a sonata aims to set forth is as imbecile as to listen to an actor and not know the language he is speaking. Americans do both, and profess to enjoy both.

But, as I have said, a stray book on music drifts in now and then— and pleasant the day that brings so penetrating and amusing a one as James Huneker's *Old Fogy*. Here is Huneker at his very darnedest: the sage in motley, the comic encyclopedia, the pundit on a spree. Here he lays about him right and left, knocking the reigning idols off their perches, resurrecting the old, old dead and trying to pump the breath into them, lambasting on one page and lauding on the next, lampooning the critics and burlesquing their rubber stamp fustian, extolling Dussek and damning Wagner, swearing mighty oaths by Mozart, and, after him, Strauss—not Richard, but Johann! The Old Fogy, of course, is the thinnest of disguises, a mere veil of gossamer for "Editor" Huneker. There is only one Huneker: *ergo,* there was never any Old Fogy. That solo Huneker, that James *a cappella,* is inimitable, incomparable, almost indescribable. On the one hand, he is a prodigy of learning, a veritable warehouse of musical information, true, half-true and apocryphal; on the other hand, he is a jester who delights in reducing all learning to absurdity. Reading him somehow suggests hearing the Fifth Symphony rescored for two fifes, one tambourine in B, one wind machine, two tenor harps, a contrabass oboe, two banjos, eight tubas and "the usual strings." The solid substance is there: every note is struck exactly in the middle—but what outlandish tone colors, what strange, unearthly sounds! It is not Beethoven, however, who first comes to mind when Huneker is at his tricks, but Papa Haydn—

the Haydn of the "Surprise" Symphony and the "Farewell." There is
the same incurable gaiety, the same magnificent irreverence, the same
masking of profundity with high spirits. Haydn did more for the symphony than any other man—but he also got more fun out of it than
any other man.

Old Fogy, of course, is not to be taken seriously: it is frankly a critical *scherzo,* an elaborate piece of fooling. But all the same a serious
idea runs through the book from end to end, and that is the idea that
music is getting too subjective to be comfortable. The makers of symphonies forget beauty altogether; their one effort is to put all their own
petty trials and tribulations into cacophony. Even so far back as Beethoven's day that autobiographical habit had begun. "Beethoven," says
Old Fogy, "is dramatic, powerful, a maker of storms, a subduer of
tempests; but his speech is the speech of a self-centered egotist. He is
the father of all the modern melomaniacs, who, looking into their own
souls, write what they see therein—misery, corruption, slighting sel-
fishness and ugliness." Old Ludwig's groans, of course, we can stand.
He was not only a great musician but also a great man. It is just as
interesting to hear him sigh and complain as it would be to hear the
private prayers of Julius Caesar. But what of Tchaikovsky, with his
childish Slavic whining? What of Liszt, with his cheap playacting, his
incurable lasciviousness, his plebeian warts? What of Wagner, with
his delight in imbecile fables, his popinjay vanity, his soul of a
grafter? What of Richard Strauss, with his warmed-over Nietzscheism,
his flair for the merely horrible? Old Fogy sweeps them all into his
ragbag. If art is to be defined as beauty seen through a temperament,
then give us more beauty and cleaner temperaments! Back to the old
gods—Mozart and Bach, with a polite bow to Brahms and a sentimental tear for Chopin! Beethoven tried to tell his troubles in his music; Mozart was content to ravish the angels of their harps. And as for
Johann Sebastian, "there was more real musical feeling, uplifting and
sincere, in the old St. Thomaskirche in Leipzig . . . than in all your
modern symphony and oratorio machine-made concerts" put together.

All this is argued, to be sure, in extravagant terms. Wagner is a
mere ghoul and impostor: *The Flying Dutchman* is no more than a
parody on Weber, and *Parsifal* is "an outrage against religion, morals
and music." Daddy Liszt is "the inventor of the Liszt pupil," a bad
piano player, "a venerable man with a purple nose—a Cyrano de

Cognac nose." Tchaikovsky is the Slav gone crazy on vodka. He transformed Hamlet into "a yelling man" and Romeo and Juliet into "two
monstrous Cossacks, who gibber and squeak at each other while reading some obscene volume." "His 'Manfred' is a libel on Byron, who was
a libel on God." And even Schumann is a vanishing star, a literary
man turned composer, a pathological case. But, as I have said, a serious idea runs through all this concerto for slapstick and seltzer siphon,
and to me, at least, that idea has a plentiful soundness. We are getting
too much melodrama, too much vivisection, too much hysteria—and
too little music. Turn from Tchaikovsky's "Manfred" or his "Pathé-
tique" to Mozart's "Jupiter," or to Schubert's "Unfinished," or Beethoven's Eighth: it is like coming out of a *kaffeeklatsch* into the open
air, almost like escaping from a lunatic asylum. The one unmistakable
emotion that much of this modern music arouses is a hot longing for
form, clarity, coherence, a tune. The snorts and moans of these pothouse Werthers are as irritating, in the long run, as the bawling of a
child, the rage of a disappointed job seeker, the squeak of a pig under
a gate. One yearns unspeakably for a composer who gives out his pair
of honest themes, and then develops them with both ears open, and
then recapitulates them unashamed, and then hangs a brisk coda to
them, and then shuts up.

(July, 1914)

An Apostle of Rhythm

The Tone Art.—Snowbirds in hell, Presbyterians in Paris, blondes
along the Niger, musical critics in the United States! All of them who
actually know what a sonata is could be numbered on the fingers of
the two hands, and of these all save a few confine themselves to transient and trivial reviewing in the newspapers. As for bound books on
music, we do not average one good one a year. James Huneker, in
fact, has produced nearly a half of all we have printed since 1890; he
is the only American musical critic who has any existence across the
ocean. Henry Edward Krehbiel, the dean of the New York critics, will

leave little behind him save some dreary records of performances, and a few elemental volumes for the newly cultured. His most respectable book, that on negro folksong, impresses one principally by its incompleteness; it is a creditable rough sketch, but surely no full-length work. The trouble with Krehbiel is that he mistakes mere diligence for criticism. He is an adept at accumulating facts, but he doesn't know how to write, and so his compositions are chaotic and tedious. W. J. Henderson, of the *Sun,* carries no such handicap. He is as full of learning as Krehbiel, as his small book on early Italian opera shows, but he also wields a slippery and intriguing pen, and could be vastly entertaining if he would. Instead, he has devoted himself chiefly to manufacturing petty school-books, and one finds little of the charm of his *Sun* articles between his covers. Lawrence Gilman? The perfect type of the *dilettante* turned professor; he says much, but has little to say. Philip H. Goepp? His three volumes on the classical symphonies are pedantic and irritating. Philip Hale? His gigantic annotations and footnotes scarcely belong to criticism at all; they are musical talmudism. Beside, they are buried in the programme books of the Boston Symphony Orchestra, and might as well be inscribed on the walls of Baalbec. As for Upton and other such fellows, they are merely musical Chautauquans, and belong to *Ladies' Home Journal* Kultur. One of them, a Harvard *maestro* named Daniel Gregory Mason, has published a book on the orchestra in which, on separate pages, the reader is solemnly presented with pictures of first and second violins!

In view of all this paucity, such a volume as *Music After the Great War,* by Carl Van Vechten, takes a considerable importance, despite its modest size and range. This Mr. Van Vechten, I believe, hires his ears and soul to *The New York Times,* and is a prophet of the extremest heterodoxy in music. His revolt, indeed, goes so far in mad, mad daring that one hears in it the gurgle of the *vin rouge* of Greenwich Village, and abroad it would probably attract the attention of the *polizei.* For example, he lifts a scornful eyebrow to Brahms, sniffs at the string quartets, and argues that the C minor symphony should be embalmed in some museum. Even Debussy begins to bore him; he has heard nothing interesting from that quarter for a long while. As for present-day Germany, he finds it a musical desert, with Arnold Schoenberg behind the bar of its only inviting *gasthaus.* Richard Strauss? Pooh! Strauss is an exploded torpedo, a Zeppelin brought to earth, "he has nothing more to say." (Even the opening of the "Al-

pine" Symphony, it would appear, is mere stick-candy.) England? Go
to! Italy? Back to the barrel-organ! Spain, Holland, Scandinavia, the
United States? It is to laugh, perchance to die! . . . Where, then, is
the *post bellum* tone poetry to come from? According to Mr. Van
Vechten, from Russia. It is the steppes of that prodigal and prodigious
empire which will produce it, or, more specifically, certain of the
fauna thereof, especially Prof. Igor Strawinsky, author of "The Night-
ingale" and of various revolutionary ballets. In the scores of Strawinsky, says Van Vechten, music takes a large leap forward. Here, at last,
we are definitely set free from melody and harmony; the tonal fabric
becomes an ineffable complex of time signatures; "all rhythms are
beaten into the ears."

But is such purged thumping actually of the future? Is it really
new? I have not yet heard these powerful shiverings and tremblings
of M. Strawinsky, but all the same I presume to doubt it. "The ancient
Greeks," says Van Vechten, "accorded rhythm a higher place than either melody or harmony." Perhaps they did, but what of it? So did the
ancient Goths and Huns, the more ancient Assyrians and Dravidians.
So do the modern niggers and New Yorkers. But do these admitted
facts dispose of the *Wohltemperirtes Clavier?* Surely not. The simple
truth is that the accentuation of mere rhythm is a proof, not of progress in music, but of a reversion to barbarism. The African savage,
beating his tom-tom, is content to go no further; the American composer of popular dance music gives him eager support. But music had
scarcely any existence as a civilized art until melody came to rhythm's
aid, and its fruits were little save a childish prettiness until harmony
began to support melody. To argue that naked rhythm, unaided by
anything save a barbaric tone-color, may now supplant them and ob-
literate them is to argue something so absurd that its simple statement
is a sufficient answer to it.

The rise of harmony, true enough, laid open a dangerous field. Its
exploration attracted meticulous and rabbinical minds; it was rigidly
mapped out, in hard, geometrical lines, by dry-as-dust professors
(think of Jadassohn, Prout!); in each succeeding age it tended to become unnavigable to the man of living ideas. But there were always
plenty of champions ready to put the pedagogues to flight—Haydn,
Mozart, Beethoven, Wagner—and surely there is no lack of them today. No melodramatic rejection of melody and harmony is necessary
to work such reforms as remain to be achieved. The dullest conserva-

tory pupil has learned how to pull the nose of Goetschius; no one
cares a hoot any more about the ancient laws of preparation and resolution; the rules grow so loose, indeed, that I myself begin to write
tone-poems. But out of this seeming chaos new laws will inevitably
arise, and though they will be much less stiff than the old ones, they
will still be coherent and logical and intelligible. One needs but glance
through such a book as René Lenormand's *Étude sur l'Harmonie
Moderne*, indeed, to see that a certain order is already showing itself,
that even Debussy and Ravel and Florent Schmitt know precisely
what they are about. And when the present boiling in the pot dies
down, the truly great musicians will be found to be, not those who
have been most extravagant, but those who have been most discreet
and intelligent—those who have most skillfully engrafted what is good
in the new upon what was sound in the old. Such a discreet one, I believe, is Richard Strauss—not a hollow iconoclast, as Strawinsky seems
to be, but an alert and skillful musician. His music is modern enough,
God knows, but he stops before it ceases to be music. One turns from a
hearing of it to a reading of it with a sense of surprise at its essential
simplicity and soundness. The performance reveals so many purple moments, so staggering an array of lusciousness, so gorgeous a music
Bull Moosery, that the ear is deceived into hearing scales and chords
that never were on land or sea. What the exploratory eye subse-
quently discovers in the score, perhaps, is no more than our stout and
comfortable old friend, the highly well-born *hausfrau*, Mme. C. Dur
—with a hooch of successive ninths in her afternoon *schokolade*, and
a vine-leaf or two of C sharp minor or B flat major in her hair.

I thus repudiate the heresies of Prof. Van Vechten, but praise him
for a brisk and stimulating little book. At all events, he has got away
from the *kindergarten*. He rises above the parlor vocalist and the au-
tomatic piano-player. Let him print more.

(July, 1916)

A First-Rate Music Critic

When Carl Van Vechten's first book, *Music After the Great War*, was published a year or so ago, I lifted a modest hymn in praise of it, and at the same time denounced the other music critics of America for the fewness of their books, and for the intolerable dulness of that few. Nine-tenths of all our tomes upon the tone art have to be imported from England, or clawed from the baffling Deutsch. Our native Hanslicks—or, at all events, all save Huneker—either confine themselves to punditic trivialities in newspapers and concert programmes or write books so leathery and preposterous that only music teachers can read them. And even Huneker, in these later years, seems to be neglecting music for the lesser arts. His last full-length book of musical criticism was his *Overtones*, dated 1912, and *Overtones* was pieced out with discourses on Flaubert and Nietzsche. Hence my rejoicing at first sight of this Prof. Van Vechten, for his maiden volume was full of interesting ideas and sound information, and it was written in a style that made reading very pleasant.

Now comes his second book, *Music and Bad Manners*—thicker, bolder, livelier, better. In it, in fact, he definitely establishes a point of view and reveals a personality, and both have an undoubted attractiveness. In it he proves, following Huneker, that a man may be an American and still give all his thought to a civilized and noble art, and write about it with authority and address, and even find an audience that is genuinely interested in it. Huneker got his first breath in Philadelphia, and still, I believe, swears off his taxes there, and keeps the family pew at St. Ostendorf's. Van Vechten, despite his Knickerbocker name, comes from an even remoter outpost—to wit, from Cedar Rapids, Iowa, in the saleratus and osteopathy belt. A strange hatching for such a nest! But nevertheless, a bird of very bright plumage, and, after Huneker, the best now on view in the tonal aviary.

The worst thing in *Music and Bad Manners* is the chapter which gives the book its title—a somewhat banal collection of anecdotes about tenors with the manners of Duroc-Jerseys and concerts made gay by rough-house, almost fit for the long-winter-evening pages of *The Musician* or *The Étude*. His second chapter, made up of idle spoofing on moving-picture music, is nearly as bad: it might have been printed in *The Outlook*. But in Chapter III he spits on his hands, as it were, and settles down to business, and the result is a long, a learned and a very instructive dissertation on modern Spanish music —a school of tone so little understood, and even so little known, that it gets but twenty lines in Grove's *Dictionary*, and is elsewhere scarcely mentioned at all. Here is useful pioneering; here is also good criticism, for it arouses the curiosity of the reader about the thing described, and makes him want to know more about it. And following it come four chapters upon various aspects of that new music which now causes such a pother, with its gossamers of seconds and elevenths, its wild, niggerish rhythms, and its barbaric Russian cadences. The Slavs are at the bottom of it; its chief prophet is Igor Strawinsky and its plenipotentiary in New York is Leo Ornstein. Dr. Van Vechten constitutes himself its literary agent, and makes out a very plausible case for it. It outrages, as yet, the ear trained in the three B.'s—but the ear grows tougher as year chases year. Who cannot remember the time when even *Til Eulenspiegel* was denounced as cacophony? Nay, there are critics alive today, and drawing pay from New York papers, who got their start bellowing for more tunes in *Die Walküre*. Under the musical bridges the water rushes like a mill-race.

I shall not attempt a summary of Van Vechten's exposition. It deserves a first-hand reading, and besides, I am still but imperfectly converted to all these new prodigies of tone, and so I might distort the tale in the telling. Long hours over the piano score of Strawinsky's *Zhar-Ptitsa* have left me in a somewhat muddled state of mind. My fingers come to grief in the very introduction; there is a rhythm in the seventh measure which, so far at least, they have failed to convey to the keys. Again, I trip over the tonality at the beginning of the first tableau, *"Zakoldovann'ii Sad Kashcheia"*: the signature is C major, but the actual key seems to be G sharp major, with a lowered third. In the third measure it fades into D major, and then into G minor, and then back into D major. Yet again, what a damnable thing is the dance of the fire-bird, *allergro rapace*. The flutes, I suppose, bear the weight of the curse in the orchestra; in the piano score there is a continuous flutish cadenza on a separate staff. God help the flutes! Yet again, how does one play the series of trills in the section called *"Nastuplenie Utra"*? Strange things, indeed, are in this ballet. Trills resolve themselves into ear-splitting double organ points in seconds. In one place there is a quintuplex shake on all five tones of the chord of the ninth, with the seventh lowered. Chords of the eleventh and thirteenth are piled upon one another; an ordinary discord sounds like a steal from Haydn; at one place, where Strawinsky actually borrows a whole figure from S. Coleridge Taylor's setting of "Many Thousands Gone," one gets the effect of a swallow of Pilsner after a hard day's work. Amazing stuff, indeed! But idiotic, unimaginable, *unmöglich?* Please, gents, no leading questions! I have not said so! By the Spring of 1920 it may all sound as flat and unprofitable as the whole-tone scale. The ear mellows. Who, today, can actually grasp the fact that Mozart was denounced for harmonic anarchies? Who can even *hear* the successive fifths in the minuet of the Jupiter symphony?

Van Vechten, as I have said, writes bouncingly and entertainingly. But like all critics he suffers from a literary disease: perhaps the critical frenzy itself is a pathological state. In his case it is the custom of putting a large part of the discourse into parentheses. His essay on Spanish music, for example, runs to 75 pages, and upon every one of them save ten there is a parenthesis, and sometimes half a dozen. He puts whole sentences within the curved lines; sometimes even whole paragraphs. A few days on Blackwell's Island would cure him of this malady; uncorrected, it puts clumsiness into what is otherwise a very graceful style. . . . The book is bound in boards of a staring pea-green. At first blush the color seems gratuitously strident, but second thoughts bring it into harmony with the music discussed within. The taste of Mr. Knopf, the publisher, is usually to be trusted. He is bold, but he always seems to know what he is doing. His career, by the way, deserves watching. In little more than a year of independent publishing he has brought together a formidable list of interesting books, and many of them appear to be selling. The publishing business has room for a man of his enterprise and intelligence. Most of the older and richer houses are run by old women in pantaloons; there is no great trade in America, indeed, which shows a vaster inbecility. Reflection and discrimination seem to have been almost completely divorced from publishing; books are printed for any and all reasons save the reason that they are worth printing. Some of the largest houses in the country devote themselves chiefly to merchanting garbage that should make any self-respecting publisher blush. If it were not for the influence of the big English publishers things would probably be even worse. They at least send over a few dozen fairly decent books every month and so save the face of the trade.

(May, 1917)

VII

Autobiographies

Mencken believed that it was well-nigh impossible for a man to write a dull book about himself. The honest writer would almost invariably tell us something that was both interesting and enlightening, and the dishonest writer would interest and entertain by the very fact of his dishonesty. Benvenuto Cellini's autobiography was no less a great work because Cellini happened to be a grandiose liar and cad. Indeed, had Cellini been more addicted to telling the homely truth than he was to showing how he was always right and his enemies wrong, his book would have been a good deal less fascinating than it is.

The fact is that Mencken was interested in people, in all kinds of people. Moreover, unlike a large number of optimists and spouters of high ideals, Mencken frankly liked people—which is not to say that he suffered fools gladly. But any man intelligent enough to tell the story of his life found a ready and receptive audience in Mencken.

Hall Caine and John D. Rockefeller

It would be difficult to imagine two men more utterly unlike in externals than Hall Caine and John D. Rockefeller, and yet the autobiographies of the pair, published recently, have more than a little in common. In each the author attempts to draw a picture of himself as he would have posterity and the celestial grand jury see him, and both pictures, naturally enough, are marked by magnificent charity. Caine, indeed, does not hesitate to hint that he is one of the first *illuminati* of the age. And John D., on his part, wants it to be understood that he is a fine old fellow, with the soft heart of a Tammany leader and the corundum virtue of an early Christian martyr. So much for the aims of Hall and John as conscious artists. Fortunately for the reader, their most elaborate effects, like those of every other artist, are conditioned and modified by touches of unconscious self-revelation. Behind the picture we always glimpse the man, and the man is often more interesting than the picture.

Caine's book is called *My Story* and is a tome of considerable bulk and dignity. He begins with an account of his childhood on the Isle of Man, and he ends with a chapter of "beautiful" reflections upon the obsequies of Wordsworth and Tennyson. The youthful Caine, it appears, was a true father to the man—a hard-working, ambitious, bumptious, assertive youngster who took his work with vast seriousness and was eager for a word of praise, however insincere. He pestered the literary lions of the day with letters; he gave them his manuscripts to read, and he filed away their good-natured commendations in his archives. Some of these commendations he prints in his book, and there they constitute an eternal proof of the folly of politeness.

With the drug-soaked and melodramatic Dante Gabriel Rossetti, Caine struck up what he seems to regard as a memorable friendship. As a matter of fact, his own story of it leads to the suspicion that Rossetti looked upon him as a sort of literary butler and private *claque*. The poet yearned for an ever-faithful audience—one that would be ready to huzzah whenever a huzzah would help his digestion. Caine filled the bill. His worship was constant and copious, for he felt that the greater the god the greater the devotee. He was ready to admire day or night. Even Rossetti's capacity for chloral excited his awe.

The autobiography of such a man must needs be an intensely interesting human document. It is not often that we can get so intimate a view of a common mind, for it is only rarely that a common mind is articulate. Suppose you could actually look into the cerebellum of the man who mows your chin, or of the woman who dusts your office, or of your trousers presser, your ward leader, your father-in-law, or any other human blank of your acquaintance: what a host of interesting

discoveries you would make! You would learn in one easy lesson why
it is that sentient beings, theoretically sane, join fraternal orders,
march in parades, go to political meetings, wear badges, read the
poems of Ella Wheeler Wilcox and weep over the plays and novels of
Hall Caine. As it is, the thing is an impenetrable mystery, and it will
remain so until someone establishes a science of comparative psychology and gives exhaustive study to the embryology of mental processes.
Meanwhile, it helps us a bit to examine the anatomy and physiology
of a mind that is obviously in tune (to borrow a phrase from wireless
telegraphy) with the mass mind of the fraternalists, the paraders, the
badge wearers. At all events, the book throws some light upon the
elusive psychic states which precede the genesis of a platitude and are
necessary to the evolution of bathos.

Caine's own story, in a word, is ten times as engrossing as any of his
novels. That he is a novelist of subtlety and skill I do not presume to
deny, but I am on safe ground, I believe, when I maintain that it
would take a whole seminary of Thackerays, working day and night,
in eight-hour shifts for a geological epoch, to create a character as interesting as Hall Caine himself.

The other book, that of Mr. Rockefeller, entitled *Random Recol-
lections of Men and Events,* is less ingenuous than Caine's, but
scarcely less readable. The Oil King is on the defensive throughout,
and in his defense he employs not only common logic and ignoble
facts, but also sophistry and paralogy of a high order. This is not sar-
casm; I mean it seriously. Logic and facts are within the reach of all,
and any numskull can show that twice two is four, but it takes ability
of a rare sort to demonstrate the inconceivable. And yet John D. does
it constantly, and with the ease of a psychical researcher proving the
existence of spooks. When he lays down, for example, the thesis that
the Standard Oil Company is a law-abiding and patriotic corporation,
he not only lays it down, but also proves it triumphantly. You may know
that he is wrong in premise and conclusion as certainly as you know
that virtue is its own punishment, and yet, when he comes to *quod
erat demonstrandum,* and looks up into your eyes with that pious
smile of his, you are literally forced to believe him, no matter how pit-
iously your tortured intelligence shrieks. If you would find his equal
in the higher chicanery of the dialectic, you must go back to St. Augustine, Tertullian, Origen, Philo Judaeus and St. Hilary of Poictiers.

This book will give you a new respect for the Oil King. He is not

merely a money grubber plus a theologian, but a man of imagination
and mental beam, full of daring and originality and skilled in all the
casuistry of the jury lawyer, the ballyhoo evangelist and the politician.
And when he abandons the hortatory mood and descends to plain exposition, he is beautifully clear and convincing. His ideas about everything he discusses, whether it be gardening, accounting, pathology or
ecclesiastic promotion, are those of a far-seeing, reflective man, and he
sets them forth in simple English. There is nothing of the visionary
about him. The one god in his Olympus is Efficiency—and Efficiency,
if you come to think of it, is a very passable divinity.

(September, 1909)

George Moore

The wizards and the munyons depart. Let in George Moore: he has
been waiting long enough. When I tell you that his *Vale* is the best of
the three volumes of his *Hail and Farewell*, I tell you enough, I hope,
to make you want to read it without further ado. Not since *Impressions and Opinions* has Moore put more charm and color into the English language; not since the famous preface to the bowdlerized American edition of *Memoirs of My Dead Life* has he been more humorous,
or more intimate, or more thoroughly delightful. One gets in this thick
volume, not only a full-length picture of Moore himself, as youth, man
and ancient, but also a series of brilliant pictures of his friends. For
example, John Millington Synge: "a thick stubbling growth of hair"
starting out of "a strip of forehead like black twigs out of the head of
a broom"; a "flat, ashen-colored face, with two brown eyes, looking at
me not unsympathetically"; a "large uncouth head"; a "ragged mus-
tache"; a pair of "great country shoes spreading over the carpet."
Somehow, I had always thought of Synge as a delicate and small-
boned fellow—a sort of sublimated clerk. But here he emerges in all
the Gothic ruggedness of a navvy, with his celluloid collar, his oafish
silences and his broad and hairy hands. Moore was somewhat doubt-
ful of Synge at the start. When the manuscript of *The Playboy of the
Western World* reached him, he made fatuous suggestions of changes

in the last act. Synge was disinclined to make them: he had already
rewritten the act thirteen times. Moore seems to have resented this
flouting of his advice, but the coolness didn't last, and the two were
good friends before Synge died.

Yeats, of course, is in almost every chapter of the book—Yeats, the
Celt *par excellence*, with his pagan love of beauty and his childish
superstitions. One day Moore and John Eglinton fell to discussing the
"one great passion" of Yeat's life. Was it innocent? Was it pure?
Moore volunteered to put the question to Yeats himself, and put it he
did. The poet answered sorrowfully: "I was very young at the time,
and was satisfied with. . . ." Moore has forgotten the exact word, but
remembers the virtuous denial. "I was sorry for Yeats," he says, "and
for his inspiration, which did not seem to have survived his youth, because it had arisen out of an ungratified desire." And then a long
chapter of unmoral moralizing, chiefly devoted to showing that too
much conscience is bad for an artist. But here, alas, I suspect alien
editing. Can it be that *Vale*, like the *Memoirs*, has had to yield to the
Chautauquan respectability of its American publishers? What of
"Euphorian in Texas," printed in the *English Review* for July? Isn't it
obviously a chapter from the book? And isn't it plainly lacking in the
book as it stands?

This "Euphorian in Texas" is incomparably of Moore, Moorean. It
tells a strange tale of a young woman from Austin, Texas, who crossed
the seas to Ireland upon a highly patriotic mission—no less, indeed,
than that of seeking a father for a Texas genius, and so giving the
commonwealth a literature. But why apply to Moore? Why not to
Meredith, to Swinburne, to Yeats, to Gosse—particularly to Gosse?
Moore mulls over the problem solemnly, and then gives it up. . . .
The lady, one hears, remained in Dublin a week or two, and then "she
smiled and went away, and this letter announcing his birth is all I
have." Other byzantine amours are in the chronicle: a great babbling
of ancient secrets. Lately I took Moore to task in a newspaper article
for all this kissing and telling. He replied: "It seems to me that an
amatory indiscretion is only possible within a zone of ten or fifteen
years; after five and twenty—certainly after thirty—love adventures
are no longer indiscretions, but matter for literary history." A curious
doctrine, indeed. The New Thought's repeal and reënactment of
"lying like a gentleman"!

(October, 1914)

Henry Ford

There is some clumsy pussyfooting in Henry Ford's *My Life and Work*—as, for example, in his discussion of his early partners—and there are chapters in which he ladles out platitudes with all the humorless passion of a Dr. Orison Swett Marden or a Dr. Frank Crane; but in the main it is a very plainspoken and intelligent book, and some of its principal ideas are of a quite extraordinary sagacity. I don't know whether the volume was written in the main by Ford himself or by his so-called collaborator, Samuel Crowther, but in any case Ford read it, approved it and signed it. A diligent study of it fills my heart with the conviction that the common view of him—that is, as of an ignoramus almost comparable to a King Kleagle of the American Legion, a chiropractor or a fresh-water university president—must be radically revised. The genesis of that common view, indeed, is almost too dubious to bear inspection: it only goes to show once more how easy it is to spread false ideas under a Republic. Ford first got into hot water by paying his slaves more than other automobile manufacturers paid them; he turned on another burner by opposing the crooks, political and financial, who shoved the American booboisie into the late war; he produced a renewed and fearful ebullition by suing the Chicago *Tribune* for lying about him, and he brought the temperature under him up to 10,000 degrees Fahrenheit by attacking the Jews. All of these acts grossly offended the camorra of patriotic usurers and shyster newspaper proprietors which now runs the country. The result was that all news about Ford—and because he made so much money he was naturally always in the news—began to take on a bilious and pessimistic flavor. The second result was and is that the average American of today, particularly if consciously respectable, regards him as a sort of mixture of Karl Marx and Billy Sunday—that is, as a fool whose notions are not only foolish, but also dangerous, and even criminal.

Well, in his book Ford strikes back at his enemies, and as a neutral in all such vast and complex combats I am bound to say that he pretty well convinces me. What would be more adept and convincing, for example, than his *reductio ad absurdum* of the whole hocus-pocus of "efficiency" engineering—his devastating demonstration that all the inventions of the "psychologists" and "sociologists" who now play lice to industry are buncombe. Here is a man who has built up one of the

largest manufacturing plants in the world, who pays more to his
workmen than any rival and sells his product cheaper, and yet he
boasts that there is not an "expert" in his whole plant, and that none
of the elaborate machinery of cost-accounting devised by such frauds
is in operation in his place. His scheme for keeping his eye on production is so astoundingly simple that, to a Rotary Club lecturer, it must
needs appear insane. Every afternoon, when work is done, the foreman of each workroom writes down the number of slaves he has had
at work during the day and the number of parts he has turned out.
Then he divides the latter by the former—and that is his whole report. If the daily figures show a rise, he is called up and ordered to
give an account of himself. If they show a decline he gets a note praising him as a competent fellow, and maybe a raise in wages. All such
austere and stenographic reports, when they reach the main office in
the evening, are put upon an adding machine and added up. If the total today is larger than yesterday, Ford finds out instantly what shops
are at fault. If it is less, he begins figuring on another cut in the price
of flivvers. Would it be possible to imagine anything simpler? Or more
workable? The disease is instantly apparent, and the diagnosis and
treatment follow immediately. Maybe there is not enough light in the
offending shop. Maybe the men working there have to take too many
steps. Maybe some of them are unfitted for their jobs, and ought to be
sent elsewhere. Maybe the materials they have to work with are inferior. Whatever the cause, it is detected and remedied the next day—
and by practical shopmen, not by "experts." These shopmen have no
luxurious offices, but keep on the jump all day. They never draw up
charts. They know nothing about abscissae. They are never given any
time off to address Summer Schools and Kiwanis Clubs.

Ford's capital discovery in manufacturing was this: that very few of
the operations in an ordinary plant require any intelligence in the
operator—in brief, that a moron is quite as useful in industry as a
Socrates. This discovery, practically applied, has got him a bad name
among economic and political sentimentalists—which is to say, among
the messianic sophomores and unhappy professors who do all the
writing for the Liberal weeklies. It is argued that Ford has made
slaves of his workingmen. Well, suppose he has? Is there any complaint from the slaves? If so, I have yet to hear of it. My spies in Detroit report that the men in the Ford plants stick to their jobs longer
than the men in the other automobile plants out there, and seem to

have more money, and are generally more contented. They drink better liquor than even judges and bishops drink in New York; they wear
good clothes and have money in the bank; communism seems to be as
dead among them as Socinianism or the Pelagian heresy; their wives
spend the afternoons window-shopping, home-brewing, or lolling in
the movie parlors. The Ford plant is an open shop, and apparently
labor-leader-proof. There is no collective bargaining, and yet there is
never any dispute about wages. No one is paid double for overtime. No
one, in fact, is paid anything for overtime; the man who works an hour
extra today gets an hour off tomorrow; if he wants to he can accumulate such extra hours, and take a whole day, or even a week. In normal times any man who applies for work, so long as he is not palpably
dying or insane, is given a job. If he is just out of the penitentiary, no
one notes it. If he has only one leg or one arm he is put at something
that a one-legged or one-armed man can do. If he is blind there is also
a place for him, and at full wages: there are more good jobs for blind
men, says Ford, than there are blind men. No matter what his experience or equipment, he is started at the bottom—that is, at $6 a day. If
he has brains, he rises quickly and automatically. If, on the contrary,
he is a vegetable he remains where he started.

As I have said, Ford's discovery that morons, under proper supervision, make good workmen has got him a good many sharp words
from the *Survey*, the *New Republic* and other such guardians of the
downtrodden. These gazettes allege, and with much show of evidence,
that he converts his men into machines—that a man who spends eight
hours a day, week in and week out, dipping pieces of steel into a vat
of enamel, or daubing grease on axles, or picking up little nuts and
screwing them on little bolts—that such a man, after a couple of
years, is a mere automaton, and hence unfitted to render a just verdict
upon the Fordney tariff or the recall of judges. A true bill, certainly.
But Ford's reply to it is simple and convincing. He is, he says, not the
Lord God Jehovah, but merely a modest manufacturer of cheap,
durable and infinitely hideous automobiles. Such fellows were made
as they are, not by him, but by the Jehovah aforesaid. They keep on
picking up nuts because they are incapable of doing anything of a
greater complexity—above all, they keep on doing it because they like
it. Ford finds that, taking his workmen as they run, only 25 per cent of
them "are even willing to be straw-bosses"—apparently the lowest
order of foremen—and that only 5 per cent "have the willingness to

accept the additional responsibility and the additional work which goes with the higher places." The vast majority of men, he says, "want to stay put. They want to be led. They want to have everything done for them and to have no responsibility. . . . The difficulty is not to discover men to advance, but men who are willing to be advanced." The truth of this is certainly known to every man who has ever employed labor in large masses. It is the unanswerable answer to all industrial sentimentalism, to every variety of economic utopianism, to democracy itself. And yet what other large employer of labor has ever said it?

But Ford's book is not given over wholly to a discussion of his great can-factory. He is most interesting and instructive, of course, when he talks of what he knows best, but he is also full of shrewdness when he alights upon other subjects, for example, the railroads and hospital management. His brief chapter upon the hospital he has founded at Detroit seems to me to be the most intelligent treatise upon the general theme that I have ever read—and I am rather more familiar than most laymen with such literature. Here the public function of a hospital is stated with admirable clarity and good sense, and the most practicable methods of discharging it are simply set forth. Very few · great American hospitals, it must be obvious, are of any tangible value to the great majority of the citizens who, whether directly or indirectly, support them. They offer free board to paupers and they offer enormously expensive board to the rich, but the average man must keep out of them if he would remain solvent. In Detroit Ford has sought to provide a hospital for this average man. His plan is excellent—and it will work. So will his plan for operating his railroad. It is sublimely simple: kick out all the financiers and put in railroad men. . . . But I had better shut off my hymn to him: he may send me a Lizzie. Such a book, for all its merits, is fundamentally a sour apple for a literary man. My taste is not for manufacturers, but for artists. Nevertheless, I beg amnesty for saying here and now that I have never read anything by George Santayana one-half so sound and important as this modest tome by the Detroit E. W. Howe.

(January, 1923)

In the Altogether

If Frank Harris' *My Life and Loves* had the imprint of a regular publisher and were on sale in the book-stores, instead of being privately printed, as it is, I suppose that the smut-snufflers of the Comstock Society would be prosecuting the publisher by now, and that pious Tammany judges would be denouncing it, while the case was still *sub curae,* in the newspapers, and that the newspapers themselves would be wallowing in the scandal, and making sure, as usual, that not a single flapper in any self-respecting finishing-school missed reading the book. Perhaps, indeed, the whole buffoonery will be upon us before these lines get into print, despite the very elaborate efforts that seem to have been made to keep the thing from getting into general circulation. If so, then I can only hope that the pornomaniacs will tell us how any normal man could achieve the task that Harris has set before himself, to wit, that of writing a complete and honest autobiography, without introducing matters of sex into the first volume. This first volume, in the present case, deals with the years before the author came to his majority. They are, as everyone knows, years of intense sexual curiosity, and, in the healthy male, of outreachings toward sexual experience. The difference between the story that Harris has to tell of them and the story that the ideal American youth of the Y.M.C.A. would have to tell is simply this: that Harris' tale is bare of suppressions, autoerotism and dirty dreams. In truth, a sort of innocence gets into it, even when it is superficially most lubricious, and one cannot escape the notion that, for that certain young man at that certain time, there was a great deal more to be got out of hearkening to the hormones than could ever have been got by hearkening to the counsels of the village pastor. Experience killed curiosity, and the death of curiosity left the mind free for graver concerns. In the midst of proceedings that certainly cannot be reconciled with the formal moral code of Christendom, Harris managed to develop his body to strength and resilience, to acquire habits of thrift and industry, to pack his mind with a vast store of positive knowledge, and to outfit himself with the tastes and ways of thought of a highly civilized man.

Moreover, all this took place in Kansas—surely a miracle, if there ever was one. Born in Ireland, the son of a naval officer of obscure career, Harris escaped to New York as a boy, had some experience there of very severe manual labor, and then somehow made his way to the

University of Kansas, at Lawrence, and there fell under the influence
of a forgotten but apparently extraordinarily accomplished pedagogue, Prof. Dr. Byron C. Smith. This first volume of his autobiography is, in a large sense, an eloquent and almost impassioned
tribute to Smith—a man who seems to have had a truly amazing capacity for awakening intellectual enterprise. He not only set his pupil
to devouring the humanities voraciously; he also implanted in him
habits of independent thinking—habits that have characterized Harris
ever since. The raw material, of course, was there—chiefly Irish facility and Irish bellicosity. But Smith converted what might have been,
after all, no more than a strange, moody cowboy into something of a
scholar, more of an artist, and even more of a man of the world. I had
never heard of him until I read this volume, but now I can see his
tracks all over Harris' later work—over the two volumes of Shakespearean criticism, over the biography of Wilde, and even over the
Contemporary Portraits, though they deal specifically with men met
long after Smith's death, of whom, in many cases, he had never heard.
It is a genuine pleasure to come upon a record of so talented a schoolmaster. The breed is certainly not notable for professional efficiency.
But here is one who found a wild young man in a Kansas village, too
much interested, perhaps, in the ladies, and made of him one of the
most original, pungent and effective critics of the life of our time.

The work, as planned, will run to seven volumes, and no doubt the
later ones will show a greater decorum than this first one. Harris did
not stay long in Kansas, or, indeed, in America. He went back to Brit-
ain, and presently became an editor of influential newspapers and
magazines, and a salient and picturesque figure in the life of London.
If he deals as frankly in his subsequent volumes with the men he met
and knew there as he here deals with his own youth, he will produce
a record of the highest historical value—a record, in fact, that will be
singular and invaluable. It is shocking, but there is very little in it that
is palpably false. No man, perhaps, will ever write an absolutely exact
history of himself, for no man ever quite knows himself. But here
Harris shows a promise of coming as near to it as is humanly feasi-
ble.

(June, 1923)

VIII

Politics and Politicians

With the possible exception of his language studies, Mencken's writings on government and politics are probably better known today than anything else he did. I have known English teachers, for example, who knew almost nothing about Mencken, but I have never met a political scientist who was unaware of Mencken's views on his subject. This is, I suppose, as it should be. Our lives, either directly or indirectly, are conditioned far more by political matters than by any other. Regrettable though this may be, it is nonetheless true.

Two essays in particular, "The Politician" and "On Government" (both in *Prejudices: Fourth Series*), provide excellent brief statements of just what Mencken thought on the subject. While he saw the need for strong governments, he also understood the inevitable process by which governments will eventually smother the civil rights of the private citizen under the guise of *protecting* those rights. In short, he early saw the cause-effect sequence that would lead to the horrifying "utopias" of Aldous Huxley and George Orwell. Finally, though Mencken seems to have considered the free man's battle against government doomed from the start, he still raised his voice in an appeal to view the battle realistically and not sentimentally. Unlike Henry Adams, who retreated into a rather self-complacent pessimism, Mencken always insisted on the need for an *active* response to politicians and politics—swinish and sordid though they may be. For instance, he always voted in local and national elections (in contrast to a man like Thoreau, who never voted). Moreover, he was often constructive in his approach to matters of public concern, particularly on the local level. As Malcolm Moos put it in his Introduction to *A Car-*

nival of Buncombe, a collection of Mencken's famous Monday articles
for the *Evening Sun:* "In his own Baltimore bailiwick he performed
yeoman duty by arousing readers to the serious problems that menaced public health, to the need for sanitary milk, to a pure water supply, and to the necessity of controlling diphtheria and typhoid."

Like all Menckenophiles, I succumb to the urge to quote. The following passages conclude his essay "On Government," published in
1924. A few words would need changing today, but not many:

This great pox of civilization, alas, I believe to be incurable, and so I propose no new quackery for its treatment. I am against dosing it, and I am
against killing it. All I presume to argue is that something would be accomplished by viewing it more realistically—by ceasing to let its necessary and
perhaps useful functions blind us to its ever-increasing crimes against the
ordinary rights of the free citizen and the common decencies of the world.
The fact that it is generally respected—that it possesses effective machinery
for propagating and safeguarding that respect—is the main shield of the
rogues and vagabonds who use it to exploit the great masses of diligent and
credulous men. Whenever you hear anyone bawling for more respect for
the laws, whether it be a Coolidge on his imperial throne or an humble
county judge in his hedge court, you have before you one who is trying to
use them to his private advantage; whenever you hear of new legislation for
putting down dissent and rebellion you may be sure that it is promoted by
scoundrels. The extortions and oppressions of government will go on so
long as such bare fraudulence deceives and disarms the victims—so long
as they are ready to swallow the immemorial official theory that protesting
against the stealings of the archbishop's secretary's nephew's mistress' illegitimate son is a sin against the Holy Ghost. They will come to an end
when the victims begin to differentiate clearly between government as a
necessary device for maintaining order in the world and government as a
device for maintaining the authority and prosperity of predatory rascals and
swindlers. In other words, they will come to an end on the Tuesday following
the first Monday of November preceding the Resurrection Morn.

The Style of Woodrow

A truly devastating piece of criticism is to be found in *The Story of a Style,* by Dr. William Bayard Hale. The style is that of poor Woodrow, and Dr. Hale operates upon it with machetes, hand grenades and lengths of gas-pipe. He is one peculiarly equipped for the business, for he was at one time high in the literary and philosophical confidence of the late Messiah, and learned to imitate the gaudy jargon of the master with great skill—so perfectly, indeed, that he was delegated to write one of the Woodrovian books, to wit, *The New Freedom,* once a favorite text of *New Republic* Liberals, deserving Democrats, and the tender-minded public in general. But in the end he revolted against both the new Euphuism and its eminent pa, and now he tackles both with considerable ferocity, and, it must be added, vast effect. His analysis of the whole Wilsonian buncombe, in fact, is downright cruel; when he finishes with it, not even a Georgia postmaster or a Palmer *agent provocateur* could possibly believe in it. He shows its ideational hollowness, its ludicrous strutting and bombast, its heavy dependence upon greasy and meaningless words, its frequent descent to mere sound and fury, signifying nothing. In particular, he devotes himself to a merciless study of what, after all, must remain the fallen Moses's chief contribution to both history and beautiful letters, *viz.,* his biography of George Washington. I have often, in the past, called attention to the incredible imbecility of this work. It is an almost inexhaustible mine of bad writing, faulty generalizing, childish pussyfooting, ludicrous posturing, and naive stupidity. To find a match for it one must try to imagine a biography of the Duke of Wellington by his barber. Well, Hale spreads it out on his operating table, sharpens his snickersnee upon his boot-leg, and proceeds to so harsh an anatomizing that it nearly makes me sympathize with the author. Not many of us—writers, and hence vain and artificial fellows—could undergo so relentless an examination without damage. But not many of us, I believe, would suffer quite so horribly as Woodrow. The book is a mass of puerile affectations, and as Hale unveils one after the other he performs a sound service for American scholarship and American letters.

I say that this book is cruel, but I must add that his laparotomies are carried on with every decorum—that he by no means rants and rages against his victim. On the contrary, he keeps his temper even when there is strong temptation to lose it, and his inquiry maintains itself upon the literary level as much as possible, without needless descents to political and personal matters. More than once, in fact, he says very kind things about Woodrow—a man probably quite as mellow and likable within as the next man, despite his strange incapacity for keeping his friends. The curiosities of his character I hope to investigate at length on some future occasion, probably in *Prejudices: Third Series.* At the moment, I can only give thanks to God that Hale has saved me the trouble of exposing the extreme badness of the Woodrovian style —a style until lately much praised by cornfed connoisseurs. Two or three years ago, at the height of his illustriousness, it was spoken of in whispers, as if there were something almost supernatural about its merits. I read articles, in those days, comparing it to the style of the Biblical prophets, and arguing that it vastly exceeded the manner of any living literatus. Looking backward, it is not difficult to see how that doctrine arose. Its chief sponsors, first and last, were not men who actually knew anything about the writing of English, but simply editorial writers on party newspapers, *i.e.,* men who related themselves to literary artists in much the same way that Dr. Billy Sunday relates himself to the late Paul of Tarsus. What intrigued such gentlemen in the compositions of Dr. Wilson was the plain fact that he was their superior in their own special field—that he accomplished with a great deal more skill than they did themselves the great task of reducing all the difficulties of the hour to a few sonorous and unintelligible phrases, often with theological overtones—that he knew better than they did how to arrest and enchant the boobery with words that were simply words, and nothing else. The vulgar like and respect that sort of balderdash. A discourse packed with valid ideas, accurately expressed, is quite incomprehensible to them. What they want is the sough of vague and comforting words—words cast into phrases made familiar to them by the whooping of their customary political and ecclesiastical rabble-rousers, and by the highfalutin style of the newspapers that they read. Woodrow knew how to conjure up such words. He knew how to make them glow, and weep. He wasted no time upon the heads of his dupes, but aimed directly at their ears, diaphragms and hearts.

But reading his speeches in cold blood offers a curious experience. It is difficult to believe that even idiots ever succumbed to such transparent contradictions, to such gaudy processions of mere counter-words, to so vast and obvious a nonsensicality. Hale produces sentence after sentence that has no apparent meaning at all—stuff quite as bad as the worst bosh of the Hon. Gamaliel Harding. When Wilson got upon his legs in those days he seems to have gone into a sort of trance, with all the peculiar illusions and delusions that belong to a frenzied pedagogue. He heard words giving three cheers; he saw them race across a blackboard like Socialists pursued by the *Polizei;* he felt them rush up and kiss him. The result was the grand series of moral, political, sociological and theological maxims which now lodges imperishably in the cultural heritage of the American people, along with Lincoln's "government for the people, by the people," etc., Perry's "We have met the enemy, and they are ours," and Vanderbilt's "The public be damned." The important thing is not that a popular orator should have uttered such grand and glittering phrases, but that they should have been gravely received, for many weary months, by a whole race of men, some of them intelligent. Here is a matter that deserves the sober inquiry of competent psychologists. The boobs took fire first, but after a while even college presidents—who certainly ought to be cynical men, if ladies of joy are cynical women—were sending up sparks, and for a long while anyone who laughed was in danger of the calaboose. Hale does not go into the question; he confines himself to the concrete procession of words. His book represents tedious and vexatious labor; it is, despite some obvious defects, very well managed; it opens the way for future works of the same sort. Imagine Harding on the Hale operating table!

(January, 1921)

Vox Populi

I

Walter Lippmann's *Public Opinion* leaves me with a feeling not unlike that which ensues upon the ingestion of near-beer. I am full, but not at all satisfied. It is a sober and earnest book and it is an extremely laborious book, but it seems to me that it gets to no recogniz-

able goal and that it throws very few new lights upon the dark and
tortuous road it traverses. What Mr. Lippmann says about public
opinion under democracy, in his volume of 418 pages, is simply that it
is ignorant, credulous, superstitious, timid and degraded—which
might have been said just as well in a hundred words. The evidences
that he amasses do not appear to be new, nor is there anything novel
about the generalizations he deduces from them. You will find the
same stuff, sometimes far more charmingly presented, in many other
books: Graham Wallas' *Human Nature in Politics*, George Santayana's
Character and Opinion in the United States, James N. Wood's *Democracy and the Will to Power*, Everett Dean Martin's *The Behavior
of Crowds*—even in Gustave Le Bon's half-forgotten pioneer treatise,
The Crowd. Mr. Lippmann was a pupil at Harvard of the late William James, and in more than one place the weight of his argument
rests upon the master's psychological realism. But his conclusions belong far more to the romantic Liberalism of half a dozen years ago
than to any system so harsh as pragmatism. His *coda*, in fact, reminds me strongly of the mystical gurgle at the end of James Bryce's
Modern Democracies. What he says, in brief, is that we must keep on
hoping that the mob will one day grow intelligent, despite the colossal
improbability of it. There have appeared in the world, at various
times since the time of Christ, occasional intelligent individuals. Even
in our own time a few have been reported. Well, then, why not assume that there will be more and more hereafter? If you do, you will
be happy. If you don't, "the Lord Himself cannot help you."

All this seems to me to be a gigantic begging of the question,
which, in plain terms, is this: how, *in spite* of the incurable imbecility
of the great masses of men, are we to get a reasonable measure of
sense and decency into the conduct of the world? The Liberal answer
(much more clearly stated by H. G. Wells in *The Outline of History*
than by Mr. Lippmann in the present book) is, in essence, simply a
variant of the old democratic answer: by spreading enlightenment, by
democratising information, by combatting what is adjudged to be
false by what is adjudged to be true. But this scheme, however persuasively it may be set forth, invariably goes to wreck upon two or
three immovable facts. One is the fact that a safe majority of the men
and women in every modern society are congenitably uneducable,
save within very narrow limits—that it is no more possible to teach
them what every voter theoretically should know than it is to teach a

chimpanzee to play the *viola da gamba*. Another is the fact that the
same safe majority, far from having any natural yearning to acquire
this undescribed body of truth, has a natural and apparently incurable
distrust of it, and seldom accepts it, even in its most elemental and obvious forms, save after desperate resistance and at the point of the
sword. A third (and it is more important than either of the other two)
is that there exists no body of teachers in Christendom capable of
teaching the truth, even supposing it to be known—that the teacher,
almost *ex officio*, seems to be sworn to corrupt it and put it down—
that the inevitable tendency of pedagogy, as Mr. Wood shows in the
book I have mentioned, is to preserve and propagate the lies that happen to be currently respectable, which is to say, that happen to be
salubrious to the current masters of the mob. In support of this last I
pass over the whole corps of professional pedagogues, who are admit-
tedly too stupid to teach the truth or even to recognize it, and point to
two teachers extraordinary, to wit, Mr. Wells and Mr. Lippmann himself. Both, during the late war, consecrated their talents to the official
enlightenment of the vulgar. Both, in the conduct of that enterprise, lent their authority and their dignity to the propagation of nonsense—some of it nonsense that was deliberately disingenuous and
unquestionably evil. One worked for the Right Hon. David Lloyd
George and the other for Dr. Wilson. Well, what is the difference between working for two such frauds and working for Senator Lusk,
Judge Gary and the Ku Klux Klan?

II

The fact is, of course, that it is absolutely hopeless to think of filling
the great masses of men with even the most elemental sense—that the
dream of Mr. Lippmann has no more probability of realization than the
dream of a man who has sniffed nitrous oxide. To discuss it seriously
is simply to talk in terms of Liberal astrology. I do not deny, to be
sure, that the great masses of men can take in certain sorts of knowledge, at least within narrow limits. Fully 80 per cent of the inhabi-
tants of the United States, within our own time, have absorbed a
number of solid facts, before unknown to them—for example, that
beer is easy to make in the kitchen, that wood alcohol has various
unpleasant physiological effects, and that it is dangerous to crank a
Ford. Probably half as many have taken in information of a somewhat
wider and more philosophical kind—for example, that the guarantees in

the Bill of Rights are merely rhetorical, that saving the world for democracy costs a great deal of money, that feeding a human infant on fried liver will not make it flourish, and that every old woman who mumbles as she shuffles along is not a witch. Go back a thousand years, and you will be able to show even greater accretions of knowledge, much of it sound. The average member of the American Legion, though the professors may report him a moron, knows more, I am convinced, than the average legionary of Caesar's Gallic army, and what he knows is better organized. The average American farmer, though he voted for Bryan, is more intelligent than the average peasant of Charlemagne's time. Even the average American Congressman, at least in matters that do not concern his business of lawmaking, probably has more useful information in him than the average member of a Tenth Century Witenagemot.

But it is easy to overestimate this growth of knowledge and intelligence among the lower orders of men, both quantitatively and qualitatively. Nine-tenths of the positive facts that such men acquire are superficial, unorganized and unimportant. For eight years past the whole American people have rocked and sweated under the incessant discussion of the fundamental problems of international politics, and vast hordes of gifted soothsayers, including Mr. Lippmann himself, have devoted themselves to spreading enlightenment on the subject. But if you go to the nearest polling place at the next election, and ask the first ten men and women in line to give you a coherent account of even the simplest of those problems, the answers that you will get from at least eight of them will be wholly idiotic. Even in more important matters the horse-power of public sagacity is vastly less than romantic democrats assume. I believe that at least a majority of the people of the United States, after a century and a half of education, still believe firmly in ghosts—and when I say at least a majority I really mean two-thirds. In the city of Baltimore, of which I am a citizen, the police lately found themselves confronting a murder mystery that was far beyond their intelligence. Quite as a matter of course they turned to a spiritualist for help, and when she laid the crime to an obviously innocent man they promptly arrested him and put him into jail. The accused was released at the order of a police commissioner who happened to be a former army colonel, and hence an agnostic in idealistic and transcendental affairs. But the point is that the great majority of Baltimorons saw nothing strange about the proceeding of the cops, and showed absolutely no indignation over it. They believed in spirits just as they had once believed in the childish gibberish of Dr. Wilson. It was a belief inherited unchanged from their savage ancestors of the European swamps. Two thousand years of so-called civilization had not changed it in the slightest. Nor has there been any change in scores of other such fundamental superstitions. The Knight of Pythias of today, setting aside a few unimportant facts, believes almost precisely what was believed by the slaves who built Cheops' pyramid.

In brief, the progress of enlightenment affects the great masses of men but little; it is a matter which concerns exclusively a small minority of men. The size of that minority is always grossly overestimated. Whole classes of men are counted in it without any inquiry as to the actual intelligence of their members. Because a man is a Ph.D. and licensed to teach Latin grammar it is assumed that he is generally intelligent—that he shares, to some extent at least, in the stupendous miscellaneous knowledge of a Virchow or a Huxley. The assumption is often false. He may be, in fact, practically an imbecile, and not infrequently he actually is. I once knew a man holding a teaching post in a respectable university who threw it up in order to become a Christian Science healer. I know a United States Senator who wears a rheumatism string. Sir Oliver Lodge believes in spooks. The President of the United States subscribes to the doctrines of the United Brethren. Dr. Wilson, for long viewed universally as a master mind, has written books that are inaccurate and nonsensical, and is so stupid that he had got to Paris before ever he heard of the secret treaties—an evidence of mental deficiency in the learned that lately gave great concern to Mr. Lippmann. I do not here argue, of course, that the intelligence of a man is to be determined by subjecting him to an examination like that recently proposed by Thomas A. Edison. Edison himself, indeed, though he could pass his own examination, must be thick-witted at bottom, for when he goes on a holiday he chooses such men as Harding and Henry Ford as his companions. But what I do argue is that no man can be said to share fully in the progress of human knowledge who is ignorant of any of its basic facts—for example, the facts that ghosts do not actually haunt graveyards, that malaria is not caused by miasmas, that printing paper money cannot make a nation rich, and that men cannot be made virtuous by law.

It is possible, of course, that many, or even all such facts have a

touch of mortality in them—that greater knowledge may conceivably
modify them, or displace them. But in so far as the human mind, in its
present stage of development, can determine, they are true today, and
their truth is accepted unquestionably by all men whose fitness for
judging them is of a special and superior character. If it be admitted
that the human intelligence can function at all, then it must be admitted that they are, to all practical intents and purposes, true. Yet
there are whole categories of such facts which the generality of human beings reject, and other whole categories of which they have
never so much as heard. It is my contention that this failure to take
them in is congenital and incurable—that only a small minority of
men are capable of grasping them at all. If that notion be sound—and
I believe that the whole of human experience supports it—then it follows that no imaginable scheme of education will ever bridge the gap
between the great masses of men and the intelligent minority. The former, by dint of terrific effort, may be gradually inoculated with certain simple facts, and so, in a sense, it may be said to make progress,
but no matter how fast it is cajoled and goaded into moving, the
minority will move ten times as fast. The gap, indeed, is constantly
widening. The distance, intellectually, between a Huxley and an Iowa
muzhik is at least ten times as great, I believe, as the distance between Socrates and the average Greek citizen of his time. The human
race, I begin to suspect, is actually splitting into two distinct species.
The one species is characterized by an incurable thirst for knowledge,
and an extraordinary capacity for recognizing and taking in facts and
evidences. The other is just as brilliantly marked by a chronic appetite
for whatever is most palpably false and a chronic distrust for whatever is most palpably true. To the second species belong the overwhelming majority of individuals under democracy, including all of
the favorite politicians, philosphers, theologians, star-gazers and di-
viners. These half-wits now run the world.

III

The dilemma is recognized by Mr. Lippmann in his book, but he
seems quite blind to the concrete problem that it presents. That problem is not to discover some way to educate the majority up to the
level of the minority—for the business, if my contention holds water,
is a physical impossibility—but to devise ways and means whereby
the minority may gain control of the majority. As things stand, it has

no such control; on the contrary, it is almost lacking in influence polit-
ically, as it is culturally. The great nations of the world are run today,
not by their first-rate men, nor even by their second-rate or third-rate
men, but by groups of professional mob-masters, all of them ignorant
and most of them corrupt. As democracy spreads, the grip of these
mob-masters becomes firmer and firmer. There was a time in the history of England when such an Englishman as Gilbert Murray or Havelock Ellis might have had some chance of rising to high office in the
state, and, what is far more important, some chance of bringing his
superior intelligence and integrity to the determination of national
policies, but that time has plainly passed. Today it is the mob that decides who shall rule, and the choice of the mob, when it is free, is always for some man who reasons in terms of its own brutish ignorance,
and shows all its disregard for decency and honor. The chief man in
England, under that system, is the Lloyd George aforesaid—a man of
whom it would be flattery to say that he has the honesty of a press-
agent and the dignity of a bawdy-house keeper. It would be difficult,
indeed, to find in the whole Empire a man who stands further from
the common concept of a statesman and a gentleman. His politics is
frankly selfish; he will sacrifice anything to have and hold his job. His
ideas, in so far as they are intelligible at all, are on the level of a stock-
broker's. His word of honor is worth absolutely nothing.

Well, how does it come that such a man reaches so high an estate in
a great nation—and in every other great nation, under democracy,
there are scoundrels to match him? It comes very simply. He is, *imprimis,* so near to the mob in his natural ways of thought—his gross
self-seeking and lack of sensitiveness, his tendency to reduce all ideas
to hollow formulae, his feeling of kinship for ignorant and degraded
men—that it is easy for him to put himself into their collective mind,
and just as easy for him to make them respond to the processes of his
own. He is, *zum zweiten,* so lacking in ordinary professional pride and
conscientiousness that he is willing to submit with alacrity to the
mob's mandates, even when he dissents from them and regards them
as dangerous and wrong. He is, *troisièmement,* enormously skilful at
appealing to the savage prejudices that lie in the depths of its consciousness, even below the level of its primitive ratiocination—the
great body of ignoble hopes and poltroonish fears out of which flow
all its customary rages and enthusiams. In brief, he is a demagogue,
and his power rests wholly upon his talent for that rôle. What keeps

him in office—and all his French, German, American and Italian peers with him—is not any special capacity for the duties of his office, nor even any special liking for them *per se,* but simply his tremendous capacity for evoking the emotions of the mob. He knows how to make it exult and he knows how to make it tremble. Knowing that much, he is master of the whole art of practical politics under democracy. No appeal to logic and facts can stay him, and no appeal to decency can daunt him.

The problem of democratic government thus narrows down to this: how is the relatively enlightened and reputable minority to break the hold of such mountebanks upon the votes of the anthropoid majority? At first glance, the thing seems to be insoluble. Of the three characters of the demagogue that I have rehearsed, the first two are quite unimaginable in any man worthy of being called a member of the enlightened minority. If his ways of thought were the ways of the mob, he would simply go over to the majority. If he had no professional pride and conscientiousness he would go the same route. So far the quest is obviously hopeless. But a third character remains, and in it I venture to find more consolation. The man of education and self-respect may not run with the mob and he may not yield to it supinely, but what is to prevent him deliberately pulling its nose? What is to prevent him playing upon its fears and credulities to good ends as a physician plays upon them by giving its members bread-pills, or as a holy clerk, seeking to bring it up to relative decency, scares it with tales of a mythical hell? In brief, what is to prevent him swallowing his political prejudices (as he now has to swallow his prejudices in other directions in the interest of public decorum) in order to channel and guide the prejudices of his inferiors? It may be, at first blush, an unsavory job—but so is delivering a fat woman of twins an unsavory job. Yet obstetricians of the first skill and repute do it—if the fee be large enough. So is hearing the confessions of Freudian old maids. Yet priests do it. So is going to war. Yet the chivalry of the world has just done it.

What I propose, in truth, has been done already—by men of very considerable intelligence, and to brilliant effect. I allude to the boob-bumping that was undertaken during the late war by certain members of the *intelligentsia*—many of them, of course, fakes, but a few of them genuine enough. These performers took to the business for motives that sometimes brought them into contact with the second character of a demagogue; that is to say, they seized the drum-stick because it was more comfortable wielding it than going into the trenches. But if we forget that possible descent from the higher integrity, the fact remains that they performed their duties very skilfully and effectively. Some of the most potent raids upon the boob emotions made during those days were planned and executed, in fact, by men who are normally too sniffish to engage in any such enterprise. All I argue is that what they did once they can do again—that if they devoted themselves to the arts of the demagogue in peace times as ardently and ingeniously as they did in war times, they would present a very formidable opposition to the standardized buncombe of the Bryans, Roosevelts, Hardings, Cabot Lodges, Cal Coolidges and other such professionals, and perhaps debauch the booboisie into accepting ideas of a relatively high soundness. Not, of course, as ideas, but as emotions. As a matter of bald sense or decency, I believe, it is a sheer impossibility to induce the mob to do or believe anything. But as a matter of fear it is possible to make it do or believe almost everything. The demagogue is a man who is privy to this fact. There will come a change in the conduct of the world when men of intelligence and integrity also become privy to it, and, being privy to it, act upon it boldly and vigorously.

IV

The thing, I need not add, is not quite so simple as I have here made it appear. Before one may scare the plain people one must first have a firm understanding of the bugaboos that most facilely alarm them. One must study the schemes that have served to do it in the past, and one must study very carefully the technic of the chief current professionals. If American political biography were worth anything at all, it would be full of sound information in this department. But, as I have so often argued in this place, it is chiefly romantic and dishonest. Abraham Lincoln, one of the most adept masters of the mob that ever lived, is depicted in all the lives of him as an idealist and visionary comparable to Abelard or Thomas à Kempis. Roosevelt, a performer so bold that sometimes even his dupes revolted, is seen in the innumerable volumes of his relatives and other *pediculidae* as a moody altruist of the foreign missions variety. What is needed is a realistic investigation of the careers of all such successful virtuosi, at home and abroad, and a scientific attempt to deduce the principles upon which they worked—above all, a scientific presentation of the fundamental mental and gastric processes of the mobs upon which they exercised their art. I hereby give public notice that I am engaged upon such a treatise, and solicit the patronage of the nobility and gentry. I have been gathering materials for it, in fact, for twenty years, and some of the principles of the new science already begin to clarify in my mind. The book, when it is finished at last, may be incomplete as to its facts and inaccurate in some of its deductions, but I offer you every assurance that it will at least be honest—that it will be grounded upon what I have actually observed, in history and in current politics, and not upon *a priori* theories. Nobody realizes better than I do that I am not the ideal author for it. My interest in politics has always been that of an observer, not that of a participant, and so I lack the delicate knowledge that comes only with personal experience. But a man up a tree, in certain human concerns, sees more than a man on the ground, and perhaps that may be true also in politics. In any case, no one else seems to be willing to do the work. The practical politicians are no doubt afraid that they would be lynched if they gave the secrets of their craft away, and the political amateurs among the *intelligentsia,* as the book of Mr. Lippmann shows, are too academic to grapple with realities. So I consecrate myself to the enterprise.[1]

(June, 1922)

[1] The "treatise" mentioned here was doubtless *Notes on Democracy* (1926).

IX

Psychology

Unlike the professional psychologist, Mencken was less interested in neurotics, psychotics, and perverts of all kinds than he was in the behavior of more normal human beings. Moreover, he considered the study of crowd psychology (which, for him, implied a study of democracy) more important than the study of individual behavior.

Because of his harsh treatment of amateurs in the field, many people have assumed that Mencken failed to comprehend the importance of psychoanalysis. Actually, as "The Advent of Psychoanalysis" clearly shows, he was among the first to applaud the work being done in Vienna and elsewhere. It is noteworthy, however, that he probably considered Havelock Ellis a greater man that Freud—largely, I suspect, because Ellis was less given to theorizing than was Freud. In "The Genealogy of Etiquette" (included in Farrell's *Prejudices: A Selection*), Mencken disparaged the Freudians in memorable fashion: "The essential doctrines of Freudism, no doubt, come close to the truth, but many of Freud's remoter deductions are far more brilliant than sound, and most of the professed Freudians, both American and European, have grease-paint on their noses and bladders in their hands and are otherwise quite indistinguishable from evangelists, corn-doctors and circus clowns."

The Taste for Romance

On the first page of *The Broad Highway*, by Jeffery Farnol, we discover that young Sir Peter Vibart must wed the Lady Sophia Sefton within one calendar year or lose the fortune of five hundred thousand pounds left by that unpleasant old cannibal, his late uncle. Of course Sir Peter objects most stubbornly; of course he is inveigled by fate into Lady Sophia's presence; of course he falls madly in love with her, and of course he marries her and annexes the cash.

It is soothing to see this good old plot on its legs again. It was a favorite during the middle Victorian period, and did valiant service not only in prose fiction, but also on the stage. Toward the beginning of the present century, however, it fell into discredit and was heaved into the literary hellbox along with the lost will plot, the stern father plot and the plot of the changelings. Let Mr. Farnol be given praise for rescuing and resuscitating it. He has adorned it in the process with new gauds. He has hung upon it a fabric of astounding incident and brilliant speech. He has written, in brief, a picaresque romance of the first quality, and there is small doubt that it will have as great a success in this fair land of ours as it has already enjoyed in England.

The taste for romance, like the taste for impropriety, is inborn in all normal human beings. Some of us, in the pride of our hearts, try to convince ourselves that we have outgrown it, that daredevil adventure can no longer thrill us, that affecting love making can no longer dim our eyes—but all in vain. The day comes when we turn inevitably from Zola to Dumas, just as the day comes when we turn from Richard Strauss to Johann and from *John Gabriel Borkman* to *Sweet Lavender*. The only difference between man and man is that one pursues the unreal incessantly, while the other chases it only in moments of weakness. Examine, for example, the vaudeville audience. It is made up in part of persons who find joy in vaudeville day in and day out, and in part of persons who like it only when they are sick, miserable, overworked or drunk. Vaudeville is romantic—and no man ever quite rids himself of romance. His head may rule his heart for a week, a month or a year—but on some fatal day or other that head of his will succumb to sorrow, weariness, alcohol, an unbalanced ration, the coo of a baby or the perfume of a woman's hair, and that heart of his will go upon a debauch straightway.

The most level-headed man is probably benefited by such a spree now and then, and fortunately enough, it is always possible to have it at will. If the natural impulse fails, alcohol will do the work very well. I made the discovery years ago that three drinks of rye whiskey would double the pleasure to be got out of *Il Trovatore*. Try it yourself. And if *Il Trovatore* is not the bill, try it on *Faust* or *Traviata* or any other such maudlin stuff—or on the plays of Charles Klein or the novels of George Barr McCutcheon or the conversation of your wife. But don't try it on *Das Rheingold* or Beethoven's Ninth Symphony or the dramas of August Strindberg or the novels of Henry James! To enjoy such things you must have your wits about you—which is precisely what you must *not* have about you to enjoy romance. Vaudeville, to a man who is both intelligent and sober, is anguish unspeakable. But vaudeville to a man who lacks either intelligence or sobriety, permanently or for the moment, is often extremely agreeable. And the same rule covers romantic fiction as well, not to mention the prattle of children, parlor melodrama, politics, homiletics and the (normally) depressing business of making love to a woman.

(May, 1911)

The New Thought, Dreams, and Christian Science

The New Thought, taking it by and large, is probably the most prosperous lunacy ever invented by mortal man. Every one of its multitudinous sub-lunacies, from psychical research to anti-vaccination, from vegetarianism to the Emmanuel Movement, and from zoöphilism to Neo-Buddhism, is gaining converts daily and making excellent profits for a horde of male, female and neuter missionaries. Why work at gravel roofing or dishwashing in the heat of the day when you can open a table tapping studio in any convenient furnished room house and rake in the willing dollars of the feeble-minded, the while you make their eyes bulge and the xanthous freckles on their necks go lemon pale? As a communicative New Thinker of my acquaintance once said, Mind is a darn powerful thing. What causes chilblains to afflict the slaves of error, banjos to tinkle in dark cabinets, veiled (and fat) she-wizards to read the number of your watch, dogs to die of

nonexistent rabies, dreams to come true? Mind! Matter is a mere symbol of Mind—a sort of effigy, shadow or greenback. And of the two
halves of Mind (for, like all other things, it has two halves) the most
potent and protean is the Subconscious. It is the Subconscious that
awakens you in the middle of the night to deliver a telepagram from
the coroner at Zanesville, O., saying that your mother-in-law, dear old
girl, has just died of lockjaw. It is the Subconscious, again, that cures
you when pink pills, camomile and five doctors have failed. It is the
Subconscious, yet again, that plucks the banjo in the cabinet and lifts
the table from the floor and strokes you with damp, uncanny hands—
while the medium's *de facto* husband, out in the anteroom, is searching your overcoat for cigars.

Such is Mind. Such is the Subconscious. Such are their tricks and
their gains. And yet, for all their potency and for all their prophets
and profits, they, too, have enemies. Lamentable—but yet a fact!
There are actually scoundrels who maintain that Eusapia Palladino,
with the lights up and her feet nailed to the floor, could not lift a
table, nor even a footstool—that a Christian Scientist, held under
water for twenty minutes, would infallibly drown—that when Katie
King looked at Sir William Crookes she could scarcely throttle her
guffaws—that psychotherapy is by Emerson's Essays out of Peruna—
that poor old Lombroso was an ass—that the influence of Mind upon
the liver is to the influence of Liver upon the mind as a wart is to
Ossa.

And now comes a new heretic—Dr. Havelock Ellis, to wit—with
the scandalous allegation that the true meaning of a dream about a
murder is not that the dreamer is soon to be married, or that his
brother Fred, in Texas, has been trampled to death by hippopotami,
or that the Athletics will win the pennant, but that deep down in the
dreamer's innards, somewhere south of his Tropic of Cancer, the cartilages of last night's lobster are making a powerful resistance to
digestion. In brief, Dr. Ellis presumes to maintain, in *The World of
Dreams,* his new book, that dreaming is a physical business, almost as
much so as snoring, and that the small part played in it by Mind is
usually that of a low comedian.

Did you ever dream that you were walking in air—that you were
going upstairs at a gallop, but with your feet just missing the stair
treads? Early in life, before I took to hard labor and ceased to dream,
I used to dream that dream very often. Other folk tell me that they

know it, too; Dr. Ellis says that it is very common in the young. Well, what causes it? The theosophists say that it is not a dream at all, but a real experience—that the astral body takes wing in the night and goes upon wild jaunts among the stars. The psychical researchers hold it to be either reminiscent or prophetic—a memory of something forgotten or a prevision of something to come. No doubt the Babists, the Swedenborgians, the Emmanuel Movers and the crystal gazers have other explanations—all more or less abstruse and all absurd. As for Dr. Ellis, he has a theory, too, but it is not abstruse a bit, and neither is it absurd.

Such dreams of flying, he says, are probably caused at bottom by respiratory and cardiac disturbances, the effect of sleeping in a constrained position. To the dulled brain goes a vague message that the lungs and heart are laboring, and at once an effort is made to account for the fact. What, in everyday experience, gives those organs their hardest strains? Why, the act of running upstairs, of course. It is the most violent exercise ever undertaken by the ordinary human being —and the young, to be sure, indulge in it more than the ancient and paunchy. So the brain, but one-tenth awake and one-twentieth intelligent, decides that a journey upstairs is under way. But how explain the element of aviation—the impression that the feet are not touching the stair treads? Easily enough. When the body is going to sleep it is the peripheral nerves—that is to say, the nerves just beneath the skin —that go to sleep first. Some time before the brain itself is quite inert, the skin has lost all sensation. By now, perhaps, you see what happens. The brain formulates a muddled idea of going upstairs, but no appropriate sensory impressions come from the feet. Therefore the idea that the feet are not touching the stairs is superimposed upon the first idea, and the result is that vague dream of walking in air which most of us know.

I have here lifted but one page from Dr. Ellis's book, and that one by no means the most interesting. He has put together what must stand for a long time as the shrewdest and most comprehensive treatise upon dreams in the English language. As those readers who have read his *Man and Woman* and his *Studies in the Psychology of Sex* are aware, he is a psychologist who adds to a native ingeniousness a thorough acquaintance with the latter day psychological literature of Germany, France and Italy. In the present book he rehearses the experiments and observations of every recent investigator of importance and weighs their ideas with judicial fairness. His own conclusions are put forth, of course, not as definite theories, but merely as hypotheses—but even when they fail to account for all of the known facts, they never go counter to any of those facts. If you are at all interested in the mechanism of existence you will find his volume enormously entertaining. He is a diligent and sapient inquirer, a brave enemy of pseudo-scientific flapdoodle, a writer of sense and charm.

Another scientific fellow with something worth hearing to say is Dr. Leon C. Prince, who riddles the sophistry of the Eddyites in *The Sense and Nonsense of Christian Science*. Dr. Prince, let it be clearly understood, is no mere heaver of half-bricks. On the contrary, he has a kindly feeling for the Christian Scientists and is ready to admit that, judged empirically, their magic is genuine enough. That is to say, he grants them some of their alleged cures—not all, by any means, but still an appreciable some. Going further, he agrees with the Christian Scientists in their philosophical idealism, in their belief that the universe was created and is maintained by intelligence, and that all material things are mere condensations, as it were, of that intelligence. But to hold to that belief, he points out, by no means involves denying the practical reality of experience. A *streptococcus* and the first reader of the Mother Church may be equally ideal and apparitional, and yet their mutual reaction is real enough—to them. Let the *streptococcus* invade the first reader and the latter will inevitably fall ill, and though it may ease his mind to deny that the *streptococcus* is there, and even help him to get well, the *streptococcus* will be there all the same.

The Christian Scientists, however, deny that it is there; and in support of their denial they argue that the apparent existence of all such carnivora is a mere illusion of mortal mind. But what is mortal mind? Nothing—or, as Mrs. Eddy once said, "nothing claiming to be something." But how can nothing produce an effect which is undoubtedly something—the effect, to wit, of being ill—the sensation of pain? The Christian Scientists reply that it can't: that this sensation is a pure illusion, that no pain is actually experienced. And here, of course, they go counter, not only to the overwhelming and indubitable experience of the human race, but also to the plain rules of common sense, for they speak of a thing as having illusions and in the next breath they declare that it does not exist. To have any experience whatever, whether real or illusory, a thing must obviously exist. Dead men, as someone has said, tell no tales, and neither do they see ghosts or suffer from imaginary pains. To be fooled a thing must first *be*. The imaginary cannot imagine. And so it follows that, if mortal mind experiences illusions, then mortal mind cannot be an illusion itself.

But halt—let us have done with such philosophical grappling! The Christian Scientists, I am well aware, have an answer to the objections I have here tried to put forward, and I, in turn, have an answer to their answer. Going further, they have an answer to my answer to their answer, and I have an answer to their answer to my answer to their answer. The debate stretches out infinitely; I prudently retire at the end of the first round, with my wind still in me, my eyes unblacked and all of my teeth in my gums. The discussion in Dr. Prince's excellent little book is far more interesting and valuable than I could hope to make it, for Dr. Prince is a better philosopher than I am, and besides, he is a fairer man. Fairness, indeed, is the hallmark of his work. The Christian Scientists will go far before they find a critic so liberal and generous, and at the same time so logical and shrewd. When you tire of novels, get his book. It is short enough to be read at one sitting, and good enough to be reread at some other sitting.

(September, 1911)

Zuleika Dobson

The good folk of the Middle Ages, tiring anon of pouring out their obeisance and their cash at the feet of their lords spiritual, had a habit of declaring an occasional hiatus or interregnum, during which the truly prudent bishop retired to some convenient catacomb or other secure place of retreat, while the town scaramouche discharged witticisms from the episcopal throne, and a red flag floated from the cathedral spire, and the baptismal font was filled with malt liquor, and all the bad boys played at "I-spy" and Crusader-and-Saracen in the nave. Such was the so-called *Festa Asinoria*, the feast of asses (or, in later times, of fools), of which you will find much indignant discourse in the ancient tomes.

It came, as a rule, once a twelve-month, usually just before Christmas, but in some dioceses it was a vagrant and movable feast, to be proclaimed and celebrated whenever the burden of reverence began to put unbearable strains upon the popular spine. Whether the ass from which the festival took its name played the role of bishop or merely that of bishop's steed—this the antiquaries fail to tell us. Sometimes perhaps the one, and sometimes the other. But at all events the long-eared animal was always the center of the merrymaking, and the rest of the merrymakers took their cue from his character. Light and cheerful doings, indeed, and full of the innocent sacrileges of those days of faith. To charge the censer with old boot heels and cows' hair, to wallop the mock bishop with slapsticks and bladders, to put geese in the chancel and dunce-caps on the sacred images, to imitate the rough sports of Gargantua in the cathedral of Notre Dame and of Pantagruel on the day of Corpus Christi—all this was part of the fun. And then, the *Festa Asinoria* being over and the common people purged of their profane bile, back they went to orderly worship, and the bishops, emerging from the bowels of the earth, once more took their lawful toll of genuflections and currency.

Well, well, a pretty tale, to be sure, but what is the moral of it? The moral—already visible to the astute—is simply this: that, far from being corrupting, it may be actually healthful now and then to ride a jackass into church. And why? Because a too steady piety, like a too steady sobriety, is dangerous to body and soul. Absolute virtue, turning upon itself, may easily become the worst of vices. A man may die of thirst even more quickly than he may die of drink. Those medieval burghers, with the rude wisdom of lowly folk, knew the fact and profited by their knowledge of it. They were always much the better, I believe, for their heathenish flings. Thus discharging, at one devastating salvo, a whole year's accumulations of profanity and indecency, of contumacy and rebellion, they were left clean of all such moral ptomaines. Not a snicker lingered; not a doubt remained in their craws. And so completely restored by their own dionysian act to a pristine docility and state of grace, they were willing and even eager to meet the exactions of their ecclesiastical superiors, and until another fit came on them their loudest bellow in the sanctuary was as the faint harmonic whisper of an undertaker.

All of us are helped by such treasons to the things we believe in, by such premeditated debauches of backsliding and ribaldry. If a *Seidel* of Pilsner is worth twenty cents to you or me, it must be worth twenty dollars to the average rabble rouser of the Anti-Saloon League; for whatever his moral horror of the great Bohemian brew, he has veins and arteries like our own, and those veins and arteries shriek piteously now and again for something with more body to it and more steam in it than well water. And if a single hearty "damn," bursting from his surcharged system, can reduce the temperature of a steamboat mate by one hundred thousandth of a degree Fahrenheit, then the same "damn," loosed by an archbishop, may conceivably save him from apoplexy. So speaks logic—and speaking so, it gives me excuse for advising you to read *Zuleika Dobson*, by Max Beerbohm, a burlesque novel. We of this club are in the habit of taking novels very seriously. We burrow, month by month, with perfectly straight faces, into their abysmal problems of psychology and physiology, of politics and sex; we engage in laborious and scientific dissections of their technique; we examine each new one in the light of the classics of its own purport and quality; we constantly assume, as a first principle, that the novel is an art form as dignified as the epic or the symphony, and that it is worth while to give time and thought to it; we insist that, whatever its play of humor, it deal earnestly with the human beings it presumes to depict; even when we ourselves indulge in titters and cat calls, it is only because we hope thus to punish trifling by the novelist himself. Therefore let us put away for a hygienic moment or two all such fine assumptions and sobrieties, and take a heretical vacation. In brief, let us guffaw a bit with Max, for this burlesque novel of his is a burlesque upon the whole art of novel writing, upon the whole science of hypothetical psychology—and what is more, it is genuinely and uproariously funny.

Naturally enough, *Zuleika Dobson* is a love story, for the novel, to nine-tenths of us, is unimaginable save as a love story, and naturally enough, the heroine is a being of stupendous beauty and of even more stupendous charm. By profession a stage magician, she is yet a lady —for isn't her grandfather warden of Judas College, Oxford?—and being a lady, she is a hundred times as seductive as if she were an ordinary houri of the boards. Before her greatest romance begins she has slain her thousands on two continents. In Paris, whither she went for a month's engagement, she struck the whole town dumb. "The jewelers of the Rue de la Paix soon had nothing left to put in their windows— everything had been bought for 'La Zuleika!' For a whole month bac-

carat was not played at the Jockey Club—every member had succumbed to a nobler passion. For a whole month the whole demi-
monde was forgotten for one English virgin." And after that first triumph capital after capital groveled at her feet. In Berlin the students
escorted her home every night with torches, and Prince Vierfünfsechs-
Siebenachtneun wooed her so wildly that the Kaiser had to lock him
up. In St. Petersburg the Grand Duke Salamander-Salamandrovitch
deluged her with precious stones and nearly died of love of her. In
Madrid the most famous living matador committed suicide in the
plaza de toros because she would not smile upon him. In Rome the
Pope launched a bull against her—and in vain. In Constantinople the
Sultan offered her Divan A-I-Center in his seraglio. In New York she
held the front pages of the newspapers for weeks and weeks and all
the millionaires of Pittsburgh combined to entertain her.

And yet when Zuleika goes to Oxford to pay a filial visit to her venerable grandpa, her own heart is still whole. Sick unto death of
homage, the thing she craves is scorn. Her dream is of a hero, young,
handsome and rich, who will look into her violet eyes—and then turn
away with a sneer. She is in search of the lordly, magnificent, tyran-
nical male, of the *Übermensch* who will conquer and subdue her, of
the master foreordained. Is he at Oxford? Is he among those pink
youths who already, before she has been in the town half an hour,
begin dashing off sonnets to her eyebrows and hexameters on her
nose? Alas, it scarcely seems probable! But halt—what of this splendid
fellow who comes galloping down the street, this Adonis upon a polo
pony, with his riband of blue and white—what, in brief, of the young
Duke of Dorset? A misogynist, indeed, to match Zuleika, the misan-
thrope! He, too, sickens of admiration, particularly of that admiration
which spans the gulf of sex. A nobleman, a millionaire and a celebrity
at three and twenty, his dream is of a woman who will not bore him
with her love. He has tasted nearly all of the sweets of life. He has
seen the world; he has taken Oxford's prizes; he has made a name for
himself in the House of Lords; he has won the Garter; he has known
passion and conquest. All he asks now is peace—and the brand of
peace he pictures to himself is that which has its roots in celibacy, in
existence *a cappella*.

Therefore when he and Zuleika face each other across the dinner
table of the innocent old warden of Judas on the evening of her ar-
rival, the ensuing duel of sex is necessarily of unexampled fury and fe-

rocity. Will Zuleika, by falling in love with the Duke, send him flying in dismay, or will the Duke, by falling in love with Zuleika, disgust her and freeze her? The gross evidence, the outward and visible play of events, seems to point to the former consummation. That is to say, the Duke, after a terrific exchange of malicious animal magnetism, suddenly dashes from the table and the house, leaving a half-peeled orange on his plate. Has Zuleika fallen in love with him and so scared him out of his boots? For the moment, yes. But when early next morning she pursues him to his rooms, bent upon worshiping him for his heartlessness, she makes the staggering discovery that his flight was really inspired not so much by fear of *her* love as by horror at his own. In brief, the Duke has fallen in love with Zuleika as she has fallen in love with him—and that very fact of course makes it impossible for her to love him further. Her quest is for a man who can resist her, for a man unshaken by her charms, for a man arctic enough to flout her and laugh "Ha, ha!" at her devotion. The more the Duke pleads his suit the less she loves him. In the end she tells him calmly that she can never, never be his.

Ah, fatal girl! Little do you reck the depth and virulence of that ducal passion! Is Dorset to be put off like a common admirer? To be sure he is not. Self-respect, duty to his noble order, the honor of his ancient race—all demand some overt act of protest, some awe inspiring and memorable signal of rebellion. What suggests itself? Suicide, of course—the last, sublime act of many a greater man. The Duke decides to drown himself—to drown himself in the river Isis on the day of the Magdalen-Judas boat race, and in the full robes and regalia of the Most Noble Order of the Garter. And to that desperate act, after one or two false starts, he actually proceeds. Just as the boats heave into view flying down the river, he wraps the mantle of his high dignity about him, cries "Zuleika!" in a loud voice, and plunges from the upper deck of the Judas houseboat. And what is more, every other undergraduate in Oxford plunges with him! All love Zuleika, and all wither in her scorn. The Duke, their leader, has shown the way. By squads and companies, by battalions and regiments, they follow him. The river is full of drowning youths. The very crews jump from the boats. And not a soul is saved!

So much for the machinery of the tale. It is in its detail of course that Max particularly shines—in the little sidelights upon Oxford legends and prejudices, in the little flings at Oxford snobs and mag-

nificoes. You will miss, I dare say, some of the best of its whimsicali-
ties, as I have doubtless done, for only an Oxford man may be expected to understand them all; but even so the book will delight you
from cover to cover. The style of Max was never more fantastically
graceful; the vocabulary of Max was never more sonorous and amazing. I rescue "dulcify," "daedal," "ineluctable," "peripety," "orgulous,"
"splendent," "meiosis," "aseity," "otiose," "commorient" and "ataraxy"
—a hundred others float down the stream. And nothing could be more
hilarious than some of the colloquies à faire: for example, that between
Zuleika and the Duke, when he tries to stagger her with his splendors,
and that between the Duke and his undergraduate followers, when he
tries to dissuade them from their last grim following, and that between Zuleika and her ancient granddad, after the Isis has swallowed
the whole youth and chivalry of Oxford. Here indeed Mr. Beerbohm
has made a first rate contribution to a department of humor which
shows remarkably few good examples in English, for though comic
novels are common among us, burlesque novels are very rare. Setting
aside Mark Twain's medieval romance and the parodies of Thackeray
and Bret Harte—and a parody of a definite novel or of a definite novelist's mannerisms is not quite the same thing as a burlesque of the
Novel—what, in truth, have we to show?

(July, 1912)

Havelock Ellis

More bosh. To wit, in *The Dream of Love and Death,* by Edward
Carpenter, an English platitudinarian who seems to be arousing a
good deal of excitement of late among the virgin reviewers. What is
genuinely valuable in the book is a wordy paraphrase of chapter
eleven of the last volume of Havelock Ellis's exhaustive *Studies in the
Psychology of Sex.* What Ellis pleads for there is a frank recognition
of the essential decency of passion, a recognition granted as a matter
of course by the Turks, the Hindoos, the Japanese and all other truly
clean-minded races. It is only among Christian peoples that so palpable a fact is denied. We alone make the supreme experience of life

a shame and a hissing, to be mentioned, when mentioned at all, as something intolerably disgraceful and degrading. Ellis, of course, speaks plainly, but Carpenter, having a chemically base audience in front of him, must needs put his argument in the form of vague hints and obfuscatory half-statements. How many readers, unacquainted with Ellis beforehand, will ever know what Carpenter is driving at on Page 41, in the paragraph beginning "And if the man"? Not many, I respectfully opine. And yet it would be unwise, I suppose, if not downright dangerous, to speak more plainly. I, myself, in this present paragraph, hem, haw and keep off the actual subject. Carpenter, at worst, has courage enough to touch its outermost frontiers. But why, having tackled so brave a job, does he then turn his book into a treatise on the occult, with anecdotes about spooks, spectral hands, poltergeists and other such preposterous fowl? Why drag in Katie King, that ancient fraud? Why try to make it appear that the properties of radium give support to the puerile tricks of spiritualist mediums? Why destroy whatever value the book may have by leading it from sense into platitudes and from platitudes into piffle?

One indubitable use, however, remains to its credit: it may inspire the more intelligent reader to go to Havelock Ellis himself and so make him drink of a spring truly Pierian. Ellis is one of the most learned and clear-minded Englishmen of our time. A psychiatrist, a psychologist and a sociologist of very high rank, he is also a charming writer and a sound critic. He is the editor of the invaluable Contemporary Science Series, and has himself contributed several volumes to it. He is one of the editors of the excellent Mermaid Series of old English dramatists. He was one of the first Englishmen to write intelligently about Ibsen. His book on the causes and processes of dreams is the best in any language. Saving only Sir Francis Galton, he has made a more valuable contribution to the statistical study of genius than any other man. His great monograph on *Man and Woman* is the starting point of every current discussion of secondary sexual differences.

But above and beyond all these works are his six volumes of *Studies in the Psychology of Sex*. Here we have the labor of years, the labor of a scientific Hercules. Every pertinent fact and observation, in whatever language, is set down, weighed, appraised. The abysmal delvings of Germans and Russians, the gay flights of Frenchmen and Italians, the tedious figurings of Englishmen and Americans, even the views and traditions of Arabs and Chinese, are put in order, compared, digested, studied. And to all this staggering welter of material, to all this homeric accumulation of data, Ellis brings the path-finding faculty of a trained and penetrating mind. He has that supreme sort of common sense which is the mother and father of genuine science. He discerns the general fact in the Alpine rubbish heap of special facts. The result is a magnificent contribution to human knowledge—a contribution not immediately assimilable, of course, by the folk of Christendom, but one that they must eventually get down, in the sugar-coated pills of lesser sages, if they are ever to shake off their abominable doctrine that the only decent way to discuss the most important of all the facts of life is by silly indirection and with nasty giggles.

(December, 1912)

Osculation Anatomized

The Labial Infamy.—Despite a great laboriousness in the collection of materials, I can find nothing that is novel and little that is sound in *A Bundle of Kisses,* by Dr. R. McCormick Sturgeon, a York, Pa., savant. Dr. Sturgeon, indeed, takes a thoroughly sentimental view of the thing he presumes to vivisect, and so his book is no more than a compendium of mush. Even when, putting on a scientific black cap, he essays to describe the act of osculation in cold terms, he gets no further than a sonorous gabble about heaving bosoms, red lips, electric sparks and such-like imaginings. The truth is that the physiology of the kiss, like its psychology, has been unaccountably neglected. What reason have we for believing, as Dr. Sturgeon says, that the lungs are "strongly expanded" during the act? My own casual observation inclines me to hold that the opposite is true: that the lungs are actually collapsed in a pseudo-asthmatic spasm. Again, what is the ground for arguing that the lips are "full, ripe and red"? The real effect of the emotions that accompany kissing is to empty the superficial capillaries and so produce a leaden pallor. As for such salient symptoms as the temperature, the pulse and the rate of respiration, the learned pundit passes them over without a word. Mrs. Elsie Clews Parsons would be a good one to write a sober and accurate treatise upon kissing. Her books upon *The Family* and *Fear and Conventionality* indicate her possession of the right sort of scientific learning and accuracy. Even better would be a tome by Havelock Ellis, say, in three or four volumes. Ellis has devoted his whole life to illuminating the mysteries of sex, and his collection of materials is unsurpassed in the world. Surely there must be an enormous mass of instructive stuff about kissing in his card indexes, letter files, book presses and archives.

Just why the kiss as we know it should have attained to its present popularity in Christendom—or, as Dr. Sturgeon puts it, its universal veneration—is one of the things past finding out. The Japanese, a very affectionate and sentimental people, do not practise kissing in any form; they regard the act, in fact, with an aversion matching our own aversion to the rubbing of noses. Nor is it in vogue among the Moslems, or among the Chinese, who countenance it only as between mother and child. Even in parts of Christendom it is girt about by rigid taboos, so that its practice tends to be restricted to a few occasions. Two Frenchmen or Italians, when they meet, kiss each other on both cheeks. One sees, indeed, many pictures of General Joffre thus bussing the heroes of Verdun; there has even appeared in print a story to the effect that one of them objected to the scratching of his moustache. But imagine two Englishmen kissing! Or two Germans! As well imagine the two former kissing the two latter! Such a display of affection is simply impossible to men of Northern blood; they would die with shame if caught at it. The Englishman, like the American, never kisses if he can help it. He even regards it as bad form to kiss his wife in a railway station, or, in fact, anywhere in sight of a third party. The Latin has no such compunctions. He leaps to the business regardless of place or time; his sole concern is with the lady. Once, in driving from Nice to Monte Carlo along the lower Corniche road, I passed a hundred or so open taxicabs containing man and woman, and fully 75 per cent of the men had their arms around their companions, and were kissing them. These were not peasants, remember, but well-to-do persons. In England such a scene would have caused a great scandal; in most American States the police would have charged the offenders with drawn revolvers.

The charm of kissing is one of the things I have always wondered at. I do not pretend, of course, that I have never done it; mere politeness forces one to it; there are women who sulk and grow bellicose unless one at least makes the motions of kissing them. But what I mean is that I have never found the act a tenth part as agreeable as poets, the authors of musical comedy librettos, and (on the contrary side) chaperons and the *gendarmerie* make it out. The physical sensation, far from being pleasant, is intensely uncomfortable—the suspension of respiration, indeed, quickly resolves itself into a feeling of suffocation—and the posture necessitated by the approximation of lips and lips is unfailingly a constrained and ungraceful one. Theoretically, a man kisses a woman perpendicularly, with their eyes, those "windows of the soul," synchronizing exactly. But actually, on account of the incompressibility of the nasal cartilages, he has to incline either his or her head to an angle of at least 60 degrees, and the result is that his right eye gazes insanely at the space between her eyebrows, while his left eye is fixed upon some vague spot behind her. An instantaneous photograph of such a maneuver, taken at the moment of incidence, would probably turn the stomach of even the most romantic man, and force him, in sheer self-respect, to renounce kissing as he has renounced leap frog and walking on stilts. Only a woman (for women are quite devoid of aesthetic feeling, as their choice of mates shows) could survive so damning a picture of the thing she venerates.

But the most embarrassing moment, in kissing, does not come during the actual kiss (for at that time the sensation of suffocation drives out all purely psychical feelings), but immediately afterward. What is one to say to the woman then? The occasion obviously demands some sort of remark. One has just received (in theory) a great boon; the silence begins to make itself felt; there stands the fair one, obviously waiting. Is one to thank her? Certainly that would be too transparent a piece of hypocrisy, too flaccid a banality. Is one to tell her that one loves her? Obviously, there is danger in such assurances, and beside, one usually doesn't and a lie is a lie. Or is one to descend to chatty commonplaces—about the weather, literature, politics, the war? The practical impossibility of solving the problem leads almost inevitably to a blunder far worse than any merely verbal one: one kisses the cutie again, and then again, and so on, and so on. The ultimate result is satiety, repugnance, disgust; even the girl herself gets enough. . . . I lament that Dr. Sturgeon discreetly dodged all such inquiries. His book will please the mushy, for it is full of saccharine evasions; but it is quite worthless as a contribution to psychology.

(August, 1916)

The Advent of Psychoanalysis

Hard upon the heels of the initiative and referendum, the Gary system, paper-bag cookery, the Montessori method, *vers libre* and the music of Igor Feodorovitch Stravinsky, psychoanalysis now comes to intrigue and harass the sedentary multipara who seeks refuge in the women's clubs from the horrible joys of home life. The thing is much more dangerous to toy with than its forerunners in Advanced Thought, and at the same time much more fascinating—dangerous because it turns the uplift inward and may lead to sudden embarrassments, and fascinating because those embarrassments have to do with the forbidden subject of sex, the one permanent interest of all who go in skirts. Already it becomes impossible for a fashionable doctor to hold his trade without setting up a psychoanalytical laboratory behind his tile-and-nickel surgery, with a rose-tinted bunch-light to tone down his bald head, and zinc etchings of Pasteur, Metchnikoff and the Mona Lisa on the walls. Appendectomy and tonsillectomy go out of vogue, along with Bulgarian bacilli and Rabindranath Tagore. Let the correct *médecin* mention a gall-stone or an adenoid, and he appears as archaic as if he mentioned boneset tea or phlebotomy. Even nervous prostration seems to be in decay, at least under its old name. In place of all such *déclassé* whimsies of the gods the truly solvent patient now suffers from a complex complex of complexes, the mildest of which causes her to imagine that she has asthma or that there are burglars in the house, and the more gaudy of which make her dream that her husband has been poisoned by a Hindu swami or that she has been carried into captivity by a moving-picture actor eight feet high and with eyes as shining as the headlights of an automobile.

Such is the new complex complex. Such is psychoanalysis, the youngest of the arts and sciences. One snickers at it as in duty bound. It passes through the stage of buncombe, ill comprehended, infested by quacks, still a bit wobbly and uncertain. The flavor of sex in it lifts the snicker to a guffaw, for whatever is sexual, to us of English speech, belongs to humor: we evade the infernal mystery by making a joke of it. But the further I proceed through the fat tomes of the psychoanalysts the more I am convinced that, in E. W. Howe's favorite phrase, there must be something in it. The early announcements of Prof. Dr. Sigmund Freud, the founder, had an appearance of extravagance, and a critical examination of them showed that, in point of fact, some of them *were* extravagant, but the more his fundamental ideas have been put to the test the more plain it has become that they are essentially sound. As developed and modified by Adler of Vienna, by Jung of Zurich, by Ferenczi of Budapest, by Bjerre of Copenhagen, by Brill of New York, by Jones of London and by scores of other widely dispersed investigators, they have come to such a stage that both their truth and their utility begin to be manifest. On the one hand they blow away the accumulated psychological rubbish of centuries, both "scientific" and popular, and on the other hand they set up a new psychology that meets the known facts exactly, and interprets them logically, and diligently avoids all the transcendental pishposh of the past. The process of thought, under this new dispensation, becomes thoroughly intelligible for the first time. It responds to causation; it is finally stripped of supernaturalism; it is seen to be determined by the same natural laws that govern all other phenomena in space and time. And so seen, it gives us a new understanding of the forces which move us in the world, and shows us the true genesis and character of our ideas, and enormously strengthens our grip upon reality.

Freud's dependence upon the concept of the subconscious has exposed his whole system to misinterpretation, for the subconscious is a favorite stage property of psychical researchers, mental healers, East Indian "philosophers" and other such mountebanks, and has thus fallen under the suspicion of the judicious. Nevertheless, the thing exists. You are trying to remember, say, a man's name or a street address, and for the life of you you can't call it up. After half an hour you give over the effort, and go about your business. Then, of a sudden, it bobs up in your memory. Where has it been meanwhile? Was it actually forgotten, as you concluded? If so, how could it reappear? Nay, brother, it was not forgotten: it was merely buried temporarily in the sub-cellars of your subconscious, which is simply another name for that part of your memory which is unconscious. You remembered all the while, but for the time you didn't know that you remembered.

Well, it is Freud's notion that this subconscious of yours is full of such obliterated memories—that it is a sort of cold-storage warehouse for all the things that you have thought in the past and then put out of mind. Some, perhaps, have quite died; you have genuinely forgotten them. But the majority live on in a state of suspended animation. A new thought or experience may suddenly revive them; they appear without apparent reason and surprise you. And even when they don't appear clearly—that is, even when you are not plainly conscious of them—they are still there, and their influence shows itself, often mysteriously, in what you *are* conscious of—in the strange ideas that flit through your mind, in the fears and prejudices that lurk there, in the fantastic dreams that you dream, in your ravings when you are delirious or drunk, in the whole contents of your mental baggage. And the more you try to hold down the lid—the more you try to convert the unpleasantly remembered into the comfortably forgotten—the more these quasi-corpses pick at their grave-clothes, and poke their heads out of their tomb, and whisper into your inner ear, and fill you with disquiet.

The fact that a good many such throttled memories must be sexual in character is so obvious that it scarcely needs statement. Under our Christian civilization the sexual impulse is constantly under suppression. Our whole culture, in fact, is largely a conspiracy against it. Not only is it opposed outwardly by a host of social taboos, most of them in conflict with nature; it is also opposed inwardly by powerful concepts of morals and decorum. No human being, in the department of sex, is absolutely unmoral, not even a Broadway actor or a Greenwich village poetess. The worst of us hesitate, at least at times. And the best of us, giving "best" its moral significance, hesitate so habitually and with such determination that in the end the very impulse of sex seems to be extinguished, and the individual ceases, obviously in act and apparently in thought, to be a mammal. But only apparently! Here is where Freud and his friends have got farthest with their revelation. On the surface all is quiet, but down in the depths a war goes on, with nature on one side and rectitude on the other, and that war casts its uncomprehended flames and uproars through the whole consciousness, and influences the whole process of thought, and leaves its influence upon every idea, and every emotion and every dream.

This, indeed, is the crux of the matter: that ideas are determined, not alone by conscious causation, but even more importantly by unconscious causation—that the mental life of every one of us is partly the logical product of our environment, and partly a reaction from the natural desires which that environment opposes. Some of the most powerful of those opposed desires, particulary when they seem to be most thoroughly obliterated, are of a sexual character: it is not indulgence that makes that lion most exigent, but self-control. But, as Adler and Jung have shown, there are other desires in us that are powerful too, and their suppression leads to similar inflammations. For example, there is the strong yearning that Schopenhauer called the will-to-live and Nietzsche the will-to-power. It is the impulse behind all our egoistic dreams, all our secret hopes and aspirations, all our reaching out for envy, respect, consideration. But like the primary impulse of sex it is opposed implacably by the discipline that is civilization; we must all learn to renounce, to take half a loaf, to practice a certain humility. Moreover, there is something worse here: we must all learn to face the fact that we are by no means the lordly creatures that we'd like to be—that other men, in this way or that, are actually better—that even the most modest ambition is impossible of full attainment.

Out of this depressing realization arises what the psychoanalysts call the inferiority complex. The idea itself, being highly unpalatable, is put out of mind, and we try to forget it. But it lingers on in the subconscious, diligently producing toxins to flood the consciousness upstairs, and the result, on the one hand, is many a bad case of worry, many a curious delusion, many an attack of neurasthenia, and on the other hand many a high faith and resolution. The psychoanalysts still devote too much time to the former department. Their main energies are yet concentrated upon studying individual patients; they try to find out why Miss —— has succumbed to nervous prostration, and Mr. —— has suddenly forgotten how to multiply 3,654 by 1,875, and Mrs. —— has such terrifying dreams. But their progress hereafter must be from the particular to the general. They must begin to prod into wider and more normal ideas—for example, the idea of Puritanism, the idea at the bottom of such irrational beliefs as that in ghosts, the idea of uplifting, the idea that the arts are immoral, all the flatulent and imperishable ideas that afflict the human race. Here is their great chance. Here they may create an entirely new science of psychology, and take the study of mind away from the absurd college professors who now make it ridiculous, and so help man to understand himself.

As I have said, the tomes of these inquirers are very bulky. Jung's *Analytical Psychology,* translated by Constance Long; his *Psychology of the Unconscious,* translated by Beatrice Hinkle; Adler's *The Neurotic Constitution,* translated by Glueck and Lind, and Hitschmann's capital exposition of *Freud's Theories of the Neuroses,* translated by C. R. Payne, are tall, stately volumes; H. W. Frink's *Morbid Fears and*

Compulsions is nearly three inches thick and weighs two-and-a-half pounds. But there is nothing dull in these books; you will surely not fall asleep over them. Nor over Freud's *Totem and Taboo,* translated by A. A. Brill, nor over his *Leonardo Da Vinci,* nor over Bjerre's *The History and Practise of Psychoanalysis,* nor over Ferenczi's *Contributions to Psychoanalysis.* Here, indeed, is a literature of singular interest. There is in it all the horror of theology and all the fascination of fiction.

(September, 1918)

The Anatomy of Ochlocracy

I

I find myself in a rather curious difficulty about *The Behavior of Crowds: A Psychological Study,* by Everett Dean Martin, for it is a book that I have long had a secret desire and intent to write myself, and Mr. Martin casts it in almost precisely the mold that I have had in mind. All that remains for me is to give three cheers for it. It is, as I have hinted, a useful, interesting and competent work, and its appearance saves me a great deal of harsh labor, and so probably prolongs my life.

The wonder is that some other literatus did not snitch my idea (and Mr. Martin's) years and years ago. What, indeed, could be more attractive to the speculative mind than the study of the vast herds whose rages and poltrooneries give the tone to what is called modern civilization? We live in such a time as never was before on land or sea. All the old restraints upon the swinishness of men in the mass are falling away, and the world is gradually coming to be run on principles borrowed from the communal ethics and politics of wolves and hyenas—nay, of rabbits and polecats. Here, obviously, is a phenomenon of the first magnitude; here is something to arrest and engross the psychologist; here is an exhibition a million times more significant than that afforded by the bubbling up of naughty nonsense out of the subconsciouses of man-crazy women. Yet the latter is investigated with the utmost painstaking by psychologists in all the countries west of the Urals, and they put their discoveries into long shelves of fat books, whereas the former is scarcely looked into at all, and even to direct attention to it constitutes a sort of indecorum. The whole literature of crowd psychology, in fact, still consists of but three books—two by Gustave Le Bon and this one by Mr. Martin, with, maybe, Trotter's war-propaganda volume as a dubious fourth. It is as if the democratic hostility to all free inquiry, to all honest examination of basic social and political facts, to all clear and courageous thinking, had thrown around democracy itself a kind of protective armor, and so protected it effectively against even the slightest challenge. No intelligent American that I know of actually believes in democracy—that is, as we suffer and endure it in the Republic—and yet no one ever makes a headlong attack upon it. It is dirty, it is dishonest, it is incompetent, it is at war with every clean and noble impulse of man—and yet the eunuchs who write our books and profess in our colleges go on assuming that it is not only immortal, but also impeccable—that to propose mopping it up by *force majeure,* as smallpox and yellow fever have been mopped up, is a sin against the Holy Ghost.

Even Mr. Martin shows a certain yielding to that weakness. More than once he proves that he is a sound American under his skin, and hence a victim of mob thinking, particularly when he mentions the late war. Worse, the cure that he offers is typically democratic, in that it rests squarely upon a logical impossibility. What he proposes, in brief, is a revival of humanism, the liberation of the individual from crowd emotions and crowd superstitions, his education as a truly civilized man. Well, how is this education going to be accomplished, and by whom? As I have been patiently demonstrating for three or four years past, the whole educational machine in the United States has fallen into the hands of the dominant mob; an American university is now operated upon exactly the same principles upon which a Rotary Club, a Chamber of Commerce or a post of the American Legion is operated. There was a time when a pedagogue of the higher sort was a relatively free agent, and he showed the virulent self-respect which always goes with free agency: he was superior to the mob and he didn't give a hoot for the mob. But the revolt under Jackson brought him down, as it brought down all other exponents of the old individualism, and already in the thirties Emerson was lamenting his downfall and urging him to rise again. He has not risen. On the contrary, he

has kept on going down. To-day he is no more fit to liberate the spirit
of youth than a one-legged man would be fit to dance a *pas seul*. He
is pre-eminently the spokesman of current orthodoxy, the willing
agent of all sorts of disgusting crowd propagandas, the servile valet of
the unintelligent and unspeakable. Before a young man of our time
may liberate his spirit and so set up shop as a free agent in the street
of ideas, he must first wrestle with his professors, and survive the savage wallops of his professors. And if, by any chance, he escapes them,
there are higher authorities who will look to him.

II

Mr. Martin's book is a good deal better than Le Bon's. For one
thing, he applies the methods of psychoanalysis to his inquiry, without
falling into the super-sexual tosh of the usual psychoanalyst. For another thing, he points out and evades an error that lies at the bottom
of all of Le Bon's reasoning; to wit, the error of assuming that crowd
thinking is confined to the actual herd, and that educated men do not
indulge in it. This, of course, is quite untrue. All of us belong to
crowds of one sort or another, and all of us, on occasion, think as
crowd men, which is to say, emotionally, orgiastically, idiotically. The
late war offered examples innumerable, and on a colossal scale. For a
year or two the whole American people constituted a gigantic lynching party, and even the most elemental reason was adjourned. It was
physically dangerous, in those days, for an American to show any sign
that he retained his good sense. Not only did the nether mob take to
the highway, but also the corps of pedagogues aforesaid, and all the
leaders in politics, and the massed clergy, and even the literati. It will
be a curious enterprise, in the years to come, to study the phenomena
thus unveiled, and so naïvely put upon indelible record. They showed
weaknesses in the national character that must needs give a great deal
of disquiet to a reflective American, imagining that any such mammal
has survived. They showed that the American people, stripped of a
few conventional restraints, are almost unanimously without courage,
without dignity, without honor and without sense. True enough, a few
men stood out against the orgy, boldly risking their scalps to save
their faces. But how many? And how many of them were genuine
Americans, within the limits of the prevailing definitions? I'd have a
hard time naming a hundred.

Mr. Martin has relatively little to say about this war mania; he seems to avoid it deliberately. Perhaps it is as well that he does. For we are at war only occasionally, and the extravagance of the bellicosity on exhibition brings its own cure: it is a self-limiting disease. The crowd phenomena of peace times are more durable and more important. Moreover, they are grounded upon precisely the same psychological facts. The first of these facts is that an individual, when he joins a crowd, whether of life-long Democrats, Methodists or professors, sacrifices his private judgment in order to partake of the power and security that membership gives him. The second is that the crowd confines its aims to one or two simple objects, and that it holds itself together by cherishing the delusion that they are all-important and pressing for attainment. The third is that its primary motive is almost always fear, or, as Mr. Martin puts it, hate. This fear, of course, is seldom plainly stated; it is almost always concealed beneath a profession of altruism. But the profession need not deceive us. A crowd is quite incapable of altruism. The most it is capable of is to help A, to whom it is indifferent, in order to hurt B, whom it fears and hates. Beyond that it cannot go. Altruism, like honor, is the exlusive possession of individuals—and of very few individuals.

For years past I have devoted odd moments to the study of the uplifters who rage in These States—the Prohibitionists, vice crusaders, book censors, Blue Sunday advocates and other such fauna. I know a great many of them, and have had rather unusual opportunities to examine them. All of them profess to be altruists, and yet all of them, at bottom, are animated by fear. Consider, for example, the old fellows who specialize in sexual suppressions—campaigns against short skirts, peek-a-boo waists, bedroom farces, dancing, spooning in the parks, naughty literature, nude statuary, and so on. Ostensibly, what they propose to do is to save the young—especially, in Comstock's phrase, "females of immature mind." Actually, their purpose is to save themselves. In other words, they are men severely menaced by the slightest sexual provocation—men of an abnormal and often bizarre eroticism—men in constant dread that they will not be able to police themselves. To you or to me, normal men, it is difficult to understand their horror of the most banal indelicacy. The spectacle of a nude statue has no more effect on me than the spectacle of a beer-keg. When a fat woman shows me her legs, I am not filled with designs for stealing her from her husband; I am filled with thanks to God that she has a husband, and that he is watchful. And when I read such a book as *Jurgen* I do not enjoy the thrills of a country lout reading *Only a Boy* or the report of the Chicago Vice Commission behind the barn; I enjoy the far more placid delights of a somewhat elderly man hearing Brahms. Hence I do not fear such things, and have no desire to put them down. But the vice crusaders, eternally harassed by their filthy imaginations and obscene lusts, *do* fear them, just as a drunkard fears the sight of an open saloon door and the lewd, suggestive scent of mint, stale beer, cloves, pretzels, salt herring and *Blutwurst*.

In a society made up of the botched ejecta of a dozen antagonistic European, Asiatic and African societies—a society so unhealthy that the great majority of its individuals, on the psychological side, are born as pathological cases—there are many men of the vice-crusading kidney—many men who have a hard time keeping their erotic impulses within the limits of ordinary decency. These men, seeking each other for support and consolation, constitute a crowd, and it functions exactly like any other crowd. That is to say, it functions orgiastically, emotionally, furiously, without rhyme or reason—above all, without honesty or honor. As Mr. Martin shows, democracy tends to become indistinguishable from government by an endless series of just such crowds. Sometimes two of them come into collision, and while they fight it out the rest of us are at peace. But more often they help one another, as the Anti-Saloon League crowd is now helping the Blue Sunday crowd. Then their imbecile schemes to make the world better —*i.e.*, to make it safer for the sick and unfit—are embodied in draconian statutes, and the rest of us, refusing quite properly to obey such statutes, are converted into outlaws. More and more every civilized man in the United States tends to become an outlaw. More and more it becomes virtually impossible for any man of decent instincts and tastes to live in the Republic without provoking the devastating wrath of one or more of its feral and predatory crowds. As democracy is perfected—by direct primaries, the initiative and referendum, the recall, and so on—it is increasingly easy for mobs recruited from the lowest depths to put their fears into laws in this manner. The story related in William Graham Sumner's famous essay, "The Forgotten Man," is thus endlessly repeated. In order to save one mob from drinking itself to death I am forbidden to refresh myself with a *Seidel* of beer or a glass of wine. In order to curb another mob's pathological lubricity I am forbidden to read certain books or to look at certain pictures. In order to sooth the consciences of yet another mob, forever tortured by thoughts of hell-fire, I am compelled to spend one day of every week in the fashion of a prisoner in a house of correction. The Forgotten Man is the peaceable man, the well-disposed man, the man of self-respect and dignity, the man healthy in mind and body. He is the arch-butt, the eternal enemy of democracy. . . .

Don't miss *The Behavior of Crowds*. There are gaps in it, but it shows the way. Let us hope that other psychologists will give up their current follies and go after Mr. Martin along that way.

(February, 1921)

X

The Critic as Demolition Expert

In an effort to review or at least notice anywhere from ten to thirty books a month, Mencken read a vast amount of trash during his years as book critic. Benjamin De Casseres commented on the high price Mencken paid to be a literary critic: "My God!, the years Mencken has spent—wasted—in mentally rolling in tons and tons of dried dung: American fiction! Can he ever be cleansed? Such is the price an honest workman must pay for thoroughness. (Dante's River of Dung —was that a vision of American fiction to come?)" With all due respect for De Casseres' sympathy, I doubt that the years were wasted. After all, Mencken's *destructive* criticism probably did more to create a sophisticated reading public than did all the constructive criticism written between 1890 and 1920. Furthermore, Mencken quite frankly delighted in applying the sword to incompetent work, particularly if it was pretentious as well as foolish. The writers he garroted were often popular at the time of their execution; they are today, almost without exception, forgotten.

Mencken employed a number of varying rhetorical devices to carry out his demolition work. He sometimes simply quoted a few lines of a work, thus allowing the author to indict himself. Then again, he sometimes paraphrased a work, making no comment on its quality. At other times he employed what might be called a "frontal assault" technique. Very seldom does anything like moral indignation mar his satire; rather, he used laughter, the greatest satiric weapon, to deflate the flatulent and waylay the idols of the marketplace. In his definition of "The Iconoclast," Mencken expressed a belief that governed a large part of all his writing: "The iconoclast proves enough when he proves

[157]

by his blasphemy that this or that idol is defectively convincing—that at least *one* visitor to the shrine is left full of doubts. The liberation of the human mind has been best furthered by gay fellows who heaved dead cats into sanctuaries and then went roistering down the highways of the world, proving to all men that doubt, after all, was safe —that the god in the sanctuary was a fraud. One horse-laugh is worth ten thousand syllogisms."

The Way to Happiness

And now let us jump from Paradise to Gehenna, which is to say, from the three excellent books we have been discussing to the Rev. Thomas Dixon's *Comrades*. The first chapters of this intolerably amateurish and stupid quasi-novel well-nigh staggered me, and it was only by tremendous effort that I got through them at all. After that, I must confess, the task became less onerous, and toward the end the very badness of the book began to exercise a nefarious fascination. I was exploring new worlds of banality, of vapidity, of melodrama, of tortured wit. I felt the thrill of the astronomer with his eye glued upon some new and inconceivable star—of the pathologist face to face with some novel and horrible *coccus*. So I now look back upon my two hours with *Comrades*, not with a shudder, but with a glow. It will lie embalmed in my memory as a composition unearthly and unique—as a novel without a single redeeming merit. It shows every weakness, fault, misdemeanor known to prose fiction, from incredible characterization to careless proofreading, and from preposterous dialogue to trashy illustrations.

No, I am not going to tell you the plot. Buy the book and read it yourself. The way to happiness lies through suffering.

(April, 1909)

To Drink or Not to Drink

Alcohol, by Dr. Henry S. Williams, is a chapbook against the most delightful of all juices. Dr. Williams is no blowzy evangelist, howling in a gospel tent, but a pathologist of learning and intelligence. The question as to whether a wine-bibber can ever hope to go to Heaven does not interest him. All he seeks to discover and set forth is the effect of alcohol upon the mental and bodily machinery. His conclusion seems to be that that effect is constantly pernicious. Even in small doses, he says, alcohol attacks the vital organs, interferes with the mental processes and promotes the growth of the germs of disease. The man who absorbs even as little as one ounce of alcohol a week is appreciably less valuable as a citizen than the man who absorbs none at all.

The Doctor's statistics are overwhelming, and his conclusions, on their face, seem to be perfectly sound; but, like all students of tables and percentages, he is often unable to see the facts for the figures. He proves, for example, that 50 per cent, more or less, of all criminals are devotees of the stein and goblet, and he seems to conclude therefrom that alcohol is responsible for 50 per cent of all crime. A moment's reflection will show the fallaciousness of this. The same mode of reasoning, indeed, will prove that alcohol is responsible for 50 per cent of all poetry, 60 per cent of all philosophy, 70 per cent of all prose fiction and 99 per cent of all music.

The notion that teetotalers, as a class, are more valuable to the race than moderate drinkers is one that we should not accept with too much alacrity. Drink, true enough, is responsible for many crimes of violence, but such crimes, in the last analysis, are less harmful to society than those done in cold blood. And your cold-blooded criminal, whether he be a burglar, a Mormon elder, or a Tammany leader, is almost always assertively sober. In its long journey down the ages, indeed, the chief burdens of the water wagon have been vileness and theology. It was a teetotaler, I have no doubt, that gave us the doctrine of infant damnation, but it was a joyful, clean-minded pothouse athlete that gave us *Much Ado About Nothing.*

Dr. Williams's proofs that total abstinence is necessary to extreme longevity are convincing without being impressive. Before the human race will accept the conclusions he draws from them, it must first accept the theory that the usefulness and agreeableness of life are to be measured by its duration, and by its duration only. No such theory is held today by sane men. We estimate an individual life, not by its length, but by its breadth. Fifty years of Shakespeare were worth more to the world than the innumerable hundreds of all the centenarians that ever lived.

I voice these modest objections, not because I hold a brief for alcohol, but because I want to show that the fearsome figures of the anti-rum crusaders are not to be taken too seriously. The ideal of human existence that they have before them is not that of intelligent, efficient men. It is too austere, too drab, too nearly bloodless. They forget that there is such a thing as an art of life—that civilization, at bottom, is really a successful conspiracy to defy and nullify the simple laws which secure the perpetuation of the protozoa. The physical act of reading a book obviously shortens life, for it not only strains the eyes but also tends to compress the lungs and other viscera and to atrophy the disused muscles of leg and arm; but the man of thirty who has read many books is more creditable to the race, all other things being equal, than the man of ninety who has merely lived ninety years. The argument for alcohol, though by no means identical, is at least similar. Its crimes cry aloud to heaven, but its services are not to be forgotten. When we are told that it makes life shorter, let us remember that, by dulling the tragedies of existence and heightening the joys, it also makes life more bearable. How saith the ancient scribe? "A short life and a merry one—"

(September, 1909)

A Novel Thus Begins

Apologies for Love—by F. A. Myers. " 'Do you remain long in Paris, Miss Wadsworth?' Earl Nero Pensive [!!!!] inquired, as he seated himself beside her. His eyes, like beaming lights out of shadowless abysm, were transfixed upon her as by magic force. . . ." Thus the story begins. God knows how it ends!

(December, 1909)

The Story of a Resourceful Wife

In *The Winning Game*, by Madge Macbeth, we come upon the sad story of a charming young American girl married to a drunken and dissolute Englishman. How to save him from his highballs and his hussies—here is a tough problem indeed! But his fair young wife solves it. Against his intolerable polygamy she proceeds by disguising herself as one of his harem beauties. When in pursuance of his routine he drags her to his den of iniquity, she strips off her disguise and sears his soul with the hot flash of her indignant eye. His lesson learned, he promises to break the seventh commandment no more. But he is still a drinking man—a lusher, in fact, with one foot constantly upon the rail. How to cure him? Again that resourceful wife of his is equal to the task. What would be easier than feigning drunkenness? She is familiar with the outward symptoms of that condition, and she gives an astonishingly realistic performance. He is horrified, disgusted—cured! Such a story!

(August, 1910)

A Non-Cure for the World's Ills

"These pages have no other general purpose than to point out that we cannot create anything good until we have conceived it." Thus the eternally diverting but never converting Gilbert K. Chesterton lays down the thesis of his latest volume of philippics and exhortations, which appears between covers of a sullen, venous red and under the characteristically modest title of *What's Wrong with the World*. That thesis is a platitude so all-fired platitudinous that it stings the roof of the mouth, but even so excessively platitudinous a platitude, as Mr. Chesterton himself somewhere admits, is often quite true. So with this one. Its truth is as obvious as the rotundity of Mr. Taft. Therefore, why rage and roar over it—to the extent of nearly four hundred pages? Suppose it to be a fact that our system of education is getting us nowhere—what of it? Maybe most of us are happy where we are! Suppose it to be a fact that our 174 warring sects are getting precious few of us into Heaven—who cares? Isn't it a fact that nine-tenths of us, like the melancholy shades in *Man and Superman,* prefer Hell? Mr. Chesterton, in brief, is quite right in his diagnosis, but he makes the tremendous error of regarding native cussedness as a curable disease. As a matter of fact, we blunder along, barking our shins at every step and walking straight into every tree, not because we need quinine, but because that is the happy-go-lucky human way. If it were not for the fun of watching the other fellow gouge out his eyes and break his neck, we might stop to lament our own lacerations. As it is, we hail life as the greatest of adventures and accept without protest the trivial fact that it is meaningless. Imagine it as the orderly and tedious march Mr. Chesterton would make it, with all hands trooping up the celestial gangplank in a lockstep, forbidden to laugh, swear or eat peanuts—sweet symbols of dissolute irresponsibility—and clubbed into line by ecclesiastics on muleback! What man worthy the name would care to live?

(January, 1911)

A Faded Charmer

The wine of Chestertonian wit begins to lose its headiness and flavor, as all wine must when the seller makes endeavor, with the aid of rain water, to turn a bottle into a butt. Mr. Chesterton started out in life with a set of striking, if invalid, ideas. They were ideas such as no other sane man had publicly maintained, or perhaps even secretly harbored, since the days of Nicholas Chryffs of Kues. Because they had been dead so long, they seemed newborn. Because they were so astoundingly unsound, they carried the queer, emotional conviction of revelations. So the world heard them avidly and called for more. But, alas for Chesterton, he had no more to offer! His whole stock was exhausted before he was halfway through his second book—but he kept on and on and on. He is still printing books today, at intervals of six months—like some faded charmer who continues to smirk at us across the footlights, and rattle her dry bones, and expose her lean calves to the ribaldry of the baldheads, long after her beauty is dead. Not that

the Fat Mullah's latest volume, *Alarms and Discursions*, is entirely
without savor. Even bad wine, shamelessly diluted, is better than
water from the rain spout. Even a faded charmer, long shorn of teeth,
eyebrows and hips, may yet wring the willing tear as Marguerite
Gautier. But out of Chesterton the old shock of pleasant surprise, the
old sting of devilish and delightful heresy, has gone. He needs a holiday, a chance to catch his breath, a rest in some philosophical sanitar-
rium, a course of intellectual wet nursing. Let him put aside his pen
for a year or so and renew his stock of ideas—preferably in the moldy
tomes of the Thomists, the Scotists and the Ockhamites, where he
seems to have got the shopworn stock that he is now trying to sell for
the fourteenth time.

(May, 1911)

Earnest Messages

Various earnest messages and calls to arms from moral, political and
sociological Iokanaans—the Hon. Robert M. La Follette, the Progressive martyr; the Hon. Stephen Coleridge, the anti-vivisectionist; the
Hon. Henry Beech Needham, the tobaccophobe, and others after their
kind. The tale that the Hon. Mr. La Follette has to tell in his *Personal
Narrative of Political Experiences* is one that must wring a pearl of
sorrow from the dryest duct. He has been the target for years, it
seems, of a hellish hierarchy of political prisoners and banditti, and on
scores of occasions they have come close to letting his soul out of his
body. The thing began far back in the eighties of the present or Christian era, and has been going on without interruption ever since. The
last to try him on a grand scale was the Hon. Theodore Roosevelt—
and with more success than most. Theodore did not wield the blud-
geon personally, but employed a gang of professional bravos from the
gashouse district, including Giff Pinchot, alias Giff the Biff; Medill
McCormick, alias the Embalmer, and Gilson Gardner, alias Cyanide
of Potassium. These Catilines gave the Hon. Mr. La Follette to understand that they were in favor of him for President of the United
States, and so he jumped into his frockcoat and made a tour of the

Chautauquas, stirring up the peasantry against Prof. Taft. The peasants were duly inflamed and things had begun to look soft, as the vaudevillians say, for the Hon. Mr. La Follette—when suddenly the loathsome conspirators landed on him with a sandbag, and when he came to his senses again he found that Theodore was running in his place, and that all his eloquence had gone for naught! Well, well, enough to make any man a bit sore! No wonder the Hon. Mr. La Follette is bitter against Theodore! So would you be, dear reader, if he had played you such a trick. But did he actually play it upon the Hon. Mr. La Follette? Alas, there is a conflict of testimony here. The La Follette men say that Bob was deceived; the Roosevelt men say that he ruined himself by his Philadelphia speech, and that the common people bellowed for Theodore. To quote Hannah More:

If the whole conclave of hell can so compromise exadverse and diametrical contraditions as to compolitise such a multimonstrous maufrey of heteroclites and quicquidlibets quietly, I trust I may say with all humble reverence they can do more than the Senate of Heaven.

So much for poor Bob and his sanguinary battles for the lowly. All the combats of the Hon. Mr. Coleridge, whose *Memories* come next, have been fought for the guinea pig. He is the *shamash* and *capo comico* of the English anti-vivisectionists, and the best years of his life have been devoted to excoriating the doctors. In this pious enterprise he has been greatly helped by the fact that he is a son of the late Lord Coleridge, Chief Justice of England, but it didn't help him much when he was haled into court by a doctor who objected to being excoriated, and a rambunctious jury mulcted him in ten thousand dollars damages. Stephen's book is made up, in the main, of witless and uninteresting anecdotes about old friends of his father—Gladstone, Manning and Jowett among them. For the rest, he devotes himself to proving that all science is evil. What is it, after all, this science? Empty bosh! A curse to man! Ah, for the good old days when the madstone was a sovereign balm for hydrophobia, and whiskey yet cured snakebite, and camomile tea was pumped into the yowling young, and London was six days a-horse from Liverpool, and all Jews and Catholics were disfranchised, and men were hanged for one hundred and fifteen different crimes, and the honest English bathed but once a year, and consumptives enjoyed the sacred right of unlimited expectoration, and doctors were ranked with barbers, and the death rate was sixty per thousand of population per annum. Darn Darwin! To Hades with Huxley! A greater man than either is the Hon. Stephen Coleridge. As he hints himself, he has "retained the old and beautiful ideals of life in a faithless world," he has "kept the essential vulgarity of science out of his life," he has a mind that is "stored with the greatest and best that has been said by the wisest and holiest of all the ages." And yet, as I have remarked, that contumacious jury found against him, and he had to disgorge for fibbing about the doctor. . . . His portrait is his frontispiece. A smug gentleman in a white necktie, smooth of gill and chin, and fast growing bald. A countenance full of conscious rectitude.

The Hon. Mr. Needham's tale of his victory over tobacco, in *Divorcing Lady Nicotine*, will doubtless give joy to those who are engaged in similar struggles, but I myself am not, and pray devoutly that I never shall be; and so I am but mildly thrilled. Mr. Needham seems convinced that tobacco was fast dragging him down to his grave. It gave him gastritis, insomnia, nightmare, incipient cancer, katzenjammer, dyspepsia, distemper and that tired feeling. No wonder he tried to escape! But hundreds of thousands of us, smoking from reveille to taps, have not got any of these diseases, nor even the dizziness and trembling of the patent medicine advertisements, and so we keep on puffing away, and propose to devote the rest of our lives to the vice. . . .

(August, 1913)

Brief Dismissals

In *Mind and Spirit,* by Thomas Kirby Davis, D.D., the reverend author starts out by arguing that the common people have more sense than "the educated, the opulent and the eminent," and on page 3 he reaches the doctrine that "the mind being inferior to the spirit, the object of all education should be to enable the spirit to dominate the mind." This will be enough for the Rev. Dr. Thomas Kirby Davis, whoever he may be. In *A Primer of Higher Space,* by Claude Bragdon, we discover a theosophist trying to prove that four-dimensional bodies exist on the "astral plane." The book has been extravagantly praised by *The New York Times*. Enough! Enough! In *Syrinx*, by Mitchell S. Buck, we have a series of Grecian rhapsodies in rhythmic prose, many of them of a considerable beauty. And in *Tender Buttons*, by Gertrude Stein, we come upon a volume of harmless and amusing balderdash by the press agent of the Futurists. Examples of this sweet stuff:

Stick stick call then, stick stick sticking, sticking with a chicken. Sticking in a extra succession, sticking in.

Enthusiastically hurting a clouded yellow bud and saucer, enthusiastically so is the bite in the ribbon.

The title of the first of these miniature prose poems is "Chicken"; that of the second is "A New Cup and Saucer." It is upon such subjects and in such advanced style that Miss Stein discourses, to the edification and delight of the emancipated and forward-looking. The New York *Sun* (quoted in the canned review) says that she is "an artist in the new use of words." In the same sense exactly the Futurists of her adoration are artists in the new use of colors and line. It is the great achievement of the Futurists that they have made painting easier for the man who doesn't know how to do it than for the man who does know how to do it. It is the great achievement of Miss Stein that she has made English easier to write and harder to read. Meanwhile, it would be interesting to get an analysis of her nonsense from Dr. A. A. Brill or some other such explorer of the esoteric significance of words.

(October, 1914)

Mush for the Multitude

Midway between the tales of persecution and passion that address themselves frankly to servant girls, country school-teachers and the public stenographers in commercial hotels and those works of popular romance which yet hang hazardously, as it were, upon the far-flung yardarms of beautiful letters—midway, as I say, between these wholly atrocious and quasi-respectable evangels of amour and derring-do, there floats a literature vast, gaudy and rich in usufructs, which outrages all sense and probability without descending to actual vulgarity and buffoonery, and so manages to impinge agreeably upon that vast and money-in-pocket public which takes instinctively a safe, middle course in all things, preferring Sousa's band to either a street piano or the Boston Symphony Orchestra, and *The New York Times* to either the *Evening Journal* or the *Evening Post,* and Dr. Woodrow Wilson to either Debs or Mellon, and dinner at six o'clock to either dinner at noon or dinner at eight-thirty, and three children (two boys and a girl) to either the lone heir of Fifth Avenue or the all-the-traffic-can-bear hatching of the Ghetto, and honest malt liquor to either Croton water or champagne, and Rosa Bonheur's "The Horse Fair" to either Corot's *"Danse de Nymphes"* or a "Portrait of a Lady" from the *Police Gazette,* and fried chicken to either liver or terrapin, and a once-a-week religion to either religion every day or no religion at all, and the Odd Fellows to either the Trappists or the Black Hand, and a fairly pretty girl who can cook fairly well to either a prettier girl who can't cook a stroke or a good cook who sours the milk.

To make an end, the public I refer to is that huge body of honest and right-thinking folk which constitute the heart, lungs and bowels of this great republic—that sturdy multitude which believes in newspapers, equinoctial storms, trust-busting, the Declaration of Independence, teleology, the direct primary, the uplift, trial by jury, monogamy, the Weather Bureau, Congress and the moral order of the world—that innumerable caravan of middling, dollar-grubbing, lodge-joining, quack-ridden folk which the Socialists sneer at loftily as the *bourgeoisie,* and politicians slobber over as the bulwark of our liberties. And, by the same token, the meridional, intermediate literature that I speak of is that literature without end which lifts its dizzy pyramids from the book-counters in the department stores, and from which, ever and anon, there emerges that prize of great price, the best-seller. The essence of this literature is sentiment, and the essence of that sentiment is hope. Its aim is to fill the breast with soothing and optimistic emotions—to make the fat woman forget that she is fat—to purge the tired business man of his bile, to convince the flapper that Douglas Fairbanks may yet learn to love her, to prove that this dreary old world, as botched and bad as it is, might yet be a darn sight worse.

I offer *The Rosary, Soldiers of Fortune, Laddie, The Helmet of*

Navarre, Little Lord Fauntleroy, Freckles, Eben Holden and V. V.'s.
Eyes as specimens, and so pass on to the latest example, to wit, *Bambi*, by Marjorie Benton Cooke. By the time this reaches you, I have no doubt, *Bambi* will be all the rage in your vicinage. You will be hearing about it on all sides. You will see allusions to it in your evening paper. You will observe it on the desk of your stenographer. Your wife (if you belong to the gnarled and persecuted sex) will be urging you to read it and mark it well. You yourself (if you are fair and have the price) will be wearing a Bambi petticoat or a Bambi collar or a pair of Bambi stockings or a Bambi something-more-intimate-still. Such, alas, is the course that best-sellers run! They permeate and poison the atmosphere of the whole land. It is impossible to get away from them. They invade the most secure retreats, even the very jails and almshouses. Serving thirty days myself, under the Sherman Act, during the late rage for *The Salamander*, I had it thrust upon me by the rector of the bastile, and had to read it to get rid of him.

Wherefore, in sympathy, as it were, I have ploughed through *Bambi* in time to tell you what it is about before you have to read it yourself, thus hoping to save you from the dangers of too much joy. It is a tale, as you may suspect, of young love, and the heroine is a brilliant young lady named Miss Francesca Parkhurst, the daughter of Professor James Parkhurst, Ph. D., the eminent but somewhat balmy mathematician. Professor Parkhurst, as Bambi herself says, knows more about mathematics than the man who invented them, but outside the domain of figures his gigantic intellect refuses to function. Thus he always forgets to go to his lecture-room unless Bambi heads him in the right direction at the right hour, and if it were not for her careful inspection of his make-up, he would often set off with his detachable cuffs upon his ankles instead of upon his wrists, and the skirts of his shirt outside instead of inside his pantaloons. In a word, this Professor Parkhurst is the standard college professor of the best-sellers—the genial jackass we know and love of old. The college professor of the stern, cold world, perhaps, is a far different creature: I once knew one, in fact, who played the races and was a first-rate amateur bartender, and there is record of another who went into politics and clawed his way to a very high office. But in romance, of course, no such heretics are allowed. The college professor of prose fiction is always an absent-minded old boob, who is forever stumbling over his own feet, and he always has a pretty daughter to swab up his waist-

coat after he has dined, and to chase away the *ganovim* who are trying to rob him, and to fill his house with an air of innocent and youthful gayety.

Naturally enough, this Professor Parkhurst of our present inquest is
not at all surprised when sweet Bambi tells him that she has decided
to marry young Jarvis Jocelyn, the rising uplifter, nor even when she
tells him that Jarvis knows nothing about it, nor even when she kid-
naps Jarvis while he is in a state of coma and sends for a preacher and
marries him on the spot, nor even when she puts him to bed *a cappella* on the third floor of the house, and devotes her honeymoon to
gathering up and sorting out the flying pages of the Great Drama that
he is writing. College professors of the standard model do not shy at
such doings. Like babies in arms, they see the world only as a series
of indistinct shadows. It would not have made much impression upon
Professor Parkhurst had Bambi invited the ashman to dinner or fla-
vored the soup with witch-hazel or come to the meal herself in a bath-
ing-suit. And so it makes very little impression upon him when she
shanghais Jarvis and internes the poor fellow in the garret and kicks
up a scandal that shakes the whole town. He is dimly conscious that
something is going on, just as an infant is dimly conscious that it is
light at times and dark at times, but further than that he recks and
wots not.

Well, well, we must be getting on! What does Bambi do next? Next
she grabs a pencil and a pad of paper and dashes off a short story of
her own, with herself, Jarvis and the professor as its characters. Then
she tires of it and puts it away. Then, one day, she picks up a New
York magazine containing an offer of $500 cash for the best short
story submitted in competition. Then she gets out her story, has it type-
written and sends it in. Then—what! have you guessed it? Clever you
are, indeed! Yes, even so: then she wins the prize. And then, tucking
Jarvis under her arm, she goes to New York and tries to sell the Great
Drama. And then she spends a week of sitting in the anterooms of
theatrical managers. And then, her story being published under a *nom
de plume,* she finds herself an anonymous celebrity and is hospitably
received by the genial Bob Davis, editor of *Munsey's.* And then another and much slimmer magazine editor—no doubt G. J. Nathan,
thinly disguised—falls in love with her and gives her many valuable
pointers. And then Charles Frohman proposes to have her story dramatized, and she lures him into offering Jarvis the job, and then

pitches in and helps to perform it. And then the play makes a tremendous hit on Broadway, and she confesses the whole plot, and Jarvis falls desperately in love with her, and we part from them in each other's arms.

A sweet, sweet story. A string of gum-drops. A sugar-teat beyond compare. Of such great probabilities, of such searching reports of human motive and act, the best-seller is all compact. If you have a heart, if you can feel and understand, if your cheers for the true, the good and the beautiful are truly sincere, then this one will squeeze a tear from your leaden eye and send it cascading down your nose. And if, on the contrary, you are one of those cheap barroom cynics who think it is smart to make game of honest sentiment and pure art, then it will give you the loud, coarse guffaw that you crave. But do not laugh too much, dear friend, however hard your heart, however tough your hide. The mission of such things as *Bambi* is, after all, no mean one. Remember the fat woman—how it will make her forget that she is fat. Remember the tired business man—how it will lift him out of his wallow and fill him with a noble enthusiasm for virtue and its rewards. Remember the flapper—how it will thrill her to the very soles of her feet and people her dreams with visions of gallant knights and lighten that doom which makes her actual beau a baseball fan and corrupts him with a loathing for literature and gives him large, hairy hands and a *flair* for burlesque shows and freckles on his neck. And so to other things.

(December, 1914)

Lachrymose Love

Have you tears? Do you leak easily? Are you a weeper? Then wrap yourself in a shower-bath curtain before you sit down to *Innocent*, by Marie Corelli, for the tale wrings the lachrymal ducts with exquisite and diabolical art. Sadness, indeed, stalks through the countryside; it is a sure cure for joy in every form. I myself, a mocker at all sweet and lovely things, a professional snickerer, a saucy fellow by trade, have moaned and blubbered over it like a fat woman at *La Dame aux*

Camélias. My waistcoat is a sponge. My beard is white with salt. My eyes are a brilliant scarlet. My nose glowers and glitters with pink flames. I have blown it two hundred and eighteen times. . . .

It is Briar Farm that sees the beginning of the business—Briar Farm, that ancient and fruitful demesne, with its Tudor manor house, its stone archways, and its air of brooding and mysterious romance. The current owner of Briar Farm is Mr. Hugo Jocelyn, a bachelor of sixty-odd years and the last of the Jocelyns, or, more accurately, de Jocelins. The original de Jocelin, the Sieur Amadis to wit, came to England in the train of that Duc d'Anjou who dared the impiety of wooing the Virgin Queen, and when the Duc returned to France he remained behind, having fallen in love with Lady Penelope Devereux, a buxom baggage of the court. But this affair, alas, ended unhappily for him, for the Lady Penelope presently married Lord Rich, and, as if that were not enough, soon afterward deserted Rich to become the white slave of Lord Mountjoy. Thus removed from his heart's desire by two obstacles, both insurmountable, the Sieur Amadis fell into a state of melancholy, and retired to what is now Briar Farm to write poetry and forget his sorrows. There, "seeking Forgetfulness" he "did fynde Peace." That is to say, he "resigned the illusions of his love" and took to wife "a simple village girl, remarkable, so it was said, for her beauty, but more so for her skill in making butter and cheese." This estimable creature could neither read nor write, but in the course of time she "gave him no less than six children, three boys and three girls, all of whom were brought up at home under the supervision of their father and mother." Thereafter, as one reads in Holy Writ, Amadis II begat Amadis III, and Amadis III begat Amadis IV, and Amadis IV begat Amadis V, and so on down to the Mr. Hugo Jocelyn aforesaid, the last of all the Jocelyns.

When the story opens this ultimate Hugo is entering the last stages of arterio-sclerosis, the reward of an outdoor and moral life, and so he thinks it high time to tell his adopted daughter, Innocent by name, the story of her life. Innocent, it appears, has hitherto regarded Hugo as a widower, not as a bachelor, and herself as his actual offspring. But not so. She was left on his hands, it appears, by a Mysterious Stranger. On a dark and stormy night? Yes; on a dark and stormy night. Hugo, his haying finished, "stood under a shed in the yard and watched the rain falling in straight sheets out of a sky as black as pitch." Suddenly the stage hands in the wings began drumming upon a soap-box with two cocoanut-shells—and there entered the Stranger, mounted and with "a bundle in front of him." The tale he told was a specious one: he had a honeyed tongue, and was as handsome as James K. Hackett. The upshot was that Hugo, the poor boob, agreed to hold the drowning baby while the Stranger rode on to keep an appointment with some neighboring Earl. . . . Six months later came a couple of banknotes in an envelope, marked "For Innocent." . . . And that is the story of Innocent Fitz-Jocelyn.

Naturally enough, poor Innocent is greatly perturbed by its unfolding. Not only does it leave her vastly in old Hugo's debt, with no means of repaying him, but in addition it makes impossible her marriage with young Robin Clifford, his nephew. "What!" she exclaims. "Marry Robin *now?* How *could* I marry Robin? I'm nothing! I'm nobody! I have not even a name!" she murmurs. "Not even a name! . . . All my life seems gone—I can't realize it! . . . Only a few moments ago I was a happy girl with a loving father, as I thought—now I know I'm only a poor nameless creature—deserted by my parents and left on your hands. Oh, Dad dear! I've given you years of trouble! It's not my fault that I am what I am!" Old Hugo, seeking to comfort her, only makes things worse. That is to say, he tells her fatuously not to take it so badly—that all the folks of the neighborhood look upon her as his illegitimate daughter. (He himself, it appears, has also had an unfortunate love affair.) But this news, of course, only makes poor Innocent weep the more. "It's far worse!" she screams. "You've branded me with shame! . . . I will not be considered your illegitimate daughter any longer! It's cruel of you to have made me live a lie!—yes, cruel!—though you've been so kind in other things. You don't know who my parents were—you've no right to think they were not honest!"

Old Hugo, suddenly realizing what a mess he has made of it, tries clumsily to comfort her and calm her, but all in vain, and within the next few weeks come three incidents that double, triple and quadruple her sorrow. The first floors her that very night. She has gone to her room to weep her eyes out, locking the door behind her. Robin Clifford, hearing her sobs, decides to climb up the wistaria vine which grows beneath her window, thus hoping to divert her with a romantic love scene. But before he can get much beyond "Soft, what light through yonder," etc., a noise is heard below, and he springs down to face the menacing figure of a man. The man is Ned Landon, a neigh-

boring villain who has long plotted to get Innocent into his loathsome
clutches, and the first words Landon utters embody a plain accusation
that Robin was aloft for no good purpose—in brief, that Innocent has
just been betrayed. "You lie!" exclaims Robin, throwing back his
shoulders. "And you shall pay for it! Come away from the house and
fight like a man! Come into the grass meadow yonder, where no one
can see or hear us. Come!" But Landon, the cur, refuses. Instead, he
turns away with a sneer, "drawing his breath quickly, and looking like
a snarling beast baulked of its prey." As for Innocent, all that remains
for her to do is to settle down for a whole night of weeping.

The second blow falls upon her a week or so later. It is the death of
old Hugo. Not wholly unexpected, it yet staggers her, and what is
more, sours her. That is to say, she not only declares flatly that she
will never marry Robin now, but she even goes to the length of
scoffing at marriage itself. "It is the common lot of women," she says,
"but why they should envy or desire it I cannot think. To give one's
self up entirely to a man's humors—to be glad of his caresses, and
miserable when he is angry or tired—to bear his children and see
them grow up and leave you for their own 'betterment,' as they would
call it—oh!—what an old, old drudging life!—a life of monotony, sickness, pain, and fatigue!—and nothing higher done than what animals
can do! There are plenty of women in the world who like to stay on
this level, I suppose—but I should not like it—I could not live in this
beautiful, wonderful world with no higher ambition than a sheep or a
cow!" Robin, luckily enough, does not hear this terrible speech, but it
almost shocks Priscilla, the ancient serving maid, out of her boots. Sorrow has made a cynic of Innocent. She has embraced the abhorrent
fallacies of Nietzsche, Schopenhauer and Emma Goldman.

But the worst is yet to come. It arrives in the person of Lady
Blythe, a worldly, wicked woman with a "low, sweet, yet cold voice,"
straight out of a play by Alfred Sutro. This Lady Blythe, supercil-
iously contemplating Innocent through her *lorgnon*, at once proceeds
to business. She is none other, it appears, than Innocent's own mother,
and she confesses her shame with sneering, scoffing *sang froid*. Was
she betrayed? Bosh! Such gabble is for cheap melodramas, moving
pictures. She and Pierce Armitage, the rising young artist, simply
came to an understanding. "We went to Devon and Cornwall, and he
painted pictures and made love to me—and it was all very nice and
pretty. Then, of course, trouble came, and we had to get out of it as

best we could—we were both tired of each other and quarreled dreadfully, so we decided to give each other up. Only *you* were in the way." Poor Innocent, hearing this unblushing confession, blanches, gasps and reels ("You remind me," says Lady Blythe maliciously, "of Sarah Bernhardt in 'La Tosca'!"). It is too, too much. It was bad enough to be illegitmate, but to be the offspring of *this* creature, of *this* hussy, of *this*—

But enough! I have brought you to Page 193, and that, in truth, is as far as I could get myself. I was then in a semi-liquid condition; I had wept buckets; the bathroom was flooded; my sobs could be heard half way to Newark. Unable to stand any more of it, I turned over a whole handful of the soaked and pulpy sheets and found myself on Page 431. . . . Alas, more sorrow. Innocent is now dying—after a long and successful career, it appears, as a novelist. Robin, still faithful, reaches her room just in time to catch her as she expires. The fragile form he clasps to his bosom is "helpless, lifeless, breathless." With "a great shuddering sob of agony" he realizes "the full measure of his life's despair." Pierce Armitage, one discovers, has turned over a new leaf since we first heard of him, and is now paying his elderly devotions to a Miss Leigh, apparently an early love. But Miss Leigh, of course, refuses to marry him, and so he and she and old Lord Blythe make "a compact of affection such as is seldom known in this work-a-day world." *Lord* Blythe? Do I not mean *Lady* Blythe? Not at all. Lady Blythe, that vile one, has vanished from the scene. Perhaps she went down with the *Empress of Ireland.* Perhaps she was killed in Flanders, fighting for her country. Perhaps—who knows?—she has run over to Biarritz with Viscount Jones, the wicked heir of the Earl of Maudlin. Again, perhaps she has entered a nunnery—or a monastery. Yet again, perhaps she is in gaol. I could go on perhapsing for page after page, but all to no purpose. The simple truth is that I do not know. . . .

(February, 1915)

XI

Literati

The following reviews, summaries, impressions, and criticisms cast light on a number of the major writers of the period covered by this collection. Nietzsche, of course, had been dead eight years when Mencken began his work on *The Smart Set*, but his books were just being translated into English; and Mencken devoted several reviews to the new translations and to explaining the Nietzschean gospel to his American readers. The writings on Twain, who died in 1910, are devoted in the main to correcting what Mencken considered a false view of his true stature. Some of the writers in this group, particularly Twain and Conrad, are also represented under various other divisions. It is noteworthy that Mencken celebrated, in his early criticism, the genius of such writers as Twain and Conrad and Nietzsche and Shaw (see the chapter on dramatists); and in his final years, he lauded Lewis, Miss Cather, Anderson, and Fitzgerald.

MARK TWAIN

Popularity Index

How long does it take a new idea to gain lodgment in the professorial mind? The irreverent ignoramus may be tempted to answer six days and six nights, or just as long as it took to manufacture and people the world; but any such answer would be a gross and obvious underestimate. Some day a painstaking statistician, putting aside his beloved death rates and export tables, will take the trouble to give us more satisfactory figures. He will determine, for example, with mathematical accuracy, just how many years, months, weeks and days elapsed between the publication of *The Origin of Species* and the abandonment of Genesis by the professor of "natural history" in, say, Amherst College. He will find out for us, again, exactly how long was required to make the first scholastic convert to Sidney Lanier's sound but revolutionary theory of English verse. And finally, he will measure for us, with a dependable tape, the hiatus between the appearance of *Huckleberry Finn* and its acceptance by any reputable professor of literature, tutor, lecturer or high school pundit as a work of art of the first rank.

This last hiatus, I suspect, was of exactly twenty-five years' length, to a day. And my suspicion is grounded upon three facts, to wit:

(A) On March 15, 1885, the first American edition of *Huckleberry Finn* was published in New York.

(B) On March 15, 1910, or just a quarter of a century later, the Adams Express Company dropped on my doorstep a copy of *Essays on Modern Novelists,* by William Lyon Phelps, a Harvard master of arts, a Yale doctor of philosophy, a former instructor in English at Harvard, and now the Lampson professor of English literature at Yale.

(C) I found in that book the first honest and hearty praise of *Huckleberry Finn,* by a college professor in good standing, that these eyes had ever encountered, and the first faint, trembling admission, by the same sort of professor, that Mark Twain was a greater artist than Oliver Wendell Holmes.

After all, the sun *do* move! After all, there is yet hope! If it is possible, in the year 1910, for a college professor to admit that Clemens was a greater artist than Holmes, without thereby imperiling his salary and the honor of his craft, then it may be possible by 1950 for him to admit that Clemens was a greater artist than Irving, than Lowell, than Fenimore Cooper, than all and sundry of the unbearable bores whose "works" are rammed into the heads of schoolboys by hunkerous pedagogues, and avoided as pestilences by everyone else.

Fortunately for Dr. Clemens, he didn't have to wait for the college professors. Long before the first of them began to harbor thoughts of treachery to the *Tales of a Traveler* and *The Last of the Mohicans,* a large number of less orthodox persons began to sense the colossal merits of *Huckleberry Finn.* One of the first of them, unless memory errs, was the late Sir Walter Besant, himself a writer of experience and very much alive to the difficulties of the trade. Back in the early '90's his remarkable analysis of the story was printed, and soon afterwards a number of distinguished English critics adopted his view of it. Then came the gradual disappearance of Mark Twain, the glorified buffoon, and the rise of Samuel Langhorne Clemens, the master of letters. He lived just long enough to see the metamorphosis of his fame accomplished. Twenty-five years ago the world roared over his extravagances and swore that they were fully as funny as the quips of Tom Hood and Petroleum V. Nasby, Bill Nye and Josiah Allen's Wife. Fifteen years ago there arose folk who were rash enough to compare him, with some hesitation, to Holmes and Sam. Foote, Farquhar and Wycherley. And finally, just before he died, it began to be bruited about that a literary artist of world rank was among us, the greatest that the United States had yet produced—a greater than all our Hawthornes and Lowellses—a peer to Swift, Fielding, and Defoe—perhaps even a peer to Cervantes, Molière and Rabelais.

There is no space here to discuss the grounds for that last theory. You will find them in parts of *A Connecticut Yankee,* in parts of *A Tramp Abroad* and other books, in every line of *Huckleberry Finn.* The pictures of the mighty Mississippi, as the immortal Huck presents them, do not belong to buffoonery or to pretty writing, but to universal and almost flawless art. Where, in all fiction, will you find another boy as real as Huck himself? In sober truth, his equals, young or old, are distressingly few in the world. Rabelais created two, Fielding one, Thackeray three or four and Shakespeare a roomful; but you will find none of them in the pages of Hawthorne or Poe or Cooper or Holmes. In Kipling's phrase, Huck stands upon his feet. Not a freckle is missing, not a scar, not a trick of boyish fancy, not a habit of boyish mind. He is, in brief, Everyboy—the archetype of all other boys— the most delightful boy that ever stole a ginger cake or tortured a cat.

(June, 1910)

Twain and Howells

The name of *My Mark Twain,* by William Dean Howells, is well chosen, for the book is less a record of events than an attempt at a personal interpretation. The Mark Twain that we see in it is a Mark Twain whose gaunt Himalayan outlines are discerned but hazily through a pink fog of Howells. There is an evident effort to palliate, to tone down, to apologize. The poor fellow, of course, was charming, and there was a lot of merit in some of the things he wrote—but what a weakness he had for thinking aloud! What oaths in his speech! What awful cigars he smoked! How barbarous his contempt for the strict sonata form! It seems incredible, indeed, that two men so unlike as Clemens and Howells should have found common material for a friendship lasting forty-four years. The one derived from Rabelais, Chaucer, the Elizabethans and Benvenuto Cellini—buccaneers of the literary high seas, loud laughers, law breakers, giants of an elder day; the other came down from Jane Austen, Washington Irving and Hannah More. The one wrote English as Michelangelo hacked marble, broadly, brutally, magnificently; the other was a maker of pretty waxen groups. The one was utterly unconscious of the means whereby he achieved his staggering effects; the other was the most toilsome, fastidious and self-conscious of craftsmen. Read the book. It will amuse you; better still, it will instruct you. If you get nothing else out of it, you will at least get some notion of the abysmal difference between the straightforward, clangorous English of Clemens and the simpering, coquettish, overcorseted English of the later Howells.

(January, 1911)

Our One Authentic Giant

I believe that *Huckleberry Finn* is one of the great masterpieces of the world, that it is the full equal of *Don Quixote* and *Robinson Crusoe*, that it is vastly better than *Gil Blas, Tristram Shandy, Nicholas Nickleby* or *Tom Jones*. I believe that it will be read by human beings of all ages, not as a solemn duty but for the honest love of it, and over and over again, long after every book written in America between the years 1800 and 1860, with perhaps three exceptions, has disappeared entirely save as a classroom fossil. I believe that Mark Twain had a clearer vision of life, that he came nearer to its elementals and was less deceived by its false appearances, than any other American who has ever presumed to manufacture generalizations, not excepting Emerson. I believe that, admitting all his defects, he wrote better English, in the sense of cleaner, straighter, vivider, saner English, than either Irving or Hawthorne. I believe that four of his books —*Huck, Life on the Mississippi, Captain Stormfield's Visit to Heaven,* and *A Connecticut Yankee*—are alone worth more, as works of art and as criticisms of life, than the whole output of Cooper, Irving, Holmes, Mitchell, Stedman, Whittier and Bryant. I believe that he ranks well above Whitman and certainly not below Poe. I believe that he was the true father of our national literature, the first genuinely American artist of the blood royal.

Such is my feeling at the moment, and such has been my feeling for many a moon. If any gentleman in the audience shares it, either wholly or with qualifications, then I advise him to buy and read the biography of Mark lately published by Albert Bigelow Paine, for therein he will find an elaborate, painstaking and immensely interesting portrait of the man, and sundry shrewd observations upon the writer.

Not that I agree with Paine in all his judgments. Far from it, indeed. It seems to me that he gets bogged hopelessly when he tries to prove that *The Innocents Abroad* is a better book than *A Tramp Abroad*, that he commits a crime when he puts *Joan of Arc* above *Huck Finn*, and that he is too willing to join Howells and other such literary sacristans in frowning down upon Mark's clowning, his weakness for vulgarity, his irrepressible maleness. In brief, Paine is disposed, at times, to yield to current critical opinion against what must be his own good sense. But when you have allowed for all this—and it is not obtrusive—the thing that remains is a vivid and sympathetic biography, a book with sound merit in every chapter of it, a mountain of difficulties triumphantly surmounted, a fluent and excellent piece of writing. Paine tells everything that is worth hearing, whether favorable to Mark or the reverse, and leaves out all that is not worth hearing. One closes the third volume with unbounded admiration for the industry of the biographer, and with no less admiration for his frankness and sagacity. He has given us a rich and colorful book, presenting coherently a wise selection from a perfect chaos of materials. The Mark Twain that emerges from it is almost as real as Huckleberry Finn.

And what a man that Mark Twain was! How he stood above and apart from the world, like Rabelais come to life again, observing the human comedy, chuckling over the eternal fraudulence of man! What a sharp eye he had for the bogus, in religion, politics, art, literature, patriotism, virtue! What contempt he emptied upon shams of all sorts—and what pity! Mr. Paine reveals for us very clearly, by quotation and exposition, his habitual attitude of mind. He regarded all men as humbugs, but as humbugs to be dealt with gently, as humbugs too often taken in and swindled by their own humbuggery. He saw how false reasoning, false assumptions, false gods had entered into the very warp and woof of their thinking; how impossible it was for them to attack honestly the problems of being; how helpless they were in the face of life's emergencies. And seeing all this, he laughed at them, but not often with malice. What genuine indignation he was capable of was leveled at life itself and not at its victims. Through all his later years the riddle of existence was ever before him. He thought about it constantly; he discussed it with everyone he knew; he made copious notes of his speculations. But he never came to any soothing custom-made conclusion. The more he examined life, the more it appeared to him to be without meaning, and even without direction; the more he pondered upon the idea of God, the more a definite idea of God eluded him. In the end, as Mr. Paine tells us, he verged toward a hopeless pessimism. Death seemed to him a glad release, an inestimable boon. When his daughter Jean died, suddenly, tragically, he wrote to her sister: "I am so glad she is out of it and safe—safe!"

It is this reflective, philosophizing Clemens who stands out most clearly in Mr. Paine's book. In his own works, our glimpses of him are all too brief. His wife and his friends opposed his speculations, perhaps wisely, for the artist might have been swallowed up in the sage. But he wrote much to please himself and left a vast mass of unpublished manuscript behind him. Certainly it is to be hoped that these writings will see the light, and before long. One book described by Mr. Paine, *Three Thousand Years Among the Microbes,* would appear to be a satire so mordant and so large in scale that his admirers have a plain right to demand its publication. And there should be a new edition, too, of his confession of doubt, *What is Man?* of which a few copies were printed for private distribution in 1905. Yet again we have a right to ask for most if not all of his unpublished stories and sketches, many of which were suppressed at the behest of Mrs. Clemens, for reasons no longer worth considering. There is good ground for believing that his reputation will gain rather than suffer by the publication of these things, and in any case it can withstand the experiment, for *Huck Finn* and *Life on the Mississippi* and *A Connecticut Yankee* will remain, and so long as they remain there can be no question of the man's literary stature. He was one of the great artists of all time. He was the full equal of Cervantes and Molière, Swift and Defoe. He was and is the one authentic giant of our national literature.

(February, 1913)

Final Estimate

I

In *The Curious Republic of Gondour,* a small volume of Mark Twain's early sketches, hitherto unpublished in book-form, there is little that is of much intrinsic value, but nevertheless it is agreeable to see the collection get between covers, for even the slightest of Mark's work has its moments and should be accessible. He wrote these pieces during the year 1870, some of them for the Buffalo *Express,* in which he had lately acquired a proprietary interest, and the others for the New York *Galaxy,* to which he began contributing a monthly department in May, 1870. Some of the other things that he did for the *Galaxy* are well known, for he reprinted them in *Sketches Old and New.* Yet others were done into a book by a Canadian pirate named Backas, and this book was republished in London. I doubt that the present volume has the *imprimatur* of the Clemens executors, or of the Harpers, who control the Mark Twain copyrights. But what if it hasn't? Mark was too vast a figure in the national letters to be edited after death by executors. Whatever he wrote, signed and published during his lifetime should be decently in print today, that readers may judge it for themselves. If, in the exercise of an incomprehensible discretion, his executors venture to suppress this or that, not as of legal right but simply because it offends their susceptibilities, then it seems to me competent for any other publisher to print it as he listeth. In the present case, as I say, no lost masterpiece is revealed, but nevertheless the stuff, in the main, is quite as good as that which got into *Sketches Old and New.* Incidentally, it shows an early flowering of two qualities that marked the great humorist very broadly in his later days, to wit, his curious weakness for the gruesome and his unshakable moral passion—his high indignation at whatever he conceived to be wrong. No one familiar with the Markian canon could possibly fail to recognize the authorship of "A Reminiscence of the Back Settlements" and "About Smells." Both the former, with its Rabelaisian sporting with the idea of death, and the latter, with its furious onslaught upon the Presbyterian Pecksniff, T. De Witt Talmage, are absolutely characteristic.

Such a collection, I repeat, has its uses, and it is a pity that it is not more extensive. The official edition of Mark, published by the Harpers, shows serious defects. For one thing, it is incomplete. For another thing, the binding is gaudy and inappropriate (though not, perhaps, so horribly hideous as the Mother Hubbard binding the Harpers put upon poor Dreiser). And for a third thing, most of the illustrations of the first editions are omitted. In a few cases this last is an improvement; the pictures in *Following the Equator,* for example, were unspeakable. But just as certainly there is something lacking in *Huckleberry Finn* when it appears without the capital drawings of Kemble, and something lacking in *A Tramp Abroad* when any of those of Brown are omitted. It would be easy to reproduce all the original illustrations; it would restore to the earlier books something that is essential to their atmosphere. But it is not done. Neither is anything approaching fair progress being made with the publication of the things that Mark left in manuscript, particularly his autobiography. He himself, I believe, desired that parts of it remain unprinted for a long while—he once proposed to the Harpers a contract providing for its publication a century after his death—but certainly there are other parts that might be done forthwith. As for me, I also grow restive waiting for *Three Thousand Years Among the Microbes,* several pages of which are printed by Albert Bigelow Paine in the appendix to his excellent biography, and for the Bessie dialogues, and for *Letters From the Earth,* and for "The War Prayer," and, above all, for "1601." The last-named was once privately printed and contraband copies are still occasionally circulated. Why not a decent edition of it? If the Comstocks are capable of sufficiently throttling their swinishness to permit the open publication and circulation of Walt Whitman's "A Woman Waits For Me," why shouldn't they consent to the printing of "1601"? Must it wait until some extraordinarily literate United States Senator reads it into the *Congressional Record?*

II

The older I grow the more I am convinced that Mark was, by long odds, the largest figure that ever reared itself out of the flat, damp prairie of American literature. He was great absolutely, but one must consider him relatively to get at the measure of his true greatness. Put him beside Emerson, or Whitman, or Hawthorne, or even Poe; he was palpably the superior of all of them. What ailed the whole quartette was a defective contact with their environment, an aloofness from the plain facts of life, a sort of incurable other-worldliness. Emerson was

always half lost in the shadows; toward the end of his life they closed
upon him completely. The ideas that he spoke for, in the main, were
ideas borrowed from men in far lands, and for all his eloquence he
never got into them any sense of their pressing importance to the men
of his own country. He was the academic theorist *par excellence*. He
inhabited a world of mystical abstractions. The very folks who yielded
most readily to his soughing phrases were furthest from grasping their
exact import; to this day he is chiefly the philosopher, not of men who
think clearly and accurately, but of half-educated dolts whose thinking is all a mellow and witless booziness. A man of extraordinary mental equipment and of even more extraordinary nobility of character,
he failed both as a great teacher and as a great artist because of his
remoteness from the active, exigent life that he was a part of. Set here
in the America of the nineteenth century, begirt by politics, railways
and commercial enterprise (and no less by revivals, cuspidors and
braggadocio), he carried on his inquiries in the manner of a medieval
monk, and his conclusions showed all the nebulousness that one associates with the monkish character. To this day his speculations have
had no appreciable influence upon American ways of thought. His
only professed disciples, in fact, are the votaries of what is called the
New Thought, and these idiots libel him quite as absurdly as the
Methodists, say, burlesque Christ.

The intellectual foreignness and loneliness of Hawthorne, Whitman
and Poe is scarcely less noticeable. They lived in the republic, but
were anything but of it. Hawthorne concerned himself with psychological problems that were not only inordinately obscure and labored,
but even archaic; his enterprise, in his chief work, might almost be
called an attempt to psychoanalyze the dead. It would be ridiculous
to say that there was anything in his books that was characteristic of
his time and his country. The gusto of a man thoroughly at home in
his surroundings was simply not in him, and it is surely not surprising
to hear that while he was physically present in America he lived like a
hermit, and that his only happiness was found abroad. Whitman was
even more solitary. The democracy he dreamed of was simply a fig-
ment of his imagination; it had no more relation to the reality sprawl-
ing before him than the Sermon on the Mount has to the practical
ethic of the average Christian ecclesiastic. His countrymen, recognizing the conflict, regarded him generally as a loafer and a scoundrel,
and it was only after foreign enthusiasts began to cry him up that he

emerged from the constant threat of going to jail. As for Poe, he was
almost the complete antithesis of a great national artist. In the midst
of the most sordid civilization ever seen on earth and in the face of a
population of utter literalists, he devoted himself grandly to *hélioga-
balisme*. His countrymen, in the main, were quite unaware of his stature while he lived. They regarded Cooper and Irving as incomparably
greater artists, and such eighth-raters as N. P. Willis as far cleverer
men. When they went to the works of Poe at all they went to them as,
a generation later, they went to Barnum's circus—that is, as to an entertainment fantastic and somehow discreditable—one to be enjoyed
now and then, but not too often. The Baptist critic, Rufus W. Gris-
wold, accurately expressed the national view; his judgment was not
challenged for years. An American boy of 1848 who had conceived the
ambition of becoming a second Poe would have been caned until his
very pantaloons took fire.

At the bottom of this isolation of Poe and Whitman and Hawthorne
and Emerson there was, of course, the dense ignorance of a nation in
a very backward state of culture; a Beethoven or a Mozart or an El
Greco, set down amid the same scenes, would have got the same cold
shoulder. But the fault, obviously, was not all on one side; the men
themselves lacked something. What that something was I have already indicated. It may be described briefly as responsiveness, observation, aliveness, a sense of reality, a joy in life. Around them roared
a great show; it was dramatic, thrilling, unprecedented; above all, it
was intensely amusing. And yet they were as unconscious of it as so
many deaf men at a combat of brass bands. Only Whitman seemed to
have the slightest notion that anything was going on—and Whitman
mistook the show for a great sacrament, a cheap and gaudy circus for
a sort of Second Coming of Christ. Well, such lofty detachment is not
the habit of great artists. It was not the habit of Shakespeare, or of
Pushkin, or of Thackeray, or of Balzac. More important to our present
purpose, it was not the habit of Mark Twain. Mark was the first of
our great national artists to be whole-heartedly and enthusiastically
American. He was the first to immerse himself willingly and with
gusto in the infinitely picturesque and brilliant life of his time and
country. He was the first to understand the common man of his race,
and to interpret him fairly, honestly and accurately. He was the first
to project brilliantly, for the information and entertainment of all the
world, the American point of view, the American philosophy of life,

the American character, the American soul. He would have been a great artist, I believe, even on the high-flung plane of Emerson or Hawthorne. He would have been *konzertmeister* even among the *umbilicarii.* But being what he was, his greatness was enormously augmented. He stands today at the head of the line. He is the one indubitable glory of American letters.

III

The bitter, of course, goes with the sweet. To be an American is, unquestionably, to be the noblest, the grandest, the proudest mammal that ever hoofed the verdure of God's green footstool. Often, in the black abysm of the night, the thought that I am one awakens me like a blast of trumpets, and I am thrown into a cold sweat by contemplation of the fact. I shall cherish it on the scaffold; it will console me in hell. But, as I have said, there is no perfection under heaven, and so even an American has his small blemishes, his scarcely discernible weaknesses, his minute traces of vice and depravity. Mark, alas, had them: he was as thoroughly American as a Knight of Pythias, a Wheeling stogie or Prohibition. One might almost exhibit his effigy in a museum as the archetype of the *Homo Americanus.* And what were these stigmata that betrayed him? In chief, they were two in number, and both lay at the very foundation of his character. On the one hand, there was his immovable moral certainty, his firm belief that he knew what was right from what was wrong, and that all who differed from him were, in some obscure way, men of an inferior and sinister order. And on the other hand, there was his profound intellectual timorousness, his abiding fear of his own ideas, his incurable cowardice in the face of public disapproval. These two characteristics colored his whole thinking; they showed themselves in his every attitude and gesture. They were the visible signs of his limitation as an Emersonian Man Thinking, and they were the bright symbols of his nationality. He was great in every way that an American could be great, but when he came to the border of his Americanism he came to the end of his greatness.

The true Mark Twain is only partly on view in his actual books— that is, in his printed books. To get the rest of the portrait you must go to Paine's exhaustive and fascinating biography—a work so engrossing as a character study that, despite its three volumes and more than 1,700 pages, I have gone through it three times. The real Mark was not the amiable jester of the white dress suit, the newspaper interviews and the after-dinner speeches. He was not the somewhat heavy-handed satirist of *A Tramp Abroad* and *Tom Sawyer*. He was not even the extraordinarily fine and delicate artist of *Joan of Arc* and *Huckleberry Finn*. Nay, he was a different bird altogether—an intensely serious and even lugubrious man, an iconoclast of the most relentless sort, a man not so much amused by the spectacle of life as appalled by it, a pessimist to the last degree. Nothing could be more unsound than the Mark Legend—the legend of the lighthearted and kindly old clown. Study the volumes of Paine and you will quickly discern its unsoundness. The real Mark was a man haunted to the point of distraction by the endless and meaningless tragedy of existence—a man whose thoughts turned to it constantly, in season and out of season. And to think, with him, was to write; he was, for all his laziness, the most assiduous of scribblers; he piled up notes, sketches of books and articles, even whole books, about it, almost mountain high.

Well, why did these notes, sketches, articles and books get no further? Why do most of them remain unprinted, even today? You will find the answer in a prefatory note that Mark appended to *What Is Man?* published privately in 1905. I quote it in full:

> The studies for these papers were begun twenty-five or twenty-seven years ago. The papers were written seven years ago. I have examined them once or twice per year since and found them satisfactory. I have just examined them again, and am still satisfied that they speak the truth. Every thought in them has been thought (and accepted as unassailable truth) by millions upon millions of men—and concealed, kept private. Why did they not speak out? Because they dreaded (*and could not bear*) the disapproval of the people around them. Why have I not published? The same reason has restrained me, I think. I can find no other.

Imagine a man writing so honest and excellent a book, imagine him examining it and re-examining it and always finding it good—and yet holding off the printing of it for twenty-five years, and then issuing it timorously and behind the door, in an edition of 250 copies, none of them for sale! Even his death did not quench his fear. His executors, taking it over as part of his goods, withheld the book for five years more—and then printed it very discreetly, with the betraying preface omitted! Surely it would be impossible in the literature of any other civilized country since the Middle Ages to find anything to match that long hesitation. Here was a man of the highest dignity in the national letters, a man universally recognized to be their chief living adornment, and here was a book into which he had put the earnest convictions of his lifetime, a book carefully and deliberately written, a book representing him more accurately than any other, both as artist and as man—and yet it had to wait thirty-five years before it saw the light of day! An astounding affair, in all conscience—but thoroughly American, messieurs, thoroughly American! Mark knew his countrymen. He knew their intense suspicion of ideas, their blind hatred of heterodoxy, their bitter way of dealing with dissenters. He knew how, their pruderies outraged, they would turn upon even the gaudiest hero and roll him in the mud. And knowing, he was afraid. He "dreaded the disapproval of the people around him." And part of that dread, I suspect, was peculiarly internal. In brief, Mark himself was also an American, and he shared the national horror of the unorthodox. His own speculations always half appalled him. He was not only afraid to utter what he believed; he was even a bit timorous about *believing* what he believed.

The weakness takes a good deal from his stature. It leaves him radiating a subtle flavor of the second-rate. With more courage, he would have gone a great deal further, and left a far deeper mark upon the intellectual history of his time. Not, perhaps, intrinsically as artist. He got as far in that direction as it is possible for a man of his training to go. *Huckleberry Finn* is a truly stupendous piece of work—perhaps the greatest novel ever written in English. And it would be difficult to surpass the sheer artistry of such things as *A Connecticut Yankee, Captain Stormfield, Joan of Arc* and parts of *A Tramp Abroad*. But there is more to the making of literature than the mere depiction of human beings at their obscene follies; there is also the play of ideas. Mark had ideas that were clear, that were vigorous, and that had an immediate appositeness. True enough, most of them were not quite original. As Prof. Schoenemann, of Harvard, has lately demonstrated, he got the notion of "The Mysterious Stranger" from Adolf Wilbrandt's *Der Meister von Palmyra;* much of *What Is Man?* you will find in the forgotten harangues of Ingersoll; in other directions he borrowed right and left. But it is only necessary to read either of the books I have just mentioned to see how thoroughly he recast everything he wrote; how brilliantly it came to be marked by the charm of his own personality; how he got his own peculiar and unmatchable eloquence into the merest statement of it. When, entering these regions of his true faith, he yielded to a puerile timidity—when he sacrificed his conscience and his self-respect to the idiotic popularity that so often more than half dishonored him—then he not only did a cruel disservice to his own permanent fame, but inflicted genuine damage upon the national literature. He was greater than all the others because he was more American, but in this one way, at least, he was less than them for the same reason. . . .

Well, there he stands—a bit concealed, a bit false, but still a colossus. As I said at the start, I am inclined year by year to rate his achievement higher. In such a work as *Huckleberry Finn* there is something that vastly transcends the merit of all ordinary books. It has a merit that is special and extraordinary; it lifts itself above all hollow standards and criteria; it seems greater every time I read it. The books that gave Mark his first celebrity do not hold up so well. "The Jumping Frog" still wrings snickers, but, after all, it is commonplace at bottom; even an Ellis Parker Butler might have conceivably written it. *The Innocents Abroad*, re-read today, is largely tedious. Its humors are artificial; its audacities are stale; its eloquence belongs to the fancy journalism of a past generation. Even *Tom Sawyer* and *A Tramp Abroad* have long stretches of flatness. But in *Huckleberry Finn*, though he didn't know it at the time and never quite realized it, Mark found himself. There, working against the grain, heartily sick of the book before it was done, always putting it off until tomorrow, he hacked out a masterpiece that expands as year chases year. There, if I am not wrong, he produced the greatest work of the imagination that These States have yet seen.

(October, 1919)

FRIEDRICH NIETZSCHE

The Prophet of the Superman

The newspaper editorial writers still turn the name of Friedrich
Wilhelm Nietzsche into "Nietzse," "Nietsche" and "Neitzche," and the
pale parsons who arise in suburban pulpits to argue for his damnation
still call him "Nishy," "Nitsky" and "Neatsky"; but all the same he
seems to be making a certain progress, even in those dull and cabbagy
streets of the world wherein English, in some form or other, is the
prevailing cackle. Thus the mere report of seeming. Behold now the
evidence: eighteen thick volumes of an Englished Nietzsche—say
some five thousand pages duodecimo—a complete version, by a corps
of twenty or more bilingual volunteers and with Dr. Oscar Levy at
the editorial desk, of all the wild German's books and pamphlets,
pasticcios and fragments, broadsides and dithyrambs—a whole library
of Nietzscheism.

Publishers, you may be sure, do not venture upon such libraries unless there is a public waiting to buy, or at least willing to sniff the
goods. Fifteen years ago, when Nietzsche still lay dying at Weimar,
the enterprise would have brought up the commercial coroner at a
gallop. There was at that time not a single whole book of his in English; a few stray selections, not too well chosen or too clearly inter-
preted, had to content the investigator who shrank from German
verbs. But when, at the beginning of the new century, death released
the philosopher from his ten years of darkness, some echo of the noise
his ideas were making in Germany began to reach us. Theodore
Roosevelt was one who heard—the *leit-motif* of *Also Sprach Zarathustra* reappeared as the fanfare in *The Strenuous Life*. And in England, George Bernard Shaw and others took up the tune; it was trans-
posed into softer keys, syncopated, developed by diminution and in-
version, commingled in timid counterpoint with gentler themes, now
and then bawled brazenly.

A demand arose slowly for more. Dr. Grace Neal Dolson, going up
for a Cornell doctorate in philosophy, wrote her pioneer handbook,
describing for students the Nietzschean ethics, the Nietzschean esthetic, the superman. The Macmillans announced an English Nietzsche in eleven volumes, and actually published five. I myself, rushing
in where angels feared to tread, concocted a Nietzschean Gemara in
the vulgate—the hot labor of a hotter summer, the butt of many a
slashing review. More learned fellows followed: Mügge, Ludovici,
Kennedy and others. Nietzschean commentaries were clawed out of
German and French; the quarterlies began to discuss *Der Antichrist;*
Shaw wrote *Man and Superman;* the orchestras played Richard
Strauss's *Zarathustra;* the custom of alluding darkly to "Nietzse,"
"Nietsche" and "Neitzsche" was inaugurated by the newspapers;
finally T. M. Foulis, the Scotch publisher, announced a complete
Nietzsche in eighteen volumes. Well, here it is after many days, the
last five volumes coming together. The Nietzsche shelf, once so small,
is now full five feet long. The prophet of the superman has ceased to
be a mere projection upon the clouds, a half-fabulous hobgoblin. People begin to read him, and even, perhaps, to understand him, for all
his unprofessorial (and hence mystifying) clarity.

"Ich bin noch nicht an der Zeit. Einige werden posthum geboren"—
"I have not yet come to my time; some men are born posthumously."
So said Nietzsche in his last book, the astounding *Ecce Homo.* That
was written in 1888. An accurate self-judgment then; and despite the
hearing he is now getting and the sudden rooting of his ideas here
and there, a judgment he might reaffirm were he still alive today. The
time for him is not yet, nor will it be tomorrow or the next day. The
races of Christendom still flirt with the theory of equality. The sponge
of democracy is not yet squeezed dry. And so we are not ready for
Nietzsche's doctrine of essential *in*equality, with its scale of natural
castes and its plea for an aristocracy uncompromising and unashamed.
Folk still gabble about brotherhood and the duty of the strong to give
of their strength to the weak, and so the law of the survival of the
fittest, for all Nietzsche's eloquence, is forbidden the house, though
made welcome in the stable. Our "good" is still "meek"; our "bad" is
still "ruthless." However much our practical acts may war upon these
definitions, we still give lip service to them. And not only lip service,
but also genuine assent and reverence, for every time we violate them
there lingers in us some sense of wrongdoing—some feeling that our

instinctive desire to get on in the world, to win advantage over the other fellow, to grab and hold the thing desirable and valuable, has led us into proceedings not altogether creditable. The man who lacks that feeling—for example, the stray Bonaparte, or Byron, or Jay Gould—takes on a sinister aspect. We may admire him and envy him, and even admit it under cross-examination, but we never wholly approve of him. Our taste among conquerors is for the conqueror who first conquers and then melts—Carnegie pensioning doddering Latinists, Grant giving his prisoners their horses, the mortgage shark on the mourner's bench. The cult of self-sacrifice, of abasement, still holds us fast.

Well, it was Nietzsche's business in the world to attack that cult, to pry into its uncelestial lineage, to expose its weakness, to point out its dangers, to protest against its effects. What he proposed, in brief, was a transvaluation of moral values—an exchange of definitions between "good" and "bad." "What is good?" he asked, and then he answered boldly: "All that increases the feeling of power, the will to power, power itself in man." And bad? "All that proceeds from weakness." True happiness, he argued, was not the child of self-sacrifice, but of victory—"of the feeling that power increases, that resistance is being overcome." His ideal was not contentment, but fresh conquest; not peace as an end in itself, but successful war; not virtue in the ordinary Christian sense, but efficiency. The law of natural selection, for all his denials of Darwin, was his one supreme mandate and revelation. "The weak and the botched," he roared, "must perish; that is the first principle of *our* humanity. And they should be *helped* to perish."

Out of this fundamental concept grew the whole of his philosophical system, with his dream of the superman as its final flower. "Man," he said, "is not a goal, but a bridge. Man is something to be surpassed. What the ape is to man, that man must be to the superman." But what was this superman that he saw in the distance? Merely man raised to perfect efficiency, to perfect accord with his environment— man completely in control of the natural and social forces making for his destruction—man absolutely healthy, absolutely unfettered, absolutely undeluded, absolutely immoral. Literalists have denounced Nietzsche savagely for this dream of his; many sheets of white paper have been spoiled in demonstrating its essential fantasy, its impossibility of realization. But there is no reason whatever to believe that Nietzsche himself took it so seriously. Certainly he had no hope that it

would condense into fact any faster than the anthropoid ancestors of
the cave man developed into Shakespeares and Huxleys. All that he
sought to do was to set before man a new ideal—an ideal as remote
and impalpable, perhaps, as the Christian ideal of a race without
thought of self, but still an ideal in measurably closer agreement with
the facts of life. His plea was ever for a square facing of reality. He
was the sworn foe of all systems in opposition to those natural laws
which control man in his myriad activities as firmly as they control the
protozoa in the sea ooze. As he was himself fond of saying, he was a
ja-sager—a yes sayer.

No doubt this brief glance at Nietzscheism has brought several objections to your tongue. If it be true, as Nietzsche argued, that the
ideal of self-sacrifice is falacious and dangerous, that it goes counter
to natural laws and makes for decadence, then how is it that it remains in such high esteem among the most alert and observant races
of the world today? And how is it that these races, in the face of its
evil influence, yet survive in full vigor and bid fair to survive for ages
to come? Such questionings are inevitable—but rest assured that
Nietzsche was not without answers to them. You will find those answers in all the volumes of his philosophical canon—answers developed at great length and meeting all imaginable objections. My advice to you, if you desire to make acquaintance with them and with
the ideas accompanying them, is that you first clear the way to understanding by reading one or other of the half-dozen handbooks now
available—books which afford a clear birdseye view of the whole
Nietzschean system. Then tackle *The Dawn of Day,* in the new and
excellent translation of J. M. Kennedy; then go to *Human All Too
Human;* and then, in order, read *The Genealogy of Morals, Beyond
Good and Evil* and *The Joyful Science.* After that you will be ready
for *The Antichrist,* which is a small pamphlet of one hundred pages or
so, and is printed, in the new edition, as the second part of the volume entitled *The Twilight of the Idols.* Then will come *Thus Spake
Zarathustra,* Nietzsche's *magnum opus* and one of the most astounding
works of our time—a book of dazzling brilliancy, alive with ideas, the
Bible of the Nietzscheans. But to understand it you must have the
other books behind you. Plunging into it as a novelty, you will infallibly find it incomprehensible.

The other books of Nietzsche are much less important than those I
have named. His early essays on Greek philosophy and esthetics, for

instance, are of interest only to the specialist in those sciences, and need not detain the general reader. So, too, the pamphlets aimed at Richard Wagner, Arthur Schopenhauer, David Strauss and others. The Nietzsche-Wagner controversy was one of the famous feuds of the seventies and eighties, albeit Nietzsche did all the fighting. For long the intimate of Wagner and Frau Cosima and an ardent propagandist for the new music, he was alienated by *Parsifal*, which he regarded as a weak and hypocritical concession to Christian mysticism, and so his appalling powers of invective were turned against the composer. When Nietzsche took the floor to denounce, it was time to send for ambulances. No man of his time, certainly no German, matched him at that black art. He devised epithets which cut like knives; his wit was of almost cannibalistic cruelty; his one aim was to flabbergast and destroy his antagonist, regardless of the means. Blasphemies, libels, bad puns, indecencies, gross personal accusations, quotations out of ten languages, elaborately artificial and offensive nicknames—all these weapons were in his arsenal. But all that fuming and fury belongs to the dead past. Wagner lives and Nietzsche lives. Neither carried any very serious wounds from the encounter. Nietzsche himself, indeed, survived to regret his extravagance, if not to retreat from his position. His old affection for Wagner returned. *"Den habe ich sehr geliebt,"* he said, almost with his last breath: "He was one I loved a lot." And in his last book, *Ecce Homo,* he even ventured upon unblushing praise of Frau Cosima!

(March, 1912)

Transvaluation of Morals

Of the late Professor Friedrich Wilhelm Nietzsche, Ph. D., of the University of Basel, one hears a lot of startling gabble in these days of war, chiefly from the larynxes of freshwater college professors, prima donna preachers, English novelists, newspaper editorial writers, Chautauqua yap-yankers and other such hawkers of piffle. He is depicted as an intellectual pestilence, a universal fee-faw-fum, a high priest of diabolism. All bowels of compassion are denied him. It is solemnly and indignantly argued, not only that he plotted and hatched the burning of Louvain (as if a special devil were needed to account for so commonplace an act of war!), but also that he left behind him detailed plans and specifications for the blowing up of all the churches of Christendom, the butchery of all their rectors and curates, and the sale into levantine bondage of all their communicants, without regard to age, virtue or sex. It is more than hinted that the Turks have adopted him as their god, vice Allah, resigned in disgust. His hand is seen in at least forty or fifty massacres of Armenians, the *pogrom* of Kishinev, the *Titanic* disaster, the cruise of the *Emden*, the eruption of Mont Pelée, the Claflin failure, the assassination of King Carlos, the defeat of the Prohibition amendment, the torpedoing of the *Audacious*, the shelling of Rheims and the Italian earthquake. He is credited with advocating a war of extermination upon all right-thinking and forward-looking men, especially his fellow Germans. He is hailed as the patron and apologist of all crimes of violence and chicane, from mayhem to simony, and from piracy on the high seas to seduction under promise of marriage. And his critics and expositors, as if to prove their easy familiarity with him, spell his name variously Nietshe, Neitzsky, Nittszke, Neitzschi, Nietschke, Neatsche, Nietzkei, Niztzsche, Nzeitsche, Neitzschy, Nietztskie and Nistskie.

I dare say you have got enough of this windy nonsense, this imbecile Nietzsche legend, and so thirst for no more of it. But an accurate and intelligent account of Nietzsche's ideas, by one who has studied them and understands them, is, as Mawruss Perlmutter would say, yet another thing again. Seek in *What Nietzsche Taught*, by Willard H. Wright, and you will find it. Here, in the midst of the current obfuscation, are the plain facts, set down by one who knows them. Wright has simply taken the eighteen volumes of the Nietzsche canon and reduced each of them to a chapter. All of the steps in Nietzsche's arguments are jumped; there is no report of his frequent disputing with himself; one gets only his conclusions. But Wright has arranged these conclusions so artfully and with so keen a comprehension of all that stands behind them that they fall into logical and ordered chains, and are thus easily intelligible, not only in themselves, but also in their interrelations. The book is incomparably more useful than any other Nietzsche summary that I know. It does not, of course, exhaust Nietzsche, for some of the philosopher's most interesting work appears in his arguments rather than in his conclusions, but it at least gives a

straightforward and coherent account of his principal ideas, and the
reader who has gone through it carefully will be quite ready for the
Nietzsche books themselves.

These principal ideas all go back to two, the which may be stated
as follows:

1. Every system of morality has its origin in an experience of utility. A
race, finding that a certain action works for its security and betterment, calls
that action good; and, finding that a certain other action works to its peril,
it calls that other action bad. Once it has arrived at these valuations it seeks
to make them permanent and inviolable by crediting them to its gods.

2. The menace of every moral system lies in the fact that, by reason of
the supernatural authority thus put behind it, it tends to remain substantially
unchanged long after the conditions which gave rise to it have been sup-
planted by different, and often diametrically antagonistic conditions.

In other words, systems of morality almost always outlive their usefulness, simply because the gods upon whose authority they are
grounded are hard to get rid of. Among gods, as among office-holders,
few die and none resign. Thus it happens that the Jews of today, if
they remain true to the faith of their fathers, are oppressed by a code
of dietary and other sumptuary laws—*i.e.*, a system of domestic
morality—which has long since ceased to be of any appreciable value,
or even of any appreciable meaning, to them. It was, perhaps, an actual as well as a statutory immorality for a Jew of ancient Palestine to
eat shell-fish, for the shell-fish of the region he lived in were scarcely
fit for human food, and so he endangered his own life and worked
damage to the community of which he was a part when he ate them.
But these considerations do not appear in the United States of today.
It is no more imprudent for an American Jew to eat shell-fish than it is
for him to eat *süss-und-sauer*. His law, however, remains unchanged,
and his immemorial God of Hosts stands behind it, and so, if he
would be counted a faithful Jew, he must obey it. It is not until he
definitely abandons his old god for some more modern and intelligible
god that he ventures upon disobedience. Find me a Jew eating oyster
fritters and I will show you a Jew who has begun to doubt very seriously that the Creator actually held the conversation with Moses described in the nineteenth and subsequent chapters of the Book of
Exodus.

It is Nietzsche's chief thesis that most of the so-called Christian
morality of today is an inheritance from the Jews, and that it is quite

as much out of harmony with the needs of our race and time as the Mosaic law which prohibits the eating of oysters, clams, swine, hares, swans, terrapin and snails, but allows the eating of locusts, beetles and grasshoppers (Leviticus, XI, 4–30). Christianity, true enough, did not take over the Mosaic code *en bloc*. It rejected all these dietary laws, and it also rejected all the laws regarding sacrifices and most of those dealing with the family relations. But it absorbed unchanged the ethical theory that had grown up among the Jews during the period of their decline—the theory, to wit, of humility, of forbearance, of non-resistance. This theory, as Nietzsche shows, was the fruit of that decline. The Jews of David's day were not gentle. On the contrary, they were pugnacious and strong, and the bold assertiveness that seemed their best protection against the relatively weak peoples surrounding them was visualized in a mighty and thunderous Jehovah, a god of wrath and destruction, a divine Kaiser. But as their strength decreased and their enemies grew in power they were gradually forced into a more conciliatory policy. What they couldn't get by force they had to get by a show of complaisance and gentleness—and the result was the renunciatory morality of the century or two preceding the birth of Christ, the turn-the-other-cheek morality which Christ erected into a definite system, the "slave-morality" against which Nietzsche whooped and raged nearly two thousand years afterward.

The whole of Nietzsche's protest may be thus reduced to a single question: Why should a strong nation of to-day continue to give lip service to a system of morality which was devised by a weak race—in his own words, a race of slaves—to conciliate and mollify its masters, and so protect it from wrath and destruction? The cause of that survival is plain enough: it lies in the fact that the supernatural authority behind the system is still accepted. The necessities of life impose upon all healthy peoples and upon all healthy individuals an incessant compromise in morality, but Christianity still remains the general idea, and every violation of it, however unescapable, is felt to be a wrong. The result is an almost universal hypocrisy. The Germans, on the one hand, argue with a great show of plausibility that their invasion of Belgium was absolutely necessary for their own security, and yet, on the other hand, they admit in so many words that it was wrong. The English, in the same way, argue that they could not avoid taking sides with the Mongolian races against the integrity of the white race, and yet they are plainly full of doubts about the morality of it, and devote all their traditional casuistry to the business of apologizing for it. And here at home we Americans go to church and call upon the Most High to stop the war forthwith—and then proceed to wring a bloody profit from the necessities of the contending nations. The best Christian among us is inevitably the most shameless hypocrite. There is probably no man in America who harbors a more genuine belief in the Christian doctrine of brotherhood and good will than the Hon. William Jennings Bryan, and yet it would be difficult to find a man who has devoted a larger part of his life to furious and merciless combat, or who seeks with greater ardor to rout, cripple and destroy his enemies. The whole uplift is Christian in theory, and yet the whole uplift is inordinately savage and vindictive in practice.

Keep all this in mind, and nine-tenths of Nietzsche becomes crystal-clear. His objection to Christianity is simply that it is mushy, preposterous, unhealthy, insincere, enervating. It lays its chief stress, not upon the qualities of vigorous and efficient men, but upon the qualities of the weak and parasitical. True enough, the vast majority of men belong to the latter class: they have very little enterprise and very little courage. For these Christianity is good enough. It soothes them and heartens them; it apologizes for their vegetable existence; it fills them with an agreeable sense of virtue. But it holds out nothing to the men of the ruling minority; it is always in direct conflict with their vigor and enterprise; it seeks incessantly to weaken and destroy them. In consequence, Nietzsche urged them to abandon it. For such men he proposed a new morality—in his own phrase, a "transvaluation of values"—with strength as its highest good and renunciation as its chiefest evil. They waste themselves to-day by pulling against the ethical stream. How much faster they would go if the current were with them! But as I have said—and it cannot be repeated too often—Nietzsche by no means proposed a general repeal of the Christian ordinances. He saw that they met the needs of the majority of men, that only a small minority could hope to survive without them. In the theories and faiths of this majority he has little interest. He was content to have them believe whatever was most agreeable to them. His attention was fixed upon the minority. He was a prophet of aristocracy. He planned to strike the shackles from the masters of the world. . . .

(March, 1915)

JAMES GIBBONS HUNEKER

Importer of Foreign Flavors

No facile blubberer, I assure you, I have yet risen from James Huneker's *New Cosmopolis* with more tears in these eyes, and wetter ones
and bigger ones, than ever a chaplain of the Junior Order of United
American Mechanics gave issue to at a forty-hack funeral. The book is
sad, affecting, almost tragic. It is written in the key of B minor, *con
malinconia*. Gloom hangs over it in opaque, cimmerian, mucilaginous
clouds, like the fumes of sulphur, bromine, and molybdenum over
Aetna, of selenium, tungsten, and praesodidymium over Krakatoa.
Now and then, true enough, a lighter mood intervenes—there are, so
to speak, *scherzo*-like episodes, waggish, optimistic, even gay—but always, as in the immortal *scherzo* of Beethoven's Fifth, one hears,
down in the bowels of them, the zugzugging of lugubrious bull-
fiddles, the complaining of a sombre and solitary *waldhorn*, the faint,
faraway mourning of Loreleis, Valkyries, Giroflé-Giroflas, Elsas, Isol-
des, *Biermädel*. It is the play of *Hamlet* in brilliant, voluptuous prose,
with the author himself as the Dane. There is in it from end to end,
for all its superficial concern with crowds and paving stones, noise and
gaudiness, a flavor of old, forgotten, far-off things, of dreams gone a-
glimmering, of joys that are no more, alas, alas!

And why not, indeed? To be Huneker in the United States is to be
a lonely rock in the illimitable expanses of the Southern Ocean, a sar-
dine in the Sahara, a snow-bird in Hell. The man is as exotic as a
samovar, as essentially un-American as a bashi-bazouk, a nose-ring or
a fugue. He is filled to the neck with strange and unpatriotic heresies.
He ranks Beethoven miles above the Hon. William Jennings Bryan,
and not only Beethoven, but also Bach and Brahms, and not only
Bach and Brahms, but also Berlioz, Bizet, Bruch, and Bülow, and perhaps even Balakirew, Bellini, Balfe, Borodin and Boieldieu. He regards
Prague as a more civilized city than Philadelphia, Otto Julius Bier-

baum as a greater author than Washington Irving, *"Künstler Leben"* as better music than "There is Sunlight in My Soul." He knows all that is worth knowing about Chopin, and probably a good deal more than is worth knowing about Czerny, but in all his chapters upon New York there is not a single mention of John McGraw. In the days when the name of Ibsen was as full of blushful impropriety as the word *drawers*, this Huneker was writing long articles upon him, lavish praises of him. When Nietzsche and the late Herr Most were generally regarded as facets of the same sinister gem, he was expounding the one and rubbing noses with the other. And now, after thirty years of such satanry, he commits his crowning offense against the Republic, his last and worst flouting of the national virtue, by filling a thick book with dithyrambs upon things to eat, hymns to the carnalities of the aesophagus and pylorus, whoops for Pilsner.

Not, of course, that he is forever at table, *mass* and eating knife before him. Anon he turns to other concerns—the charm of the Dutch woods, the marble palaces at Newport, the gorgeous pile of buildings on the Hradcany at Prague, the church bells of Belgium, the street cries of Madrid, the bad pictures at Dublin, the immortal dead of Vienna. But these, after all, are merely interludes, digressions—as the tourist advertisements say, side trips. The thread of his narrative is a thread of nutriment. His philosophizing always comes back, however far it may roam, to such ease as a man finds in his inn. "The stomach of Vienna," he says, "first interested me, not its soul." And so, after a dutiful bow to St. Stephen's ("Old Steffel," as the Viennese call it), he proceeds to investigate the paprika-chicken, the *gulyas*, the *risi-bisi*, the *apfelstrudel*, the *kaiserschmarn* and the native and authentic *Wienerschnitzel*. And from food to drink—specifically, to the haunts of Pilsner, to "certain semi-sacred houses" where the ritual of beer-drinking is observed, to the shrines at which beer-fanatics meet, to "a little old house near a Greek church" where "the best-kept Pilsner in Vienna may be found."

Think of it! The best-kept Pilsner in Vienna! The very phrase amazes and enchants. It suggests the best caviare in Russia, the best oysters in Baltimore (now, by the way, a mere tradition), the worst actor on Broadway, the most virtuous angel in Heaven. Such superlatives are almost unimaginable. And yet—so rare is perfection in this weary world!—the news swiftly follows, unexpected, disconcerting, that the best Pilsner in Vienna is now far short of the ideal. For some

undetermined reason—the influence of the American tourist? the de-
cay of the Austrian national character?—the Vienna *Bierwirte* now
freeze and paralyze it with too much ice, so that it chills the nerves it
should caress, and fills the heart below with heaviness and repining.
Avoid Vienna if you are one who understands and venerates the great
Bohemian brew! And if, deluded, you find yourself there, take the first
D-Zug for Prague, that lovely city, for in it you will find the Pilsen
Urquell, and in the Pilsen Urquell you will find the best Pilsner in
Christendom—its color a phosphorescent, translucent, golden yellow,
its foam like whipped cream, its temperature exactly and invariably
right. Not even at Pilsen itself (which the Bohemians call Plzen) is
the emperor of malt liquors more stupendously grateful to the palate.
Write it down before you forget: the Pilsen Urquell, Prague, Bohe-
mia, 120 miles S.S.E. of Dresden, on the river Moldau (which the na-
tives call the Vltava). Ask for Fräulein Ottilie. Mention the name of
Herr Huneker, the American *schriftsteller*.

Of all the eminent and noble cities between the Alleghenies and the
Balkans, Prague seems to be Herr Huneker's favorite. He calls it
poetic, precious, delectable, original, dramatic—a long string of adjectives, each argued for with eloquence that is unmistakably sincere. He
stands fascinated before the towers and pinnacles of the Hradcany, "a
miracle of tender rose and marble white with golden spots of sunshine
that would have made envious Claude Monet." He pays his devotions
to the Chapel of St. Wenceslas, "crammed with the bones of buried
kings," or, at any rate, to the shrine of St. John Nepomucane, "composed of nearly two tons of silver." He is charmed by the beauty of
the stout, black-haired, red-cheeked Bohemian girls, and hopes that
enough of them will emigrate to the United States to improve the
fading pulchritude of our own houris. But most of all he has praises
for the Bohemian cuisine, with its incomparable apple tarts, its
chicken liver in casserole, its dumplings of cream cheese and its
muffins stuffed with poppy-seed jam, and for the magnificent, the
overpowering, the ineffable Pilsner of Prague. This Pilsner motive runs
through his book from cover to cover. In the midst of Dutch tulip-
beds, Dublin cobble-stones, Madrid sunlight and Atlantic City leg-
shows, one hears it insistently, deep down in the orchestra. The cellos
weave it into the polyphony, sometimes clearly, sometimes in scarcely
recognizable augmentation. It is heard again in the wood-wind; the
bassoons grunt it thirstily; it slides around in the violas; it rises to a

stately choral in the brass. And chiefly it is in minor. Chiefly it is
sounded by one who longs for the Pilsen Urquell in a far land, and
among barbarous and teetotaling people, and in an atmosphere as
hostile to the recreations of the palate as it is to the recreations of the
intellect.

As I say, this Huneker is a foreigner, and hence accursed. Just what
strange, heathen race he belongs to I don't know: perhaps he is a
Czech, a Basque, a Crim Tartar, a Walloon. The legend that he is
Irish is as absurd as the political theory that he is an American. The
naïf romanticism of the Celt is not in him; he leans frankly toward a
more sniffish and earthly philosophy. No one has ever heard of an
Irish epicure, nor of an Irish *flâneur,* nor, for that matter, of an Irish
contrapuntist. The arts of the voluptuous category are unknown west
of Cherbourg. But whatever the gentleman's racial origins and affilia-
tions, he is obviously one who has made, in his day, a very valuable
contribution to American letters, and, more important still, to American thought. The sheer charm of his style has won him readers in
many a far-flung outpost of our morals-ridden and desolate civilization, and under cover of that charm he has diligently poisoned the
American mind with heretical ideas. As yet, of course, his influence is
scarcely perceptible. One might throw a thousand bricks in any American city without hitting a single man who could give an intelligible
account of either Hauptmann or Cézanne, or of the reasons for holding Schumann to have been a greater composer than Mendelssohn.
The boys in our colleges are still taught that Whittier was a great poet
and Fenimore Cooper a great novelist. Nine-tenths of our people—
perhaps ninety-nine-hundredths of our native-born—have yet to see
their first good picture, or to hear their first symphony. Our Chamberses and Richard Harding Davises are national figures; our Norrises
and Dreisers are scarcely heard of. The "dean of American letters,"
though a competent craftsman and capable of sound work, writes
from the standpoint of a somewhat jocose old woman. Of the two undoubted world figures that we have contributed to letters, one was allowed to die like a stray cat up an alley and the other was mistaken
for a cheap buffoon. Criticism, as we understand it, is what a Frenchman, a German or a Russian would call donkeyism, booming emptiness, puerile pedantry. In all the arts we still cling to the ideals of the
dissenting pulpit, the public cemetery, the electric sign, the bordello
parlor.

But for all that, I hang to an incorrigible optimism, and one of the chief causes of that optimism is the fact that Huneker, after all these years, yet remains unchanged. A picturesque and rakish fellow, a believer in joy and beauty, a disdainer of petty bombast and moralizing, a sworn friend of all honest purpose and earnest striving, he has given his life to an educational work that must needs bear fruit hereafter. While the college pedagogues of the Brander Matthews type still worshipped the dead bones of Scribe and Sardou, Robertson and Bulwer-Lytton, he preached the new and revolutionary gospel of Ibsen. In the golden age of Rosa Bonheur's "The Horse Fair," he was expounding the principles of the post-impressionists. In the midst of the Sousa marches he whooped for Richard Strauss. Before the rev. professors had come to Schopenhauer, or even to Spencer, he was hauling ashore the devil-fish, Nietzsche. No stranger poisons have ever passed through the customs than those he has brought in his baggage. No man among us has ever urged more ardently, or with sounder knowledge or greater persuasiveness, that catholicity of taste which stands in direct opposition to American narrowness, ignorance and vulgarity. Himself a man of enormous hospitality to new ideas, whatever their origin, he has made a long and gallant effort to ram some of that hospitality into his countrymen. Superficially, he seems to have failed. But under the surface, concealed from a first glance, he has undoubtedly left his mark. To be a civilized man in America is measurably less difficult than it used to be, say in 1890. One may at least speak of *Die Walküre* without being laughed at as a maniac, and go to see *Hedda Gabler* without being turned out of one's club, and argue that Huxley got the better of Gladstone without being challenged at the polls. I know of no man who has done more to bring about this change than James Huneker.

(July, 1915)

Huneker's Confessions

I lift the following from the next to the last page of the second and last volume of James Gibbons Huneker's autobiography, *Steeple-jack:*

Need I tell you that my cosmopolitanism peeled off like dry paint from a cracked wall when President Wilson proclaimed our nation at war? I shall never forget the amazed expression of Colonel Roosevelt as I admitted that I was in Paris when I attained my majority, and did not cast a vote in our Presidential election. And he was justified in his gesture of disapproval. . . .

In other words, vote for some puerile ass—and spoil a Huneker. Worse, spoil a litterateur. For Paris made Huneker, as *Steeple-jack* shows very plainly, and it was Huneker more than any other who delivered the national letters from the old camorra of schoolmarms, male and female. There were other critics in the nineties, perhaps, who knew more than he, and there were others whose judgments were more careful and accurate, but there was no other who brought to the dull critical business more of the charm and lightness of the Frenchman—there was no other who made of criticism so fine and delightful an adventure. Before his day criticism had been a means of improving the mind: its aim was to convert the reader into a New England bluestocking. After he got his gait it became a means of expanding the soul: its aim was to make the reader a civilized man. Obviously, Huneker did not acquire this point of view, this method of attack, this charm and plausibility, in his native Philadelphia. It was then, as it is now, a cultural slum; fully two-thirds of the old friends he mentions as having made it bearable in his youth were foreigners, and some of them could scarcely speak English. Nor did he pick up his manner in New York, for it was not until later that New York knew him. Where he got it was in Paris—the Paris of Verlaine and Villiers de l'Isle Adam, of Flaubert and Jules Le Maitre, of Renoir and Manet, of the Symbolists and the Parnassians, of Zola and Guy de Maupassant, of all sorts of savory pots, of endless babble about the seven arts, of heroic revolt against the professors and their superstitions. Huneker brought back from Paris a completely un-American state of mind, and successfully implanted it in the national skull. . . . The President of the United States, while he was beyond the seas, was Rutherford B. Hayes. His first vote would have been cast for James A. Garfield. Or for some tawdry Pennsylvania congressman, a brother to the ox and the ass. Or for some thieving swine of a Philadelphia common councilman. . . .

Let us draw the arras. Roosevelt, too, had charm. In his presence reason tottered on its throne. He was a rabble-rouser so powerful that he could fetch even Huneker. No doubt he was helped by the Pilsner famine: the interview took place late in the war. A Huneker emptied of Pilsner was a Huneker denaturized and not himself. I noticed it at the time. One day my blood froze with horror as the author of *Icono-clasts* walked into a public bar-room wearing the gilt-edged purple of the National Institute of Arts and Letters, then but lately conferred upon him by Robert W. Chambers, Chimmie Fadden Townsend, and Prof. Dr. Balderdash, of Harvard. No doubt he thought I was moved by his gruesome description of his malaises—a chronicle to make a hospital interne break down and sob. But what actually blanched my nose was the spectacle of that pathetic gaud—a rosette stuck into the beard of Brahms—Richard Strauss awarded the Order of the Silver Pumpernickel, eighth class. It was a symptom, and should have in-spired me to shoot him on the spot, thus putting him out of his agony, for which he falsely blamed uric acid. Imagine the anguish of the transmogrification: the playboy of the arts, for years so innocent, so puckish, so ribald, so happy, transformed into a literary Knight of Pyth-ias, a peer of Hamilton Wright Mabie, an honorary pallbearer of letters!

Well, I forgive him. I am not God, but a poor and miserable sinner. There was a day when I came so near lecturing at Princeton that the memory of it converts my spine into an icicle. Every man to his own villainy. Huneker reserves his for the last chapter of his fat, two-barrelled book. What goes before is always amusing, and frequently brilliant—Huneker in his best form, full of learning masquerading as badinage, sound criticism disguised as agreeable gossip. Now and then, true enough, a too great amiability gets into it, and third-raters are given more politeness than they deserve. But an autobiography is not the verdict of a coroner's jury: a man is surely justified in devoting at least a part of it to praising his friends, *i.e.*, the men and women who have made life agreeable for him, and so enabled him to do his work. Huneker's friends run all the way from Shaw and the de Reszkes to obscure music critics of obscure *Käseblätter* and almost anonymous music teachers in Philadelphia. He has led a curiously full life, seeing cities, meeting men and women, taking graceful headers into art after art, never neglecting either the spirit or the aesophagus.

He came out of an extraordinary household—a father of fine taste and intellectual enterprise, a mother full of wit and learning and yet without the faintest trace of the *bas bleu*. The father is always secondary, culturally as well as biologically; it is the mother that counts. Huneker's seems to have been as remarkable a woman as Dreiser's, without the tragic melancholy but with all of the fine feeling. He pays his tribute to her, simply and eloquently. If she lived into his maturity, it is a safe guess that his career did not surprise her. She knew that she had an extraordinary son, and she let him rear himself in an extraordinary fashion, mingling music and law in a fearful stew, consorting with fiddlers and metaphysicians, boldly flinging himself upon Paris before he was out of his nonage.

The book, as I say, is agreeable stuff, though there are gaps that I should like to see filled and chapters that rub my fur the wrong way. Here and there the bow is drawn until it begins to squeak; adventures of the imagination creep into the adventures of the real Huneker. But this is as it should be, for the imagination is as much a part of the man as the liver or lights, and in the case of such a man as Huneker it is a good deal more. I like best the earlier parts—the days of all-night piano-thumping in Philadelphia, then, it appears, quite as dull as now, but with an inner circle of musicians to make a scarlet spot in the gloom. Music was Huneker's first love, and it remains his last. He has toyed with painting, with sculpture and with books and plays, but no one familiar with his long row of volumes can be in any doubt as to where his heart is, and always has been. He confesses boldly to an ancient and unshaken ambition: to be a fine tickler of the white keys and black, a concert pianist in the grand manner. An easy and lordly life, progressing incessantly from city to city, from country to country, from continent to continent, observing the gals and the monumental remains, eating strange dishes and catching cold in strange drafts, making Brahms and Chopin live again. But the gods withheld the blue ticket and gave him one of green—the union card of the critic. He has been, and is, a marvelously diligent workman, turning out column after column, and book after book. But surely no mere plodder. In every line there is the mark that no one else can make. In every book there is the incomparable charm of a lively and unusual personality, of roguish wit, of solid learning, of sound relish for what is good.

(December, 1920)

OSCAR WILDE

A Note on Oscar Wilde

We have forgotten long since that Francis Bacon was a thief, and we have begun to forget that William Wycherley was a white slave; and so it is not unreasonable to suppose that we shall forget, too, some day that Oscar Wilde was careless of the decencies. The process of forgetting, it is even probable, is already in progress, for didn't the first citizens of London not long ago give a public dinner to Robert Ross for his fidelity to Wilde as friend and protector? Once that process is complete, the residuum will be a great reputation, for while it may be admitted freely that Wilde was not a genius of the first rank, the fact that he stood very near the top of the second rank cannot be denied. He restored wit to the English drama, whence it had departed with Sheridan's youth; he made sound and permanent contributions to English criticism; and he left behind him more than one example of inspired English verse.

A new and complete edition of his works, edited by Mr. Ross, is now under way, and as a sort of herald the volume containing his poems is sent out ahead—*The Poems of Oscar Wilde*, Complete and Authorized. There is no need to consider them in detail. Not a few of them—"Ave Imperatrix," "The Ballad of Reading Gaol" and "Easter Day," for example—are already firmly lodged in the anthologies. They are striking and beautiful poems, with music in them and the great human note. Elsewhere the familiar faults of Wilde—his posing, his strutting, his tinsel—mar his fine stanzas, but in the worst that he wrote there is proof that he is not to be punished, dead, by oblivion for the crimes that he paid for, living, in intolerable suffering.

(January, 1910)

The Accounting of a Tartuffe

Regarding that small and shrinking minority of writers who are worth reading at all, it may be said that some of them improve the mind by giving away information and others charm it by giving away themselves. To the first class belong the authors of *Who's Who in America*, the *Encyclopaedia Britannica*, *The Origin of Species*, *Greenleaf on Evidence*, *Every Man His Own Bartender* and the Book of Genesis. To the second class belong the authors of *Science and Health*, *Three Weeks*, the Book of Revelation and *L'Evolution Créatrice*, the contributors to the *Nation* and the *Congressional Record*, and such expansive fellows as Jean-Jacques Rousseau, Benvenuto Cellini, Dr. Orison Swett Marden, Samuel Pepys, James Boswell, J. Gordon Cooglar and Richard Harding Davis. Now add to this second class, and not far behind Benvenuto, Lord Alfred Douglas, author of *Oscar Wilde and Myself*.

Douglas, I daresay, knew Wilde better than any other member of that queer bodyguard which slobbered over him and buzzed around him in his days as a London celebrity—certainly better than Frank Harris, or Robert Sherard, or Lionel Johnson, or Walter Pater, or Gomez Carillo, or André Gide, or even Robert Ross. The two men were together almost daily for at least three years on end; they lunched together, they dined together, they went visiting together, they had what was virtually a common purse. Douglas was Wilde's favorite feeder and *claqueur;* he knew when to laugh at a Wilde epigram, and, what is more important, when *not* to laugh at a Wilde apothegm; his rank filled Wilde with a subtle and grateful sense of social importance; he was on good terms with all the lords and ladies that Wilde yearned to know; he had nothing to do all day but play the disciple, flatterer and sedulous ape. No man ever had a better chance to get at the truth about another, to see things not perceptible to the general public, to come away with a report full of novelty and veracity. But does he make that report in his book? Does he offer us anything important that is new, or anything trivial that is interesting? He does not. The one fact he brings forth that hasn't been a commonplace for years is this: that Wilde had bad teeth and they were "the sorrow of his life." This, and nothing more!

But when I say nothing more, I mean, of course, nothing more about Wilde. As a Wilde book, the volume is a complete failure. The

paper on which it is printed might have been used far more profitably
to stuff hotel pillows. But as a Douglas book it is an enormous success.
It draws Douglas sharply, vividly, mercilessly. It lets a bright and tell-
tale light into his mind. It exposes him as one of the most amusing
low comedians of literary history: a pious and sniveling obfuscator, a
shifty and wholly unconscionable special pleader, a crafty beggar of
questions, a master of innuendo and denial, a veritable prince of
Pecksniffs. One grows fascinated after a while by the whole-hearted
malice of the fellow. It seems to be his sworn purpose to depict Wilde
as the worst scoundrel that ever lived, and not only as the worst
scoundrel, but also as the hollowest fraud. His thesis, reduced to a few
words, is a sweeping denial that his old idol had any virtue or merit
whatever, either as literary artist or as man. Wilde's waistcoats and his
plays are alike damned and torn to tatters. His epigrams are denounced as but one degree better than his morals and his teeth. His
style is ridiculed, flouted, denied. His estheticism is sneered at as a
thing of rags and patches, a senseless compound of misunderstood
borrowings. He is branded a plagiarist, a snob, a glutton, a sycophant,
a liar, a trickster, a deadbeat, a common rogue. Even his family is laid
upon the block and treated to the ax: his father, it appears, was once
"prosecuted for insulting a lady patient," and "heaven alone knows
who his grandfather was."

In all this debauch of denunciation there is one discordant note, one
solitary interlude of praise. Its mark and beneficiary is "The Ballad of
Reading Gaol"—"a sustained poem of sublimated actuality and of a
breadth and sweep and poignancy such as had never before been attained in this line." This single poem, we are told, "will last"; on it
alone "his reputation among posterity will stand." And why? Turn to
page 124 and you will find the reason. It is because *Douglas helped
Wilde to write it!* Nay; not merely *helped* him: even *wrote* a good
part of it—and that, no doubt, the best part! "There are passages," we
are told, "which he lifted holus-bolus from a poem of my own." What
poem? The name is not given—but be sure that it existed and exists.
Douglas, it appears, was a specialist in the ballad form, whereas
Wilde "knew next to nothing of its possibilities." And so, upon the
framework of "Eugene Aram," with occasional bows to "The Ancient
Mariner," "The Ballad of Reading Gaol" was made, with Wilde sup-
plying the jail life and Douglas the balladry! . . .

I go no further into this most amazingly impudent and unpleasantly amusing book. It deserves a first-hand inspection; it is one of the really curious volumes of the year. Let it be said in passing that behind all of Douglas' affectation of Baracca Class virtue and behind all of his imbecile denial of any virtue whatever in Wilde, there is at least the excuse (if not the justification) of a couple of sound grievances. On the one hand, it is an undoubted fact that Wilde put some nasty things about him into *De Profundis*, written in prison, and then accepted money from him later on, concealing the fact of the manuscript's slanderous character. And on the other hand, it is an undoubted fact that the donkeyish British courts played a sorry trick upon him when they refused him permission to quote from that manuscript in his defense (it has never been published in full), while allowing opposing attorneys to read from it in open court in the course of his various recent lawsuits. But these grievances, though they may explain his rage, by no means explain away his pious cannibalism upon the Wildean cadaver, his wholesale revilings, his show of injured innocence. The book remains a brilliant and pitiless character study, no less vivid because it is unconscious. It is a full-length portrait of a virtuoso of buncombe, a brummagem martyr, a master pettifogger and Tartuffe.

(November, 1914)

Portrait of a Tragic Comedian

The Preface to Frank Harris' two-volume biography of Oscar Wilde bears date of 1910, and on the title page the author appears as his own publisher, and even as his own printer. A curious proof of the potency of prudery in the Anglo-Saxon countries! For six years, it would seem, this highly dramatic and significant story of a first-rate artist's rise and fall has been seeking a publisher on both sides of the Atlantic, and now at last, despite the dignified position of the author and his obvious competence to write such a book with discretion and understanding, he is forced to print it privately and from a house in Washington Square! Strange tales go about of its adventures in New York. One publisher, after others had failed, accepted it and had it set up—but when he submitted the sheets to those who have authority in such matters he was warned that its publication would land him in jail. He thereupon had the work revised, and with all passages taken out that could reasonably offer offense to even the most prudish, it was submitted again. He was then plainly given to understand that its publication in any form would expose him to prosecution, and so he was forced to abandon it. Harris himself seems to look forward to some sort of Puritan attack, and in preparation for it rehearses the reasons which moved him to write and print the book—his long and intimate friendship with Wilde; the importance of the man, not only as an individual artist, but also as an influence in English letters; the palpable inaccuracy and inadequacy of the existing studies of him; the need of a simple and truthful account of his grotesque mock trials in the English courts; the growth of a huge body of fantastic fables about him, and particularly about his last days; the sound principle that even the worst of offenders deserves to have his case presented by one who is not his sworn foe. He might have added, in further defense of his boldness, his own unusual charm as a writer, for his book is not only the most comprehensive and informative volume on Wilde that has yet appeared, but also, and by long odds, the most skillfully written. It is, indeed, an excellent biography, intimate, sympathetic and yet rigidly honest, and whatever its theoretical shortcomings in moral eyes it at least stands up as a piece of writing.

And why have the publishers been so reluctant to publish it, and the guardians of the public rectitude so eager to suppress it? For the life of me I can't make out. Saving one chapter, I can find nothing in it to lift the eyebrow of any sane adult, and even there Harris does no more than allow Wilde to say a few words (they are empty and unconvincing enough, surely) in his own cause. The truth is told, but it is told cleanly, reticently, with due reserve. I myself, after having read every word of the two volumes, come away in complete ignorance of the precise act for which Wilde was condemned to such barbaric tortures in prison. It may have been one thing, or it may have been some other and quite different thing—both disgusting enough, in all conscience, but neither a penal offense in most civilized countries, and neither so rare in our own land that we can afford to go through any hocus-pocus of holy horror. In my native State, not six months ago, the leader of the vice crusade, a Methodist clergyman in high standing, was taken in such *Schweinerei* in the central lamasery of the

Young Men's Christian Association, and had to be spirited out of the jurisdiction by his fellow apostles of purity. But when the newspapers, scenting a smutty trial, set up a demand for his indictment and extradition, it was found, to everyone's astonishment, that the offense of which he was accused was not indictable, and so the State Legislature rushed through a special prohibitory act, that the recreant clergy and laity might be better handled hereafter. It was for this indecency, or for something substantially equivalent to it, that Wilde was given two years in solitary confinement, and one long year of it without books, without writing implements, without decent medical attention, and even without sufficient food. It is Harris' offense, if he has committed any offense, that he went to Wilde's rescue when the burdens of his punishment grew maddening and intolerable, that he helped him through the cruel difficulties of the years following his release, and that he now puts himself into jeopardy to tell the man's story as he knows it, carefully and completely, concealing nothing that is salient and significant, and yet making no cheap show of what is merely nasty.

That story, I need scarcely say, is anything but edifying. One rises from it, indeed, with the impression that the misdemeanor which caused Wilde's actual downfall was quite the least of his onslaughts upon the decencies—that he was of vastly more ardor and fluency as a cad and a poltroon than ever he became as an immoralist. No offense against what the average civilized man regards as proper and seemly conduct is missing from the chronicle. Wilde was a fop and a snob, a toady and a social pusher, a coward and an ingrate, a glutton and a grafter, a plagiarist and a mountebank; he was jealous alike of his superiors and of his inferiors; he was so spineless that he fell an instant victim to every new flatterer; he had no sense whatever of monetary obligation or even of the commonest duties of friendship; he lied incessantly to those who showed him most kindness, and tried to rob some of them; he seems never to have forgotten a slight or remembered a favor; he was as devoid of any notion of honor as a candidate for office; the moving spring of his whole life was a silly and obnoxious vanity. It is almost impossible to imagine a fellow of less ingratiating character, and to these endless defects he added a physical body that was gross and repugnant, but through it all ran an incomparable charm of personality, and supporting and increasing that charm was his undoubted genius. Harris pauses more than once to

hymn his capacity for engaging the fancy. He was a veritable specialist in the amenities, a dinner companion *sans pair*, the greatest of
English wits since Congreve, the most delightful of talkers, an artist to
his finger-tips, the prophet of a new and lordlier aesthetic, the complete antithesis of English stodginess and stupidity. Born out of his
time, as he himself was fond of saying, he was even more an exile
from his true country. The London of the eighties was as immovably
hostile to such a man as the Germany of the seventies was to Nietzsche. It could see him only as an extravagant buffoon, a preacher of
the fantastic and dubious, one to be regarded with a wary eye; and so
it was very quick, in the old, old Puritan way, to explain his strangeness in terms of villainy, and to fall upon him, once the chance
offered, with an enthusiasm almost religious. Wilde was guilty without
a doubt; we have, indeed, his plain confession in this book; but all the
same he was not tried but lynched, and no gabble about substantial
justice will ever rub out that discreditable fact.

Harris tells us that he was personally convinced of Wilde's innocence until after the first trial. It is the hardest thing in the book to
believe, for surely no one else in the London of that day labored under any such delusion, and Harris himself mentions many anterior circumstances that gave him suspicion. The point, however, is scarcely
worth making. The important thing is the light that the confession
threw upon Wilde's character. Harris had already advised him to flee
to France, knowing full well the impossibility of breasting a high tide
of Puritan indignation; he now renewed his arguments with all the
persuasiveness he could muster, for he saw clearly that, at the second
trial, Wilde would fall an easy victim to the prosecution's lawyers, and
that the jury's disagreement in the first trial would not be repeated. In
order to facilitate the proposed escape (Wilde was out on bail), he
borrowed a steam yacht from a friend, and anchored it with steam up
at Erith on the lower Thames. More, he had a carriage in waiting, and
made arrangements which practically amounted to official connivance.
But Wilde could never get up sufficient courage for the enterprise.
Once he was actually in the carriage, but at the last moment an
astounding cowardice seized him, and he demanded to be taken to his
brother's house. "I would as soon take you to prison!" exclaimed Harris. But Oscar stood to his decision. His mood was one of utter inertia;
he preferred waiting and doing nothing to the easy way to freedom.
Later on, Harris tackled him again, but with equal lack of success.

Fear had reduced him to a pitiful state, indeed; he could do nothing
save bury his head in the sand; the days of his trial and conviction,
and even the first days of his penal servitude, passed over him as in a
dream; it would be difficult to imagine a picture of more pathetic
weakness.

The story of Wilde's two trials and of the cruelties rained upon him
in prison gives a serious shaking up to all our old notions of English
justice and decency. Both trials were tragic farces. Notorious rogues
and blackmailers were admitted as witnesses, a half-witted young man
was solemnly put upon the stand, and the newspapers inflamed the
jury with extraordinary denunciations of the accused, many of them,
as Harris shows, inspired by persons as guilty as the prisoner. Not-
withstanding all this clamour for his blood, the first jury disagreed.
But the second was more responsive to opinion, and so Wilde was
railroaded to prison. On the day after his sentence forty well-known
men about town sat down to a public banquet in celebration of the
event—"a feast," as Harris says, "to celebrate the ruin and degradation
of a man of genius." The leading spirit in this great moral banquet
was Charles Brookfield, the present English censor of plays. Brookfield
was the author of *Dear Old Charlie,* the most indecent comedy seen
on the London boards in years. But he constituted himself the unoffi-
cial prosecutor of Wilde, and gathered the highly dubious evidence on
which he was convicted. Later on, when Brookfield was rewarded
with the censor's post for his high services to public morality, some
humorous London manager revived *Dear Old Charlie,* and it had a
hilarious run. The piece had been licensed by Brookfield's predecessor,
and he was unable, under the law, to withdraw the license. But poor
Wilde was dead before ever this last act of the tragic farce was played
out.

Despite the fact that a Royal Commission had already protested
against the penalty as barbarous and unreasonable, Wilde was condemned to two years' penal servitude, and the first of them was spent
in what was virtually solitary confinement. The prison food was revolting and insufficient; silence was enforced by severe punishments; the
prisoner was forbidden to read or to write. His health broke down
under this drastic régime and he lost forty pounds in weight; but the
governor of the prison and the prison doctor refused him any relief.
Harris, meanwhile, was in South Africa. On his return he visited
Wilde, and then lodged a protest with Sir Ruggles Brise, the head of

the Prison Commission. Brise turned out to be a humane man, and at once ordered a relaxation of the killing discipline. Wilde was given pen, ink and paper, and soon began work on *De Profundis.* Brise went still further. He told Harris that he was in favor of reducing Wilde's sentence, and that he would urge the Home Secretry to reduce it if it were not for fear of Puritan objections in Parliament. To meet this situation Harris suggested that a petition be prepared, signed by the leading authors of England. Brise jumped at the suggestion, and proposed George Meredith as the first signer. But when Harris approached Meredith the latter curtly refused. So did Professor Churton Collins. So, it appears, did Swinburne. Harris went from door to door. He found them all closed against him. There was no Christian charity on tap in England. Worse, there was no courage. Most of these magnificoes based their refusal frankly on the ground that it would be dangerous to hold out a hand to Wilde, with the state of public opinion what it was. Harris himself and Professor Tyrell, of Trinity College, Dublin, seem to have been the only ones with valour enough to face that storm—not forgetting the Rev. Stewart Headlam, "who was an English clergyman, and yet, wonder of wonders, a Christian."

So Wilde served his two years, not escaping a single day. Once he was released the Puritan rage against him revived, and he went to France. Had he been given, in those days, a helping hand, it is highly probable that he would have pulled himself together and spent the rest of his life in diligent and valuable work. To a few relatively happy months of this period, indeed, belong his best writings—"The Ballad of Reading Gaol" and parts of *De Profundis.* But what he actually got, save from a few faithful friends, was contumely of an unmeasured and almost unbelievable sort; he was firmly lodged in the Puritan valhalla of devils, and no extravagance of hatred was too much for him. The result was that, after a gallant new start, he slipped back into his old associations, and presently he was living in squalid idleness in Paris, drunken, dirty and indecent. It was then that all the worst weaknesses of the man came out. He borrowed money right and left, wasted his days in filthy debauchery, and played ingrate and traitor to his best friends. The experience of Harris was perhaps typical. During his Paris days Wilde devised an excellent scene for a play, but found himself unable to complete it. He proposed to Harris that they collaborate on it, and after long negotiations, during which

Wilde's unfitness for the task became manifest, Harris ended by buy-
ing the idea from him for £50. The money paid, Harris went back to
London, completed the play—it was called *Mr. and Mrs. Daventry*—
and sold it to Mrs. Patrick Campbell. Wilde, hearing of this, now demanded more money, and Harris, to pacify him, gave him another
£50. But the worst was to come. The moment the play was announced,
various actors and actresses came forward with the claim that Wilde
had sold his idea to them, and investigation showed that he had actually done so, and on a large scale. Mrs. Brown Potter, Beerbohm Tree,
George Alexander and Ada Rehan were among these claimants; some
had paid Wilde as much as £100. Worse still, he acknowledged the
swindle without shame, and even denounced Harris for depriving him
of "a certain income"!

After this curious episode he went downhill rapidly, and was soon
quite unable to do any work at all. His sole means of support was the
charity of his friends, and to the business of wheedling money out of
them he devoted all of his surviving energies. The end that now rapidly approached was of a sort to delight the Puritan heart. Wilde had
suffered a fall in prison and one of its results was an abscess of the
ear. In addition, he was in the last stages of chronic alcoholism, and
beside, was victim to an unmentionable disease, the product of his
vices. He died in a little hotel in a by-street, with only two friends,
Robert Ross and Reginald Turner, at his side. The death-bed scenes
were full of horror; he seemed doomed to go out of life in abominable
filthiness. The body was buried in quicklime, like that of the hanged
man in "The Ballad of Reading Gaol." Years later Ross went to Paris
with Wilde's son to have it reinterred in Père Lachaise. When it was
dug up it was found that the quicklime had failed to act; the features
were still recognizable. "At once Ross sent the son away, and when
the sextons were about to use their shovels, he ordered them to desist,
and descending into the grave, moved the body with his own hands
into the new coffin in loving reverence."

So much for the life and death of Oscar Wilde. Harris gives no
space to a criticism of his books, and I follow his example. Thanks to
the labors of Ross, they are now to be had in an excellent complete
edition of fourteen volumes. Innumerable other editions exist (some
of them boldly pirated), but that of Ross is better than all the rest.
Much that is hollow and feeble is in those fourteen volumes—
epigrams that strain and creak, poems that are all a brittle sounding,

an aesthetic theory that floats upon the surface and is chiefly borrowed to boot. But there are other things, and rare and precious things—the best wit that England has produced since the Restoration, three or four incomparably amusing plays, the noblest ballad in English, some essays that have left their mark, a story or two of the first rank, an endless stream of good writing. Wilde, beyond all things, was a stylist, and perhaps the greatest of his time. His epigrams may lose their tang, his plays may go out of fashion, even *De Profundis* and "The Ballad of Reading Gaol" may cease to move, but so long as there is an art in our resilient and glowing English speech, he will live as one who knew pre-eminently how to use it. The charm of his style is in the very least of his writings—his squibs, the speeches in his plays, his letters to the newspapers. He could no more put words together without making music than he could face a temptation without yielding to it. Our depressing Puritan philosophy is against such men. It distrusts the artist with a great distrust; it sees in him a prophet of that innocent gusto, that pagan joy in life, which is its chief abomination; it is always ecstatically eager to discover him a criminal, and to fall upon him with the utmost rigors of its savage justice. Wilde was in the wrong country and the wrong time. The Irishman of genius should not go to England, but to France.

Harris, as I say, has done a good job in this life of his friend, no matter how much specialists in righteousness may belabor it with incomprehensible objurgations. He has told the truth about Wilde's stupendous weaknesses, but he has also managed to convey some understanding of the man's unquenchable attractiveness. There was never another quite like Oscar. His very grotesqueries somehow brought him friends, and not all his rogueries and indecencies could ever drive them away. "One can be sure," says Harris, speaking of Ross' last services, "that the man who won such fervid self-denying tenderness, had deserved it, called it forth by charm of companionship, or magic of loving intercourse." Harris' book is yet another proof. It is a grim and unsentimentalized record, but there is shot through it the enchantment of a personality that, after all, must have had something fine and inspiring in it—of a man who, for all his vileness, was at least far better than the Pecksniffs who tore him to pieces.

(September, 1916)

H. G. WELLS

H. G. Wells *Redivivus*

Two years and two months ago, addressing the chosen of God from this pulpit, I announced the decease and preached the funeral sermon of H. G. Wells as a novelist. Let that sermon stand. Wells the novelist is still dead—dead as Haman, dead as Friedrich Barbarossa, dead as the Constitution of the United States. But out of the tomb, wearing all the glittering raiment of the departed, there crawls the murderer, to wit, Wells the forward-looker, the popular philosopher, the advanced thinker, the amateur politician, the soothsayer in general practice. This literary felon I am bound to abhor, for Wells the novelist was a performer very much to my taste, but all the same I am not one to deny his talents. On the contrary, I believe that, within the limits presently to be set forth, he owns and operates one of the most active and penetrating intelligences in function in the England of today—that he is an enormously clever, well-taught, reflective, courageous and original fellow—a man with a head worth a pile of Chesterton heads as high as the Trafalgar monument, or a pile of Lloyd George or Asquith heads as huge as the Alps. Before these lines reach the news-stands he will probably be in our midst, haranguing crowds of lady intelligentsia in stuffy halls and excessively pawed by the Ex-Zionists and scab-Irish of the Sulgrave Foundation, the Anglo-Saxon Union and other such patriotic sodalities. I am not among those who will wait upon him. My supply of gin is running so low that I have had to give up entertaining pilgrim literati. But I shall be glad to see him among us none the less. At least once or twice a week, while he is here, he will say something genuinely worth hearing—something sharp and novel, of an order of utterance never encountered in the halls of our colonial legislature at Washington, or in the columns of *The New York Times* or the *Saturday Evening Post*. Now and then, forgetting politeness—even forgetting

his large trade in the Republic and the principles of sound *Geschäft*
—he will tell the boobery the truth—that is, *his* truth, the truth as he,
Wells, sees it.

This truth, of course, may not be mine, or yours. All of us, even on
the rare occasions when we try to think fairly and honestly, have to
think within the limits of our congenital prejudices and current interests. No man suffering for a drink can take a detached and politico-
economical view of Prohibition; no man married to a virago can ever
quite enjoy the passionate poetry of Algernon Charles Swinburne. I
have prejudices as an American, as a High Church Presbyterian, as a
Brahmsianer, as a magazine editor, as a capitalist, and as a literary
popinjay. I detest men who put cologne water on their pocket hand-
kerchiefs, and hence am blind to much that is high and noble in the
French genius. Blonde, scanty eyebrows revolt me, and so I rejoice
every time that I hear that another Dane has been hanged. I was
born, for well or for ill, with a fixed conviction that anyone who spells
all right as one word, *alright,* may be trusted to blow into his soup to
cool it, and so I always decline dinner invitations from such persons,
and from their relatives and friends. I believe, as I believe in infant
damnation, that all Methodists are scoundrels, and the more you
prove that a given one isn't, the more I am convinced that he is.
Wells, for all his intellectual suppleness and cunning, has prejudices of
precisely the same sort; it is a common human bond between us, like
our joint incapacity to move our ears. Many of these prejudices arise
out of the simple fact that he is an Englishman—that he was brought
up amid certain general ideas, certain ways of looking at things, certain fundamental assumptions. Others owe their origin to the special
circumstance that, as Englishmen estimate such distinctions, he is an
Englishman of the lower classes—one shut off from a large and important body of privileges and immunities—a man facing peculiar obstacles in his struggle toward power and eminence among his compatriots. To be an Englishman is to be born with an incurable prejudice
in favor of certain notions in government, *e.g.,* debate, representation,
majority rule, compromise, the whole machinery of parliamentarism.
And to be of the lower classes in any civilized country is to be born
with an even firmer prejudice in favor of certain other notions, *e.g.,*
human equality, the virtues of education, the eternal immorality of
whatever is aristocratic, the substantial truth of the Sermon on the
Mount. You will find both prejudices lavishly displayed from end to

end of Wells's new and extremely shrewd and valuable work, *The Outline of History*.

To a great many Americans, of course, these prejudices will not be apparent, for they themselves share them. The typical American of the more violently correct sort, as I have often pointed out, is simply a sort of imitation Englishman—a botched and third-rate Englishman —in brief, an Englishman of the lower classes. This is particularly true of two classes of Americans: the generality of social pushers (which means practically the whole of the rising commercial group), and the generality of the learned. Social distinction, in the United States, stops short almost exactly where it stops for Englishmen who have got rich by trade; it may imitate all the forms of the English aristocracy, but it must surmount a definite wall before it is actually recognized by the English aristocracy. So with eminence among the learned. To receive an LL.D. from Harvard is substantially equal to receiving an LL.D. from such an English university as Leeds or Manchester; beyond there is always the infinitely higher dignity of recognition from Cambridge or Oxford. Thus Wells, when he writes the history of the world in the terms of an Englishman who, whatever his intrinsic learning and intelligence, is still distinctly the inferior of, say, the Duke of Norfolk, Prof. Dr. Gilbert Murray, or even the Right Hon. Winston Churchill, is also writing it in the terms of an ordinary respectable American. This explains the lavish and usually wholly uncritical praise that has been heaped upon his book. It is a very interesting, intelligent and instructive book; it comes near being a genuinely great book; but there are still a number of fundamental defects in it as truthful history, and all of them arise out of Wells's inborn and ineradicable prejudices.

I shall not rehearse them in detail; you will read the *Outline* assuredly, and so discover them for yourself. Nevertheless, a few hints may be of service. There is, first of all, the prejudice of a typically democratic man against every tendency to transfer sovereignty from the people to an individual—the chronic incapacity of such a man to understand such regal egoists as Alexander, Julius Cæsar, Charlemagne, Frederick the Great, and Napoleon I. Wells is not merely against all these great conquerors; he is extravagantly unjust to them; he simply cannot understand them. And in order to carry off his libel of them, he is forced into not a few obvious absurdities, *e.g.*, the doctrine that military genius is a thing of a very low intellectual order, and scarcely to be distinguished from a talent for ordinary crime. This, of course, is quite idiotic. To plan and execute such an enterprise as Napoleon's invasion of Italy, or the battle of Tannenberg, or even Kitchener's Khartum campaign, actually calls into play so vast a mass of accurate information, so crafty a capacity for co-ordinating it and systematizing it, and so great an ingenuity in applying it effectively that the whole process takes on an unmistakable intellectual dignity, as much so as the process of writing a symphony, or isolating a new element, or calculating the time of an eclipse. Such things may be accomplished by men who are immoral, by men who are cynical, by men who do not fear God, but they are certainly not accomplished by men who are stupid. Yet Wells dismisses the whole boiling of great captains as mere brigands, of as little sober significance in the history of the world as a bad belly-ache is of sober significance in the history of an individual. And by the same token he is grossly unfair to the sort of men who deduce philosophical ideas from the acts of such captains—for example, Bismarck and Machiavelli. Here the historian is always a slave to the democrat—that is, to the man who believes, not in salient and extraordinary men, but in the huge, brutish masses of ordinary men.

The same interloper appears every time Wells turns from the interpretation of the past to the forecasting of the future. The thing he dreams of is a sort of universal democracy, with all the affairs of the world ordered by the will of a vague and shifting majority. But he sees, of course, that the success of any such scheme must depend upon the possession of quick and accurate information by the people, and, more important still, upon their capacity to make use of it in a rational manner. Therefore, he is an enthusiastic advocate of popular education, and insists that it be made very much cheaper and more widespread than it is today. But here he overlooks a capital fact, and that is the fact that popular education, no matter what efforts are made to improve it, must inevitably remain but little more than a device for perpetuating the ideas that happen to be official—in other words, the nonsense regarded as revelation by the powers currently in control of the state. Education in the true sense—education directed toward awaking a capacity to differentiate between fact and appearance—is and always will be a more or less furtive and illicit thing, for its chief purpose is the controversion and destruction of the very ideas that the majority of men—and particularly the majority of official and powerful men—regard as incontrovertibly true. To the extent that I am genuinely educated, I am suspicious of all the things that the average citizen believes and the average pedagogue teaches. Progress consists precisely in attacking and disposing of these ordinary beliefs. It is thus opposed to education, as the thing is usually understood, and so there should be no surprise in the fact that the generality of pedagogues, like the generality of politicians and superpoliticians, are bitter enemies to all new ideas.

Think of what the average American schoolboy is taught today, say of history or economics. Examine the specific orders to teachers issued from time to time by the School Board of New York City—a body fairly representative of the forces that must always control education at the cost of the state. Surely no sane man would argue that the assimilation of such a mess of evasions and mendacities will make the boy of today a well-informed and quick-minded citizen tomorrow, alert to error and wary of propaganda. The plain fact is that such an education is itself a form of propaganda—a deliberate scheme to outfit the pupil, not with the capacity to weigh ideas, but with a simple appetite for gulping ideas ready-made. The aim is to make "good" citizens, which is to say, docile and uninquisitive citizens. Let a teacher let fall the slightest hint to his pupils that there is a body of doctrine opposed to the doctrine he is officially ordered to teach, and at once he is robbed of his livelihood and exposed to slander and persecution. The tendency grows wider as the field of education is widened. The college professor of Emerson's day was more or less a free agent, at all events in everything save theology; today his successor is a rubber-stamp, with all the talent for trembling of his constituent gutta-percha. In the lower schools the thing goes even further. Here (at least in New York) the teachers are not only compelled to stick to their text-books, but also to pledge their professional honor to a vast and shifting mass of transient doctrines. Any teacher who sought to give his pupils a rational view of the late Woodrow at the time Woodrow was stalking the land in the purloined chemise of Moses would have been dismissed from his pulpit, and probably jailed. The effects of such education are already distressingly visible in the Republic; let Dr. Wells give an eye to them when he is among us. Americans, in the days when their education stopped with the three R's, were a self-reliant, cynical, liberty-loving and extremely rambunctious people. Today, with pedagogy standardized and a school-house in every third block, they are the herd of sheep (*Ovis aries*).

Thus Wells's peruna fails to convince me; I doubt seriously that it would cure the patient. He believes in it simply because believing in it is an invariable part of the mental baggage of a democrat. Most of his other errors are due to his virtues as a British patriot. In discussing the war, despite a laudable and very palpable effort to be fair, he sometimes falls into distressing imbecilities, as, for example, when he argues that British imperialism was inspired by German imperialism and is an imitation of it. But this is not nearly so often as it might be. The whole war section, in fact, is immeasurably above anything that any American of like origin and surroundings would be capable of. It will probably be years before an American historian shows a fifth of the decency that Wells shows. Our college professors of history are still writing of the war in terms of the Liberty Loan posters, the editorials in *The New York Times,* the fulminations of the Creel Press Bureau, and the snuffling nonsense of the great Presbyterian. Here Wells displays once more, conclusively and sickeningly, how much higher all discussions of public matters range in England than they do in America. I know of no American who could have planned a work so bold and comprehensive—a work involving so colossal a synthesis of human knowledge and opinion in a field so tangled and so wide. And I know of none who could have executed it with such unfailing learning, such charming persuasiveness, and, above all, so much of honesty, dignity and sense.

(March, 1921)

JOSEPH CONRAD

Probing the Russian Psyche

The real objection to melodrama, when everything has been said, is not that its effects are too staggering but that its causes are too puny. The melodramatist, for all his exuberance of fancy, seldom shows us a downright impossible act; what he does constantly show us is an inadequate and in consequence a logically impossible motive.

Basil Montmorency, the tall, saturnine gentleman in the elegant dress suit with the shiny patent leather shoes and the cushions of gray above his ears—Basil Montmorency, that exquisite, that accursed fellow, binds the shrieking Lottie Sweeney to the rails, with the Cannon Ball Express bearing down at ninety miles an hour. Why? The melodramatist offers two reasons, the first being that Basil is Satan plus Don Juan, and the second being that Lottie has resisted his morganatic advances. We laugh thereat—laugh because our eyes reveal to us that Basil is far more the floorwalker, the head barber, the Knight of Pythias than the Satan or Don Juan—laugh because our experience of life teaches us that men do not bind women to railroad tracks for any such silly reason.

But women are undoubtedly done to death in that way—not every day, perhaps, but now and then. Men bind them, trains run over them; newspapers discuss the crime, the pursuit of the felon, the ensuing jousting of the jurisconsults. Why, then, do men bind them? The true answer, when it is forthcoming at all, is always much more complex than the melodramatist's answer. It may be so enormously complex, indeed, as to transcend all the normal laws of cause and effect —an answer made up largely, or even wholly, of the fantastic, the astounding, the unearthly reasons of lunacy. And that is the chief, if not the only difference between melodrama and reality. The events, the effects of the two may be, and often are identical. It is only in their underlying causes that they are dissimilar and incommensurate.

By all of which it appears that the selfsame incident or series of incidents in a work of fiction may bear either one of two diametrically
opposite aspects. If it is properly prepared for and accounted for, if it
comes at the end of a chain of connected and comprehensible though
perhaps amazing and unprecedented causes, then it has reality in it
and belongs of a right in any serious study of man and his ways. But
if it is unprepared and unaccountable, a bolt from the psychological
blue, an incident *in vacuo,* then it misses reality altogether and is fit
only for melodrama.

Here you have, in brief, the point of distinction between the great
stories of Joseph Conrad, a supreme artist in fiction, and the trashy
best sellers of the literary artisans. Conrad, like the artisans, has a liking for the spectacular, the nerveracking event. His tales are full of assaults, batteries, assassinations. He takes us through shipwrecks, revolutions, anarchist plottings, uproars of all imaginable sorts. But always his events have elaborate and plausible causes behind them—
always he tries to show us, not only the thing done, but also the why
of it and the wherefore. His *Nostromo,* in its externals, is merely a tale
of South American turmoil, and not unrelated to *Soldiers of Fortune.*
But what great differences between the methods, the points of view,
the psychological materials of the two stories! Davis is content to
show us the overt act; Conrad goes behind it for the motive, the
process of mind. The one achieves an agreeable romance, and an
agreeable romance only; the other achieves an extraordinarily incisive
study of the Latin-American temperament—a study of the ideals and
passions which lead presumably sane men to pursue each other like
wolves, and of the reaction of that incessant pursuit upon the men
themselves. I do not say that Conrad is always accurate. I do not
know, in point of fact, whether he is or isn't. But I do say that he is
wholly convincing, that the men he sets into his scene hang together;
that the explanations he offers for their acts are at least plausible;
that the effects of those acts, upon actors and immediate spectators
alike, are such as might be reasonably expected to follow; that the
final impression is one of almost uncanny reality.

Such is his manner in all of his great stories. Sometimes, as in "The
Point of Honor" and "The End of the Tether," his chief concern is
with the obscure genesis, in human emotion or ideation, of an extraordinary event; at other times, as in *Typhoon* and "Youth," his main endeavor is to determine the effect of such an event upon the mind and

soul of man; at still other times, as in *Almayer's Folly* and *Lord Jim*, he makes his slow way from one event to another through a maze of mingled consequences and causes. But always it is the process of mind rather than the actual act that interests him; always he is trying to account for the thing visible to the eye; always he is trying to penetrate the actor's mask and interpret the actor's frenzy. That is what makes him a literary artist of the first calibre, whatever his occasional failings in mere craftmanship. And that is what gives importance and distinction and high quality to the latest of his books, *Under Western Eyes*, for all its irritating *ritardandos*, its circumlocutions, its infelicities of phrase. Conrad, though he writes in English, is a Pole. I have been told that he knew no English until he was at the end of his 'teens; that when he came to write he was a long time deciding between English, French and some third language, probably Polish or Russian. The result of his multilingual thinking is often visible in his prose. He fishes patiently, laboriously for the right phrase; it may be, when he finds it, a French phrase or a Polish phrase, clumsy when done into English. And his whole manner is extraordinarily deliberate; he hangs over an idea until he has made it plain, however slight its relative importance, however damaging the delay to the dramatic rhythm of the narrative. But if you accept all this as a necessary concession to a great artist's faults, if you take him as he stands, infinitely painstaking, infinitely analytical, you must grant him, in the end, the virtue of accomplishing something magnificent by all that assiduity. The first time I read *Lord Jim* it exasperated me, the second time it fascinated me, the third time it staggered me. It is, in a sense, unique in English fiction. It is Dumas and Stevenson raised to the dignity of Athenian tragedy.

Under Western Eyes lacks something of that fine perfection. It suffers, to begin with, from the general defect of being less interesting than *Lord Jim*. Its events are less goldenly romantic, less heroic; its personages, despite a plentiful picturesqueness, have none of the barbaric exaltation and glamour of Jim himself, of Dain Waris, Doramin, Tamb' Itam and the Rajah Allang, of Stein, Cornelius and Cornelius's Jewel. Moreover, its central situation comes perilously near to banality. Even in the best-sellers the hero who finds his true love among the womenfolk of his enemy has long gone stale. But with all of these demerits vividly in mind, the story yet produces an effect of powerful drama, of undoubted actuality. It is the general effect rather than the special effect, the background rather than the incident, that enlists

Conrad's attention. He is trying to set before us, not so much the story of one man as a study of the Russian national character, with all its queer mingling of Western astuteness and Oriental fogginess, its crazy tendency to go shooting off into the interstellar spaces of an incomprehensible mysticism, its general transcendence of all that we Celts and Saxons and Latins hold to be true of human motive and human act. Russia is a world apart: that is the sum and substance of the tale. "It is unthinkable"—I quote from Page 24—"that any young Englishman (or American, or Dane, or Spaniard, for that matter) should find himself in Razumov's situation. . . . He would not think as Razumov thought at this crisis of his fate. . . . By an act of mental extravagance he might imagine himself arbitrarily thrown into prison; but it would never occur to him, unless he were delirious (and perhaps not even then) that he could be beaten with whips as a practical measure either of investigation or of punishment."

This Razumov, then, is a young Russian, a student at the University of St. Petersburg; a pushing, hard reading, ambitious fellow; the illegitimate and unacknowledged son of a great personage. He is too busy to have much concern with the Utopia making of his fellows; he knows vaguely what they are about and he is polite to them, but no definite group, whether of action or of mere fustian, has him on its roll. His dream is of some safe professorship and the fame of a pundit. His secret sympathy is with the existing order, as becomes a man of good blood. Into the room of this rather colorless young man there bursts one evening a disheveled brother student, Victor Victorovitch Haldin by name, with a startling appeal for help. M. de P——, the Minister President, chief recruiting officer for Siberia and the gallows, has been done to death on the street. "It was I," says Haldin deliberately, proudly, "who removed De P——." But why come to Razumov? Why ask help of the one man least likely to give it with enthusiasm? "Because," says Haldin, "you are the last that could be suspected—should I get caught. . . . And it occurred to me that you—you have no one belonging to you—no ties, no one to suffer if this came out. . . . There have been enough ruined Russian homes as it is."

So the problem faces poor Razumov—to save Haldin, or to betray him? He decides, weakly dubious, upon the first course. There is a drunken sledge driver, one Ziemianitch, to be sought out and instructed. Ziemianitch is to wait for Haldin at a certain street corner, half an hour after midnight. Razumov starts out to find the fellow:

Ziemianitch is dead drunk, resistant to blows and bawling. Razumov
wanders about the streets, half crazed with doubts and dreads. On the
one hand, there is his chivalrous duty to Haldin, the only human being in all the world who has ever put trust in him; on the other hand
there is that mirage of a professorship and a long life of ease, and a
chance, perhaps, to do a real service to Russia. He is won over, in the
end, by the professorship. He goes to Prince K——, boldly asserting,
though not in words, the tie of blood; and he and Prince K—— go to
General T——, a magnifico above and beyond all mere police. Then
he returns to his room and tells the waiting Haldin that Ziemianitch
will be in readiness. Haldin, at midnight, slinks out into the bitter
cold. . . . Four days later he is hanged.

And now we plunge headlong into the dark depths of the Russian
character. Razumov has done something for God and the Czar, but
the reward of such services, in Russia, is not the frank one of the
West. General T——, inscrutable behind his beard, mingles ever so
discreet questions with his spoken thanks. Councilor Mikulin, a famous
searcher of hearts, a master of delicate cross-examinations, is called up
to help. Why did Haldin go to Razumov's room? On what pretext did
Razumov induce him to stay there three hours? Razumov has said
nothing about the visit to Ziemianitch, nothing about his uncertainty;
his story makes him a betrayer from beginning to end. But the eternal
suspiciousness of the men in uniform, if it does not actually penetrate
that deception, at least comes close to it, jostles it, marks out its outlines. The test, finally, is put to poor Razumov. He is offered the
greatest of all payment for his night's work—a chance to serve the
Czar again. The old comrades of Haldin know only that he sheltered
the fugitive; the betrayal is laid at other doors. The ideal man for police work of the highest sort! The ideal man to "flee" from Russia,
closely "pursued" by Mikulin's men—to invade Geneva and the colony
of exiles there, and send back news by way of a safe agent in Vienna!

And so the end approaches. Razumov, cornered, is forced to accept the commission, with all its torturing difficulties and shames. In
Geneva are Haldin's mother and sister, tragic figures in that parliament of frauds and fools. Around them revolve the "thinkers" and
"leaders" of the revolution—writers for obscure, forbidden newspapers, planners of diableries for lesser spirits to carry out, attitudinizers
and platitudinarians—ten charlatans to one honest man. Razumov,
thrown into this rabble, turns to the brave and sorrowing Nathalie

quite naturally, and is in love with her before he knows it—but let us stay our snickers! It is not because he falls in love with Nathalie that he makes his staggering confession—not primarily, at any rate. One somehow feels that. The confession was foreordained, Nathalie or no Nathalie, as the logical climax of the emotional hurricane through which he has passed. His life has gone to pieces; his dream of a sedate professorship, of an old age full of ease and honor, is done; henceforth he is to be the slave of Mikulin; for his lamented service to the Czar he must bear forever his share of the heavy burden of the Czar. So there is no true surprise, at the end, when he stalks into the meeting of maniacs and mountebanks and there invites destruction. Nor is there any surprise when that destruction takes a fantastic and horrible, an essentially Russian form—Nikita, the "police killer," springing forward like a tiger, Razumov's head in his hairy hands, Razumov's eardrums broken, his legs yanked out of joint by main strength, his senseless form thrown out into the street, for a streetcar crew to blunder upon in the gray dawn—and Nikita cackling over the business: "He'll never be any use for a spy to anyone! . . . I have burst the drums of his ears. Oh, you may trust *me!* I know the trick. He, he, he! I know the trick!"

If you know Conrad, you also know, of course, that all this is not the story of *Under Western Eyes,* but only the gross framework of that story. The real concern of the author is with the genesis and conflict of ideas in the mind of Razumov. What he is always trying to make clear is that Razumov is essentially a Russian, that his ideation follows routes unfamiliar, and often almost impassable, to the man of the West. The thing, in brief, is a study in national or rather in racial psychology. Its aim is to give us more or less clearly a notion of the processes of thought which eventuate in the astounding Russian act— the elaborately planned, artistically perfect, wholly savage assassination; the piling up of spy upon spy, of spy upon the spy of spy; the childlike following of false and motley leaders; the sudden appearance of the Tartar chieftain, fresh from the steppes, in the frock coat of the bespectacled doctor of philosophy. The characters of the tale, for all their *bizarrerie,* never lose plausibility. Razumov's slow progress, through doubt and terror, to what must be accepted, perhaps, as actual insanity, has the convincing flow of an equation. And the impostors at Geneva, conscious and unconscious, are sketched with almost Molièresque brilliancy. It is not, to be sure, Conrad at his greatest; as

I have said, *Lord Jim* is a far more arresting piece of work. But it is certainly Conrad at a level of achievement which not many other men of the day ever reach. If by any chance you don't know this extraordinary Pole, now is the time to subscribe. *Under Western Eyes* represents him fairly enough. Along with *Nostromo, The Secret Agent,* and his own share of *Romance,* it may stand for the average Conrad, the Conradic mean. Above and beyond tower the heights—"Youth", *Heart of Darkness, Typhoon,* "The End of the Tether," "Falk" and *Lord Jim*—a series shaming all praise. If I had to choose four stories of Conrad and let all the rest go, I should choose "Youth," *Heart of Darkness, Typhoon* and "Falk." If I had to choose four stories among all written in English since 1888 and let the rest go, "Youth" and "Falk" would be two of them.

(January, 1912)

Conrad's Self-Portrait

Now for Conrad, who comes forward, as if yielding in advance to his impending popularity, with a volume called *A Personal Record,* in which he describes the genesis of *Almayer's Folly,* his first novel, and sweeps his incredible youth with a philosophical glance. The son of a Polish aristocrat, and bred to carry on the family trade of political martyrdom, he astounded his relatives toward the end of his school days by demanding that they let him go to sea. Why to sea? Whence the origin of that exotic yearning? Poland was not a land of sailors. There was no record, in all the family archives, nor in those of friends and neighbors, of one who had dallied with ships. Nor was there even a history of a romantic invasion from without: no wandering mariner had penetrated that far country, to spin his yarns and set the boy afire. But nevertheless young Joseph declared for the sea, and after a due period of deliberation and opposition the family council surrendered and negotiations were opened with a mysterious M. Solary, of Marseilles, who knew ship captains and could berth an apprentice. A change of flags from the Tricolor to the Union Jack followed soon—"if a seaman, then an English seaman"—and ten years later Mr. Joseph

Conrad Korzeniowski, now Mr. Joseph Conrad, stood upon the quarterdeck of his own ship, a master in the British merchant service. And a master he remained until *Almayer's Folly* won him fame and sent him ashore to write *An Outcast of the Islands* and *Lord Jim* and "Youth" and *Typhoon* and all the rest of those enthralling and memorable tales.

Conrad's book of fact is as formless as his fiction. He begins it in the middle and does not go back to the beginning until it is half done. We see him get his master's certificate long before we see him get his first glimpse of the sea. We hear how *Almayer's Folly* was written long before we hear a word about Almayer. On one page it is the year 1873 and young Joseph is descending the Furca Pass with his tutor. On the next page it is the year 1812 and Mr. Nicholas B——, granduncle to Joseph and *officier d'ordonnance* to Marshal Marmont, is retreating from Moscow and eating a dog *en route*. (Granduncle to Joseph, but father to Falk!) So the book appears as one proceeds, a string of dissentient episodes, a mixture of reminiscence and self-explanation, a thing of no apparent coherence or direction. But how vivid the picture when it is closed and put away! How magnificently Conrad has drawn himself, as he drew Almayer, Jim, MacWhirr, Kurtz, Nostromo and Falk in days gone by! The notes of experience in "Youth," *Heart of Darkness* and *Typhoon*, and above all, in *The Mirror of the Sea*, fall into their ordered places; chaos becomes symmetry; a real man emerges.

And that real man, if I make no mistake, is the greatest artist writing in English today. Don't think that I here fall into a merely rhetorical hurrah, all sound and no sense. I am not forgetting Hardy and *Jude the Obscure*, nor Moore and his superb memoirs, nor Kipling and *Kim*, nor Wells and *The New Machiavelli*, nor James and *What Maisie Knew*, nor the honest stuff in the midst of Bennett's tinsel, nor the early work of Howells, nor the high points of such men as De Morgan, Chesterton, Masefield, Galsworthy and Shaw. But put the best of Kipling beside "Youth" or *Heart of Darkness* or *Typhoon*, and you begin to sense Kipling's deficiencies. In one detail or another many of our current scriveners are far beyond Conrad. James, Wells and Kipling have vastly more humor; Howells and Hardy are nearer to the usual, the typical; Moore writes incomparably better English. But take him as he stands, Conrad shows more draft and beam than any of these. Better than the best of them he penetrates to the central fact of human existence—the fact, to wit, that life is meaningless, that it has no purpose, that its so-called lessons are balderdash—the capital discovery of our day and generation—the one supreme truth that must eventually revise and condition every other truth. In his stories you will find, for the first time in the history of the world, romance set free from sentimentality. He is, in short, not only a great artist, but also a great artistic revolutionist, and some day he will get his due. Meanwhile, as I have said, the great American public, overlooking entirely the very virtue which sets him above and apart from the whole rabble of popular authors, threatens to take him to its arms as a new and delectable Stevenson, a super-Richard-Harding-Davis, a Dumas *de luxe*. Let it embrace him; he will survive the squeeze. And he will also survive his brief day.

(October, 1912)

Victory

Can it be that Joseph Conrad connives at the current effort to make a popular novelist of him? Is it possible that the austere author of *Chance* and *Lord Jim* has determined after all these years to buck and best the Indiana genii? Does he actually lend a covert hand to those shameless Barabbases of Garden City, L. I., who advertise him as if he were some new brand of breakfast food or touring car, and republish his incomparable masterpieces in rows of pretty volumes, and bedizen the slip-covers thereof with encomiums by James Huneker, Edwin Björkman, J. B. Kerfoot, Edwin Markham, H. L. Mencken and other such tasters and snouters of good, bad and indifferent books? One blushes to think of that sort of debauchery. It goes against tradition and the grain. But here, alas, is the damning evidence. Here, to wit, is *Victory*, a bouncing and straightforward tale of love and villainy, a yarn as swift and compact as the veriest piece of trade goods, a fiction that even a tired business man might conceivably enjoy and understand. Gone are all the Conradean indirections of yesteryear: the backings and fillings, the endless interludes and by-the-ways, the amazing snarls and subtleties. In place of them there is a narrative

that gets under way on the very first page and proceeds uninter-
ruptedly to a *sforzando* and melodramatic close. It moves; it throbs; it
grips. And the thing in it that does the gripping is not a meticulous
and merciless anatomizing of motive and emotion, as in *Lord Jim*, or
Almayer's Folly, or *Under Western Eyes*, but a skilful and deliberate
piling up of dramatic suspense, as in *Germinal*, or *McTeague*, or (one
almost adds) *Treasure Island*. In brief, the story sets a new style for
Conrad, and one obviously likely to increase his audience. Not even
"Falk" or *Typhoon* has more naked action in it.

The scene is again the Eastern islands that the great Pole long ago
preëmpted for his own, and the central figure is one Baron Alex [*sic*]
Heyst, a wandering and enigmatical Swede. Of the origin and early
history of this Heyst we never learn very much; when we meet him he
has been drifting up and down those sapphire seas for years, and the
one public enterprise of his life, the Tropical Belt Coal Company, has
already gone to smash. All that remains of the Tropical Belt Coal
Company is a pair of bungalows and a rickety jetty on a certain small
and remote island—an island made visible (and sinister and hostile)
for miles around by the volcano that glowers at one end of it. It is
here, in one of the bungalows, that Heyst finally makes his home. Out
from London, by Gibraltar, Suez, Aden, Colombo and Singapore,
come certain huge packing cases, and out of the packing cases come
books, furniture, plate and pictures. One of the pictures is a fine portrait of Heyst's father. He hangs it in the living-room of his bungalow
and beneath its inscrutable gaze he dines in solitary state every evening, attended by his one servant and companion, a silent Chinaman
named Wang. Once in a great while, having mysterious business to
transact with merchants and bankers, Heyst hails a passing trading
ship from his jetty and makes a visit to Sourabaya, the parched capital
of one of the far-flung Dutch Indies. There he puts up at Schomberg's
Hotel and for a brief space gives the bibulous clerks and supercargoes
of the port something to gossip about.

It is Schomberg (fat, carnal, timorous, a lieutenant of the reserve)
who sets in train the events that make up the story of Heyst's undoing. A highly dubious "ladies'" orchestra has come to Sourabaya, offi-
cered by a greasy German disguised as Signor Zangiacomo, and
Schomberg has installed it in an alleged concert hall adjoining his hotel. There it butchers Verdi and Meyerbeer of an evening, while the
clerks and supercargoes swill gin-fizzes and ogle its constituent artists.

Upon one of these artists, Alma by name, Schomberg himself casts a lascivious eye. He has a wife, true enough, and she is constantly visible in the background, but, as he himself says, he is devoid of conventional prejudices and superstitions—and Sourabaya is anything but a Methodist port. But this Alma, strangely enough, is not much impressed by the honor that Schomberg proposes to confer upon her. On the contrary, she regards his gross lovemaking with the utmost aversion, and in the end she is so terrified by it that she appeals to Heyst for help. Heyst is no ladies' man, but *noblesse oblige!* One morning, before the oafish Schomberg is astir, he puts Alma into a boat and departs with her for his island, and there, in that God-forsaken Eden, they make shift to marry each other, and, what is more, to fall in love. Alma is a simple girl and Heyst is a handsome man. Heyst is a simple fellow and Alma is a pretty girl.

Schomberg, back in Sourabaya, rages and gnashes his teeth like Gerald Basingstoke or Desperate Desmond. More, he babbles his woes to all who will give him ear, and so gradually builds up a tremendous fiction of Heyst's villainy. He accuses the Swede of swindles and chicaneries innumerable, and even of a treacherous murder. He pictures the island of Alma's sanctuary as a sort of piratical retreat, with the profits of a thousand foul deeds hidden in its caves. And he tells the tale so often that he not only comes to believe it himself, but gives it wide currency in the archipelago, so that Heyst grows into a sort of legendary billionaire, a tropical Monte Cristo. Finally, from Schomberg's lips, it reaches one Martin Ricardo, a touring faro dealer and general blackleg, and from Ricardo it is transmitted to his master, the elegant Mr. Jones. This Mr. Jones is a gentleman adventurer whose field is the world. He has a past in Central America and another in the ports of the Eastern Mediterranean; it is now his ambition to engage the goddess of chance in South Africa. To finance this enterprise hard cash is necessary—and Heyst is reputed to have it by the bag. So Mr. Jones and Ricardo, accompanied by an anthropoid Central American who serves them as valet, cook and first murderer, set out in an open boat for Heyst's island.

What follows is melodrama so rapid, so gorgeous, so inordinate that I make no effort to reduce it to a dead summary. Thrill follows thrill in staggering succession. Conrad applies to the unfolding of it all the resources of his extraordinary art, and particularly all his gift for the dark, the threatening, the sinister. From the moment that Jones and Ricardo reach the crazy jetty, sun-blistered, purple-faced, half dead of thirst—from this moment to the last scene of all, with Heyst dead, Alma dead, Jones and Ricardo dead, the apeman dead and Wang vanished into the jungle, there is no halting or turning aside in this inexorable tragedy of blood. Put upon paper by a lesser man it would become a mere penny-dreadful, almost a burlesque. But as it is told by Conrad it takes on the Homeric proportions of an epic, a saga. The thing is more than melodramatic; it is shocking, appalling, dreadful. Told, as I say, in a straightforward, almost bald manner, with no apparent effort to build up effects, it yet leaves upon the mind a picture almost as vivid and as haunting as that left by *Heart of Darkness*. Jones, indeed, is a worthy companion for Mr. Kurtz. In both of them one glimpses depravity grown so vast that it takes on an aspect of the heroic. And in both of them, at bottom, there is humor—humor infinitely ironic, infinitely horrible.

Perhaps you read *Victory* in the February number of *Munsey's*, where it was printed with a few slight omissions. If not, then my advice is that you get the book and prepare yourself for a new order of adventure in fiction. It is, at one stroke, an authentic contribution to the Conrad canon, despite its novelty of plan and treatment, and an example of unadorned story-telling that challenges the most galloping of the best-sellers on their own ground. Perhaps, as I have hinted, it represents a deliberate effort by Conrad to yield something to the limitations of that wider audience which now drapes itself about him. But more likely it is an answer to those critics who have hitherto charged him with falling a victim to his own meticulousness. Frank Norris, it will be recalled, once played the same trick upon those who derided his realism and set him down as one incapable of managing a simple romance. That trick took the form of *Blix*, a sugar-teat so charmingly sweet that it made all the other sugar-teats seem sour. In the same way *Victory* makes all the other thrillers seem empty and paralytic. Read it after *Nostromo*, or after—well, say the latest Oppenheim: in either case it will hold you enthralled to the end and send you away with the feeling that you have given your time to something in the front rank of current English fiction. The one obvious blemish upon it is an omission. Why does Conrad forget the volcano, that glowering symbol of the whole sordid drama? One hears a good deal of it at the start. It dominates and menaces Heyst's lonely island; it is the beacon that brings Jones and Ricardo to the crazy jetty. And then, unaccountably, one hears of it no more.

There is another Conrad book in the month's hatching, but this time

it is merely a reprint. He calls it *A Set of Six,* and it consists of five
longish short stories and a novelette. The latter, here called "The
Duel," was published separately as "The Point of Honor" in 1908, and
the whole collection was printed in England under its present title
about the same time. "The Duel" is one of the sardonic fancies that
Conrad delights in. Two officers of Napoleon's army, coming to a dispute over a trifle, fight a duel. The result is inconclusive and they
presently fight again. Shortly afterward they meet a third time, and
thenceforth, for almost half a century, they are eternally at each
other's throats. The original cause of their quarrel soon fades into the
background; in the course of time, indeed, they actually forget it. But
with sword, cutlass and pistol, on horseback and afoot, they pursue
their incomprehensible feud with grim and laborious ferocity, until, in
the end, they are so old that they can scarcely lift their arms. No
more penetrating *reductio ad absurdum* of the punctilio could be
imagined. It is a brilliant answer to those carpers who have denied
Conrad a feeling for humor. He is, in point of fact, as profound a
humorist as Ibsen, and he clothes his jocosities in the same deceptive
irony.

Of the five shorter stories in the volume the most remarkable, perhaps, is "Gaspar Ruiz," a romantic tale of a South American revolution. It is a sort of by-product, I suspect, of *Nostromo,* which pre-
ceded it in publication by four years. Both are attempts to depict the
civilization of the yellow republics as it really is—not as the democracy it calls itself, nor even as a colorable parody of democracy, but as
a medieval feudalism. This Gaspar Ruiz is a strong man who forces
himself upward from the bottom—a colossal, gargantuan figure, terrible in both love and war. The manner of his death is astoundingly
novel and shocking. Confronted in battle by a superior force and having no mount for his one piece of artillery, he—but I am not going to
spoil the story for you by telling you too much of it. It will thrill you,
I am sure, and so will "The Brute," another of the six, and perhaps
"An Anarchist" also. The two remaining are rather less striking, but
Conrad at his feeblest is still vastly ahead of most other story-tellers at
their best. A brief note by the author is printed as a preface to the
volume.

(April, 1915)

A Good Book on Conrad

Conrad Again—The best study of Joseph Conrad that has yet appeared is to be found in a little book by Wilson Follet, lately privately printed by Doubleday, Page & Company. Why privately? God knows. Perhaps because this same firm publishes Richard Curle's highly unsatisfactory tome on Conrad—10 per cent sound criticism and the rest wind and moonshine. Ask for a copy of the Follet book at once; it is for free distribution so long as the supply lasts. It is full of sharp observation and intelligent discussion. I recall a haunting saying: "Under all his stories there ebbs and flows a kind of tempered melancholy, a sense of seeking and not finding. . . ." Nothing could better describe the effect of such tales as *Almayer's Folly*, *Nostromo* and *Lord Jim*. Even "Youth," though it interprets and celebrates the indomitable, yet has defeat and tragedy in it; one sees the breakup of middle age beyond the Homeric endeavors of one-and-twenty. . . . Mr. Follet finds the cause of Conrad's preference for *adagio* in the circumstances of his own life—his double exile, first from Poland and then from the sea. But this is surely stretching the facts until they squeak. Neither exile, in truth, was enforced, nor is either irrevocable. Conrad has been back to Poland, and he is free to 'round the Horn again whenever the spirit moves him. Far better to look for the springs of his melancholy in that deepest-lying race philosophy which seems to engulf all reflective men soon or late. I mean resignationism.

All philosophies and all religions come to resignationism at the last. Once it takes shape as the concept of Nirvana, the desire for nothingness, the will to not-will. Again, it is fatalism in this form or that—Mohammedanism, Agnosticism, . . . Presbyterianism! Yet again, it is the "Out, out, brief candle!" of Shakespeare, the *"Vanitas vanitatum; omnia vanitas!"* of the Preacher. Or, to make an end, it is millennium-ism, or the theory that the world is going to blow up to-morrow, or the day after, or two weeks hence, and that all sweating and striving are thus useless. Search where you will, near or far, in ancient or in modern times, and you will never find a race or an age that gave more than a passing bow to optimism. Even Christianity, starting out as "glad tidings," has had to take on protective coloration to survive, and to-day its chief professors moan and blubber like Iokanaan in Herod's rain-barrel. The sanctified are few and far between. The vast majority of us must suffer in hell, just as we suffer on earth. The divine grace, so omnipotent to save, is withheld from us. Why? There, alas, is your insoluble mystery, your riddle of the universe. . . .

This conviction that human life is a seeking without a finding, that its purpose is impenetrable, that joy and sorrow are alike meaningless, you will see written largely in the work of all great artists. It is obviously the final message, if any message is to be sought there at all, of the nine symphonies of Ludwig van Beethoven. It is the idea that broods over Wagner's Ring, as the divine wrath broods over the Old Testament. In Shakespeare, as Shaw has demonstrated, it amounts to a veritable obsession. What else is there in Turgenieff, Dostoievski, Andrieff? Or in the Zola of *L'Assommoir, Germinal, La Débâcle,* the whole "Rougon-Macquart" series? (The Zola of *Les Quatres Evangiles,* and particularly of *Fécondité,* turned uplifter and optimist, and became ludicrous.) Or in Hauptmann, or Hardy, or Sudermann (I mean, of course, Sudermann the novelist; Sudermann the dramatist is a mere mechanician). . . . The younger men of today, in all countries, seem to cherish this philosophy of impotence and surrender. Consider the last words of *Riders to the Sea.* Or Gorky's *Nachtasyl.* Or Frank Norris' *McTeague.* Or Dreiser's *Jennie Gerhardt.* Or George Moore's *Sister Theresa.* Or Conrad's *An Outcast of the Islands.*

Conrad, more than any other of the men I have mentioned, grounds his whole work upon a sense of this "immense indifference of things." The exact point of the story of Kurtz, in *Heart of Darkness,* is that it is pointless, that Kurtz's death is as meaningless as his life, that the moral of such a sordid tragedy is a wholesale negation of all morals. And this, no less, is the point of the story of "Falk," and of that of Almayer, and of that of Jim. Mr. Follet (he must be an American!) finds himself, in the end, unable to accept so profound a pessimism unadulterated, and so he injects a gratuitous and mythical optimism into it, and hymns Conrad "as a comrade, one of a company gathered under the ensign of hope for common war on despair." With the highest regard, Pish! Conrad makes war upon nothing; he is preeminently *not* a moralist. He swings, indeed, as far from moralizing as is possible, for he does not even criticise God. His undoubted comradeship, his plain kindliness toward the souls he vivisects, is not the child of hope but of pity. Like Mark Twain he might well say: "The more I see of men, the more I laugh at them—and the more I pity them." He is *simpatico* precisely because of his infinite commiseration. . . . I have said that he does not criticise God; one may imagine him even pitying God. . . .

As for Conrad the literary artist (opposing him here to Conrad the humanist), one cause of the startling vividness that he gets into his narrative is to be found in the dimness that he so deliberately leaves there. A paradox, of course, but I do not devise it for its own sake, believe me. What I mean to say is that Conrad always shows us a picture that is full of the little obscurities, the uncertainties of outline, the mysterious shadings-off, that we see in the real world around us. He does not pretend to the traditional omniscience of the novelist. He is not forever translating the unknowable in motive and act into ready formulae; instead, he says frankly that he does not know, or, at best, "I believe," or "perhaps," or "Marlow thinks it possible." A trick? To be sure. But also much more than a trick, for its constant repetition not only constitutes a manner but also indicates a state of mind. Conrad knows his characters too well to explain them too glibly. They are too real to him (and to us) to be made quite understandable. They keep to the end all of that fine mysteriousness which forever hangs about those who are nearest and dearest to us. . . . A man may profess to understand the President of the United States, but he seldom alleges, even to himself, that he understands his wife.

(January, 1916)

Conrad Revisited

I put in a blue afternoon last week re-reading Joseph Conrad's *Youth*. A *blue* afternoon? What nonsense! The touch of the man is like the touch of Schubert. One approaches him in various and unhappy moods: depressed, dubious, despairing; one leaves him in the clear, yellow sunshine that Nietzsche found in Bizet's music. But here again the phrase is inept. Sunshine suggests the imbecile, barnyard joy of the human kohlrabi—the official optimism of a steadily delighted and increasingly insane Republic. What the enigmatical Pole has to offer is something quite different. If its parallel is to be found in music, it is not in Schubert, but in Beethoven—perhaps even more accurately in Johann Sebastian Bach. It is the joy, not of mere satisfaction, but of understanding—the profound but surely not merry delight which goes with the comprehension of a fundamental fact—above all, of a fact

that has been coy and elusive. Certainly the order of the world that
Conrad sets forth with such diabolical eloquence and plausibility is no
banal moral order, no childish sequence of virtuous causes and edifying effects. Rather it has an atheistic and even demoniacal smack: to
the earnest Bible-student it must be more than a little disconcerting.
The God he visualizes is no loving papa in a house-coat and carpet-
slippers, inculcating the great principles of Christian ethics by applying occasional strokes *a posteriori*. What he sees is something quite
different: an extremely ingenious and humorous improvisatore and
comedian, with a dab of red on his nose and maybe somewhat the
worse for drink—a furious and far from amiable banjoist upon the human spine, and rattler of human bones. Kurtz, in *Youth*, makes a capital banjo for that exalted and cynical talent. And the music that issues
forth—what a superb *Hexentanz* it is!

One of the curiosities of critical stupidity is the doctrine that Conrad is without humor. No doubt it flows out of a more general error:
to wit, the assumption that tragedy is always pathetic, that death itself
is inevitably a gloomy business. That error, I suppose, will persist in
the world until some extraordinarily astute mime conceives the plan of
playing *King Lear* as a farce—I mean deliberately. That it *is* a farce
seems to me quite as obvious as the fact that *Romeo and Juliet* is another, this time lamentably coarse. To adopt the contrary theory—to
view it as a great moral and spiritual spectacle, capable of purging
and uplifting the psyche like marriage to a red-haired widow or a
month in the trenches—to toy with such notions is to borrow the critical standards of a party of old ladies weeping over the damnation of
the heathen. In point of fact, death, like love, is intrinsically farcical
—a solemn kicking of a brick under a plug-hat—and most human
agonies, once they transcend the physical—*i.e.*, the unescapably real
—have far more of irony in them than of pathos. Looking back upon
them after they have eased one seldom shivers: one smiles—perhaps
sourly but nevertheless spontaneously. This, at all events, is the notion
that seems to me to be implicit in every line of Conrad. I give you
Heart of Darkness as the archetype of his whole work and the key-
stone of his metaphysical system. Here we have all imaginable human
hopes and aspirations reduced to one common denominator of folly
and failure, and here we have a play of humor that is infinitely mordant and searching. Turn to pages 136 and 137 of the American edition—the story is in the volume called *Youth*—: the burial of the

helmsman. Turn then to 178–184: Marlow's last interview with Kurtz's
Intended. The farce mounts by slow stages to dizzy and breath-taking
heights. One hears harsh roars of laughter, vast splutterings of transcendental mirth, echoing and re-echoing down the black corridors of
empty space. The curtain descends at last upon a wild dance in a
dissecting-room. The mutilated dead rise up and jig. . . .

It is curious, re-reading a thrice-familiar story, how often one finds
surprises in it. I have been amazed, toward the close of "The End of
the Tether," to discover that the *Fair Maid* was wrecked, not by the
deliberate act of Captain Whalley, but by the machination of the unspeakable Massy. How is one to account for so preposterous an error?
Certainly I thought I knew "The End of the Tether" as well as I knew
anything in this world—and yet there was that incredible misunder-
standing of it, lodged firmly in my mind. Perhaps there is criticism of
a sort in my blunder: it may be a fact that the old skipper willed the
thing himself—that his willing it is visible in all that goes before—that
Conrad, in introducing Massy's puerile infamy at the end, made some
sacrifice of inner veracity to the exigencies of what, at bottom, is
somewhat too neat and well-made a tale. The story, in fact, belongs to
the author's earlier manner; I guess that it was written before "Youth"
and surely before *Heart of Darkness*. But for all that, its proportions
remain truly colossal. It is one of the most magnificent narratives, long
or short, old or new, in the English language, and with "Youth" and
Heart of Darkness it makes up what is probably the best book of
imaginative writing that the English literature of the twentieth century can yet show. Conrad has learned a great deal since he wrote it,
true enough. In *Lord Jim,* in *Victory,* and, above all, in *A Personal
Record* there are momentary illuminations, blinding flashes of brilliance that he was incapable of in those days of experiment; but no
other book of his seems to me to hold so steadily to so high a general
level—none other, as a whole, is more satisfying and more marvellous.
There is in *Heart of Darkness* a perfection of design which one encounters only rarely and miraculously in prose fiction: it belongs rather to music. I can't imagine taking a single sentence out of that stupendous tale without leaving a visible gap; it is as thoroughly *durch
componiert* as a fugue. And I can't imagine adding anything to it,
even so little as a word, without doing it damage. As it stands it is
austerely and beautifully perfect, just as the slow movement of the
Unfinished Symphony is perfect.

I observe of late a tendency to examine the English of Conrad rather biliously. The folly is cultivated chiefly in England, where, I suppose, chauvinistic motives enter into the matter. It is the just boast of great empires that they draw in talents from near and far, exhausting the little nations to augment their own puissance; it is their misfortune that these talents often remain defectively assimilated. Conrad remains the Slav after all these years; the people of his tales, whatever he calls them, are always as much Slavs as he is; the language in which he describes them retains a sharp exotic flavor. But to say that this flavor constitutes a blemish is to say something so preposterous that only schoolmasters and their dupes may be thought of as giving it credit. The truly first-rate writer is not one who uses the language as such dolts demand that it be used; he is one who reworks it in spite of their prohibitions. It is his distinction that he thinks in a manner different from the thinking of ordinary men; that he is free from that slavery to embalmed ideas which makes them so respectable and so dull. Obviously, he cannot translate his notions into terms of everyday without doing violence to their inner integrity: as well ask a Richard Strauss to funnel all his music into the chaste jugs of Prof. Dr. Jadassohn. What Conrad brings into English literature is a new concept of the relations between fact and fact, idea and idea, and what he contributes to the complex and difficult art of writing English is a new way of putting words together. His style amazes and irritates pedants because it does not roll along in the old ruts. Well, it is precisely that rolling along in the old ruts that he tries to avoid—and it is precisely that avoidance which makes him what he is. What lies under most of his alleged sins seems to me to be simple enough: he views English logically and analytically, and not through a haze of senseless traditions and arbitrary taboos. No Oxford mincing is in him. If he cannot find his phrase above the salt, he seeks it below. His English, in a word, is innocent. And if, at times, there gets into it a color that is strange and even bizarre, then the fact is something to rejoice over, for a living language is like a man suffering incessantly from small internal hemorrhages, and what it needs above all else is constant transfusions of new blood from other tongues. The day the gates go up, that day it begins to die.

A very great man, this Mr. Conrad. As yet, I believe, decidedly understimated, even by many of his advocates. Most of his first acclaimers mistook him for a mere romantic—a talented but somewhat uncouth follower of the Stevenson tradition, with the orthodox cutlass exchanged for a Malay *kris*. Later on he began to be heard of as a linguistic and vocational marvel: it was astonishing that any man bred to Polish should write English at all, and more astonishing that a country gentleman from the Ukraine should hold a master's certificate in the British merchant marine. Such banal attitudes are now archaic, but I suspect that they have been largely responsible for the slowness with which his fame has spread in the world. At all events, he is vastly less read and esteemed in foreign parts than he ought to be, and very few Continental Europeans have risen to any genuine comprehension of his stature. When one reflects that the Nobel Prize has been given to such third-raters as Knut Hamsun and Rabindranath Tagore, with Conrad disdainfully passed over, one begins to grasp the depth and density of the ignorance prevailing in the world, even among the relatively enlightened. One *Lord Jim,* as human document and as work of art, is worth all the works produced by all the Hamsuns and Tagores since the time of Rameses II. It is, indeed, an indecency of criticism to speak of such unlike things in the same breath: as well talk of Brahms in terms of Mendelssohn. Nor is *Lord Jim* a chance masterpiece, an isolated peak. On the contrary, it is but one unit in a long series of extraordinary and almost incomparable works—a series sprung suddenly and overwhelmingly into full dignity with *Almayer's Folly.* I challenge the nobility and gentry of Christendom to point to another Opus 1 as magnificently planned and turned out as *Almayer's Folly.* The more one studies it, the more it seems miraculous. If it is not a work of absolute genius then no work of absolute genius exists on this earth.

(December, 1922)

THEODORE DREISER

A Modern Tragedy

If you miss reading *Jennie Gerhardt,* by Theodore Dreiser, you will miss the best American novel, all things considered, that has reached the book counters in a dozen years. On second thought, change "a dozen" into "twenty-five." On third thought, strike out everything after "counters." On fourth thought, strike out everything after "novel." Why back and fill? Why evade and qualify? Hot from it, I am firmly convinced that *Jennie Gerhardt* is the best American novel I have ever read, with the lonesome but Himalayan exception of *Huckleberry Finn,* and so I may as well say it aloud and at once and have done with it. Am I forgetting *The Scarlet Letter, The Rise of Silas Lapham* and (to drag an exile unwillingly home) *What Maisie Knew?* I am not. Am I forgetting *McTeague* and *The Pit?* I am not. Am I forgetting the stupendous masterpieces of James Fenimore Cooper, beloved of the pedagogues, or those of James Lane Allen, Mrs. Wharton and Dr. S. Weir Mitchell, beloved of the women's clubs and literary monthlies? No. Or *Uncle Tom's Cabin* or *Rob o' the Bowl* or *Gates Ajar* or *Ben Hur* or *David Harum* or *Lewis Rand* or *Richard Carvel?* No. Or *The Hungry Heart* or Mr. Dreiser's own *Sister Carrie?* No. I have all these good and bad books in mind. I have read them and survived them and in many cases enjoyed them.

And yet in the face of them, and in the face of all the high authority, constituted and self-constituted, behind them, it seems to me at this moment that *Jennie Gerhardt* stands apart from all of them, and a bit above them. It lacks the grace of this one, the humor of that one, the perfect form of some other one; but taking it as it stands, grim, gaunt, mirthless, shapeless, it remains, and by long odds, the most impressive work of art that we have yet to show in prose fiction—a tale not unrelated, in its stark simplicity, its profound sincerity, to *Germinal* and *Anna Karenina* and *Lord Jim*—a tale assertively American in its

scene and its human material, and yet so European in its method, its
point of view, its almost reverential seriousness, that one can scarcely
imagine an American writing it. Its personages are few in number,
and their progress is along a path that seldom widens, but the effect
of that progress is ever one of large movements and large masses. One
senses constantly the group behind the individual, the natural law behind the human act. The result is an indefinable impression of bigness,
of epic dignity. The thing is not a mere story, not a novel in the ordinary American meaning of the word, but a criticism and an interpretation of life—and that interpretation loses nothing in validity by
the fact that its burden is the doctrine that life is meaningless, a tragedy without a moral, a joke without a point. What else have Moore
and Conrad and Hardy been telling us these many years? What else
does all the new knowledge of a century teach us? One by one the old
ready answers have been disposed of. Today the one intelligible answer to the riddle of aspiration and sacrifice is that there is no answer
at all.

"The power to tell the same story in two forms," said George Moore
not long ago, "is the sign of the true artist." You will think of this
when you read *Jennie Gerhardt,* for in its objective plan, and even in
its scheme of subjective unfolding, it suggests *Sister Carrie* at every
turn. Reduce it to a hundred words, and those same words would also
describe that earlier study of a woman's soul, with scarcely the change
of a syllable. Jennie Gerhardt, like Carrie Meeber, is a rose grown
from turnip seed. Over each, at the start, hangs poverty, ignorance,
the dumb helplessness of the Shudra—and yet in each there is that
indescribable something, that element of essential gentleness, that in-
nate, inward beauty which levels all caste barriers and makes Esther a
fit queen for Ahasuerus. And the history of each, reduced to its elements, is the history of the other. Jennie, like Carrie, escapes from
the physical miseries of the struggle for existence only to taste the
worse miseries of the struggle for happiness. Not, of course, that we
have in either case a moral, maudlin fable of virtue's fall; Mr. Dreiser,
I need scarcely assure you, is too dignified an artist, too sane a man,
for any such banality. Seduction, in point of fact, is not all tragedy for
either Jennie or Carrie. The gain of each, until the actual event has
been left behind and obliterated by experiences more salient and poignant, is rather greater than her loss, and that gain is to the soul as
well as to the creature. With the rise from want to security, from fear

to ease, comes an awakening of the finer perceptions, a widening of
the sympathies, a gradual unfolding of the delicate flower called personality, an increased capacity for suffering—and so in the end, when
love slips away and the empty years stretch before, it is the awakened
and supersentient woman that pays for the folly of the groping, bewildered girl. The tragedy of Carrie and Jennie, in brief, is not that
they are degraded but that they are lifted up, not that they go to the
gutter but that they escape the gutter.

But if the two stories are thus variations upon the same sober
theme, if each starts from the same place and arrives at the same dark
goal, if each shows a woman heartened by the same hopes and tortured by the same agonies, there is still a vast difference between
them, and that difference is the measure of the author's progress in his
art. *Sister Carrie* was a first sketch, a rough piling-up of observations
and impressions, disordered and often incoherent. In the midst of the
story of Carrie, Mr. Dreiser paused to tell the story of Hurstwood—an
astonishingly vivid and tragic story, true enough, but still one that
broke the back of the other. In *Jennie Gerhardt* he falls into no such
overelaboration of episode. His narrative goes forward steadily from
beginning to end. Episodes there are, of course, but they keep their
proper place, their proper bulk. It is always Jennie that holds the attention; it is in Jennie's soul that every scene is ultimately played out.
Her father and mother, Senator Brander the god of her first worship,
her daughter Vesta and Lester Kane, the man who makes and mars
her—all these are drawn with infinite painstaking, and in every one of
them there is the blood of life. But it is Jennie that dominates the
drama from curtain to curtain. Not an event is unrelated to her; not a
climax fails to make clearer the struggles going on in her mind and
heart.

I have spoken of reducing *Jennie Gerhardt* to a hundred words.
The thing, I fancy, might be actually done. The machinery of the tale
is not complex; it has no plot, as plots are understood in these days of
"mystery" stories; no puzzles madden the reader. It is dull, unromantic
poverty that sends Jennie into the world. Brander finds her there,
lightly seduces her, and then discovers that, for some strange gentleness within her, he loves her. Lunacy—but he is willing to face it out.
Death, however, steps in; Brander, stricken down without warning,
leaves Jennie homeless and a mother. Now enters Lester Kane—not
the villain of the books, but a normal, decent, cleanly American of the

better class, well to do, level-headed, not too introspective, eager for the sweets of life. He and Jennie are drawn together; if love is not all of the spirit, then it is love that binds them. For half a dozen years the world lets them alone. A certain grave respectability settles over their relation; if they are not actually married, then it is only because marriage is a mere formality, to be put off until tomorrow. But bit by bit they are dragged into the light. Kane's father, dying with millions, gives him two years to put Jennie away. The penalty is poverty; the reward is wealth—and not only wealth itself, but all the pleasant and well remembered things that will come with it: the lost friends of other days, a sense of dignity and importance, an end of apologies and evasions, good society, the comradeship of decent women— particularly the comradeship of one decent woman. Kane hesitates, makes a brave defiance, thinks it over—finally yields. Jennie does not flood him with tears. She has made progress in the world, has Jennie; the simple faith of the girl has given way to the pride and poise of the woman. Five years later Kane sends for her. He is dying. When it is over, Jennie goes back to her lonely home, and there, like Carrie Meeber before her, she faces the long years with dry eyes and an empty heart. "Days and days in endless reiteration, and then—"

A moral tale? Not at all. It has no more moral than a string quartet or the first book of Euclid. But a philosophy of life is in it, and that philosophy is the same profound pessimism which gives a dark color to the best that we have from Hardy, Moore, Zola and the great Russians—the pessimism of disillusion—not the jejune, Byronic thing, not the green sickness of youth, but that pessimism which comes with the discovery that the riddle of life, despite all the fine solutions offered by the learned doctors, is essentially insoluble. One can discern no intelligible sequence of cause and effect in the agonies of Jennie Gerhardt. She is, as human beings go, of the nobler, finer metal. There is within her a great capacity for service, a great capacity for love, a great capacity for happiness. And yet all that life has to offer her, in the end, is the mere license to live. The days stretch before her "in endless reiteration." She is a prisoner doomed to perpetual punishment for some fanciful, incomprehensible crime against the gods who make their mirthless sport of us all. And to me, at least, she is more tragic thus than Lear on his wild heath or Prometheus on his rock.

Nothing of the art of the literary lapidary is visible in this novel. Its form is the simple one of a panorama unrolled. Its style is unstudied to the verge of barrenness. There is no painful groping for the exquisite, inevitable word; Mr. Dreiser seems content to use the common, even the commonplace coin of speech. On the very first page one encounters "frank, open countenance," "diffident manner," "helpless poor," "untutored mind," "honest necessity" and half a dozen other such ancients. And yet in the long run it is this very *naïveté* which gives the story much of its impressiveness. The narrative, in places, has the effect of a series of unisons in music—an effect which, given a solemn theme, vastly exceeds that of the most ornate polyphony. One cannot imagine *Jennie Gerhardt* done in the gipsy phrases of Meredith, the fugual manner of James. One cannot imagine that stark, stenographic dialogue adorned with the brilliants of speech. The thing could have been done only in the way that it has been done. As it stands, it is a work of art from which I for one would not care to take anything away—not even its gross crudities, its incessant returns to C major. It is a novel that depicts the life we Americans are living with extreme accuracy and criticises that life with extraordinary insight. It is a novel, I am convinced, of the very first consideration.

(November, 1911)

The Creed of a Novelist

I

The similarity between the fundamental ideas of Joseph Conrad and those of Theodore Dreiser, so often exhibited to the public gape in this place, is made plain beyond all shadow of cavil by the appearance of Dreiser's *A Hoosier Holiday*, a volume of mingled reminiscence, observation, speculation and confession of faith. Put the book beside Conrad's *A Personal Record*, and you will find parallels from end to end. Or better still, put it beside Hugh Walpole's little volume, *Joseph Conrad*, in which the Conradean metaphysic is condensed from the novels even better than Conrad has done it himself: at once you will see how the two novelists, each a worker in the elemental emotions, each a rebel against the prevailing cocksureness and superficiality, each an alien to his place and time, touch each other in a hundred ways.

"Conrad," says Walpole (himself a very penetrating and competent novelist), "is of the firm and resolute conviction that life is too strong, too clever and too remorseless for the sons of men." And then, in amplification: "It is as though, from some high window, looking down, he were able to watch some shore, from whose security men were forever launching little cockleshell boats upon a limitless and angry sea. . . . From his height he can follow their fortunes, their brave struggles, their fortitude to the very end. He admires that courage, the simplicity of that faith, but his irony springs from his knowledge of the inevitable end." . . . Substitute the name of Dreiser for that of Conrad, with *A Hoosier Holiday* as text, and you will have to change scarcely a word. Perhaps one, to wit, "clever." I suspect that Dreiser, writing so of his own creed, would be tempted to make it "stupid," or, at all events, "unintelligible." The struggle of man, as he sees it, is more than impotent; it is meaningless. There is, to his eye, no grand ingenuity, no skillful adaptation of means to end, no moral (or even dramatic) plan in the order of the universe. He can get out of it only a sense of profound and inexplicable *dis*order, of a seeking without a finding. There is not only no neat programme of rewards and punishments; there is not even an understandable balance of causes and effects. The waves which batter the cockleshells change their direction at every instant. Their navigation is a vast adventure, but intolerably fortuitous and inept—a voyage without chart, compass, sun or stars. . . .

So at bottom. But to look into the blackness steadily, of course, is almost beyond the endurance of man. In the very moment that its impenetrability is grasped the imagination begins attacking it with pale beams of false light. All religions, I dare say, are thus projected from the soul of man, and not only all religions, but also all great agnosticisms. Nietzsche, shrinking from the horror of that abyss of negation, revived the Pythagorean concept of *der ewigen Wiederkunft*—a vain and blood-curdling sort of comfort. To it, after a while, he added explanations almost Christian—a whole repertoire of whys and wherefores, aims and goals, aspirations and significances. Other seers have gone back even further: the Transcendentalists stemmed from Zeno of Elea. The late Mark Twain, in an unpublished work, toyed with a characteristically daring idea: that men are to some unimaginably vast

and incomprehensible Being what the unicellular organisms of his
body are to man, and so on *ad infinitum.* Dreiser occasionally dallies
with much the same notion; he likens the endless reactions going on in
the world we know, the myriadal creation, collision and destruction of
entities, to the slow accumulation and organization of cells *in utero.*
He would make us specks in the insentient embryo of some gigantic
Presence whose form is still unimaginable and whose birth must wait
for eons and eons. Again, he turns to something not easily distinguish-
able from philosophical idealism, whether out of Berkeley or Fichte it
is hard to make out—that is, he would interpret the whole phenomenon of life as no more than an appearance, a nightmare of some un-
seen sleeper or of men themselves, an "uncanny blur of nothingness"
—in Euripides' phrase, "a tale told by an idiot, dancing down the
wind." Yet again, he talks vaguely of the intricate polyphony of a cosmic orchestra, cacophonous to our dull ears. Finally, he puts the observed into the ordered, reading a purpose in the displayed event:
"life was intended as a spectacle, it was intended to sting and hurt."
. . . But these are only gropings, and not to be read too critically.
From speculations and explanations he always returns, Conrad-like, to
the bald fact: to "the spectacle and stress of life." The bolder flights
go with the puerile solutions of current religion and morals. Even
more than Conrad, he sees life as a struggle in which man is not only
doomed to defeat, but denied any glimpse or understanding of his antagonist. His philosophy is an agnosticism that has almost got beyond
curiosity. What good would it do us, he asks, to know? In our ignorance and helplessness, we may at least get a slave's comfort out of
cursing the gods. Suppose we saw them striving blindly too, and
pitied them?

II

The function of poetry, says F. C. Prescott, in *Poetry and Dreams*
(a book so modest and yet so searching that it will be years before
the solemn donkeys of the seminaries ever hear of it), is to conjure up
for us a vivid picture of what we want, but cannot get. The desire is
half of the story, but the inhibition is as plainly the other half, and of
no less importance. It is this element that gives its glamour to tragedy;
the mind seizes upon the image as a substitute for the reality, and the
result is the psychical *katharsis* described by Aristotle. It is precisely
by the same process that Dreiser and Conrad get a profound and mel-

SMART SET CRITICISM   [251]

ancholy poetry into their books. Floating above the bitter picture of
what actually is, there is always the misty but inordinately charming
picture of what might be or ought to be. Here we get a clue to the
method of both men, and to the secret of their capacity for reaching
the emotions. All of Conrad's brilliant and poignant creatures are
dreamers who go to smash upon the rocks of human weakness and
stupidity—Kurtz, Nostromo, Lord Jim, Almayer, Razumov, Heyst,
even Whalley and MacWhirr. And so with Carrie Meeber, Jennie Gerhardt, Frank Cowperwood and Eugene Witla. They are not merely
vivid and interesting figures; they are essentially tragic figures, and in
their tragedy, despite its superficial sordidness, there is a deep and
ghostly poetry. "My task," said Conrad once, "is, by the power of the
printed word, to make you hear, to make you feel—it is, above all, to
make you *see*." Comprehension, sympathy, pity—these are the things
he seeks to evoke. And these, too, are the things that Dreiser seeks to
evoke. The reader does not arise from such a book as *Sister Carrie*
with a smirk of satisfaction, as he might from a novel by Howells or
James; he leaves it infinitely touched. . . .

Mr. Walpole, in his little book, is at pains to prove that Conrad is
neither realist nor romanticist, but an intricate combination of both.
The thesis scarcely needs support, or even statement: *all* imaginative
writers of the higher ranks are both. Plain realism, as in the early
Zola, simply wearies us by its futility; plain romance, if we ever get
beyond youth, makes us laugh. It is their artistic combination, as in
life itself, that fetches us—the subtle projection of the muddle that is
living against the orderliness that we reach out for—the eternal war of
aspiration and experience—the combat of man and his destiny. As I
say, this contrast lies at the bottom of all that is vital and significant in
imaginative writing; to argue for it is to wade in platitudes. I speak of
it here simply because the more stupid of Dreiser's critics—and what
author has ever been hoofed by worse asses!—insist upon seeing him
and denouncing him as a realist, and as a realist only. One of them,
for example, has lately printed a long article maintaining that he is
blind to the spiritual side of man altogether, and that he accounts for
his characters solely by some incomprehensible "theory of animal be-
haviour." Could one imagine a more absurd mouthing of a phrase?
One is almost staggered, indeed, by such critical imbecility, even in a
college professor. The truth is, of course, that all of Dreiser's novels
deal fundamentally with the endless conflict between this "animal be-

haviour" and the soarings of the spirit—between the destiny forced
upon his characters by their environment, their groping instincts, their
lack of courage and resourcefulness, and the destiny they picture for
themselves in their dreams. This is the tragedy of Carrie Meeber and
Jennie Gerhardt. The physical fact of their "seduction" (they are willing enough) blasts them doubly, for on the one hand it brings down
upon them the conventional burden of the pariah, and on the other
hand the worldly advancement which follows widens their aspiration
beyond their inherent capacities, and so augments their unhappiness.
It is the tragedy, too, of Cowperwood and Witla. To see these men as
mere melodramatic Don Juans is to fall into an error almost unimaginably ridiculous. The salient fact about them, indeed, is that they are
not mere Don Juans—that they are men in whom the highest idealism
strives against the bonds of the flesh. Witla, passion-torn, goes down
to disaster and despair. It is what remains of the wreck of his old
ideals that floats him into peace at last. As for Cowperwood, we have
yet to see his actual end—but how plainly its shadows are cast before!
Life is beating him, and through his own weakness. There remains for
him, as for Lord Jim, only the remnant of a dream.

III

With so much ignorant and misleading criticism of him going
about, the appearance of *A Hoosier Holiday* should be of service to
Dreiser's reputation, for it shows the man as he actually is, stripped of
all the scarlet trappings hung upon him by horrified lady reviewers,
male and female. The book, indeed, is amazingly naif. Slow in tempo,
discursive, meditative, it covers a vast territory, and lingers in far
fields. One finds in it an almost complete confession of faith, artistic,
religious, even political. And not infrequently that confession comes in
the form of somewhat disconcerting confidences—about the fortunes
of the house of Dreiser, the dispersed Dreiser family, the old neighbors in Indiana, new friends made along the way. As readers of *A
Traveller at Forty* are well aware, Dreiser knows little of reticence,
and is no slave to prudery. In that earlier book he described the people he encountered exactly as he saw them, without forgetting a vanity or a wart. In *A Hoosier Holiday* he goes even further: he specu-
lates about them, prodding into the motives behind their acts, wondering what they would do in this or that situation, forcing them
painfully into laboratory jars. They become, in the end, not unlike

characters in a novel; one misses only the neatness of a plot. Strangely enough, the one personage of the chronicle who remains dim throughout is the artist, Franklin Booth, Dreiser's host and companion on the long motor ride from New York to Indiana, and the maker of the book's excellent pictures. One gets a brilliant etching of Booth's father, and scarcely less vivid portraits of Speed, the chauffeur; of various persons encountered on the way, and of friends and relatives dredged up out of the abyss of the past. But of Booth one learns little save that he is a Christian Scientist and a fine figure of a man. There must have been much talk during those two weeks of careening along the highroad, and Booth must have borne some part in it, but what he said is very meagrely reported, and so he is still somewhat vague at the end —a personality sensed, but scarcely apprehended.

However, it is Dreiser himself who is the chief character of the story, and who stands out from it most brilliantly. One sees in the man all the special marks of the novelist: his capacity for photographic and relentless observation, his insatiable curiosity, his keen zest in life as a spectacle, his comprehension of and sympathy for the poor striving of humble folks, his endless mulling of insoluble problems, his recurrent Philistinism, his impatience of restraints, his suspicion of messiahs, his passion for physical beauty, his relish for the gaudy drama of big cities, his incurable Americanism. The panorama that he enrolls runs the whole scale of the colors; it is a series of extraordinarily vivid pictures. The sombre gloom of the Pennsylvania hills, with Wilkes-Barre lying among them like a gem; the procession of little country towns, sleepy and a bit hoggish; the flash of Buffalo, Cleveland, Indianapolis; the gargantuan coal-pockets and ore-docks along the Erie shore; the tinsel summer resorts; the lush Indiana farmlands, with their stodgy, bovine people—all of these things are sketched in simply, and yet almost magnificently. I know, indeed, of no book which better describes the American hinterland. Here we have no idle spying by a stranger, but a full-length representation by one who knows the thing he describes intimately, and is himself a part of it. Almost every mile of the road travelled has been Dreiser's own road in life. He knew those unkempt Indiana towns in boyhood; he wandered in the Indiana woods; he came to Toledo, Cleveland, Buffalo as a young man; all the roots of his existence are out there. And so he does his chronicle *con amore,* with many a sentimental dredging up of old memories, old hopes and old dreams.

Strangely enough, for all the literary efflorescence of the Middle West, such pictures of it are very rare. I know, in fact, of no other on the same scale. It is, in more than one way, the heart of America, and yet it has gone undescribed. Dreiser remedies that lack with all his characteristic laboriousness and painstaking. When he has done with them, those drowsy villages and oafish country towns have grown as real as the Chicago of *Sister Carrie* and *The Titan*. One sees a land that blinks and naps in the sunshine like some great cow, udders full, the cud going—a land of Dutch fatness and contentment—a land, despite its riches, of almost unbelievable stupidity and immobility. We get a picture of a typical summer afternoon; mile after mile of farms, villages, little towns, the people sleepy and empty in mind, lolling on their verandas, killing time between trivial events, shut off from all the turmoil of the world. What, in the end, will come out of this over-fed, too-happy region? Ideas? Rebellions? The spark to set off great wars? Or only the silence of decay? In Ohio industry has already in-vaded the farms; chimneys arise among the haystacks. And so further west. But in Indiana there is a back-water, a sort of American Midi, a neutral ground in the battles of the nation. It has no art, no great in-dustry, no dominating men. Its literature, in the main, is a feeble romanticism for flappers and fat women. Its politics is a skeptical op-portunism. It is not stirred by great passions. It knows no heroes. . . . What will be the end of it? Which way is it heading?

IV

Save for passages in *The Titan, A Hoosier Holiday* marks the high tide of Dreiser's writing—that is, as sheer writing. His old faults are in it, and plentifully. There are empty, brackish phrases enough, God knows—"high noon" among them. But for all that, there is an unde-niable glow in it; it shows, in more than one place, an approach to style; the mere wholesaler of words has become, in some sense, a con-noisseur, even a voluptuary. The picture of Wilkes-Barre girt in by her hills is simply done, and yet there is imagination in it, and touches of brilliance. The sombre beauty of the Pennsylvania mountains is viv-idly transferred to the page. The towns by the wayside are differen-tiated, swiftly drawn, made to live. There are excellent sketches of people—a courtly hotel-keeper in some God-forsaken hamlet, his self-respect triumphing over his wallow; a group of babbling Civil War veterans, endlessly mouthing incomprehensible jests; the half-grown

beaux and belles of the summer resorts, enchanted and yet a bit staggered by the awakening of sex; Booth *père* and his sinister politics;
broken and forgotten men in the Indiana towns; policemen, wait-
resses, farmers, country characters; Dreiser's own people—the boys and
girls of his youth; his brother Paul, the Indiana Schneckenburger and
Francis Scott Key, author of "On the Banks of the Wabash"; his sisters
and brothers; his beaten, hopeless, pious father; his brave and noble
mother. The book is dedicated to this mother, now long dead, and in
a way it is a memorial to her, a monument to affection. Life bore
upon her cruelly; she knew poverty at its lowest ebb and despair at its
bitterest; and yet there was in her a touch of fineness that never
yielded, a gallant spirit that faced and fought things through. *Une
âme grande dans un petit destin:* a great soul in a small destiny! One
thinks, somehow, of the mother of Gounod. . . . Her son has not forgotten her. His book is her epitaph. He enters into her presence with
love and with reverence and with something not far from awe. . . .

In sum, this record of a chance holiday is much more than a mere
travel book, for it offers, and for the first time, a clear understanding
of the fundamental faiths and ideas, and of the intellectual and spiritual background no less, of a man with whom the future historian of
American literature will have to deal at no little length. Dreiser, as
yet, has not come into his own. In England his true stature has begun
to be recognized, and once the war is over I believe that he will be
"discovered," as the phrase is, in Germany and Russia, and perhaps in
France. But in his own country he is still denied and belabored in a
manner that would be comic were it not so pathetically stupid. The
college professors rail and snarl at him in the *Nation* and the *Dial;* the
elderly virgins of the newspapers represent him as an iconoclast, an
immoralist, an Anti-Christ, even a German spy; the professional
moralists fatuously proceed to jail him because his Witlas and his
Cowperwoods are not eunuchs—more absurdly still, because a few
"God damns" are scattered through the 736 crowded pages of *The
"Genius."* The Puritan fog still hangs over American letters; it is for-
mally demanded that all literature be made with the girl of sixteen in
mind, and that she be assumed to be quite ignorant of sex. And the
orthodox teachers sing the hymn that is lined out. In Prof. Fred Lewis
Pattee's *History of American Literature Since 1870,* just published,
there is no mention of Dreiser whatever! Such novelists as Owen Wister, Robert W. Chambers and Holman F. Day are mentioned as

"leaders"; substantial notices are given to Capt. Charles King, Blanche Willis Howard and Julian Hawthorne; five whole pages are dedicated to F. Marion Crawford; even Richard Harding Davis, E. P. Roe and "Octave Thanet" are soberly estimated. But not a line about Dreiser! Not an incidental mention of him! One recalls Richardson's *American Literature,* with its contemptuous dismissal of Mark Twain. A sapient band, these college professors!

But the joke, of course, is not on Dreiser, but on the professors themselves, and on the host of old maids, best-seller fanatics and ecstatic Puritans who support them. Time will bring the Indianan his revenge, and perhaps he will yield to humor and help time along. A Dreiser novel with a Puritan for its protagonist would be something to caress the soul—a full-length portrait of the Eternal Pharisee, a liming of the Chemically Pure, done scientifically, relentlessly, affectionately. Dreiser knows the animal from snout to tail. He could do a picture that would live. . . .

(October, 1916)

De Profundis

March 15.

It is easy enough to understand the impulse which prompted Dreiser to write *Hey Rub-a-Dub-Dub,* his new book, of essays and fulminations all compact. There come times in every sentient man's life when he must simply unload his ideas, or bust like a star-shell in the highroad. If he is at that end of the scale which touches the rising ladder of the *Simiidae* he becomes a Socialist on a soap-box or joins the Salvation Army; if he is literate and has a soul he writes a book. Hence the great, whirring, infernal machines which chew up the forests of Canada, now and then salting the dose with the leg or arm of a Canuck. Hence the huge ink industry, consuming five million tons of bone-black a year. Hence democracy, Bolshevism, the moral order of the world. Hence sorrow. Hence literature.

In every line of *Hey Rub-a-Dub-Dub* there is evidence of the au-

thor's antecedent agony. One pictures him sitting up all night in his
sinister studio down in Tenth Street, wrestling horribly with the insoluble, trying his darndest to penetrate the unknowable. One o'clock
strikes, and the fire sputters. Ghosts stalk in the room, fanning the yellow candle-light with their abominable breath—the spooks of all the
men who have died for ideas since the world began—Socrates, Savonarola, Bruno (not Guido, but Giordano), Ravaillac, Sir Roger Case-
ment, John Alexander Dowie, Dr. Crippen. Two o'clock. What, then,
is the truth about marriage? Is it, as Grover Cleveland said, a grand
sweet song, or is it, as the gals in the Village say, a hideous mockery
and masquerade, invented by Capitalism to enslave the soul of
woman—a legalized *Schweinerei,* worse than politics, almost as bad as
the moving-pictures? Three o'clock. Was Marx right or wrong, a seer
or a mere nose-puller? Was his name, in fact, actually Marx, or was it
Marcus? From what ghetto did he escape, and cherishing what
grudge against mankind? Aha, the Huneker complex: *cherchez le
Juif!* (I confess at once: my great-grandpa, Moritz, was rector of the
Oheb Shalon *Schul* in Grodno). Three o'clock. . . .

Back to Pontius Pilate! *Quod est veritas?* Try to define it. Look into
it. Break it into its component parts. What remains is a pale gray va-
por, an impalpable emanation, the shadow of a shadow. Think of the
brains that have gone to wreck struggling with the problem—cere-
brums as large as cauliflowers, cerebellums as perfect as pomegran-
ates. Think of the men jailed, clubbed, hanged, burned at the stake
—not for embracing error, but for embracing the *wrong* error. Think
of the innumerable caravan of Burlesons, Mitchell Palmers, Torque-
madas, Cotton Mathers. . . . Four o'clock. The fire burns low in the
grate. A gray fog without. Across the street two detectives rob a
drunken man. Up at Tarrytown John D. Rockefeller snores in his
damp Baptist bed, dreaming gaudily that he is young again and
mashed on a girl named Marie. At Sing Sing forty head of Italians are
waiting to be electrocuted. There is a memorial service for Charles
Garvice in Westminster Abbey. The Comstocks raid the Elsie books.
Ludendorff is elected Archbishop of Canterbury. A poor working-girl,
betrayed by Moe, the boss's son, drowns herself in the Aquarium.
It is late, ah me: nearly four thirty. . . . Who the deuce, then, is God?
What is in all this talk of a future life, infant damnation, the Ouija
board, Mortal Mind? Dr. Jacques Loeb is the father of a dozen bull-
frogs. Is the news biological or theological? What became of the Albi-

genses? Are they in heaven, in purgatory or in hell? . . . Five o'clock.
Boys cry the *Evening Journal*. Is it today's or tomorrow's? The question of transubstantiation remains. There is, too, neo-transcenden-
talism. . . . In Munich they talk of *Expressionismus*. . . . Poof! . . .

It is easy, as I say, to imagine a man beset by such reflections, and
urged irresistibly to work them out on paper. Unluckily, the working
out is not always as simple a business as it looks. Dreiser's first impulse as novelist, I daresay, was to do it in novels—to compose fictions
full of ideas, saying something, teaching something, exposing something, destroying something. But the novelist also happened to be an
artist, and at once the artist entered an effective caveat against that
pollution. A work of art with ideas in it is as sorry a monster as a
pretty girl full of Latin. The aim of a work of art is not to make one
think painfully, but to make one feel beautifully. What is the idea in
Jennie Gerhardt? Who knows but God? But in *Jennie Gerhardt* there
is feeling—profound, tragic, exquisite. It is a thing of poignant and
yet delicate emotions, like Brahms' Fourth Symphony. It lies in a sort
of intellectual fourth dimension. It leaves a memory that is vivid and
somehow caressing, and wholly free from doubts, questionings, head-
scratchings. . . . So Dreiser decided to make a serious book of it, a
book of unalloyed ratiocination, a book in the manner of Herbert
Spencer. The result is *Hey Rub-a-Dub-Dub*—solemn stuff, with never
a leer of beauty in it—in fact, almost furious. Once or twice it grows a
bit lyrical; once or twice it rises to the imaginatively grotesque. But in
the main it is plain exposition—a book of speculation and protest. He
calls it himself "a book of the mystery and terror and wonder of life."
I suspect that he lifted this subtitle from an old review of H. L. M. If
so, then welcome! From him I have got more than is to be described
in words and more than I can ever pay.

But what of the thing itself? Is it good stuff? My feeling is that it
isn't. More, my feeling is that Dreiser is no more fitted to do a book of
speculation than Joseph Conrad, say, is fitted to do a college yell. His
talents simply do not lie in that direction. He lacks the mental agility,
the insinuating suavity, the necessary capacity for romanticising a syllogism. Ideas themselves are such sober things that a sober man had
better let them alone. What they need, to become bearable to a human race that hates them and is afraid of them, is the artful juggling
of a William James, the insurance-agent persuasiveness of an Henri
Bergson, the boob-bumping talents of a Martin Luther—best of all,

the brilliant, almost Rabelaisian humor of a Nietzsche. Nietzsche went out into the swamp much further than any other explorer; he left such pallbearers of the spirit as Spencer, Comte, Descartes and even Kant all shivering on the shore. And yet he never got bogged, and he never lost the attention of his audience. What saved him was the plain fact that he always gave a superb show—as good, almost, as a hanging. He converted the problem of evil into a melodrama with nine villains; he made of epistemology a sort of intellectual bed-room farce; he amalgamated Christianity and the music of Offenbach. . . . Well, Dreiser is quite devoid of that gift. Skepticism, in his hands, is never charming; it is simply despairing. His criticism of God lacks ingenuity and audacity. Earnestly pursuing the true, he too often unearths the merely obvious, which is sometimes not true at all. One misses the jauntiness of the accomplished duellist; his manner is rather that of the honest householder repelling burglars with a table-leg. In brief, it is enormously serious and painstaking stuff, but seldom very interesting stuff, and never delightful stuff. The sorrows of the world become the sorrows of Dreiser himself, and then the sorrows of his reader. He remains, in the last analysis, the novelist rather than the philosopher. He is vastly less a Schopenhauer than a Werther.

(May, 1920)

ANATOLE FRANCE

A Gamey Old Gaul

Consider now, beloved, Monsieur Jacques-Anatole Thibault France *de l'Académie Française*, an ancient of three score and ten, a veritable patriarch of letters, the *doyen* of French authors, but still full of the joy of life, the Old Adam, the unquenchable gayety of the Gaul: as Nietzsche would say, still fit for dancing with arms and legs. Old Anatole, indeed, goes back to the dark ages, almost to the crusades. He was a boy of four years, and perhaps already reading Rabelais, when Louis Philippe escaped from France under the name of Mr. Smith. He was old enough to take a hand in the mafficking when they brought the glad news from Solferino. He was a young literary buck, engaged upon his first book, in the palmy days of Hortense Schneider, and no doubt loved her in a distant and respectful manner. He was a famous man before Zola, to wit, in 1871, when *Le Crime de Sylvestre Bonnard* did the business for him. When he got his lift into the Academy such men as Octave Feuillet and Émile Augier were just dropping out. He is actually a year older than Sarah Bernhardt, impossible though it may seem.

And yet, as I say, the fires of youth are still in the veteran. His Indian Summer is pert, sunshiney, Spring-like. He leaps and cavorts. One heard of him, a month or two ago, making demands on some astonished recruiting sergeant that he be enlisted, armed and sent to the front, there to do summary execution upon the invading Goths. He prayed for the proud privilege of cutting off the Kaiser's ears, of being the first upon the walls of Berlin, of diving headlong into a lake of Tedesco blood. All this, it appears, was denied him: he was put to the more sober job of adding up figures in the Paymaster's office. But no denials, you may be sure, will ever cure him of the *cacoëthes scribendi;* he will keep on writing until that dark (and, let us hope, distant) day when the inexorable embalmer casts upon him a sinister

and appraising eye. In proof whereof here is the last fruit of his
fancy: *The Revolt of the Angels,* the liveliest and most delightful
piece of fooling that I have seen in many a long day, a book of wag-
gery and gusto all compact, a literary *scherzo* that warms the cockles
of the heart.

It is the angel Abdiel who gives the signal for the revolt, or, as he
chooses to be called on the earthly plane, Arcade. This Arcade is
guardian angel to young Maurice d'Esparvieu, a somewhat frivolous,
and even loose fellow, but nevertheless a faithful son of the Church.
The house of d'Esparvieu, indeed, has long basked in the radiance of
the faith. From the Concordat of 1801 down to the fall of the Second
Empire its devotion, perhaps, was more formal than real: its first aim,
during those years, was to set a good example. But the rise of the
Third Republic sent it genuinely to its knees, and in young Maurice,
as in M. René, his father, and Madame, his mother, no doubt lingers.
He finds it impossible, true enough, to maintain that personal rectitude which his spiritual adviser, M. l'Abbé Patouille, commends as
ideal. There is, for example, the matter of his relations to his mother's
maid, Mlle. Odile. There is, again, his affair with Mme. de la Ver-
delière. There is, yet again, his affair with Mme. Gilberte des Aubels.
There is, fourthly, his affair with Mlle. Bouchotte, the singer of
Apache songs. And so on and so on—lamentable episodes, alas, of life
in a large city! But meanwhile, you may be sure, Maurice does not
forget his duties. He is often at mass in the morning. He serves as a
stretcher-bearer at Lourdes. He is horrified by Socialists, Freemasons,
atheists. He harkens docilely to the Abbé Patouille. He inspires a
considerable affection in his guardian angel, the aforesaid Arcade.

This affection, unfortunately, works Arcade's downfall, for it brings
him frequently to the d'Esparvieu mansion in the shadow of St.
Sulpice, and in the d'Esparvieu mansion, filling the whole of the
second story, there is the famous library of Maurice's great-grand-
father, Baron Alexandre-Bussart d'Esparvieu, Vice-President of the
Council of State under the Government of July, member of the Academy of Moral and Political Sciences, and author of an "Essay on the
Civil and Religious Institutions of Nations"—a huge collection of three
hundred and sixty thousand volumes, embracing all the books worth
reading, in all the sacred and profane languages, upon natural, moral,
political, philosophical and religious science. This library, under the
direction of M. Sariette, librarian, is kept up to the minute. Not only

all the old books are in it, but also all the new ones of worth, each added as it is published. And it is because he unwisely peeps into these new ones, seeking entertainment and instruction while Maurice is in bed, that good Arcade takes into his soul the heresies of Darwin, Huxley, Spencer, Weismann, Harnack, Strauss, Renan and the rest, and so becomes filled with gnawing doubts about the divinity of that vasty Ialdabaoth whom he serves, and ends by flopping to a skepticism which bars him forever from the court of Heaven, and leaves him a starving and garrulous agitator in Paris.

Worse, there are more like him. For example, Prince Istar, a fallen Cherub, now a maker of bombs on the left bank of the Seine. And Zita, an ex-angel of the softer sex, beautiful and full of plots. And Nectaire, the old gardener, once Alaciel, of the celestial hierarchy. And many another, male and female. They form a colony near Val de Grâce. They hold a monster mass-meeting on the banks of the Seine at La Jonchère—watched assiduously by spies from the prefecture of police. They take an oath to "scale the mountain of Ialdabaoth, and hurl down the walls of jasper and porphyry, and plunge the tyrant of Heaven into eternal darkness." And then—

But I have told you enough. You see the way the chronicle is heading. I command it to you again before leaving it. It is written with unfailing address, ingenuity and charm. The characters are well imagined; the incidents, for all their grotesquerie, still show an ingratiating reasonableness; there is a constant play of tart, Rabelaisian humor. Old Anatole, indeed, is the natural heir of François in our time. He has something of the same hand for elaborate, elephantine satire; he is full of the same amazing erudition, the same overwhelming allusiveness; he has the same keen eye for all that is empty and ridiculous in theological and ecclesiastical rumble-bumble. With it all, he is a far more delicate artist than Rabelais, though, of course, by no means so colossal a humorist. He never stoops to grossness, even in the midst of his most daring fooling. His urbanity never gives way to the staggering savagery of Pantagruel's creator. In its essence, to be sure, *The Revolt of the Angels* is one of the most impious books ever written, but you will search it in vain for any obvious violation of the decencies. It is, in brief, the clowning of an artist and a gentleman. Put it on your book list, by all means. Alone of all the volumes I have read of late, it belongs unmistakably to literature.

(January, 1915)

WILLA CATHER

Her First Novel

Alexander's Bridge, by Willa S. Cather, has the influence of Edith
Wharton written all over it, and there is no need for the canned review on the cover to call attention to the fact—the which remark, let
me hasten to add, is not to be taken as a sneer but as hearty praise,
for the novelizing novice who chooses Mrs. Wharton as her model is
at least one who knows a hawk from a handsaw, an artist from an
artisan. The majority of beginners in this fair land choose E. Phillips
Oppenheim or Marie Corelli; if we have two schools, then one is the
School of Plot and the other is the School of Piffle. But Miss Cather,
as I have said, is intelligent enough to aim higher, and the thing she
offers must be set down a very promising piece of writing. Its chief
defect is a certain triteness in structure. When Bartley Alexander, the
great engineer, discovers that he is torn hopelessly between a genuine
affection for his wife, Winifred, and a wild passion for his old flame,
Hilda Burgoyne, it seems a banal device to send him out on his greatest bridge a moment before it falls, and so drown him in the St. Lawrence. This is not a working out of the problem; it is a mere evasion of
the problem. In real life how would such a man solve it for himself?
Winifred, remember, is in Boston and Hilda is in London, and business takes Bartley across the ocean four or five times a year. No doubt
the authentic male would let the situation drift. In the end he would
sink into the lean and slippered pantaloon by two firesides, a highly
respectable and reasonably contented bigamist (unofficially, of
course), a more or less successful and satisfied wrestler with fate. Such
things happen. I could tell you tales. But I tell them not. All I do is to
throw out the suggestion that the shivering of the triangle is far from
inevitable. Sometimes, for all the hazards of life, it holds together for
years. But the fictioneers are seldom content until they have destroyed
it by catastrophe. That way is the thrilling way, and more important
still, it is the easy way.

Aside from all this, Miss Cather gives a very good account of herself indeed. She writes carefully, skillfully, artistically. Her dialogue has life in it and gets her story ahead. Her occasional paragraphs of description are full of feeling and color. She gives us a well drawn picture of the cold Winifred, a better one of the emotional and alluring Hilda and a fairly credible one of Bartley himself—this last a difficult business, for the genius grows flabby in a book. It is seldom, indeed, that fiction can rise above second rate men. The motives and impulses and processes of mind of the superman are too recondite for plausible analysis. It is easy enough to explain how John Smith courted and won his wife, and even how William Jones fought and died for his country, but it would be impossible to explain (or, at any rate, to convince by explaining) how Beethoven wrote the Fifth Symphony, or how Pasteur reasoned out the hydrophobia vaccine, or how Stonewall Jackson arrived at his miracles of strategy. The thing has been tried often, but it has always ended in failure. Those supermen of fiction who are not mere shadows and dummies are supermen reduced to saving ordinariness. Shakespeare made Hamlet a comprehensible and convincing man by diluting that half of him which was Shakespeare by a half which was a college sophomore. In the same way he saved Lear by making him, in large part, a silly and obscene old man—the blood brother of any average ancient of any average English taproom. Tackling Caesar, he was rescued from disaster by Brutus's knife. George Bernard Shaw, facing the same difficulty, resolved it by drawing a composite portrait of two or three London actor-managers and half a dozen English politicians.

(December, 1912)

Willa Cather vs. William Allen White

Two new novels, *My Ántonia*, by Willa Sibert Cather, and *In the Heart of a Fool*, by William Allen White, bear out in different ways some of the doctrines displayed in the earlier sections of this article. Miss Cather's book shows an earnest striving toward that free and dignified self-expression, that high artistic conscience, that civilized

point of view, which Dr. [Van Wyck] Brooks dreams of as at once
the cause and effect of his fabulous "luminosity." Mr. White's shows
the viewpoint of a Chautauqua spell-binder and the manner of a
Methodist evangelist. It is, indeed, a novel so intolerably mawkish and
maudlin, so shallow and childish, so vapid and priggish, that its accumulated badness almost passes belief, and if it were not for one
thing I should be tempted to spit on my hands and give it such a slating that the very hinges of this great family periodical would grow
white-hot. That thing, that insidious dissuader, is not, I lament to report, a saving merit. It is something far different: it is an ineradicable
suspicion that, after all, the book is absolutely American—that, for all
its horrible snuffling and sentimentalizing, it is a very fair example of
the sort of drivel that passes for "sound"" and "inspiring" in our fair republic, and is eagerly praised by the newspapers, and devoured voraciously by the people. One may observe this taste sadly, but it is
rather vain to rail against it. The leopard is chained to his spots, and
the dog to his fleas. This is the aesthetic echo and reflection of Christian Endeavor and the direct primary; this is what the public wants.
And this is why the English sniff when they look our way.

I shall not afflict you with the details of the fable. It is, in essence,
the usual and inevitable thing of its kind. On the one side are the Hell
Hounds of Plutocracy, and their attendant Bosses, Strike Breakers,
Seducers, Nietzscheans, Free Lovers and Corrupt Journalists. On the
other side are the great masses of the plain people, and their attendant Uplifters, Good Samaritans, Poor Working Girls, Inspired
Dreamers and tin-horn Messiahs. These two armies join battle, the
Bad against the Good, and for 500 pages or more the Good get all the
worst of it. Their jobs are taken away from them, their votes are bar-
tered, their women are debauched, their poor orphans are turned out
to starve. But in the third from the last chapter someone turns on a
rose spot-light, and then, one by one, the rays of Hope begin to shoot
across the stage, and as the curtain falls the whole scene is bathed in
luminous ether, and the professor breaks into "Onward, Christian Soldiers" on the cabinet-organ, and there is happy sobbing, and an upward rolling of eyes, and a vast blowing of noses. In brief, the finish
of a Chautauqua lecture on "The Grand Future of America, or, The
Glory of Service." Still more briefly, slobber.

It is needless to add that Dr. White is a member of the American
Academy of Arts and Letters. Nor is it necessary to hint that Miss

Cather is not. Invading the same Middle West that engages the Kansas tear-squeezer and academician, and dealing with almost the same people, she comes forward with a novel that is everything that his is not—sound, delicate, penetrating, brilliant, charming. I do not push the comparison for the mere sake of the antithesis. Miss Cather is a craftsman whom I have often praised in this place, and with increasing joy. Her work, for ten years past, has shown a steady and rapid improvement, in both matter and manner. She has arrived at last at such a command of the mere devices of writing that the uses she makes of them are all concealed—her style has lost self-consciousness; her feeling for form has become instinctive. And she has got such a grip upon her materials—upon the people she sets before us and the background she displays behind them—that both take on an extraordinary reality. I know of no novel that makes the remote folk of the western prairies more real than *My Ántonia* makes them, and I know of none that makes them seem better worth knowing. Beneath the swathings of balderdash, the surface of numskullery and illusion, the tawdry stuff of Middle Western *Kultur,* she discovers human beings embattled against fate and the gods, and into her picture of their dull struggle she gets a spirit that is genuinely heroic, and a pathos that is genuinely moving. It is not as they see themselves that she depicts them, but as they actually are. To representation she adds something more. There is not only the story of poor peasants, flung by fortune into lonely, inhospitable wilds; there is the eternal tragedy of man.

(February, 1919)

Youth and the Bright Medusa

. . . The same high competence marks *Youth and the Bright Medusa,* by Willa Cather. The book is made up of eight stories, and all of them deal with artists. It is Miss Cather's peculiar virtue that she represents the artist in terms of his own thinking—that she does not look *at* him through a peep-hole in the studio-door, but looks *with* him at the life that he is so important and yet so isolated and lonely a part of. One finds in every line of her writing a sure-footed and civilized culture; it gives her an odd air of foreignness, particularly when she discusses music, which is often. Six of her eight stories deal with musicians. One of them, "Coming, Aphrodite!" was published in this great moral periodical last August. Another, "Scandal," was printed in *The Century* during the Spring, to the envious rage of Dr. Nathan, who read it with vast admiration and cursed God that it had escaped these refined pages. Four others are reprinted from the *The Troll Garden*, a volume first published fifteen years ago. These early stories are excellent, particularly "The Sculptor's Funeral," but Miss Cather has learned a great deal since she wrote them. Her grasp upon character is firmer than it was; she writes with much more ease and grace; above all, she has mastered the delicate and difficult art of evoking the feelings. A touch of the maudlin lingers in "Paul's Case" and in "A Death in the Desert." It is wholly absent from "Coming, Aphrodite!" and "Scandal," as it is from *My Ántonia*. These last, indeed, show utterly competent workmanship in every line. They are stories that lift themselves completely above the level of current American fiction, even of good fiction. They are the work of a woman who, after a long apprenticeship, has got herself into the front rank of American novelists, and is still young enough to have her best writing ahead of her. I call *My Ántonia* to your attention once more. It is the finest thing of its sort ever done in America.

(December, 1920)

JAMES BRANCH CABELL

A Refined Scoffer

Of literary reputations a number of distinct varieties are to be distinguished. There is, first of all, the sort of reputation that is high both vertically and horizontally—the sort that tends to convert itself into a racial myth, unchallenged and even unexamined—to wit, the reputation of a Shakespeare, a Goethe, a Molière, a Dante, a Schiller, or, to drop a peg or two, a Tolstoi, a Hugo or a Mark Twain. Secondly there is the kind that has a wide base but dissolves in sniffs above—the reputation of a Brieux, a Harold Bell Wright, a Lew Wallace, a Richard Harding Davis, an Elbert Hubbard, a Conan Doyle or a D'Annunzio. Thirdly, there is the kind that is brilliant above but shadowy below—the reputation of a Henry James, a Huysmans, a Lafcadio Hearn, a Schnitzler, a Joseph Conrad or a George Gissing. Fourthly, there is the kind that is shadowy up and down—a thing less of public bruitings than of cautious whispers—a diffident, esoteric, Hugo-Wolfish variety—*e.g.*, the reputation of a Max Stirner, an Henri Becque, a Marie Henri Beyle or an Ambrose Bierce. . . .

Bierce is dead, and in America, at least, the post is vacant. I have a fancy that James Branch Cabell will enter into enjoyment of its prerogatives and usufructs. All efforts to make him popular will fail inevitably; he is far too mystifying a fellow ever to enchant the simple folk who delight in O. Henry, Kathleen Norris and Henry van Dyke. Moreover, he writes too well; his English is too voluptuous to be endured; there is nothing ingratiatingly mushy and idiotic about it. Nor is he likely to be embraced by such *intelligentsia* as disport in the literary weeklies and the women's clubs, for he is not a Deep Thinker, but a Scoffer, and, worse, he scoffs at Sacred Things, including even American Ideals. Nay, there is no hope for Cabell in either direction. If he ever had a chance, his new book, *Jurgen*, has ruined it. *Jurgen*, estimated by current American standards, whether of the boobery or of the super-boobery, is everything that is abhorrent. On the negative side, it lacks all Inspiration, all Optimism, all tendency to whoop up the Finer Things; it moves toward no shining Goal; it even neglects to denounce Pessimism, Marital Infidelity, Bolshevism, the Alien Menace and German *Kultur*. And on the positive side it piles up sins unspeakable: it is full of racy and mirthful ideas, it is brilliantly written, it is novel and daring, it is ribald, it is heretical, it is blasphemous, it is Rabelaisian. Such a book simply refuses to fit into the decorous mid-Victorian pattern of American letters. It belongs to some outlandish literature, most probably the French. One might imagine it written by a member of the French Academy, say Anatole France. But could one imagine it written by a member of the American Academy of Arts and Letters, say Bliss Perry? The thought is not only fantastic; it is almost obscene.

Cabell came near sneaking into refined society, a few years ago, as a novelist. Several of his novels, like the earlier pieces of Hergesheimer, trembled on the verge of polite acceptance. Both writers were handicapped by having ears. They wrote English that was delicately musical and colorful—and hence incurably offensive to constant readers of Rex Beach, Thomas H. Dixon, and *The New York Times*. Hergesheimer finally atoned for his style by mastering the popular novelette formula; thereafter he was in the *Saturday Evening Post* and the old maids who review books for the newspapers began to praise him. A few weeks ago I received an invitation to hear him lecture before a Browning Society; in a year or two, if he continues to be good, he will be elected to membership in the National Institute of Arts and Letters, in full equality with Ernest Poole, Oliver Herford, Henry Sydnor Harrison and E. W. Townsend, author of *Chimmie Fadden*. Cabell, I fear, must resign himself to doing without the accolade. *Beyond Life* spilled many a bean; beneath its rumblings one discerned more than one cackle of satanic laughter. *Jurgen* wrecks the whole beanery. It is a compendium of backward-looking and wrong-thinking. It is a devil's sonata, an infernal *kindersinfonie* for slapstick, seltzer-siphon and bladder-on-a-string. . . . And, too, for the caressing violin, the lovely and melancholy flute. How charmingly the fellow writes! What a hand for the slick and slippery phrase he has! How cunningly he winds up a sentence, and then flicks it out with a twist of the wrist—a shimmering, dazzling shower of nouns, verbs, adjectives, adverbs, pronouns and prepositions! . . .

It is curious how often the gift of irony is coupled with pedantry. Think of old François and his astounding citations from incredible authorities—almost like an article in a German medical journal. Or of Anatole France. Or of Swift. Cabell, in *Jurgen,* borrows all the best hocus-pocus of the professors. He reconstructs an imaginary medieval legend with all the attention to detail of the pundits who publish college editions of *Aucassin et Nicolette;* until, toward the end, his own exuberance intoxicates him a bit, he actually makes it seem a genuine translation. But his Jurgen, of course, is never a medieval man. No; Jurgen is horribly modern. Jurgen is you and I, or you and me, as you choose. Jurgen is the modern man in reaction against a skepticism that explains everything away and yet leaves everything inexplicable. He is the modern man in doubt of all things, including especially his own doubts. So his quest is no heroic enterprise, though it takes him over half the earth and into all the gaudiest and most romantic kingdoms thereof, for the thing that he seeks is not a great hazard and an homeric death but simply ease and contentment, and what he comes to in the end is the discovery that they are nowhere to be found, not even in the arms of a royal princess. Jurgen acquires the shirt of Nessus and the magical sword Caliburn; he becomes Duke of Logreus, Prince Consort in Cocaigne, King of Eubonia, and Emperor of Noumaria; he meets and loves the incomparable Guenevere in the moonlight on the eve of her marriage to King Arthur; he unveils the beauty of Helen of Troy; he is taught all the ineffable secrets of love by Queen Anaïtis; he becomes a great poet; he sees strange coasts; he roams the whole universe. But in the end, he returns sadly to a world "wherein the result of every human endeavor is transient and the end of all is death," and takes his old place behind the counter of his pawnshop, and resumes philosophically his interrupted feud with his faded wife, Dame Lisa.

In brief, a very simple tale, and as old in its fundamental dolorousness as arterio-sclerosis. What gives it its high quality is the richness of its detail—the prodigious gorgeousness of its imagery, the dramatic effectiveness of its shifting scenes, the whole glow and gusto of it. Here, at all events, it is medieval. Here Cabell evokes an atmosphere that is the very essence of charm. Nothing could be more delightfully done than some of the episodes—that of Jurgen's meeting with Guenevere in the Hall of Judgment, that of his dialogue with old King Gogyrvan Gawr, that of his adventure with the Hamadryad, that of

the ceremony of the Breaking of the Veil, that of his invasion of the
bed-chamber of Helen of Troy. The man who could imagine such
scenes is a first-rate artist, and in the manner of their execution he
proves the fact again. Time and again they seem to be dissolving,
shaking a bit, going to pieces—but always he carries them off. And
always neatly, delicately, with an air. The humor of them has its
perils; to Puritans it must often seem shocking; it might easily become
gross. But here it is no more gross than a rose-window. . . . Toward
the end, alack, the thing falls down. The transition from heathen
Olympuses and Arcadies to the Christian Heaven and Hell works an
inevitable debasement of the comedy. The satire here ceases to be
light-fingered and becomes heavy-handed: "the religion of Hell is patriotism, and the government is an enlightened democracy." It is almost like making fun of a man with inflammatory rheumatism. Perhaps the essential thing is that the book is a trifle too long. By the
time one comes to Calvinism, democracy and the moral order of the
world one has begun to feel surfeited. But where is there a work of
art without a blemish? Even Beethoven occasionally misses fire. This
Jurgen, for all such ifs and buts, is a very fine thing. It is a great pity
that it was not written in French. Done in English, and printed in
These States, it somehow suggests Brahms scoring his Fourth Symphony for a Jazz band and giving it at an annual convention of the
Knights of Pythias.

(January, 1920)

SHERWOOD ANDERSON

Something New under the Sun

Of these [books under review] the most original and remarkable is the Anderson book, a collection of short stories of a new order, including at least half a dozen of a very striking quality. This Anderson is a man of whom a great deal will be heard hereafter. Along with Willa Sibert Cather, James Branch Cabell and a few others, he belongs to a small group that has somehow emancipated itself from the prevailing imitativeness and banality of the national letters and is moving steadily toward work that will do honor to the country. His first novel, *Windy McPherson's Son*, printed in 1916, had plenty of faults, but there were so many compensating merits that it stood out clearly above the general run of the fiction of its year. Then came *Marching Men*, another defective but extremely interesting novel, and then a book of dithyrambs, *Mid-American Chants*. But these things, for all their brilliant moments, did not adequately represent Anderson. The national vice of ethical purpose corrupted them; they were burdened with *Tendenz*. Now, in *Winesburg, Ohio*, he throws off that handicap. What remains is pure representation—and it is representation so vivid, so full of insight, so shiningly life-like and glowing, that the book is lifted into a category all its own. Nothing quite like it has ever been done in America. It is a book that, at one stroke, turns depression into enthusiasm.

In form, it is a collection of short stories, with common characters welding them into a continued picture of life in a small inland town. But what short stories! Compare them to the popular trade goods of the Gouverneur Morrises and Julian Streets, or even to the more pretentious work of the Alice Browns and Katharine Fullerton Geroulds. It is the difference between music by a Chaminade and music by a Brahms. Into his brief pages Anderson not only gets brilliant images of men and women who walk in all the colors of reality; he also gets a profound sense of the obscure, inner drama of their lives. Consider, for example, the four-part story called "Godliness." It is fiction for half a page, but after that it seems indubitable fact—fact that is searching and ferret-like—fact infinitely stealthy and persuasive—the sort of fact that suddenly changes a stolid, inscrutable Captain MacWhirr into a moving symbol of man in his struggle with the fates. And then turn to "Respectability," and to "The Strength of God," and to "Adventure," and to "The Teacher." Here one gets all the joy that goes with the discovery of something quite new under the sun—a new order of short story, half tale and half psychological anatomizing, and vastly better than all the kinds that have gone before. Here is the goal that *The Spoon River Anthology* aimed at, and missed by half a mile. Allow everything to the imperfection of the form and everything to the author's occasional failure to rise to it: what remains is a truly extraordinary book, by a man of such palpably unusual talent that it seems almost an impertinence to welcome him.

(August, 1919)

The Two Andersons

Of all American novelists, past or present, Sherwood Anderson is probably the one whose struggles to express himself are the most interesting. Even more than Dreiser he is beset by devils that make the business difficult for him. What ails him primarily is the fact that there are two Andersons, sharply differentiated and tending to fall into implacable antagonisms. One is the artist who sees the America of his day as the most cruel and sordid, and yet at the same time as the most melodramatic and engrossing of spectacles—the artist enchanted by the sheer barbaric color of it all, and eager to get that color into living pages—the artist standing, as it were, above the turmoil, and intent only upon observing it accurately and presenting it honestly, feelingly and unhindered. The other is a sort of uncertain social reformer—one appalled by the muddle of ideas and aspirations in the Republic, and impelled to do something or say something, however fantastic, however obvious, to help along the slow and

agonizing process of reorganization—in brief, a typical American of
the more reflective sort, full of inchoate visions and confused indigna-
tions. The combat between the two was visible in Anderson's first
novel, *Windy McPherson's Son,* a book that started off so vigorously
and brilliantly as a work of art that most readers overlooked its subsequent transformation into a furious but somewhat unintelligent tract.
In *Marching Men,* after a brief struggle, the second Anderson won
hands down, and the thing degenerated into formal prophecy, often
hard to distinguish, toward the end, from burlesque. This defeat,
however, did not destroy the first Anderson, the artist Anderson; on the
contrary, it seems to have stimulated him enormously. In *Winesburg,
Ohio,* which followed, he drove his enemy quite off the field. The result was a book of high and delicate quality, a book uncorrupted by
theories and moral purposes, a book that stands clearly above anything
of its sort in latter-day American literature, saving only Dreiser's
Twelve Men. It will be appreciated at its true worth, I believe, in the
years to come. At the moment its peculiar excellencies are obscured by
its very unusualness—its complete departure from all the customary
methods and materials of prose fiction among us. Study it, and you will
get some smell of the fiction of the future. If the great American novelists visioned by Carl Sandburg ever escape from Chautauqua and
Atlanta, they will learn much more from *Winesburg* than ever they
learn from Howells and Henry James.

In *Poor White,* Anderson's latest book, there is a sort of compromise,
but with most of the advantages going to the artist. It, too, has its
ideas, its theory, but that theory relates itself to the demonstrable
facts of the past and not to the shadowy possibilities of the future, as
was the case in *Marching Men.* What Anderson seeks to set forth is
the demoralizing effect of the introduction of the factory system into
the rural Middle West. It came at a time when the old struggle with
the soil had reached success. The land was under the yoke; the yokels
were secure at last, and learning to take their ease, and beginning to
feel around for new enterprises; the day was one which might have
seen the birth of an art and a civilization. But then came the factory,
and with it a revival of the sordid combat. Rich farmers, ripe to hear
ideas, to hatch aspirations, to dream dreams, now became stock-
holders in tile-factories and shingle-mills, and at once plunged back
into their old hoggishness. The countryside was polluted, the towns
were made hideous, the people were poisoned with ignoble aims.

Worse, this new struggle was not a self-limiting disease, like the old struggle against Indians, wolves, cyclones, mud and tree-stumps. There could be no end to it. One factory would bring another factory. One success would breed an insatiable thirst for another and larger success. Thus Arcady succumbed to Youngstown and Zanesville, and the pioneer, a poet as well as a peasant, ceased to be either, and became a filthy manufacturer of muck and money.

Anderson lights up the process by carrying an imaginative and unchanging man through it. This man is Hugh McVey, a dreamer of the machines. His dreams attract the fathers of the factory system; they can be converted into money; he is dragged out of his ivory tower and put to labor in a machine-shop. But he never really succumbs. To him his successive inventions—preposterous potato-planters, coal-unloaders and other such ghastly monsters—always remain far more visions than realities. In the end he fades gently from the scene, uncomprehended and forgotten by the usurers he has enriched. A curious love affair is his final experiment. The girl is a peasant suffering all the pangs of the newly intellectual. She grasps ineptly at a culture that always eludes her. One wonders what she and McVey will make of life, the one so eager and the other so melancholy and resigned. The answer would be clearer if McVey himself were clearer. I have a notion that Anderson makes his unlikeness to the general a bit too pronounced; Norris fell into the same error in *The Octopus*. It is hard to imagine a man so absolutely out of contact with his environment—so enchanted by his visions that he scarcely sees John Doe and Richard Roe on the street. But McVey, after all, is only a sort of chorus to the main drama. That drama is set forth with a tremendous meticulousness and a tremendous force. The people who enter into it have a superb reality. There is a great brilliancy of detail. More, the inner structure of the thing is sound; Anderson has learned how to hold himself upon the track. Altogether, the best novel that he has done—not better than *Winesburg* certainly, but far better than *Marching Men* and *Windy McPherson's Son*. The Anderson promise begins to be fulfilled. Here is a serious novelist who must be taken seriously. . . .

(December, 1920)

Muddleheaded Art

Sherwood Anderson's *Many Marriages*, his first long story in three years, exemplifies very forcibly two of the faults that I have often mentioned in discussing him in this place in the past: first, his apparent inability to manage the machinery of a sustained narrative, and second, his tendency to grow vague and nonsensical when he abandons simple representation and ventures into the field of what is called ideas. It seems to me that no writer now in practice in America can write a better short story than Anderson. He not only sees into character with sharp and awful eyes; he is also extraordinarily adept at handling a simple situation. If any better short story than "I Am a Fool" has been printed in English for five years past, then it must be "I Want to Know Why"—and both of them are by Anderson. But when he tackles a novel, as he has now done four times, he begins to wobble after he has hauled his protagonist through the opening situation, and before the end he usually tries to reinforce his fading story with ideational flights that have nothing clearly and necessarily to do with it and are commonly only defectively rational and intelligible, and so the whole thing goes to pot. This failing spoiled *Windy McPherson's Son* which began brilliantly; it spoiled *Marching Men,* which began yet more brilliantly; it spoiled *Poor White,* which held up until very near the end; it now spoils *Many Marriages*, which starts out better, even, than any of the others.

The problem before Anderson here is to depict and account for a dramatic episode in the life of a hitherto commonplace man, one John Webster, a washing-machine manufacturer in a small Wisconsin town—his desertion of his wife and daughter, and his elopement with one Natalie Swartz, a dull, uncharming girl in his office, daughter to a small German saloonkeeper and an Irish *Saufschwester.* The bald episode is handled with great deftness and plausibility. The successive steps are not only fully accounted for; they also take on an air of inevitability; one feels, like Webster himself, that he is moved by forces beyond him, that he could not turn back if he would. Natalie is as unappetizing as a lady embalmer; every vestige of prudence in him bids Webster to halt; nevertheless, he is drawn into his banal and ruinous romance by invisible and irresistible chains. But, having got so far, Anderson is not content to shut down and call it a day. Instead, he proceeds to outfit Webster with a stock of theories and intuitions that are as vague as the ideas of a New Thought healer—ideas by Freud out of Greenwich Village, by the Doukhobors out of the behaviorist psychology—and presently he ceases altogether to be John Webster, of Wisconsin, and becomes a character in a play by Maeterlinck.

What, in brief, is his fundamental notion? As I understand it, peering for its outlines through the hazes surrounding it, it is the notion that men and women are in bondage to their bodies—that they will never be genuinely free until they get rid of the shames laid as burdens upon Mother Eve. To the end of getting rid of them before departing with Natalie, Webster strips off his union suit and parades before his wife and daughter in the uniform of an artist's model. His wife, shocked beyond endurance by this spectacle and by his statement that, when he first had the honor of viewing her, she was in the same state herself, retires to the next room and swallows a dose of poison. But his daughter, perhaps because she not only hears the words reported to us by the author, but also has the advantage of seeing his facial expression and gestures, seems to understand him and agree with him. Finally, his exposition completed, he resumes his clothes, leaves the house, and proceeds upon his adulterous journey with Natalie, whose drunken mother, having denounced her unjustly for unchastity for years, is now confronted at last with the proof that nature, in the long run, always imitates art—in brief, that lying about a dog makes him bite.

This theory of somatic servitude that Webster expounds is, as I say, extremely nebulous and tantalizing. I am what may be called a professional consumer of ideas; I have read Immanuel Kant, and followed him; I have even read Mary Baker G. Eddy and followed her; but the Websterian exegesis, I must confess, is mainly beyond me. In so far as it is intelligible to me at all, it seems to be simply the old doctrine that we'd all blush less and be happier if we went naked; in so far as it gets past that point it casts itself into terms of a metaphysic that I am frankly not privy to. But even more puzzling than its own intrinsic substance is the question of its applicability to the situation before us. Let us grant that Webster's wife is hopeless—that not even an act of God could make her rise to the philosophizing of her husband. It thus appears reasonable that he should leave her. But why should he run off with Natalie, who is apparently ten times worse? Is it because Natalie is a simpler and more innocent animal than his wife, and will thus refrain from plaguing him with inhibitions, as his wife has done? Then why seek to adorn that elemental fact with so formidable a soliloquy and so startling a dumbshow? And if, unknown to us, there is something in Natalie that attracts a philosopher—if she is actually a more seemly mate for poor John than Mrs. Webster—then why not show what that something is? . . .

Well, perhaps I labor the thing too hard. The inexplicable, after all, occurs in life every day; it belongs in novels, along with everything else that is real. But when it plays so important a rôle that any reader not gifted with clairvoyance must needs halt and scratch his nose—when the distraction that it presents breaks down an otherwise well-ordered and interesting narrative, and reduces reading to a bewildered sort of speculation—then there is excuse for filing a polite caveat. Anderson is so accurate an observer of the inner weaknesses and aspirations of man, and particularly of the more simple varieties of man, and he has so fine a gift for setting forth his observations in a succinct, novel and effectively dramatic manner that it is irritating to see him leaving the light for the shadows, and blundering absurdly in regions where the roads, even when they exist, are obviously not on his map. *Many Marriages* is boldly planned and it is full of brilliant detail, but as a whole it seems to me to be the author's worst failure. The opaque theorizing of Greenwich Village is in it. If there is a lesson in it, it is the lesson that Freud should have made sure that his customers were familiar with the elements of high-school psychology before he began instructing them in his non-Euclidian psychology.

(July, 1923)

SINCLAIR LEWIS

The Story of an American Family

After all, Munyon was probably right: there is yet hope. Perhaps
Emerson and Whitman were right too; maybe even Sandburg is right.
What ails us all is a weakness for rash over-generalization, leading to
shooting pains in the psyche and delusions of divine persecution. Observing the steady and precipitate descent of promising postulants in
beautiful letters down the steep, greasy chutes of the *Saturday Evening Post*, the *Metropolitan*, the *Cosmopolitan* and the rest of the
Hearst and Hearstoid magazines, we are too prone, ass-like, to throw
up our hands and bawl that all is lost, including honor. But all the
while a contrary movement is in progress, far less noted than it ought
to be. Authors with their pockets full of best-seller money are bitten
by high ambition, and strive heroically to scramble out of the literary
Cloaca Maxima. Now and then one of them succeeds, bursting suddenly into the light of the good red sun with the foul liquors of the
depths still streaming from him, like a prisoner loosed from some obscene dungeon. Is it so soon forgotten that Willa Cather used to be
one of the editors of *McClure's?* That Dreiser wrote editorials for the
Delineator and was an editor of dime novels for Street & Smith? That
Huneker worked for the *Musical Courier?* That Amy Lowell imitated
George E. Woodberrry and Felicia Hemans? That E. W. Howe was
born a Methodist? That Sandburg was once a Chautauqua orator?
That Cabell's first stories were printed in *Harper's Magazine?* . . . As
I say, they occasionally break out, strange as it may seem. A few
months ago I recorded the case of Zona Gale, emerging from her
stew of glad books with *Miss Lulu Bett*. Now comes another fugitive,
his face blanched by years in the hulks, but his eyes alight with high
purpose. His name is Sinclair Lewis, and the work he offers is a novel
called *Main Street*. . . .

This *Main Street* I commend to your polite attention. It is, in brief, good stuff. It presents characters that are genuinely human, and not only genuinely human but also authentically American; it carries them through a series of transactions that are all interesting and plausible; it exhibits those transactions thoughtfully and acutely, in the light of the social and cultural forces underlying them; it is well written, and full of a sharp sense of comedy, and rich in observation, and competently designed. Superficially, the story of a man and his wife in a small Minnesota town, it is actually the typical story of the American family—that is, of the family in its first stage, before husband and wife have become lost in father and mother. The average American wife, I daresay, does not come quite so close to downright revolt as Carol Kennicott, but that is the only exaggeration, and we may well overlook it. Otherwise, she and her Will are triumphs of the national normalcy—she with her vague stirrings, her unintelligible yearnings, her clumsy gropings, and he with his magnificent obtuseness, his childish belief in meaningless phrases, his intellectual deafness and nearsightedness, his pathetic inability to comprehend the turmoil that goes on within her. Here is the essential tragedy of American life, and if not the tragedy, then at least the sardonic farce; the disparate cultural development of male and female, the great strangeness that lies between husband and wife when they begin to function as members of society. The men, sweating at their sordid concerns, have given the women leisure, and out of that leisure the women have fashioned disquieting discontents. To Will Kennicott, as to most other normal American males, life remains simple; do your work, care for your family, buy your Liberty Bonds, root for your home team, help to build up your lodge, venerate the flag. But to Carol it is far more complex and challenging. She has become aware of forces that her husband is wholly unable to comprehend, and that she herself can comprehend only in a dim and muddled way. The ideas of the great world press upon her, confusing her and making her uneasy. She is flustered by strange heresies, by romantic personalities, by exotic images of beauty. To Kennicott she is flighty, illogical, ungrateful for the benefits that he and God have heaped upon her. To her he is dull, narrow, ignoble.

Mr. Lewis depicts the resultant struggle with great penetration. He is far too intelligent to take sides—to turn the thing into a mere harangue against one or the other. Above all, he is too intelligent to take the side of Carol, as nine novelists out of ten would have done. He sees clearly what is too often not seen—that her superior culture is, after all, chiefly bogus—that the oafish Kennicott, in more ways than one, is actually better than she is. Her war upon his Philistinism is carried on with essentially Philistine weapons. Her dream of converting a Minnesota prairie town into a sort of Long Island suburb, with overtones of Greenwich Village and the Harvard campus, is quite as absurd as his dream of converting it into a second Minneapolis, with overtones of Gary, Ind., and Paterson, N. J. When their conflict is made concrete and dramatic by the entrance of a *tertium quid,* the hollowness of her whole case is at once made apparent, for this *tertium quid* is a Swedish trousers-presser who becomes a moving-picture actor. It seems to me that the irony here is delicate and delicious. This, then, is the end-product of the Maeterlinck complex! Needless to say, Carol lacks the courage to decamp with her Scandinavian. Instead, she descends to sheer banality. That is, she departs for Washington, becomes a war-worker, and rubs noses with the suffragettes. In the end, it goes without saying, she returns to Gopher Prairie and the hearth-stone of her Will. The fellow is at least honest. He offers her no ignominious compromise. She comes back under the old rules, and is presently nursing a baby. Thus the true idealism of the Republic, the idealism of its Chambers of Commerce, its Knights of Pythias, its Rotary Clubs and its National Defense Leagues, for which Washington froze at Valley Forge and Our Boys died at Château-Thierry—thus this genuine and unpolluted article conquers the phoney idealism of Nietzsche, Edward W. Bok, Dunsany, George Bernard Shaw, Margaret Anderson, Mrs. Margaret Sanger, Percy Mackaye and the I.W.W.

But the mere story, after all, is nothing; the virtue of the book lies in its packed and brilliant detail. It is an attempt, not to solve the American cultural problem, but simply to depict with great care a group of typical Americans. This attempt is extraordinarily successful. The figures often remain in the flat; the author is quite unable to get that poignancy into them which Dreiser manages so superbly; one seldom sees into them very deeply or feels with them very keenly. But in their externals, at all events, they are done with uncommon skill. In particular, Mr. Lewis represents their speech vividly and accurately. It would be hard to find a false note in the dialogue, and it would be impossible to exceed the verisimilitude of the various extracts from the Gopher Prairie paper, or of the sermon by a Methodist dervish in the

Gopher Prairie Wesleyan cathedral, or of a speech by a boomer at a banquet of the Chamber of Commerce. Here Mr. Lewis lays on with obvious malice, but always he keeps within the bounds of probability, always his realism holds up. It is, as I have said, good stuff. I have read no more genuinely amusing novel for a long while. The man who did it deserves a hearty welcome. His apprenticeship in the cellars of the tabernacle was not wasted. . . .

(January, 1921)

Portrait of an American Citizen

The theory lately held in Greenwich Village that the merit and success of *Main Street* constituted a sort of double-headed accident, probably to be ascribed to a case of mistaken identity on the part of God—this theory blows up with a frightful roar toward the middle of *Babbitt*. The plain truth is, indeed, that *Babbitt* is at least twice as good a novel as *Main Street* was—that it avoids all the more obvious faults of that celebrated work, and shows a number of virtues that are quite new. It is better designed than *Main Street;* the action is more logical and coherent; there is more imagination in it and less bald journalism; above all, there is a better grip upon the characters. If Carol Kennicott, at one leap, became as real a figure to most literate Americans as Jane Addams or Nan Patterson; then George F. Babbitt should become as real as Jack Dempsey or Charlie Schwab. The fellow simply drips with human juices. Every one of his joints is movable in all directions. Real freckles are upon his neck and real sweat stands out upon his forehead. I have personally known him since my earliest days as a newspaper reporter, back in the last century. I have heard him make such speeches as Cicero never dreamed of at banquets of the Chamber of Commerce. I have seen him marching in parades. I have observed him advancing upon his Presbyterian tabernacle of a Sunday morning, his somewhat stoutish lady upon his arm. I have watched and heard him crank his Buick. I have noted the effect of alcohol upon him, both before and after Prohibition. And I have seen him, when some convention of Good Fellows was in town, at his innocent sports in the parlors of brothels, grandly ordering wine at $10 a round and bidding the professor play "White Wings."

To me his saga, as Sinclair Lewis has set it down, is fiction only by a sort of courtesy. All the usual fittings of the prose fable seem to be absent. There is no plot whatever, and very little of the hocus-pocus commonly called development of character. Babbitt simply grows two years older as the tale unfolds; otherwise he doesn't change at all— any more than you or I have changed since 1920. Every customary device of the novelist is absent. When Babbitt, revolting against the irksome happiness of his home, takes to a series of low affairs with manicure girls, grass-widows and ladies even more complaisant, nothing overt and melodramatic happens to him. He never meets his young son Teddy in a dubious cabaret; his wife never discovers incriminating correspondence in his pockets; no one tries to blackmail him; he is never present when a joint is raided. The worst punishment that falls upon him is that his old friends at the Athletic Club—cheats exactly like himself—gossip about him a bit. Even so, that gossip goes no further; Mrs. Babbitt does not hear it. When she accuses him of adultery, it is simply the formal accusation of a loving wife: she herself has absolutely no belief in it. Moreover, it does not cause Babbitt to break down, confess and promise to sin no more. Instead, he lies like a major-general, denounces his wife for her evil imagination, and returns forthwith to his carnalities. If, in the end, he abandons them, it is not because they torture his conscience, but because they seem likely to hurt his business. This prospect gives him pause, and the pause saves him. He is, beside, growing old. He is 48, and more than a little bald. A night out leaves his tongue coated in the morning. As the curtain falls upon him he is back upon the track of rectitude—a sound business man, a faithful Booster, an assiduous Elk, a trustworthy Presbyterian, a good husband, a loving father, a successful and unchallenged fraud.

Let me confess at once that this story has given me vast delight. I know the Babbitt type, I believe, as well as most; for twenty years I have devoted myself to the exploration of its peculiarities. Lewis depicts it with complete and absolute fidelity. There is irony in the picture; irony that is unflagging and unfailing, but nowhere is there any important departure from the essential truth. Babbitt has a great clownishness in him, but he never becomes a mere clown. In the midst of his most extravagant imbecilities he keeps both feet upon the ground. One not only sees him brilliantly; one also understands him; he is made plausible and natural. As an old professor of Babbittry I welcome him as an almost perfect specimen—a genuine museum piece. Every American city swarms with his brothers. They run things in the Republic, East, West, North, South. They are the originators and propagators of the national delusions—all, that is, save those which spring from the farms. They are the palladiums of 100 per cent Americanism; the apostles of the Harding politics; the guardians of the Only True Christianity. They constitute the Chambers of Commerce, the Rotary Clubs, the Kiwanis Clubs, the Watch and Ward Societies, the Men and Religion Forward Movements, the Y.M.C.A. directorates, the Good Citizen Leagues. They are the advertisers who determine what is to go into the American newspapers and what is to stay out. They are the Leading Citizens, the speakers at banquets, the profiteers, the corruptors of politics, the supporters of evangelical Christianity, the peers of the realm. Babbitt is their archetype. He is no worse than most, and no better; he is the average American of the ruling minority in this hundred and forty-sixth year of the Republic. He is America incarnate, exuberant and exquisite. Study him well and you will know better what is the matter with the land we live in than you would know after plowing through a thousand such volumes as Walter Lippmann's *Public Opinion*. What Lippmann tried to do as a professor, laboriously and without imagination, Lewis has here done as an artist with a few vivid strokes. It is a very fine piece of work indeed.

Nor is all its merit in the central figure. It is not Babbitt that shines forth most gaudily, but the whole complex of Babbittry, Babbittism, Babbittismus. In brief, Babbitt is seen as no more than a single member of the society he lives in—a matter far more difficult to handle, obviously, than any mere character sketch. His every act is related to the phenomena of that society. It is not what he feels and aspires to that moves him primarily; it is what the folks about him will think of him. His politics is communal politics, mob politics, herd politics; his religion is a public rite wholly without subjective significance; his relations to his wife and his children are formalized and standardized; even his debaucheries are the orthodox debaucheries of a sound business man. The salient thing about him, in truth, is his complete lack of originality—and that is precisely the salient mark of every American of his class. What he feels and thinks is what it is currently proper to feel and think. Only once, during the two years that we have him under view, does he venture upon an idea that is even remotely original—and that time the heresy almost ruins him. The lesson, you may be sure, is not lost upon him. If he lives, he will not offend again. No thought will ever get a lodgment in his mind, even in the wildest deliriums following bootleg gin, that will offer offense to the pruderies of Vergil Gunch, president of the Boosters' Club, or to those of old Mr. Eathorne, president of the First State Bank, or to those of the Rev. Dr. John Jennison Drew, pastor of the Chatham Road Presbyterian Church, or to those of Prof. Pumphrey, head of the Zenith Business College, or even to those of Miss McGoun, the virtuous stenographer. He has been rolled through the mill. He emerges the very model and pattern of a forward-looking, right-thinking Americano.

As I say, this *Babbitt* gives me great delight. It is shrewdly devised; it is adeptly managed; it is well written. The details, as in *Main Street*, are extraordinarily vivid—the speech of Babbitt before the Zenith Real Estate Board, the meeting to consider ways and means of bulging the Chatham Road Sunday-school, the annual convention of the real-estate men, Babbitt's amour with the manicure-girl, the episode of Sir Gerald Doak, the warning visit when Babbitt is suspected of Liberalism, the New Thought meeting, the elopement of young Theodore Roosevelt Babbitt and Eunice Littlefield at the end. In all these scenes there is more than mere humor; there is searching truth. They reveal something; they mean something. I know of no American novel that more accurately presents the real America. It is a social document of a high order.

(October, 1922)

F. SCOTT FITZGERALD

Two Years Too Late

F. Scott Fitzgerald, in *Flappers and Philosophers,* offers a sandwich made up of two thick and tasteless chunks of *Kriegsbrod* with a couple of excellent sardines between. In brief, a collection that shows both the very good and the very bad. The best story in it, I think, is "Benediction," which, when it was first printed in *The Smart Set,* brought down the maledictions of the Jesuits and came near getting the magazine barred from the Knights of Columbus camp-libraries. Re-reading it, I can see no reason why any intelligent Catholic should object to it in the slightest. It is a well-written story, a story with an air to it, and it is also a story that rings true. I commend it to the rev. clergy; they will enjoy it. From "Benediction" the leap to "The Off-shore Pirate" and other such confections is like the leap from the peaks of Darien to the slums of Colon. Here is thin and obvious stuff, cheap stuff—in brief, atrociously bad stuff. Fitzgerald is curiously ambidextrous. Will he proceed via the first part of *This Side of Paradise* to the cold groves of beautiful letters, or will he proceed via "Head and Shoulders" into the sunshine that warms Robert W. Chambers and Harold MacGrath? Let us wait and see. And meanwhile, let us marvel at the sagacity of a publisher who lets a young author print *Flappers and Philosophers* after *This Side of Paradise.* If it were not two years too late I'd almost suspect a German plot.

(December, 1920)

A Step Forward

F. Scott Fitzgerald's *The Beautiful and the Damned [sic]* is an *adagio* following the *scherzo* of *This Side of Paradise*. It starts off ingratiatingly and disarmingly, with brilliant variations upon the theme of the *scherzo*, but pretty soon a more sombre tune is heard in the bull-fiddles, and toward the end there is very solemn music, indeed —music that will probably give a shock to all the fluffier and more flapperish Fitzgeraldistas. In brief, a disconcerting peep into the future of a pair of the amiable children dealt with in *This Side of Paradise*. Here we have Gloria Gilbert, the prom angel, graduating into a star of hotel dances in New York, and then into a wife, and then into the scared spectator of her husband's disintegration, and then, at the end, into a pathetic trembler on the brink of middle age. And here we have Anthony Patch, the gallant young Harvard man, sliding hopelessly down the hill of idleness, incompetence, extravagance and drunkenness. It is, in the main, Anthony's story, not Gloria's. His reactions to her, of course—to her somewhat florid charm, her acrid feminine cynicism, her love of hollow show and hollower gayety, her fear of inconvenient facts—are integral parts of the intricate machinery of his decay, but one feels that he would have decayed quite as rapidly without her, whatever may be said for the notion that a wife of another sort might have saved him. There is little that is vicious about Anthony; he is simply silly—the fearful end-product of ill-assorted marriages, a quite typical American of the third generation from shirt-sleeves. The forthright competence of his old grandfather, Adam J. Patch, the millionaire moralist, has been bred out of the strain. Into it have come dilutions from a New England blue-stocking and worse. He is hopeless from birth.

The waters into which this essentially serious and even tragic story bring Fitzgerald seemed quite beyond the ken of the author of *This Side of Paradise*. It is thus not surprising to find him navigating, at times, rather cautiously and ineptly. The vast plausibility that Dreiser got into the similar chronicle of Hurstwood is not there; one often encounters shakiness, both in the imagining and the telling. Worse, the thing is botched at the end by the introduction of a god from the machine: Anthony is saved from the inexorable logic of his life by a court decision which gives him, most unexpectedly and improbably, his grandfather's millions. But allowing for all that, it must be said for

Fitzgerald that he discharges his unaccustomed and difficult business with ingenuity and dignity. Opportunity beckoned him toward very facile jobs; he might have gone on rewriting the charming romance of *This Side of Paradise* for ten or fifteen years, and made a lot of money out of it, and got a great deal of uncritical praise for it. Instead, he tried something much more difficult, and if the result is not a complete success, it is nevertheless near enough to success to be worthy of respect. There is fine observation in it, and much penetrating detail, and the writing is solid and sound. After *This Side of Paradise* the future of Fitzgerald seemed extremely uncertain. There was an air about that book which suggested a fortunate accident. The shabby stuff collected in *Flappers and Philosophers* converted uncertainty into something worse. But *The Beautiful and the Damned* [*sic*] delivers the author from all those doubts. There are a hundred signs in it of serious purpose and unquestionable skill. Even in its defects there is proof of hard striving. Fitzgerald ceases to be a *Wunderkind,* and begins to come into his maturity.

(April, 1922)

XII

Miscellany

The following are a hodgepodge of reviews or asides or estimations
that could not be fitted into any of the chapters which I have, admit-
tedly, arbitrarily chosen to encompass Mencken's *Smart Set* criticism.
The review of M. Gancel's book provides Mencken with the chance to
give, among other things, his recipe for crab *à la créole*. "The Nature
of Vice" shows Mencken in a uniquely Menckenian mood—seriously
engaged in conversation with his reader and at the same time pulling
his leg. In "Novels to Reread," Mencken takes the reader into his
study and rambles on for a few minutes about books in general and
Conrad in particular, concluding with a hymn to *Huckleberry Finn*.
"A Review of Reviewers" is more tomfoolery—but what delightful and
engaging tomfoolery! Every author dreams of reviewing his own
book; Mencken does it here, allowing other reviewers to provide him
with the lines upon which to hang his clothes. In "An Autobiographical Note" are seeds that grew, twenty-five years later, into the oak
of *Happy Days* (see the chapter entitled "In the Footsteps of Guten-
berg"). "The Incomparable Billy" puts a garish light on one of Mencken's favorite Americans. Though he was revolted by what he called
the bellicose stupidity of evangelical Christians, Mencken sat beneath
a sweating, screaming Billy Sunday for four nights running, no doubt
relishing every heave and howl of the American Savonarola. "The
Irish Renaissance" is but one of many appraisals of Irish letters that
Mencken wrote between 1908 and 1924. In the same article, Mencken
looked back over his eight and a third years on *The Smart Set*, noting
the wonders that time had wrought and assessing the changes on the
literary map. The man, or woman, who reads the first few hundred

words of the essay without bursting into laughter at least once is in need of mortuary attention. The advice Mencken gives Negro authors makes that piece worthy of restoration. Finally, "Scherzo for the Bassoon" puts a spotlight on Aldous Huxley, just then beginning his remarkable career.

A Book for the Gourmet

Ordering eggs *à la* Nordenskjold, what may one expect to find in the plate when the velvet-footed waiter totes it in? What is the exact composition of sauce *financiére*, of cocky-leeky soup, of chicken *portugaise*, of brook trout *argenteuil*, of a *bomb westphalienne?* No doubt every true lover of fine victuals is constantly pestered by such problems. The bill of fare is a perpetual mystery. It is useless to seek to master it by sitting up nights with a French dictionary, for the nouns and adjectives upon it have esoteric and unearthly meanings, entirely unconnected with the meanings attached to them in ordinary French prose. One learns, perhaps, from Cassell, that *chiffon* means a rag, a scrap, a trinket, a frippery; but that knowledge gives one no clue to the fact that eggs *chiffonade* are eggs heaved into the frying pan, or pot, or broiler, or oven, or whatever it is they use to cook eggs, in company with a handful of chopped herbs, including sorrel. Sorrel seems to be the essential ingredient, but sorrel, in French, is *oseille*. And so the inquirer is baffled.

It is to relieve the world of this burden that M. Joseph Gancel, the eminent chef of the Hotel Belleclaire, has composed and published his *Ready Reference of Menu Terms,* an exhaustive and excellent encyclopedia of the whole subject, and the fruit, as M. Gancel says with all due modesty, of thirty-five years of hard service in the most artistic kitchens of Europe and America and of intimate association with the most learned chefs of the age. M. Gancel dedicates his work to twenty-nine of these artists, mentioning them by name in alphabetical order —from M. Anjard of the Waldorf-Astoria to M. Vautrin of the Pavilion d'Armenonville in Paris, and including that serene highness among cooks, M. Letors, chief of the culinary studios of M. le Baron de Roth-

schild of Vienna. It is a book of overwhelming merits, a book fairly
bulging with information. It gives the formulae of 150 separate and
distinct sauces, of 400 omelettes, of no less than 600 soups! What is to
be said of such a one-volume library, of such a bottomless pit of learning? The reviewer stands flabbergasted, paralyzed, silent.

But let us peep within. At once we penetrate the secret of cocky-
leeky soup. It is a strong aqueous solution of the juices of chicken and
veal, brought to a boil and garnished with cubes of chicken meat,
leeks, and celery—a savory and tasty mess, you may bet your bottom
dollar. I should like to tackle a hogshead of cocky-leeky soup on a
brisk and windy day—a day of the tingling, appetizing sort. It would
also delight me to encounter, on any old day, a platter covered by an
omelette *havanaise,* with its dice of chicken livers boiled in milk, its
fragments of sweet pepper and its rich, red tomato sauce. Yet again,
who could resist a ration of lamb *impératrice,* with its stuffing of pul-
verized chicken and forcemeat, its sprinkling of truffles, its foliage of
celery and its sauce *suprême*—or a plate of veal Metternich, with its
decorations of red cabbage and chestnuts, and its *soubise* sauce, with
paprika and rice? M. Gancel is not only accurate, but also eloquent.
His terse, epigrammatic style touches the heart.

Did I say "accurate"? Alas, even the most accurate man sometimes
goes astray! Here is M. Gancel, a veritable Voltaire of cookery, telling
us that crab *à la créole* is merely a dish of crab meat drenched in
creole sauce! Far from it, indeed! The essential thing in concocting
crab *à la créole* is to mix the crab meat and the *à la créole* thoroughly
and to cook them *together,* pouring out the mixture, when it has begun to steam, upon thin slices of dry toast. That is the way crab *à la
créole* is made down in Baltimore, where the art of cooking crabs
reaches its highest perfection. A dish of crab meat, with creole sauce
poured over it, is called there, not crab *à la créole,* but "crab meat
with creole sauce." In true crab *à la créole* the mixture is infinitely intimate. Every last flake of crab meat is surrounded by its own fragments of onion, green pepper, mushroom and tomato, and the juices
of these exquisite herbs go straight through it. A dish of that sublime
invention drives dull care away. It is, perhaps, the most magnificent
victual yet devised by mortal man—and it costs but forty cents. One
may have a gallon of it, with half a dozen twelve-and-a-half-cent
cigars and a case of beer, for $2.85.

M. Gancel is wrong again when he says that soft crabs before being fried, should be dipped in a mixture of milk and flour, or breaded in the English fashion. The English know nothing whatever about frying soft crabs, and neither do the cooks of New York. If a waiter should set before a Baltimore epicure a plate of soft crabs fried in flour or bread crumbs, there would be at once the bloodcurdling sound of a waiter's skull cracking beneath the impact of a chair leg. Such pollutions of the heavenly soft crab are regarded along the Chesapeake with an aversion approaching acute dementia. Every Ethiopian cook of both shores is well aware that there is but one way to cook the soft crab, which way consists of pinning the live reptile, by means of a large sauerkraut fork, to a slice of breakfast bacon, and of holding the two, with the bacon up, over a quick fire. The bacon melts and its aromatic juices flood the Mediterranean of the crab and run down its legs, and it promptly dies of joy. Then the epicure engulfs it—before it has a chance to grow cold. Painful to the crab? Perhaps! But it's art!

Maybe, however, I am unjust to the excellent M. Gancel. After all, he tries to tell us in his book, not how crabs *should* be cooked, but how they *are* cooked. He is not responsible for the crimes of culinary anarchists, the blunders of ignoramuses. His aim is to give the public a sort of new Rosetta Stone for the interpretation of menu card Egyptian, and that aim he achieves in a comprehensive and masterly manner.

(November, 1910)

The Nature of Vice

Let us now, ladies and gentlemen, besot ourselves with prose fiction—the last debauch of that sort, I promise you faithfully, for several months at least.

Not that I myself dislike novels, or hold the vice of reading them to be worse than any other vice. Far from it, indeed. As a lifelong student of immorality in all its branches, I know very well (or I ought to know, if I don't) that between one vice and another there is no difference of degree, but only a difference of kind. One is just as bad as another—and just as good; just as deplorable—and just as satisfying. They bear the relation, one to the other, not of czar and peasant, whale and protozoön, Ossa and wart, but of free and equal citizens in an ideal republic. And that equality, I am convinced, has its roots in the fact that all of them, at bottom, are alike harmless. The essence of a vice, in brief, is not in its actual character, not in any inherent evil quality, but in its mere excessiveness, its hint of hoggishness.

I take, for example, the vice of drink—a target of moralists for un-numbered years—the cause, we are told, of 88 per cent of all maladies of the veins and arteries, of 91 per cent of all lunacies and phobias, of 78 per cent of all felonies, of 64 per cent of all divorces—the author of and excuse for the Salvation Army, acetanilid, the hot towel of the barber shops, the exhorting ex-drunkard, the Blue Laws, *Ten Nights in a Barroom,* the Anti-Saloon League of America, local option, the blind pig, the free lunch, organized charity, *katzenjammer* and a host of other hideous and horrific things. But of what elements does the vice of drink consist? Inspection shows that there are two: (*a*) the act of taking a drink, and (*b*) the multiple repetition of the act. Let us represent the first by x and the second by y. Now multiply the one by the other and we have $x \times y$, or xy—which thus becomes the symbol of and for the vice itself, the mathematical sign of drunkenness, the souse swastika. Well, which of the two elements is the essential one, the vicious one? Certainly not x. To take a drink, in itself, is not harm-ful. I myself do it now and then, and yet I am neither an apoplectic, a maniac, a felon or a divorcé. My personal experience, indeed, is that the ingestion of alcohol, in the modest quantities I affect, is not only not damaging but actually very beneficial. It produces in me a feeling of comfort, of amiability, of toleration, of mellowness. It makes me a more humane and sympathetic, and hence a happier, man. I am able, thus mildly etherized, to enjoy and applaud many things which would otherwise baffle and alarm me—for example, the tenor voice, Mary-land cooking, cut flowers, the Chopin nocturnes and the young of the human species. And that effect is not merely idiosyncratical, but uni-versal. It appears in all normal men. Alcohol in small doses dilutes and ameliorates our native vileness. Behind the spirit of Christmas are the spirits of Christmas. It is the suave gin rickey, the ingratiating whiskey sour, that gives 90 per cent of all civilized lovers the valor to make the last enslaving avowals—or, to be more accurate, that pro-duces the state of egoistic inflation which serves in valor's stead. And later on it is the more fiery whiskey straight that steels the bridegroom to face the baleful glitter of the parson's eye.

Thus it appears that drink, *per se,* is not a viper. On the contrary, it is a sweet singing canary, a faithful house dog, a purring cat upon a hearth rug. And thus it also appears that the member which makes xy lamentable is not x but y. But what is y? Merely a symbol for excess, the mathematical sign of superfluity—in brief, n. Merely a symbol—a scratch upon paper—and yet how nefarious, how demoniacal! Make x represent anything you please, however innocent, however lovely— and naughty y is still able to give a sinister quality to xy. Try it with shaving. One shave—a pleasant business, sanitary and caressing. But y shaves in succession—a debauch, a saturnalia, a delirium! Or plati- tudes. A platitude here and there, discreetly inserted, deftly screened —who shall say that it does not give discourse an air? But y plati- tudes, an orgy of platitudes—in short, a sermon by a bishop, a polit- ical platform, a newspaper editorial—and how the tortured intellect revolts! And so with novels. To read a novel or two now and then is to do only what civilization demands of us all. One must know what Ar- nold Bennett is writing of late, what Thackeray and Zola wrote, even what Dickens wrote. But to read novels, good and bad, incessantly; to wallow in them, to gulp down whole counters of them, with all their split infinitives, their "as thoughs," their gold and scarlet covers, the astounding pictures of A. B. Wenzell, their canned reviews, their pal- lid lecheries, their brummagem epigrams—to do all that is to practice a vice as bad as winebibbing, even as bad as teetotaling. The devil is in it. Voluptuous, it leads to perdition.

(February, 1912)

Novels to Reread

So much for the novels that have come to me this month—five mildly good ones and sixteen bad ones, not to mention the half-dozen so wholly bad that I haven't even mentioned them. My advice to you, if you yearn for fiction on these lazy afternoons, is that you pass over all of them, and go to the better things of yesteryear. Have you ever read *McTeague*, by Frank Norris? You have heard a lot about it, of course, and maybe, in the amiable American style, you have *talked* a lot about it, but have you ever read it? If not, then read it forthwith:

you can get it for fifty cents. And if you *have* read it, then read it again: it is worth it. I do not say the same of Norris's other work—barring, perhaps, *Blix*, an excellent sentimental comedy, a thing of young love and honest kisses. *The Pit*, when I last looked into it, failed of its old thrill, and *The Octopus* bored me with its far-fetched mysticism. So with *A Man's Woman, Moran of the Lady Letty* and the short stories in *A Deal of Wheat:* I fear that their day is already done. But *McTeague* remains—a truly distinguished piece of writing, a wonderfully painstaking and conscientious study of a third rate man, a permanent and valuable contribution to our national literature. I do not think that Mr. Howells has ever done anything more American, or anything more worthy. Certainly you will find no match for it in the work of Mrs. Wharton, not forgetting *Ethan Frome*, nor in the work of Prof. Herrick, nor in that of Mr. Churchill, nor in that of Miss Johnston. Its one indubitable rival is *Sister Carrie*—and both suffer, curiously enough, from the same fault: a lack of unity in design. Both have their backs broken in the middle. Each is made up of two stories, ineptly welded together. Each reveals a great talent not yet quite sure of itself.

A number of other American books, much talked of a dozen years ago, suggest themselves for re-reading. One of them is Stephen Crane's *The Red Badge of Courage,* a story greatly overpraised at the start and now undeservedly neglected. I haven't seen a copy in a bookstore for three or four years. But it is still well worth reading, and so are all of Crane's other war stories—for example, those in the volume entitled *The Little Regiment.* Even better are the three little masterpieces in *The Monster,* and particularly "The Blue Hotel," a grotesque, sardonic, memorable tale—one, indeed, that Joseph Conrad might have written. It is a long, long while since I last read it, but I still see clearly the wild snowstorm in that lonely prairie town, and the cerulean ugliness of the Palace Hotel, and the offhand incomprehensible doing to death of the nameless Swede. Crane got something rare and difficult into that modest story, and that was the sense of brooding disaster, of cruel and immutable fate, of the eternal meaninglessness of life—in five words, tragedy in the Greek sense. He got the same note into "The Monster," that incomparable tale of horror, and into many of his war stories, whether of fiction or of fact. Poe usually missed it: most of his tragedies are merely melodramas. But you will find it running from end to end of Joseph Conrad. *Heart of*

Darkness is as real a tragedy as *The Seven Against Thebes*. So is *Lord Jim*. So is "Falk." So, for that matter, is *Almayer's Folly*.

Which leads me to recommend Conrad to you again, with an apology if I bore you with too many references to him. If you do not know him at all, you can do no better than begin with "Youth," perhaps the best short story ever written in English. Here, indeed, is the perfect short story—a veritable slice of life, the picture of a soul on trial, the drama of Everyman upon a superbly mounted stage—a tale inimitably succinct, sympathetic, archetypical and penetrating. Believe me, the best of Kipling might borrow something from "Youth." The best of Kipling was done while Kipling still had youth himself. It is full of the jauntiness of youth, the charm of youth, the high hope of youth—but it is also full of the blindness of youth. Conrad wrote when he was already a man of middle age—a man looking back, with joy and a clear understanding, upon the memorable moods and gropings of those far-off but unforgotten days. The result is that his story is not merely a chronicle of youth but also an interpretation of youth. It illuminates a universal experience, here lifted to pulsing drama, by the light of a profound philosophy. To read it is, in some sense, to live again. And that, I think, is the highest praise that can be laid upon a work of the imagination.

Bound in the same volume with "Youth" are two other magnificent short stories, *Heart of Darkness* and "The End of the Tether," both unutterably tragic and both written with such supreme art that all criticism must be silent before them. One cannot describe such stories: as well attempt to describe the last movement of the Fifth Symphony. All three show an elephantine lack of form, a Jovian disdain of all the ancient conventions of story telling. "Youth" is a story within a story— a clumsy device, here made more clumsy by the obvious absence of all necessity for it. *Heart of Darkness* carries the same burden. "The End of the Tether" starts in the middle and then goes onward in both directions. But once you get the swing of Conrad, you will lose all sense of these awkwardnesses. Whatever the rights and wrongs of the matter, by canons made and provided, that is the way he writes—and that is the way he writes masterpieces. A detailed account of the technical errors and absurdities in *Lord Jim* would fill another book of its size, but *Lord Jim* remains nearly perfect nevertheless. And for all its amazing slowness of tempo, its baffling halts and interlardings, the effect of *Typhoon* is that of stupendous and appalling action, of a huge play of irresistible forces, of a leaping, living thing. Such is the magic of this Mr. Joseph Conrad Korzeniowski, "late master in the merchant service." At the start, I dare say, you may miss some of it. Its very strangeness requires some degree of preparation, of initiation. But soon or late, I believe and hope, it will grip you and overwhelm you.

But let me have done with Conrad and suggest a few more books before I close. Why not Henry James's *What Maisie Knew*—a perfect comedy, a riotous and delightful piece of Olympian foolery—and happily free from Mr. James's more recondite snarls of speech. It is worth a dozen best-sellers of the current crop. It has more good fun in it, and more shrewdness, and more civilized entertainment than all the masterworks of the Athertons and Sinclairs, the Herricks and Frank Danbys, the Phillpottses and Mrs. Humphry Wards, taken together. It is a first rate piece of writing by a first rate man. So is Kipling's *Kim:* you will like it on second reading better than on first reading, and still better on third reading. So is George Moore's *Evelyn Innes*, not to mention his *Sister Theresa*. Have you ever read his *Memoirs of My Dead Life*—not the bowdlerized American edition, but the English edition? If not, go order it from your bookseller. It is out of print and growing rare. A copy will cost you $7.50. It is worth at least $7.60. You will find thirteen stories in it, half fiction and half fact—and at least four of them are worthy to rank with the best of our day. Read "The Lovers of Orelay." If you are a sinner, it will ease your conscience. If you are a saint, it will cure you.

And Zola's *Germinal*, and Moore's *A Mummer's Wife*, and Dreiser's *Jennie Gerhardt*, and Max Beerbohm's *Zuleika Dobson*, and Bennett's *Whom God Hath Joined*, and George Ade's *In Babel*, and Sudermann's *The Indian Lily*, and Bojer's *The Power of a Lie*, and London's *The Call of the Wild*, and Meredith's unfinished *Celt and Saxon* —all good books, too little praised, too little read. They will fill your holidays with delight; they will give you pleasant memories. And *Huckleberry Finn*—I was almost forgetting *Huckleberry Finn!* What? You have read it? Of course you have! But such books are not sent into the world to be read once. As well read the Book of Mark once, or *Hamlet*, or *Alice in Wonderland!* I myself have read old *Huck*—but I won't tell you the number of times. I pull down the frayed volume every spring and read it again. I have been doing it every spring since I was nine years old. I expect to be doing it down the slippered sixties, into the rheumatic seventies. I enjoy it more every year. I wouldn't trade that one book—it is a genuine First Edition!—for the whole works of Dickens, Bulwer-Lytton and Nathaniel Hawthorne, plus Dr. Eliot's five-foot shelf, plus the *Encyclopaedia Britannica,* plus the Koran and the Zend-Avesta, plus all the best-sellers done in Indiana since the Mexican War.

(July, 1913)

A Review of Reviewers

Laboring in this proud, esthetic galley (as I made mention last month), since the year 1908 of the present or Christian era, I have naturally passed through many curious adventures and endured many vicissitudes. Once I was indicted for mayhem upon a best-seller; another time a lady poet tried to kiss me in a public barroom; on four or five occasions I have had to borrow money to get my lingerie out of the laundry; and eighteen times I have been blackballed in literary and sporting clubs. But one of the experiences that I have constantly missed, for all this excess of physical and metaphysical hazards, has been that of reviewing one of my own books, or, to be more accurate, that of exposing and denouncing the reviews of it by other reviewers. No less than four times during the six years my facile pen has achieved a new and praiseworthy volume, and every time it has been fallen upon and put to the torture by a horde of ignorant assassins, male and female; and yet, as I say, I have always throttled my wrath and held my peace, thus sacrificing justice to a false sense of delicacy, and the truth to an insincere and hypocritical modesty.

But no more. The time has come to turn over a new leaf. And the chance conveniently offers itself in the fact that the last fruit of my fancy, to wit, *Europe After 8:15,* is not, properly speaking, mine at all, for two-thirds of it was written by a syndicate consisting of Willard Wright and the estimable G. J. Nathan, and so I represent only an inconsiderable minority of it, and am thus free to speak of it with easy grace. This I do at once, remarking simply that it is a book of merit, with a lot of valuable information in it, not to mention the charm of style.

Its purpose, I need not add (for no doubt you have already read it, and what is more, enjoyed it and told your friends about it), is to depict, in a suave and ingratiating manner, the postprandial divertissements of five European capitals—Vienna, Munich, Berlin, London and Paris—and, in particular, such of them as do not lie floridly upon the surface. And behind that first purpose, there is the second one of poking a bit of harmless fun at the Americanos who snout through Europe in search of levantine seductions, seeing a Lola Montez in every milliner's apprentice along the Rue de la Paix, and the gay life in the stodgy Münchener's nightly stevedoring of his gallon of *Dunkel* —the Americanos who "open wine" for the drabs of all Christendom and half of Islam at the Bal Tabarin and the Moulin Rouge, and jump upon the tables and cheer when the Berlin pseudo-orchestras play *"O Tannenbaum"* or *"Heil dir im Siegerkranz,"* and pronounce *"Hofbräu"* as if it were spelled "Huff-brow" and "Louvre" as if it were an inflected form of liver, and come home smelling abominably of bad perfumes and worse liqueurs, and full of hair-raising anecdotes for the brethern of the vestry, and a dim understanding that Rubens was an Italian architect of 150 B.C., and a profound conviction that all Europeans, including even Gerhart Hauptmann, take tips.

Thus privy to the aim and purport of the book, and not without some sense, let me hope, of its virtue as literature, what have you to say of the critic of the Chicago *News,* who finds that it is "frankly and at times aggressively vulgar," and who moralizes upon the "crudeness" of the authors? And what of the critic of the New York *Herald,* who pooh-poohs it in a superior fashion, and opines that "one man might have done the work in a better style"? And what of the critic of the Detroit *News,* who denounces it for "a vague and poisonous atmosphere of cultured indifference, the taking for granted of a certain moral attitude on the part of the reader, the unspoken assumption of ethical callousness, the same spirit that marked the work of the decadents of the last century"? And what of that fourth critic—not to be identified, for the name of his low gazette has departed from the clipping—who reviles the authors for their "talk of restaurants and intoxicants," and is shocked because "immoralities are hinted at broadly"? And what of that fifth and last rapscallion, anonymous for the same reason, who bellows against the book because "there is nothing in it to lead the reader into profitable thought," and no mention from end to end of either the Sistine Madonna or the Paris morgue?

As for me, I reply to these carpers and moralists in the only way

countenanced by the critical punctilio. That is to say, I mount the ros-
trum, put on the black cap and proceed to pronounce a curse upon
them. May they pass through eternity in a bottomless pit of Indiana
best-sellers, doomed forever to read six a day! May they be racked
and stretched until they are as tall as the novel heroes in the illustrations of Howard Chandler Christy, and with heads as small! May they
be condemned to indissoluble marriage with heroines by George Barr
McCutcheon, the least auburn of them with hair as red as the binding
of *Who's Who in America!* May they be misquoted unendingly upon
the slip covers of eighth-rate novels, with all their careful qualifications stricken out! May their typewriters break down with press time
but an hour away and the foreman of the composing room shrieking
at the door! May the proofroom mutilate their grammar and make
mincemeat of their parts of speech! May the galley boys pie their
standing matter at least once a week, and may type lice devour what
is left! May the make-up men of their degraded and ornery *Zeitungs*
mix up their cut lines with those of the sporting editors, printing Jack
Johnson for William Dean Howells, and Mrs. Jack for Edith Wharton!
May they get at least fifty abusive letters from publishers in every
mail, and a hundred from poets! May they revolt against orders from
the business office, and be shot at sunrise for their contumacy! May
they yield to a petty and puerile vanity and write books themselves
—and send them to me for review!

So; the solemn business is over. The punishment has been fitted to
the crime. Let us turn now from all these revolting foes of the bozart
and hear the sweeter words of critics of a higher sagacity. For example, the gentleman of the Philadelphia *North American,* who finds
that the work is marked by "breezy, racy, amusing descriptive narrative," and that it is "a most delightful little volume, full of mirthful
glee." "Mirthful glee," I suspect, is tautological, for the essence of glee
is mirth—but who cares a hoot for tautology? Away with it! It is a
brother to sociology, an aunt to penology; in brief, a pseudo-science,
pursued only by college professors and quacks. Nor am I going to set
up a quarrel with the fair critic of *Vogue,* who says that when "the
three authors are older they will drop, no doubt, a little of their somewhat startling brilliancy of style." Well, well, who knows? We must all
grow old, to be sure, and age brings decay. A sad thought, but why
repine? Let us be glad of such rare and valuable gifts while we have
them, and blush prettily and deprecatingly when they are praised.

The *Vogue* lady goes on in the same agreeable key:

"They have told of what they saw with an abounding freshness of style, without indecent suggestiveness under their frank phrasing, and with eyes not only for what is genuinely beautiful in the physical aspects of urban nights, but for what is simple, sweet and cleanly charming in its human elements."

Thanks, Mlle. Collègue! Thou hast come nearer to our hearts than any other!

Various other critics, with perhaps equal good will, fall short of this sympathetic accuracy. He of the San Francisco *Chronicle* calls it "a very readable book," and then has done. He of the Minneapolis *Journal* calls it "smartly intellectual" and "a model of flippant erudition." He of the Detroit *Free Press* (maybe the same fellow, for literary criticism is now syndicated at wholesale, like the pictures of Mutt and Jeff) uses exactly the same words. He (or she) of the Portland *Oregonian* calls it "buoyant," which is from the OF "*boye*"—a fetter or halter, and means "having the power or tendency to float or keep afloat." He of the Oakland (California) *Tribune* says that it has an "interesting title" and will delight the "seeker for the original and bizarre." He of the Brooklyn *Eagle* calls it "a burlesque of late hours." He of the Cincinnati *Times-Star* finds that it is "as gay as the life they [the authors] saw—and the reader will be convinced that they saw some gay life." And finally, to jump the others, there is William Marion Reedy, of the St. Louis *Mirror*, who heads his notice, "Three Bad Boys' Wicked Books," and delivers himself as follows:

I was going aboard this year, but I've read the book and now won't. I feel like I've had a whiz through all the capitals of Europe in the most excellent company of fellows who didn't need any guides. The capitals yielded all their charms, some slightly secret, and I've breathed an air of freedom innocent of puritanism one can't have in lid-ridden St. Louis. . . . Reading Mencken, Nathan and Wright, one realizes that the rottenest thing about American cities is the coercion of gaiety after dark by hypocritic prudery. . . . How John Lane could have published *Europe After 8:15* without the fear of Comstock in his heart passes my comprehension. . . . It isn't every book one can close with such a sense of sin, I can tell you—and not the sin of wasting time, either!

Hoch, Reedy! An honest and friendly fellow! The ideal critic! Take his advice and—borrow the book! But lest you fall into the perplexities of some of the other critics, I had better tell you just how it was

manufactured. (The critic of the New York *Herald*, baffled by the
problem of joint authorship, concludes, as we have seen, that "one
man might have done the work in better style." The critic of the Philadelphia *North American*, knowing something of Nathan's morals,
sees Wright and me as "Nathan-led." The critic of the Los Angeles
Times argues that "the style of Mencken, Nathan and Wright is much
alike, but if one has consistently [American for constantly, regularly,
habitually] read *The Smart Set* it is not difficult, at least, to be confident in guessing.")

But, as I say, the truth is simple and had better be told. Nathan did
the chapters on Paris and Berlin; Wright did that on Vienna and most
of that on London; I did that on Munich, the first three and last two
paragraphs of that on London, and the Preface in the Socratic Manner. This to settle bets in the Sunday schools, and to aid the lady who
keeps the card catalogue of the Jamestown (N.Y.) Public Library.
And in parting, a grateful kiss to the critic of the St. Louis *Post-
Dispatch*, who says that "the cleverest part of the book is the preface,"
and another to the critic of the Los Angeles *Times*, who says that it is
"worth the price of admission alone." I am with you, gents! And
Nathan and Wright would be with you, too—if they could rid themselves of passion and prejudice and get down to the facts.

(October, 1914)

An Autobiographical Note

(*Sentimental Interlude.*—In my case it was the Ellicott City *Times*.
Ellicott City hangs precariously upon the steep banks of the upper
Patapsco, perhaps twenty-five miles from Chesapeake Bay, and is one
of the oldest and hilliest country towns of Maryland. Most of its
houses are built massively of nigger-head granite and go back to the
thirties. Some of them, plastered against the hillsides, are four or five
stories high in front and no more than half a story behind. There are
authentic legends of pigs in their backyards falling down their chimneys, and not only pigs, but even children! Main Street runs down the
bottom of a narrow gulch, and the B. & O. trains from Baltimore,

coming up the crooked and beautiful Patapsco valley, cross the gulch upon an old iron culvert. At this crossing, with its roots in Main Street but with its roof topping the trains, there is an ancient warehouse—a structure so gaunt and so weatherbeaten that it almost suggests the ruins of a medieval castle. A long balcony, making out from the track level, clings to the side of it. Upon that balcony, back in 1888 or 1889, I acquired incurably the itch of ink, the *cacoëthes scribendi,* for at the end of it was the joint editorial room, business office, composing room and press room of the Ellicott City *Times,* and through an open window, on lazy summer afternoons, one might observe a tramp printer sticking type, and Josh Lynch, the brisk young foreman, making up handbills for the farmers, and the farmers themselves being entertained by the editor. A lordly life! Gaping there, I fell in love with it—with the busyness and ease of it, the inky smells of it, the whole glamour of it. And so, when Christmas came, I intrigued for a printing press, and soon I was writing and printing a paper of my own, and ever since then, in one way or another, I have been hard at it. . . . Years afterward Josh and I were thrown together, and many were the Sunday magazine pages that we made up in hostile collaboration, and many the schooners that we emptied after work was done. A great adventure awaited us: the Baltimore fire of 1904. But that story I reserve for my autobiography. In it a whole chapter will be devoted to Josh's wild ride in a rickety express wagon with fifty galleys of hand-set type—a ride twice as thrilling as that of the Walküre and four times as worthy of immortality. . . . Both Josh and I have taken on weight in late years. We grow, in fact, more and more ovoid, bulgy, sot. Worse, he has deserted the column rule and the footstick and is now a respectable bureaucrat in a plug hat. But I—well, I am enlisted for the war. I shall keep on eating ink until I die.)

(April, 1915)

The Incomparable Billy

One William T. Ellis, an author, lately filled the *Bulletin* of the Authors' League with moving bellows against a publisher, alleging atrocities of the classical sort, but worse. The name of this Ellis arrests me; I seem to remember him as one who loves his fellow men to distraction, and gallops to save them from hell for modest honoraria. Isn't he the same, in fact, who is staff expert in piety to the Philadelphia *North American,* that loveliest flower of consecrated journalism? Isn't he Ellis the jitney Savonarola, the eminent wholesaler in Sunday-school lessons, the endless perspirer for the Uplift, the author of *Men and Missions* and other great doxological works? Isn't he the ecstatic one who hymned the late vice crusade in lascivious Atlanta—now, alas, almost forgotten!—as "more fun than a fleet of air-ships," and urged the moral sportsmen of other towns to go to it? I suspect that he is, and if so I have venerated him for years. Let a tear fall for him. If he does not gild his tale of woe, his hornswoggling was cruel, indeed. . . .

But enough of this grand young man. He appears in the chronicle only incidentally, and as complaining of his royalties on his *magnum opus, Billy Sunday: the Man and His Message.* This great critical biography, he says, has sold 300,000 copies within a year!—and is still going like Coca-Cola in "dry" Georgia! . . . Har, har, me luds! Where are your best-sellers now? What becomes of McCutcheon, MacGrath, Chambers, the Glyn? Who will now whisper the figures for *Pollyanna, Trilby, Eben Holden, Dora Thorne?* More, this Ellis tome is but one of several on the same subject. I have another before me; it is *The Real Billy Sunday,* by the Rev. Dr. Ram's Horn-Brown, and if the signs and portents go for anything, it has sold even better than the Ellis book. The plates, indeed, show signs of usage; it has been rolled off by the hundred thousand. And in the city where I bought it, just outside the gates of Dr. Sunday's vast arena of God, the official bookseller told me that it was the best-seller of them all, and worth ten times the dollar that he asked for it.

Nevertheless, the fellow had a heart and so offered me *lagniappe.* He was sworn on the Four Gospels, he said, to sell the book for no less than a dollar, but if I would take it without parley, passing over the Ellis book, he would give me something instructive as makeweight. This something as makeweight turned out to be a gaudy pamphlet entitled *Fighting the Traffic in Young Girls, or, War on the White Slave Trade,* by Ernest A. Bell, "secretary of the Illinois Vigilance Association, superintendent of Midnight Missions, etc." Another great tussler for rectitude. The Ellis, no doubt, of Cook county. The beyond-Parkhurst. But himself, it would appear, rather daring, and to the evil-minded, perhaps even somewhat racy. Several of the full-page half-tones give us flaming views of brothel parlors, with the resident staff at persiflage with the visiting fireman; another shows the exterior of "a gilded palace of sin," with a stained glass *porte-cochère;* yet another (a photograph) shows a plump *geisha,* in skirts almost as short as a débutante's, in the lewd act of plaiting her hair. In a fourth appears "the white slave clearing-house," with a gospel meeting going on across the street. In a fifth we are introduced to a lady uplifter "pleading with a lost one to give up her sinful life," the "lost one" being by far the better looking. In a sixth we see a white slave trader plying his abominable arts upon a simple country girl in an ice-cream parlor. In a seventh—

But I spare you any further carnalities in effigy. The text of the work is horrifying enough. Not only Dr. Bell himself, but various other virtuosi, each of learning and cunning, encourage the popping eyeball. One of them is the Hon. Edwin W. Sims, district attorney in Chicago during the palmy days of the white slave uproar, and secretary to the immortal Chicago Vice Commission, whose report was barred from the mails by super-uplifters at Washington. The unctuous Sims protests that he has "strong personal feelings against appearing in print in connection with a subject so abhorrent," but swallows them in order to warn all country girls that "the ordinary ice-cream parlor is very likely to be a spider's web." Another "expert" is Principal D. F. Sutherland, "of Red Water, Texas," who tells the sad story of the kidnapping of Estelle Ramon, of Kentucky, and of her rescue by the valiant William Scott, an old beau. Many more are mentioned on the title-page, but I fail to find their contributions inside. The explanation appears in an advertisement on the back cover. This advertisement shows that the present volume is no more than a sort of bait or pilot for a larger work of the same title, the which sells to connoisseurs at a dollar and a half. ("Fastest selling book of the age! Agents wanted! Write for terms and outfit!") A chance for the young gentlemen of the Y.M.C.A. to dedicate themselves to Service. Pornography for the plain people. . . . Too late, alas, too late! The copyright of the oleaginous Bell is dated 1910. That was the golden age of vice crusading, the year of unparalleled harvests for the snouting fraternity. To-day only the old-fashioned believe in white slavery; there are other bugaboos for the progressive. No wonder Dr. Sunday's bookseller was so free with his *lagniappe!* . . .

As for the actual Sunday book, dated 1914, it already tells an old
story, for the sweating doctor has since done such press-agenting as
not even a whole library of books could do, and his public eminence
in these States is scarcely less exalted than that of Col. Roosevelt, Jess
Willard, Henry Ford and the Kaiser. Dr. Horn-Brown reviews his career in phrases of laudation—a career of double distinction, for he was a
celebrated baseball-player before he became the American St. Paul.
(Joseph Smith, William Miller, Mary Baker G. Eddy, John Alexander
Dowie, Sam Jones, William A. Sunday: we have produced some noble
theologians!) His paternal grandfather was a Pennsylvania Dutchman
named Sontag, but on the distaff side he stems from Lord William Corey
"who married the only daughter of Sir Francis Drake." The family of
Corey de Pittsburgh de Reno is apparently the *jüngerer Linie*. Bill, our
present hero, was converted in Chicago, at the Pacific Garden Mission, in 1886 or thereabout, and after getting clear of his baseball con-
tracts became assistant secretary of the Chicago Y.M.C.A. Then he got
a job as advance man for J. Wilbur Chapman, an itinerant evangelist.
When Chapman retired, in 1896, Sunday took over his trade, and has
since gone steadily ahead. For fifteen years he worked the watertanks,
snaring the sinful tobacco chewers for the heavenly choir. Then he
struck out for bigger game, and today he performs only in the main
centers of population. He has saved Philadelphia, Baltimore, Kansas
City and Pittsburgh; he is headed for Boston, Chicago and New York.
He has been lavishly praised by the President of the United States, is
a Freemason and a Doctor of Divinity, and has enjoyed the honor of
shaking me by the hand.

So much for the facts of his career, and the book of Dr. Horn-
Brown. In laborious preparation for the review of that book I went to
hear the whooping doctor himself. I found him vastly more interesting
than any tome that these old eyes have rested upon in many a day.
He was engaged, as I entered his vast bull-ring for the first time, in
trying to scare a delegation of Civil War veterans into some realization, however faint, of the perils of hell, and when I took my seat in
the pen reserved for the *literati*, directly under the eaves of his pulpit,
I was sprinkled copiously with the dew of his frenzy. On it came,
dribble, dribble, splash, splash, every time he executed one of his terrifying revolutions. It was like holding the bottle for a Russian dancer
with a wet sponge strapped to his head. Of a sudden he would rush to

the edge of the platform—his pulpit is as long as a barroom, but is without rails—, scream hysterically, and then bring himself up with a jolt and spin 'round like a top, his arms flung out and saline globules leaping from his brow in a pelting shower. He shed, I daresay, at least eight ounces of sweat between 7:45 and 9:00 P.M., and though he mopped his brow constantly and tried to be polite, a good deal of it escaped into the air, and so begemmed my critical gown. . . . Revolting details, but the love of all truth is above all prudery!

Of the *sforzando* doctor's actual discourse, that night or on the other nights I heard him, I have only a faint memory. Some sweet mush about the joys of heaven, with dogs and children playing on the grass; a long review of the life and times of King Solomon, with incidental railings against money; the orthodox arguments against ethyl alcohol, of no effect upon my thirst; high words against deacons who roll their eyes on Sunday and rob the widow on Monday; the joys of hell in detail, with not a singe omitted—all the orthodox camp-meeting stuff, howled from a million stumps by Methodist dervishes since the days of Wesley, and before them by Puritans of one sort or another since the croakings of the captive in Herod's rain-barrel. Out of all this I could get nothing; it was as empty of ideas as an editorial in the Boston *Transcript*. But away with ideas, and their pursuit. It was not by ideas that the downpouring doctor bemused those sinful veterans, and white-faced shop girls, and quaking Sunday School teachers, and staggered fat women; it was by his sheer roar and outcry. He survives in the cortex, not intellectually or visually, but purely aurally—as an astounding and benumbing noise, a riot of unearthly sound, an ear-torturing cacophony. Time and again he would have to pause for breath. Time and again he would make a megaphone of his hands to give the yell more pedal. Time and again you could see the elect in the front rows shrink and quiver beneath the gargantuan wallop of his shouts. I have fought through four wars; I have been a boilermaker; I have heard *"Feuersnot."* But never have I eared such a flabbergasting caterwauling; never have I suffered such a racking of the fenestra rotunda. It penetrates the capital ivory like a bullet, and sets up a raging pyemia. Sunday tells the simplest anecdote with the triumphant yelp of Satan sighting another archbishop in the chute. He utters such bald words as "Yes" and "No" with all the withering passion that the Old Guard put into its naughty reply at Waterloo. In

the midst of a quite banal sentence his voice flies off into a shrill fal-
setto, and he clubs the side of his desk as if it were the very door of
hell.

No wonder the candidates down in the arena are raised to incan-
descence, and begin screaming to be saved! Imagine the balcony
scene in *Romeo and Juliet* with Juliet bellowing like Klytämnestra in
the last round of *Elektra*, and Romeo howling up at her like an auctioneer, and both swinging Indian clubs, and revolving like pinwheels,
and sweating like the colored waiters in a Pullman diner! Imagine
"Nearer, My God, To Thee" accompanied by anvils, tom-toms, ophicleides, bass-drums and artillery, and a committee sticking pins into
the tenors to make them squeal! No wonder the frontal celluloid is
pierced and set afire! No wonder the devil flees in alarm, and takes
refuge in some quiet Unitarian church! . . . Losing, alackaday, not
much! Robbed of very little appetizing stock! The converts, indeed,
are but feeble specimens of God's handiwork. Those I saw seemed anthropoid, but no more. In all my life I have never looked into more
stupid and miserable faces. At least half of the aspirants for harps
were adolescent and chlorotic girls; most of the males were of the
sort one finds in water-front missions and at Salvation Army Christmas dinners. Even an osteopath, glancing at the former, would have
noted a deficiency in haemoglobin, a disturbance below the dia-
phragm and above the neck, a profound veneration for moving picture actors. Some of them seemed to be flirting with tuberculosis;
many of them had heads of curious shape and eyes that did not
match; nearly all looked pitifully poor and wretched and godforsaken.
Of such, perhaps, are the kingdom of heaven. They, too, have immortal souls, as much so as Claude Debussy, General Carranza or the
Hon. Josephus Daniels. Let us hope, at all events, that somewhere or
other they will get square meals, and less work, and a chance to be
care-free, and sinful, and happy.

Such is my memory of four nights of the Rev. Dr. Billy Sunday,
now the emperor and pope of all our uplifters, the beyond-Gerald
Stanley Lee, the super-Herbert Kaufman, the Augustine of American
theology, the heir of Bryan, Dowie and Barnum. Let it stand as a review of Dr. Horn-Brown's instructive book, the which I commend to
your study. Buy a couple of copies. Give one to your pastor, that honest man. But if it sets him to whooping like Sunday, then I advise you,
in all charity, to have your gunmen do execution of the *lex non scripta*

upon him. You will never stand such *fortissimos*—as a steady diet.
Now and then, like laparotomy or mania-à-potu, a benign stimulant,
but not for every Sunday! . . . I depart from the Doctor Seraphicus
et Ecstaticus with a specimen of his official hymnology. The copyright
is owned by his kappelmeister, the Rev. Dr. Homer A. Rodeheaver
(plain "Rody" to the purged), but I take a chance. So:

> Do not wait until some deed of greatness you may do,
>   Do not wait to shed your light afar:
> To the many duties ever near you now be true,
>
> Brighten the corner where you are!
> Brighten the corner where you are!
> Some one far from harbor you may guide across the bar,
> Brighten the corner where you are!

The words, it appears, are by Miss Ina Dugley Ogdon. Ina has the
gift. Let her plod at her art; she will go far.

(July, 1916)

The Irish Renaissance

The Irish talent for impossibilities reveals itself fully in beautiful
letters. The tasters of books tell us that romance is dead; the Irish revive the corpse and set it to dancing. They tell us that the grip of the
epic is gone; the Irish resurrect Diarmuid and Grania, Naisi and
Deirdre, and make them as real as Tom Jones. They tell us that sym-
bolism passed with *When We Dead Awaken;* the Irish fill their poems
with overtones and their very plays with spectral shapes. They tell us
that no great literature is ever written in a tongue foreign to its makers; the Irish invade the language of the conqueror with Gaelic idioms
and Gaelic modes of thought, and make a new English that is as sonorous and as savory as Marlowe's. They tell us that letters cannot prosper in the turmoil of politics; the Irish turn from the land laws to
prosody without batting an eye, and stop a peasant comedy to shoot a
red-coat, and face a firing-squad with sheaves of sonnets under their
arms.

A people of fantastic and almost unearthly quality; a race that never was on land or sea! Its literature is at once the oldest and the youngest in Europe. Its grand tales of enchantment antedate the Niebelungenlied; its new tales of wonder postdate Walter Pater. The heirs of the scholars who taught Christendom how to write Latin verse in the fourth century now teach Anglo-Saxondom how to write English prose. Where is there another land with so fabulous a literary history—a history so high in its peaks at beginning and end and so low in its dark valleys between? A hundred years ago, even sixty or seventy years ago, no one read a genuinely Irish book. The literature of the country, in so far as it was known at all, was dismissed as barbarous and contemptible; it seemed no more than a mess of picaresque ballads and wild fairy tales, not always in good taste. But today, thanks to the labors of a few learned and devoted men, the old epics loom up in all the glow and majesty of the *Odyssey,* and out of the inspiration of the heroic past there has arisen a new literature that is as fecund, as various and as unmistakably national as any in Europe. Yeats and Dunsany are miles apart, and yet both are as Irish as Paddy's pig. Lady Gregory and Æ are separated even farther, and yet the essential Gaelicism of the one is as plain as the Gaelicism of the other. A school? A movement? Bosh! As well try to put Zola and Ellen Key, or Nietzsche and Tolstoi into double harness. What we have here is not merely a school or a movement, but a literature.

As I say, you will search far before you find parallels for its paradoxes. Perhaps there is one in Flanders, with Maeterlinck and Verhaeren writing French to match the French. Perhaps there is another in Norway, with Danish turned upon the Danes by Ibsen and Björnson. But in both cases literature had to wait until the turmoils of politics had died down, and men began to forget that their tongue was the tongue of a foreign foe. In Ireland there has been no forgetting. The fathers of the new literature, indeed, were political agitators almost more than they were literary pioneers. They essayed to dethrone England, English, the English and all Englishdom. They turned to the ancient demi-gods as to inspiring heroes of nationality; they called upon the Gael to be a Gael once more. One and all, they learned Gaelic, thought in Gaelic, made Gaelic at once their symbol and their weapon. But the forces they faced were too sturdy for them. The English language engulfed them in its gigantic and irresistible tide; they were forced, willy-nilly, to yield to it; they ended by making it their own. No stranger surrender has ever been seen, and no stranger conquest by the conquered. The neo-Celts, pumping not only their materials, but even their forms out of Gaelic, have emptied into English the most lavish stream of new idioms and new rhythms that it has received since the days of Elizabeth. The style of such writers as Yeats, Æ, Lady Gregory, Dunsany, and above all, Synge, is not merely a development of old styles, a refinement of Wilde and Pater, a tickling up of Arthur Symons; it is something quite new under the sun and as golden and gorgeous as the music of trumpets. He who has inner ears must needs rejoice in it forever; it is a debauch of lovely phrases; there is in it a ripple of endless surprises. No man who is genuinely an artist will ever write English hereafter without giving an ear to it, and borrowing from it, and owing inspiration to it.

As *cognoscenti* are aware, this grand revival of letters in Ireland has not gone unsung. It has, in fact, had processions of brass bands to whoop up its progress. Its chief protagonists, especially Yeats, George Moore and Lady Gregory, have revealed a fine gift for *réclame;* they have got into the newspapers of all the world, and made themselves talked of. It has provoked bitter and profitable animosities; the glare of politics has been thrown upon it from time to time; even the huge slaughter of the war has contrived to augment its romance. More important still, it has been fortunate enough to bring out, almost by accident, two or three talents of the very highest consideration, and the noise that these talents have made has directed attention to the whole movement. The natural consequence has been a great deal of writing about it—books, pamphlets and articles; polemics, expositions and interpretations; defenses and denunciations; bosh and tosh unending. On the dramatic side alone it has engendered three times as much criticism as drama.

But until the present there was no single book that told the whole story of the revival in a coherent and accurate manner—that traced its origin and growth with sure knowledge, and discussed its leading figures with any understanding of their real purposes and relations, and separated the facts about them from the chaff of report and surmise. That lack is now supplied, in part, by *Literature in Ireland,* by Thomas MacDonagh, and in completeness by *Ireland's Literary Renaissance,* by Ernest A. Boyd. The book of MacDonagh covers the field of neo-Celtic poetry, and, by an easy transition, the field of neo-Celtic prose style; the book of Boyd covers the whole progress of the new literature, from its beginnings in the translations of Mangan, Ferguson and O'Grady to its flowering in the tales and plays of Dunsany, the plays and travel sketches of Synge, the imaginary histories of George Moore and the poems of Yeats, Colum, Hyde and MacDonagh. Boyd brought to the business exactly what it required, for he had behind him not only a thorough aquaintance with the whole body of the new literature, down to its most inconsiderable journalism, but also a personal intimacy with most of its leading spirits, and a sound comprehension of the remainder. His volume is judicious, sympathetic, informative and readable; it strikes the right middle course between punditic tediousness and gossipy garrulity. It puts him into equal fellowship with the best of the new Irish poets, dramatists and novelists, for he is the first historical (as opposed to polemical) critic that the movement has produced, and his first book is so intelligently done that it will be a difficult thing for his successors to surpass it. . . .

Much misleading writing has resulted from the confusion of the Irish literary renaissance, as we know it today, with the original neo-Celtic movement, which still survives among the intransigeants, and has been much prospered by the rebellion of last Easter. The two, despite their common sources and their possession of many principles and champions in common, are really quite distinct, for most of the new writers, while not forgetting their debt to Gaelic, accept the accomplished fact that Gaelic is dying out, whereas the more furious of the neo-Celtic patriots still cherish a hope of reviving it, and look to Irish freedom to get it on its legs again. The latter are thus not only not in accord with the former, but even in antagonism to them, for they see in the acceptance of English an abandonment of one of the most precious of Irish heritages. But this antagonism, after all, is more academic than real, for more than once, with Hibernian versatility, the same man has belonged to both camps, and the leader about whom the Gaelic movement chiefly revives, Dr. Douglas Hyde, is also the father of the Gaelicized English in which the best works of the revival are written. Mr. Boyd gives an example of Dr. Hyde's pioneering in his *Love Songs of Connacht* (1893):

If I were to be on the Brow of Nefin and my hundred loves by my side, it is pleasantly we would sleep together like the little bird upon the bough. It is your melodious wordy little mouth that increased my pain and a quiet sleep I cannot get until I shall die, alas!

Here, obviously, is the pattern that Synge and Lady Gregory followed—the pattern brought to a perfection of design in the speeches of Christy Mahon and Pegeen Mike in *The Playboy of the Western World,* in the gabble of the old paupers in *The Workhouse Ward,* and, above all, in the unforgettable phrases of Maurya in *Riders to the Sea.* Mr. MacDonagh discusses its genesis at great length, and shows its dependence upon the idioms of Gaelic; Mr. Boyd traces its growth after Hyde's discovery of its possibilities. Synge, perhaps, did not borrow directly from Hyde, but he at least borrowed Hyde's trick of listening to the people of the countryside. Here we have, not an exact rendering of Gaelic idioms in a foreign tongue, but an effort to set down and preserve the peasants' difficulties with and blunderings in that tongue. It is thus from the true Irish, the countryfolk of Ireland, that the new dialect derives. There is as much of their naif mysticism and their homely humor in it as of their actual speech. It is racy of the soil. But there has been added to it an element that the soil never could have produced, and that is the element of conscious artistry, of aesthetic sensibility and sophistication. The new Irish are genuine artists. They hear and feel the most delicate overtones of speech. Their ears are as sensitive as Elizabethan ears to the slightest whisperings of beauty in words.

Of the two books now in court, Boyd's and MacDonagh's, you will find Boyd's by far the more informative and useful. MacDonagh confines himself to a relatively narrow field. It is Irish verse that chiefly interests him, for he was a poet himself and a good one, and his execution after the Easter rebellion was a heavy loss to letters. To appreciate him to the full, perhaps, one must be an Irishman; his very criticism is full of a Celtic twilight; he never proceeds by direct statement when he can proceed by allusion. There is a charm in all that, and Boyd misses it, but he makes up for it by marshaling his facts clearly and by writing in a straightforward and understandable manner. His book is particularly valuable for its illumination of the days of beginning. The greater part of new Irish criticism has concerned itself with end products, and especially with end products in the theater. Boyd avoids this false emphasis, and keeps the dramatic writings of the movement in their proper place. They are, of course, important; they include some of the best stuff that Young Ireland has given forth. But they have got so much attention that there is danger of forgetting the Irish poets and novelists and essayists, and the work of the dramatists themselves in other fields. These lacks are met by the two volumes before us. They are interesting and valuable books. . . .

(March, 1917)

Taking Stock

I nursed a secret hope that last month's article would bring me a wreath of ivy from the Authors' League of America, or, at all events, an invitation to guzzle *vin rouge* with the Poetry Society, for it was not only intrinsically meritorious, but it also had a certain historical and military interest, for it was my one hundredth mensual discourse in this place. No such celebration of the anniversary having been forthcoming, I herewith recall it myself. It is not often, on this bleak western front of civilization, that a critic holds a trench so long. The hazards of the trade are numerous and flabbergasting. The authors one puts to the torture have a habit of making furious and unexpected reprisals; the publishers undertake countless counter-offensives; there come fearful squawks from Old Subscribers when their prejudices are violated or their pet fictioneers are nailed to the wall; even the best of editors, in the midst of such a din, grows skittish at times, and wonders if a change of critics would not help his digestion. All in all, a harsh and forbidding life, and yet, after eight and a third years, I still pursue it, and if all goes well I hope to print my thousandth article in February, 1991. In those eight and a third years I have served under four editors, not including myself; I have grown two beards and shaved them off; I have eaten 3,086 meals; I have made more than $100,000 in wages, fees, refreshers, tips and bribes; I have written 510,000 words about books and not about books; I have received, looked at, and thrown away nearly 3,000 novels; I have been called a fraud 700 times, and blushed at the proofs; I have had more than 200 invitations to lecture before women's clubs, Chautauquas, Y.M.C.A.'s, chambers of commerce, Christian Endeavor societies, and lodges of the Elks; I have received 150 pounds of letters of sweet flattery; I have myself written and published eight books, and reviewed them all favorably; I have had seventeen proposals of marriage from lady poets; I have been indicted by grand juries eight times; I have discovered thirty bogus geniuses; I have been abroad three and a half times, and learned and forgotten six foreign languages; I have attended 62 weddings, and spent nearly $200 for wedding presents; I have gained 48 pounds in weight and lost 18 pounds, and have grown bald and gray; I have been converted by the Rev. Dr. Billy Sunday, and then recanted and gone back to the devil; I have worn out nine suits of clothes; I have narrowly escaped marriage four times; I have had lumbago and neuralgia; I have taken to horn-rimmed spectacles; I have eluded the white-slave traders; I have fallen downstairs twice; I have undergone nine surgical operations; I have read the *Police Gazette* in the barber-shop every week; I have shaken hands with Dr. Wilson; I have upheld the banner of the ideal; I have kept the faith, in so far as I could make out what it was; I have loved and lied; I have got old and sentimental; I have been torpedoed without warning.

Ah, the wonder and glory of life! The procession of the equinoxes! The mystery of tears and laughter! The toxic gurgle of a kiss! The way flowers shoot up, and horned cattle gambol in the fields! Eight and a third years seems a short while, and yet it has fetched me out of youth into middle age, and left my heart as bulged and battered as a gladiator's ear. Eight and a third years ago "Floradora" was still the rage, and the *New Republic* was unheard of, and Pilsner came in by every ship, and the muckrakers yet drove a fine trade, and Dr. Wilson was happy and untempted at Princeton, and Major-General Roosevelt was a simple colonel of cavalry d. R. a. D., and Díaz was on deck in Mexico, and beefsteak was still 23 cents a pound, and God was in His heaven, and all was well with the world. Where are the charming young authoresses who came to *The Smart Set* office in the autumn of 1908, the cuties who tripped in with their ingratiating smiles and their manuscripts under their arms; the sweet ones who were startled to find that a critic of the bozart could be so toothsome a youth, and so beautifully polite? Married, thirty, fat, sour, abhorrent! Where are the poets who sent in notice that I was a *Schuft*, and that their dithyrambs would survive my snickers? Dried up, blown away, forgotten, accursed! Where are the new geniuses who inflamed the skies that year —the revolutionary novelists, the novel soothsayers? Done, desolated, damned! Where are all the Great Thinkers that Col. Roosevelt used to introduce with such loud whoops—the faunal naturalists, the Pastor

Wagners, the Warrington Dawsons, the exotic poets? Passed on, alas, passed on! I remember great vogues, excitements, turmoils—for Bergson, for W. B. Trites, for Eucken, for Gorky, for Maeterlinck, for Arnold Bennett, for Leonard Merrick, for Chesterton, for Mathilde Serao, for Synge, for H. G. Wells, for William James, for Alfred Noyes, for Robert W. Service, for Signorina Montessori, for Ellen Key, for Chekoff, for Dr. Cook, for that poetizing jail-bird out West (I have even forgotten his name!) . . . *Dominus dedit, Dominus abstulit! Mais où sont les neiges d'antan! . . . Wein nicht, Süsschen, 's giebt gar kein Use!* . . .

I glance back through my first compositions for this sodality and find some strange things. For example, this in the initial article: "Mary Roberts Rinehart is a new writer." Again, a solemn tirade against the platitudinousness of Upton Sinclair: evidently new in 1908. Yet again, good counsel to Mlle. Marie Corelli: "I should advise her to spend six months in the chorus of a Broadway operetta." Operetta? They still existed eight and a third years ago! . . . In No. 2, a long hymn to Joseph Conrad, the opening anthem of a cantata yet going on. Conrad, in 1908, was scarcely more than a name on this side of the water, and only a hushed whisper on the other side. All of his greatest stories had been written, but they had dogged about from publisher's office to publisher's office, and each successive book had come out with a new imprint. Run your eye down the list: Macmillan, Appleton, Dodd-Mead, Scribner, Doubleday, McClure, Putnam—seven different publishers for his first seven books! He was a long time getting down, but down he went in the end. Today his works are offered to *cognoscenti* in an elegant series of navy-blue, limp-leather volumes: very roycrofty, indeed. I am almost tempted to lay in a set. Not only does it soothe the cultured eye, but it would also save wear and tear of the first editions, which are now soaring in value. My natural sagacity, which functions in profane affairs as well as in *belles lettres,* led me to accumulate them while they still sold at par, and they now fortify me against the *Canis lupus. Almayer's Folly,* published at six shillings, is worth from $25 to $35, according to your passion for it. *The Nigger of the "Narcissus",* in good condition, would probably bring more. Even so recent a book as *Some Reminiscences,* published in 1912, carries a premium of $10 or $12. The whole set was offered a year or so ago for $150. I doubt that it could be brought together today for less than $225. The graft of book reviewers, if they have foresight, is thus seen to be very fair. A forward-looker, I have acquired wealth, and eat and drink, perhaps, more than is strictly decent.

And Dreiser! Back in 1908 only *Sister Carrie* was behind him, and even *Sister Carrie* was but little known, for the first edition had been suppressed by a snuffling publisher, and the second edition had but recently reached the book-stalls. That first edition is now so rare that collectors bid against one another for every stray copy that shows itself. It would be a good idea to hunt up the old plates and print a forgery; nine collectors out of ten have been pleasantly deceived by the forged first edition of Thackeray's *Second Funeral of Napoleon*. Such risks add to the charm of book collecting, for every professor of the art believes firmly that he himself is beyond being fooled, and so it joys him to think of the swindles perpetrated on the other fellow. Incidentally, I know a dealer who lately bought a fine copy of the original *Sister Carrie* for twenty-five cents. He found it in a junk-shop, and leaped from the place like an archdeacon stung by wasps the moment the transaction was closed. Human-like, he couldn't help boasting about his coop, and so I was able, on juridic grounds, to beat him down to a couple of dollars for the prize. I in my turn then emitted oxygen, where upon a kind friend, unsuccessful in his own hunt for the book, affably accepted it from me as a present. I had, of course, another copy; I shall leave it to some orphan asylum when I die, and so help to save Dreiser from hell. The Comstocks, as I write, bawl for his blood on the ground that Eugene Witla, in *The "Genius,"* is a mammal, and occasionally looses a big, big damn. By the time this article is printed, he may be safely roosting in some kindly jail, with leisure to read his own books. If he gets more than six months he will have time to finish them. Then, perhaps, he will fall to work upon a novel in strict accord with the prevailing Methodist canon—a novel whose males confine their carnalities to sly glances at servant girls, and to fighting their way into Billy Sunday meetings "for men only," and to the diligent study of such literature as "What a Girl of 45 Should Know," and II Samuel, xi, 2–27. . . .

I am often asked if I enjoy my job, and reply frankly that I do. There is, at all events, constant variety in it; a surprise is always around the corner; that is a dull month which doesn't produce two or three genuinely interesting books. I glance back over eight and a third years and recall such things as Sundermann's *The Indian Lily*, and Anatole France's *The Revolt of the Angels*, and Lord Dunsany's *The*

Book of Wonder, and Arnold Bennett's *The Old Wives' Tale,* and
Dreiser's *The Titan,* and H. G. Wells' *Ann Veronica,* and Mrs. Wharton's *Ethan Frome,* and Max Beerbohm's *Zuleika Dobson,* and Conrad's *Victory*—I glance back and decide at once that my time has not
been wasted. It is a superlative pleasure to dredge such glowing and
memorable books out of the stream of drivel and commonplace, the
endless avalanche of balderdash by the Oppenheims and Chamberses,
the Bindlosses and Hall Caines, the Corellis and Phillpottses, the jitney Richard Harding Davises and the second-table O. Henrys. Sound
literature, indeed, is being produced in this, our age. The rate of emission of good books is more rapid than ever before. Moreover, it
seems to me that discrimination is increasing, despite the flood of
shoddy wares. There is still a vast market for such sentimental slobber
as one finds in the *Pollyannas* and *Bambis,* but it is no longer mistaken for great art, as was done with the slobber of Dickens. We have
as many boob-thrillers and mountebanks as ever before, but we do
not revere Hall Caine as Bulwer-Lytton was revered. We yet have
rages for sensational poets, but they do not last as long as the rage for
Byron, nor do so many folk succumb to them. Puritanism still wars
upon all art among us, but its arm grows weak and the devices on its
banners are laughed at. I doubt that any truly first-rate book has gone
unrecognized for twenty years past; I doubt that any first-rate book
has gone unpublished. If a new Samuel Butler should print a new
Erewhon tomorrow, even the *Nation* would be aware of it within a
year.

The United States, of course, produces relatively little sound writing
of its own, but it has at least grown eagerly hospitable to the sound
writing that is produced elsewhere. Our thirst for foreign novelties, in
truth, is almost as avid as the Germans'. Scarcely a month goes by
that some new Selma Lagerlöf or Leonid Andreyieff or Émil Verhaeren or Mathilde Serao or Henri Bergson is not discovered, devoured and hymned. The Americanos got down Ibsen long before the
English; the first performance of an Ibsen play in English, indeed,
was given in Louisville back in 1882. They embraced Synge while the
Dublin mob was yet heaving benches at him. They saw the first adequate performances of Shaw. They were bemused by the moonshine
of Maeterlinck before France gave him a thought. They are hot for
English novelists who are scarcely heard of at home. . . . One of the
causes of this alacrity of welcome, perhaps, lies in the somewhat ap-

palling mediocrity of our domestic produce in beautiful letters. Our
books, in the main, lack genuine distinction; they just miss rousing
the imagination. The country, for example, is full of novelists who
have shown promise and then failed. Robert Herrick is one. He began
auspiciously, but today he wallows in claptrap. His trouble is plain
enough: he is clever, but not profound; he has facility, but he lacks
ideas. Edith Wharton is another. She rose to the peak of *Ethan Frome*
and then settled down into a valley of fustian. A third is Robert
Grant. He flew all the signals of great talent—and then hauled them
in. Howells, James Lane Allen, John Luther Long, Hamlin Garland
and the rest of that elder company have run their race. Churchill has
succumbed to the national platitudinousness. Miss Cather and Mrs.
Watts have yet to strike twelve. Stephen French Whitman, Ernest
Poole, Henry Milner Rideout, Owen Johnson and a dozen others of
their quality seem to be done for; the lure of the *Saturday Evening
Post* has finished most of them.

But let us not wail and gnash our teeth. We still have Dreiser, and
despite *The "Genius,"* he will probably do his best work hereafter. He
is the one novelist among us who shows no response whatever to the
variable kinds of public favor; he hacks out his path undeterred by
either praise or blame; a sort of blind fury of creation seems to move
him. And we still have two or three other men who are sound artists,
and yet as American as trading stamps or chewing gum: Booth Tarkington, George Ade, Harry Leon Wilson. All have yielded themselves
to temptation; all have stooped for the shekel. And yet, when everything has been said, Ade's *Fables in Slang* come near being the best
comic writing of our time in any language, and Tarkington's *Penrod* is
a book that will long outlive Tarkington, and Wilson has done things
in *Bunker Bean* and again in *Ruggles of Red Gap* that belong to satire
at its best, and hint clearly at what he could do on a larger scale if he
would only spit on his hands and make the effort.

I speak only of novelists. Of poets and other such lesser fauna, I
shall discourse, perchance, at some later conference.

(March, 1917)

The Negro as Author

The Shadow, by Mary White Ovington, is a bad novel, but it is interesting as a first attempt by a colored writer to plunge into fiction in the grand manner. Hitherto black America has confined itself chiefly to polemics and lyrical verse, not forgetting, of course, its high achievements in the sister art of music. James W. Johnson's *Biography of an Ex-Colored Man* is not, at bottom, a novel at all, but a sort of mixture of actual biography and fantasy, with overtones of sociology. Mrs. Ovington issues a clearer challenge. Her book shows the familiar structure of the conventional novel—and a good deal of the familiar banality. At the very start she burdens herself with a highly improbable and untypical story. Perhaps she will answer that it once happened in real life. If so, the answer is no answer. I once knew a German saloon-keeper who drank sixty glasses of beer every day of his life, but a novel celebrating his life and eminent attainments would have been grossly false. The serious novel does not deal with prodigies; it deals with normalities. Who would argue that it is a normal phenomenon for a white girl to grow up unrecognized in a negro family, for her to pass over into her own race at twenty, for her to conceive a loathing for the scoundrelism and stupidity of the whites, and for her to prove it by going back to her black foster-relatives and resolving melodramatically to be "colored" herself thereafter? The thing is so hard to believe, even as a prodigy, that the whole story goes to pieces. Struggling with its colossal difficulties—they would daunt a Conrad or even a Bennett—Mrs. Ovington ends by making all of her characters mere word-machines. They have no more reality than so many clothing-store dummies or moving-picture actors.

Nevertheless, the author shows skill, observation, a civilized point of view. Let her forget her race prejudices and her infantile fables long enough to get a true, an unemotional and a typical picture of her people on paper, and she will not only achieve a respectable work of art, but also serve the cause that seems to have her devotion. As she herself points out, half of the difficulties between race and race are due to sheer ignorance. The black man, I suppose, has a fairly good working understanding of the white man; he has many opportunities to observe and note down, and my experience of him convinces me that he is a shrewd observer—that few white men ever fool him. But the white man, even in the South, knows next to nothing of the inner

life of the negro. The more magnificently he generalizes, the more his
ignorance is displayed. What the average Southerner believes about
the negroes who surround him is chiefly nonsense. His view of them is
moral and indignant, or, worse still, sentimental and idiotic. The great
movements and aspirations that stir them are quite beyond his comprehension; in many cases he does not even hear of them. The thing
we need is a realistic picture of this inner life of the negro by one who
sees the race from within—a self-portrait as vivid and accurate as Do-
stoyevsky's portrait of the Russian or Thackeray's of the Englishman.
The action should be kept within the normal range of negro experience. It should extend over a long enough range of years to show
some development in character and circumstance. It should be presented against a background made vivid by innumerable small details.
The negro author who makes such a book will dignify American literature and accomplish more for his race than a thousand propagandists
and theorists. He will force the understanding that now seems so
hopeless. He will blow up nine-tenths of the current poppycock. But
let him avoid the snares that fetched Mrs. Ovington. She went to
Kathleen Norris and Gertrude Atherton for her model. The place to
learn how to write novels is in the harsh but distinguished seminary
kept by Prof. Dr. Dreiser.

Another somewhat defective contribution to negro literature, this
time by a white author, is *The Negro Faces America*, by Herbert J.
Seligmann. The author's aim is, first, to rehearse the difficulties confronting the emerging negro of the United States, particularly in the
South, and, secondly, to expose the shallowness and inaccuracy of
some of the current notions regarding negro capacities and negro
character. Most of this balderdash, of course, originates in the South,
where gross ignorance of the actual negro of today is combined with a
great cocksureness. But *all* of the prevailing generalizations, even in
the South, are not dubious, and Mr. Seligmann weakens his case
when he hints that they are. For example, there is the generalization
that the average negro is unreliable, that he has a rather lame sense of
the sacredness of contract, that it is impossible to count upon him
doing what he freely promises to do. This unreliability, it seems to me,
is responsible for a great deal of the race feeling that smoulders in the
South. The white man is forced to deal with negroes daily, and it irritates him constantly to find them so undependable. True enough, it is
easy to prove that this failing is not met with in negroes of the upper

classes, and it may be even argued plausibly that it is not intrinsically a negro character—that the pure and undebauched African is a model of honor. But the fact remains that the Southern whites have to deal with the actual negroes before them, and not with a theoretical race of African kings. These actual negroes show defects that are very real and very serious. The leaders of the race, engrossed by the almost unbearable injustices that it faces, are apt to forget them. Here is a chance for its white friends to do it a genuine service. What it needs most, of course, is a fair chance in the world, a square deal in its effort to rise, but what it needs after that is honest and relentless criticism. This criticism is absent from Mr. Seligmann's book. The negro he depicts is an innocent who never was on land or sea.

(October, 1920)

Scherzo for the Bassoon

Aldous Huxley's *Chrome Yellow*, if it be called a novel, violates all of the rules and regulations that I have just laid down so smugly. But why call it a novel? I can see absolutely no reason for doing so, save that the publisher falls into the error in his slipover, press-matter and canned review. As a matter of fact, the book is simply an elaborate piece of spoofing, without form and without direction. It begins, goes on aimlessly, and then suddenly stops. But are only novels fit to read? Nay; try *Chrome Yellow*. If it does not make you yell with joy, then I throw off the prophetical robes forever. It is a piece of buffoonery that sweeps the whole range from the most delicate and suggestive tickling to the most violent thumping of the ribs. It has made me laugh as I have not laughed since I read the Inaugural Harangue of Dr. Harding.

This Huxley, in truth, is a fellow of the utmost shrewdness, ingenuity, sophistication, impudence, waggishness and contumacy—a literary atheist who is forever driving herds of sheep, hogs, camels, calves and jackasses into the most sacred temples of his people. He represents the extreme swing of the reaction against everything that a respectable Englishman holds to be true and holy. The attitude is no pose, as it would be among the fugitives from the cow states in Greenwich Village; it comes to him legitimately from his grandfather, Thomas Henry Huxley, perhaps the roughest and most devastating manhandler of gods ever heard of in human history. Old Thomas Henry was a master of cultural havoc and rapine simply because he never grew indignant. In the midst of his most fearful crimes against divine revelation he maintained the aloof and courtly air of an executioner cutting off the head of a beautiful queen. Did he disembowel the Pentateuch, to the scandal of Christendom? Then it was surely done politely— even with a certain easy geniality. Did he knock poor old Gladstone all over the lot, first standing him on his head and then bouncing him upon his gluteus maximus? Then the business somehow got the graceful character of a *Wienerwalz*. Aldous is obviously less learned than his eminent grandpa. I doubt that he is privy to the morphology of *Astacus fluviatilis* or that he knows anything more about the Pleistocene or the Middle Devonian than is common gossip among Oxford barmaids. But though he thus shows a falling off in positive knowledge, he is far ahead of the *Ur*-Huxley in worldly wisdom, and it is his worldly wisdom which produces the charm of *Chrome Yellow*. Here, in brief, is a civilized man's *reductio ad absurdum* of his age— his contemptuous kicking of its pantaloons. Here, in a short space, delicately, ingratiatingly and irresistibly, whole categories and archipelagoes of contemporary imbecilities are brought to the trial by wit. In some dull review or other I have encountered the news that all the characters of the fable are real people and that the author himself is Denis, the minor poet, who loses his girl by being too cerebral and analytical to grab her. Nonsense! Huxley, if he is there at all, is Scogan, the chorus to the whole drama, with his astounding common sense, his acidulous humor, and his incomparable heresies.

(May, 1922)

XIII

Epilogue

Fifteen Years

I

I began to write these book articles for *The Smart Set* in November, 1908—that is, the first of them appeared in the magazine for that month. Since then, counting this one, I have composed and printed no less than one hundred and eighty-two—in all, more than nine hundred thousand words of criticism. An appalling dose, certainly! How many books have I reviewed, noticed, praised, mocked, dismissed with lofty sneers? I don't know precisely, but probably fully two thousand. But how many have I *read?* Again I must guess, but I should say at least twice as many. What? Even so. The notion that book reviewers often review books without having read them is chiefly a delusion; it may happen on newspapers, but certainly not on magazines of any pretensions. I remember printing notices of a number of books that were so dull, at least to me, that I couldn't get through them, but in every such case I printed the fact frankly, and so offered no complete judgment. Once, indeed, I read part of a book, wrote and printed a notice denouncing it as drivel, and then, moved by some obscure, inner necessity, returned to it and read it to the end. This experience gave me pause and taught me something. One cylinder of my vanity—the foul passion that is responsible for all book reviewers above the rank of slaves, as it is for all actor-managers, Presidents and archbishops—urged me to stick to my unfavorable notice, but the other cylinder urged me to make handsome amends. I did the latter, and trust that

God will not forget it. I trust, too, that He will not overlook my present voluntary withdrawal from this pulpit. The insurance actuaries say that my expectation of life is exactly twenty-five years; in twenty-five years I might write and print three hundred more articles —another million and a half words. If I now resign the chance and retire to other scenes, then perhaps it may help me a few inches along the Eight-Fold Path. Men have been made saints for less.

II

Among the thousands of letters that have come to me from my customers and the public generally during the fifteen years of my episcopate have been a great many of a uraemic and acerbitous flavor, and not a few of these have set up the doctrine that whoever nominated me for my job was an idiot. To this day, curiously enough, I don't know who he was. At the time the poisoned pen was offered to me, I was not in practice as a literary critic, and had not, in fact, done much book reviewing. My actual trade was that of an editorial writer on a provincial newspaper, then in sad decay, and the subjects that I was told off to treat were chiefly (*a*) foreign politics, a topic then disdained by most American editorial writers, and (*b*) such manifestations of the naive and charming communal life of the Republic as are now grouped under the general head of Babbittry. I had a good time in that newspaper job, and invented a large vocabulary of terms of abuse of my countrymen; a number of these terms have since passed into the American language and are now used even by Babbitts. But I never reviewed books save when the literary critic of the paper was drunk, and that was not often. Some years before I had been the dramatic critic, but that office was already filled by another, to the great relief of the local Frohmans. Those were the palmy days of Augustus Thomas, Clyde Fitch and the dramatized novel. Mansfield was still the emperor of the American stage, Nazimova was a nine-days' wonder, Belasco was almost universally regarded as a Master Mind, and the late Joseph Jefferson still wobbled around the provinces with his tattered scenery and his company of amateurish sons, sons-in-law, cousins and second cousins. I am fond of recalling (to the disquiet of Comrade Nathan, who believed in the Belasco hocus-pocus so late as 1907, and once actually praised Nazimova's Nora in *A Doll's House*) that my observations upon these half-forgotten worthies brought many an indignant manager to the business office of my paper, and

filled me with a fine sensation of bellicose sagacity. Some time ago I
unearthed a bundle of clippings of my old dramatic notices, and their
general sapience amazed and enchanted me. It was like meeting a
precious one of 1902 and finding her still slim and sweet, with night-
black hair and eyes like gasoline pools on wet asphalt. Once, aroused
to indignation by my derision of his mumming, Mansfield wrote me a
letter denouncing me as an ass and inviting me to dinner. But I was
not quite ass enough to accept his invitation. The fashionable way to
fetch an anarchistic provincial critic in those days was to hire him as a
press-agent; it is, in fact, still done. But I always had a few dollars in
my pocket, and so resisted the lure. But by and by I tired of the theater, and took to writing facetious editorials, many of which were never
printed. To this day I dislike the showhouse, and never enter it if I
can help it.

But to return to my story. The assistant editor of *The Smart Set,* in
1908, was the late Norman Boyer, with whom, eight years before, I
had worked as a police reporter in Baltimore. One day I received a
polite note from him, asking me to wait upon him on my next visit to
New York. I did so a few weeks later; Boyer introduced me to his
chief, Fred Splint, and Splint forthwith offered me the situation of
book reviewer to the magazine, with the rank and pay of a sergeant of
artillery. Whose notion it was to hire me—whether Boyer's, or Splint's,
or some anonymous outsider's—I was not told, and do not know to
this day. I had never printed anything in the magazine; I had not, in
fact, been doing any magazine work since 1905, when I abandoned
the writing of short-stories, as I had abandoned poetry in 1900. But
Splint engaged me with a strange and suspicious absence of parley,
Boyer gave me an armful of books, the two of us went to Murray's for
lunch (I remember a detail: I there heard the waltz, "*Ach, Frühling,
wie bist du so schön!*" for the first time), and in November of the
same year my first article appeared in this place. I have not missed an
issue since. But now I shuffle off to other scenes.

III

Glancing back over the decade and a half, what strikes me most
forcibly is the great change and improvement in the situation of the
American imaginative author—the novelist, poet, dramatist, and
writer of short-stories. In 1908, strange as it may seem to the literary
radicals who roar so safely in Greenwich Village today, the old tradi-

tion was still powerful, and the young man or woman who came to New York with a manuscript which violated in any way the pruderies and prejudices of the professors had a very hard time getting it printed. It was a day of complacency and conformity. Hamilton Wright Mabie was still alive and still taken seriously, and all the young pedagogues who aspired to the critical gown imitated him in his watchful stupidity. This camorra had delivered a violent wallop to Theodore Dreiser eight years before, and he was yet suffering from his bruises; it was not until 1911 that he printed *Jennie Gerhardt*. Miss Harriet Monroe and her gang of new poets were still dispersed and inarticulate; Miss Amy Lowell, as yet unaware of Imagism, was writing polite doggerel in the manner of a New England schoolmarm; the reigning dramatists of the nation were Augustus Thomas, David Belasco and Clyde Fitch; Miss Cather was imitating Mrs. Wharton; Hergesheimer had six years to go before he'd come to *The Lay Anthony;* Cabell was known only as one who provided the text for illustrated gift-books; the American novelists most admired by most publishers, by most readers and by all practicing critics were Richard Harding Davis, Robert W. Chambers and James Lane Allen. It is hard, indeed, in retrospect, to picture those remote days just as they were. They seem almost fabulous. The chief critical organ of the Republic was actually the Literary Supplement of *The New York Times*. The *Dial* was down with diabetes in Chicago; the *Nation* was made dreadful by the gloomy humor of Paul Elmer More; the *Bookman* was even more saccharine and sophomoric than it is today; the *Freeman,* the *New Republic* and the *Literary Review* were yet unheard of. When the mild and *pianissimo* revolt of the middle 90's—a feeble echo of the English revolt—had spent itself, the Presbyterians marched in and took possession of the works. Most of the erstwhile *révoltés* boldly took the veil—notably Hamlin Garland. The American Idealism now preached so pathetically by Prof. Dr. Sherman and his fellow fugitives from the Christian Endeavor belt was actually on tap. No novel that told the truth about life as Americans were living it, no poem that departed from the old patterns, no play that had the merest ghost of an idea in it had a chance. When, in 1908, Mrs. Mary Roberts Rinehart printed a conventional mystery story which yet managed to have a trace of sense in it, it caused a sensation. (I reviewed it, by the way, in my first article.) And when, two years later, Dr. William Lyon Phelps printed a book of criticism in which he actually ranked Mark Twain alongside Emerson and Hawthorne, there was as great a stirring beneath the college elms as if a naked fancy woman had run across the campus. If Hergesheimer had come into New York in 1908 with *Cytherea* under his arm, he would have worn out his pantaloons on publishers' benches without getting so much as a polite kick. If Eugene O'Neill had come to Broadway with *The Emperor Jones* or *The Hairy Ape,* he would have been sent to Edward E. Rose to learn the elements of his trade. The devilish and advanced thing, in those days, was for a fat lady star to give a couple of matinées of Ibsen's *A Doll's House.*

A great many men and a few women addressed themselves to the dispersal of this fog. Some of them were imaginative writers who found it simply impossible to bring themselves within the prevailing rules; some were critics; others were young publishers. As I look back, I can't find any sign of concerted effort; it was, in the main, a case of each on his own. The more contumacious of the younger critics, true enough, tended to rally 'round Huneker, who, as a matter of fact, was very little interested in American letters, and the young novelists had a leader in Dreiser, who, I suspect, was quite unaware of most of them. However, it was probably Dreiser who chiefly gave form to the movement, despite the fact that for eleven long years he was silent. Not only was there a useful rallying-point in the idiotic suppression of *Sister Carrie;* there was also the encouraging fact of the man's massive immovability. Physically and mentally he loomed up like a sort of headland—a great crag of basalt that no conceivable assault seemed able to touch. His predecessor, Frank Norris, was of much softer stuff. Norris, had he lived longer, would have been wooed and ruined, I fear, by the Mabies, Boyntons and other such Christian critics, as Garland had been wooed and ruined before him. Dreiser, fortunately for American letters, never had to face any such seduction. The critical schoolmarms, young and old, fell upon him with violence the moment he appeared above the horizon of his native steppe, and soon he was the storm center of a battle-royal that lasted nearly twenty years. The man himself was stolid, granitic, without nerves. Very little cunning was in him and not much bellicose enterprise, but he showed a truly appalling tenacity. The pedagogues tried to scare him to death, they tried to stampede his partisans, and they tried to put him into Coventry and get him forgotten, but they failed every time. The more he was reviled, sneered at, neglected, the more resolutely he stuck to his formula. That formula is now every serious American novelist's formula. They all try to write better than Dreiser, and not a few of them succeed, but they all follow him in his fundamental purpose—to make the novel true. Dreiser added something, and here following is harder; he tried to make the novel poignant—to add sympathy, feeling, imagination to understanding. It will be a long while before that aim is better achieved than he achieved it in *Jennie Gerhardt*.

IV

Today, it seems to me, the American imaginative writer, whether he be novelist, poet or dramatist, is quite as free as he deserves to be. He is free to depict the life about him precisely as he sees it, and to interpret it in any manner he pleases. The publishers of the land, once so fearful of novelty, are now so hospitable to it that they constantly fail to distinguish the novelty that has hard thought behind it from that which has only some Village mountebank's desire to stagger the booboisie. Our stage is perhaps the freest in the world—not only to sensations, but also to ideas. Our poets get into print regularly with stuff so bizarre and unearthly that only Christian Scientists can understand it. The extent of this new freedom, indeed, is so great that large numbers of persons appear to be unable to believe in it; they are constantly getting into sweats about the few taboos and inhibitions that remain, for example those nourished by Comstockery. But the importance and puissance of Comstockery, I believe, is quite as much overestimated as the importance and puissance of the objurgation still hurled at sense and honesty by the provincial prophets of American Idealism, the Genius of America, and other such phantasms. The Comstocks, true enough, still raid an occasional book, particularly when their funds are running low and there is need to inflame Christian men, but that their monkeyshines ever actually *suppress* a book of any consequence I very much doubt. The flood is too vast for them. Chasing a minnow with desperate passion, they let a whole school of whales go by. In any case, they confine their operations to the single field of sex, and it must be plain that it is not in the field of sex that the hottest battles against the old American tradition have been fought and won. *Three Soldiers* was far more subversive of that tradition than all the stories of sex ever written in America—and yet *Three*

Soldiers came out with the imprint of one of the most respectable of
American publishers, and was scarcely challenged. *Babbitt* scored a
victory that was still easier, and yet more significant, for its target was
the double one of American business and American Christianity; it set
the whole world to laughing at two things that are far more venerated
in the United States than the bodily chastity of women. Nevertheless,
Babbitt went down so easily that even the alfalfa *Gelehrten* joined in
whooping for it, apparently on the theory that praising Lewis would
make the young of the national species forget Dreiser. Victimized by
their own craft, the *Gelehrten* thus made a foul attack upon their own
principles, for if their principles did not stand against just such anarchistic books, then they were without any sense whatever, as was and
is, indeed, the case.

I shall not rehearse the steps in the advance from *Sister Carrie*, suppressed and proscribed, to *Babbitt*, swallowed and hailed. The important thing is that almost complete freedom now prevails for the serious artist—that publishers stand ready to print him, that critics exist
who are competent to recognize him and willing to do battle for him,
and that there is a large public eager to read him. What use is he
making of his opportunity? Certainly not the worst use possible, but
also certainly not the best. He is free, but he is not yet, perhaps, worthy of freedom. He lets the popular magazine, the movie and the
cheap-John publisher pull him too hard in one direction; he lets the
vagaries of his politics pull him too hard in another. In my first article
in this place I predicted the destruction of Upton Sinclair the artist by
Upton Sinclair the visionary and reformer. Sinclair's bones now bleach
upon the beach. Beside them repose those of many another man and
woman of great promise—for example, Winston Churchill. Floyd Dell
is on his way—one novel and two doses of Greenwich Village psychology. Hergesheimer writes novelettes for the *Saturday Evening
Post*. Willa Cather has won the Pulitzer Prize—a transaction comparable to the election of Charles W. Eliot to the Elks. Masters turns
to prose fiction that somehow fails to come off. Dreiser, forgetting his
trilogy, experiments rather futilely with the drama, the essay, free
verse. Fuller renounces the novel for book reviewing. Tarkington is
another Pulitzer prizeman, always on the verge of first-rate work but
always falling short by an inch. Many of the White Hopes of ten or
fifteen years ago perished in the war, as surely victims of its slaughter
as Rupert Brooke or Otto Braun; it is, indeed, curious to note that

practically every American author who moaned and sobbed for democracy between the years 1914 and 1919 is now extinct. The rest
have gone down the chute of the movies.

But all this, after all, may signify little. The shock troops have been
piled up in great masses, but the ground is cleared for those that follow. Well, then, what of the youngsters? Do they show any sign of
seizing their chance? The answer is yes and no. On the one hand there
is a group which, revolving 'round the *Bookman,* talks a great deal
and accomplishes nothing. On the other hand there is a group which,
revolving 'round the *Dial, Broom* and the *Little Review,* talks even
more and does even less. But on the third hand, as it were, there is a
group which says little and saws wood. I have, from time to time,
pointed out some of its members in this place. There seems to be
nothing in concert between them, no sign of a formal movement, with
its *blague* and its bombast, but all of them have this in common: that
they owe both their opportunity and their method to the revolution
that followed *Sister Carrie.* Most of them are from the Middle West,
but they are distinct from the Chicago crowd, now degenerated to
posturing and worse. They are sophisticated, disillusioned, free from
cant, and yet they have imagination. The raucous protests of the
evangelists of American Idealism seem to have no more effect upon
them than the advances of the Expressionists, Dadaists and other such
café-table prophets. Out of this dispersed and ill-defined group, I believe, something will come. Its members are those who are free from
the two great delusions which, from the beginning, have always
cursed American letters: the delusion that a work of art is primarily a
moral document, that its purpose is to make men better Christians
and more docile cannon-fodder, and the delusion that it is an exercise
in logic, that its purpose is to prove something. These delusions, lingering beyond their time, are responsible for most of the disasters visible in the national literature today—the disasters of the radicals as
well as those of the 100 per cent dunderheads. The writers of the future, I hope and believe, will carefully avoid both of them.

V

Inasmuch as I was immersed from the start in the struggle that I
have briefly described, it is but natural that my critical treatises
should have seemed, to many worthy souls, unduly tart, and even, in
some cases, extravagantly abusive and unjust. But as I re-examine

them in these closing days of my pastorate, I can't escape the feeling
that that view of them is itself somewhat bilious. Tart, yes. But unjust—well, certainly not often. If I regret anything, it is that I have
been, more than once, unduly tolerant. The spectacle of a man hard
and earnestly at work is one that somehow moves me; I am often
blinded to the falseness of his purpose by the agony of his striving. It
is a sentimentality that quickly damages critical honesty, and I have
succumbed to it more than once. I have overpraised books, and I have
applauded authors incautiously and too soon. But, as the Lord God
Jahveh is my judge and I hope in all humility to be summoned to sit
upon His right hand upon the dreadful and inevitable Day of Judgment, when all hearts are bared and virtue gets its long-delayed reward, I most solemnly make my oath that, with the single exception
noted on a previous page, I can't remember a time when I ever
printed a slating that was excessive or unjust. The quacks and dolts
who have been mauled in these pages all deserved it; more, they all
deserved far worse than they got. If I lost them customers by my performances I am glad of it. If I annoyed and humiliated them I am
glad of it again. If I shamed any of them into abandoning their
quackery—but here I begin to pass beyond the borders of probability,
and become a quack myself. Regarding false art, cheap cant, pious
skullduggery, dishonest pretense—regarding all these things my position is this: that their practitioners have absolutely no rights that anyone is bound to respect. To be polite to them is not to be tolerant; it is
simply to be silly. If a critic has any duty at all save the primary duty
to be true to himself, it is the public duty of protecting the fine arts
against the invasion of such frauds. They are insidious in their approach; they know how to cajole and deceive; unchallenged, they are
apt to bag many victims. Once they are permitted to get a foothold,
however insecure, it becomes doubly hard to combat them. My
method, therefore, has been to tackle them at first sight and with an
axe. It has led to some boisterous engagements, and, I sincerely hope,
to a few useful unmaskings. So engaged, I do not hesitate to admit
that I have been led by my private tastes quite as much as by any
sense of professional duty. The man who tries to subjugate beautiful
letters to the puerile uses of some bucolic moral scheme, or some nonsensical notion of the national destiny, or some petty variety of new-
fangled politics is a man who is congenitally and incurably offensive
to me. He has his right, true enough, to be heard, but that right is
not properly exercised in the field of *belles lettres*.

VI

A hundred times, during these fifteen years, I have been made aware painfully of a great gap in our domestic *apparatus criticus,* and I still wonder that no competent clerk of letters has ever thought to fill it. I allude to the lack of a comprehensive and intelligent history of American literature. Why does it remain unwritten? The existing books are all either conventional texts for the instruction of school-boys, or histories of single periods, *e.g.,* Tyler's excellent work on the Colonial literature and Pattee's unimaginative but nevertheless often shrewd monograph on the period from 1870 to 1900. The *Cambridge History of American Literature* by no means meets the need. It is, in detail, accurate enough, and it shows some original exploration of the sources, but its defect is that it does not indicate the direction of the main currents, nor the non-literary forces behind them—that it is too much a series of essays on salient men, and views them only too often as phenomena *in vacuo.* Whole sections of the field are not entered at all—and often they are extremely interesting sections. Many of them are along the borders, with religion, politics or race enmity just over the fence. So far as I know, no literary historian, writing about Poe, has ever thrown up the fact that he came to manhood just as Andrew Jackson mounted the tin throne at Washington. Yet it seems to me to be a fact of capital importance; it explains many things about Poe that are otherwise inexplicable.

Poe, indeed, is a colossus who has never had a competent historian. His biographers have spent themselves upon vain efforts to find out the truth about his periodical drunkenness and his banal love affairs; meanwhile, the question of his artistic origins, like the question of his influence, is passed over with a few platitudes. The current doctrine in the high-schools seems to be that he was a superb poet and the inventor of the short story, or, at all events, of the tale of mystery and horror. He was actually neither. Nine-tenths of his poetry is so artificial that it is difficult to imagine even college tutors reading it voluntarily; as for his tales, they have long since passed over to the shelf of juveniles. But Poe was nevertheless a man with a first-rate head on him, and it seems to me that he proved it abundantly in his criticism, which the pedagogues now neglect. This criticism was not only revolutionary in its own time; it would have continued to seem revolutionary, had it been read, down to a few years ago. Who could imagine anything more subversive of the professorial categories—more direct, clear and hard-hitting, more fatal to literary cheese-mongers, more disconcerting to every hollow pretense and quackery. How did Poe come to write it? What set him on the track? And by what process was the whole body of it so neatly buried the moment he gasped out his last breath?

The equally strange case of Emerson I have discussed more than once in the past, but an adequate treatise upon him, alive and dead, yet remains to be written. It was obviously Emerson's central aim in life to liberate the American mind—to set it free from the crippling ethical obsessions of Puritanism, to break down herd thinking, to make liberty more real on the intellectual plane than it could ever be on the political plane. It is his tragic fate to be mouthed and admired today chiefly by persons who have entirely misunderstood his position—in brief, by the heirs and assigns of the very prigs and dullards he spent his whole life opposing. Certainly it would be difficult to imagine a greater irony than this. Emerson paved the way for every intellectual revolt that has occurred since his time, and yet he has always been brought into court, not as a witness for the rebels, but as a witness for the militia and the police. Three-fourths of the books and monographs written about him depict him as a sort of primeval Dr. Frank Crane; he was actually the first important American to give a hand to Whitman. . . . And Whitman himself! Who will work up the material so laboriously and competently unearthed by Prof. Holloway? . . . Who, indeed, will write the first history of American literature that fits such men as Poe, Emerson and Whitman into their true places, and reveals the forces that shaped them and describes accurately the heritage that they left to their countrymen? . . . I ask the question and pass on.

SOLI DEO GLORIA!

(December, 1923)

Index